Restorative Justice

Restorative Justice
Integrating Theory, Research, and Practice

Aida Y. Hass-Wisecup
MISSOURI STATE UNIVERSITY

Caryn E. Saxon
MISSOURI STATE UNIVERSITY

CAROLINA ACADEMIC PRESS
Durham, North Carolina

Library of Congress Cataloging-in-Publication Data

Names: Hass-Wisecup, Aida Y., author. | Saxon, Caryn E., author.
Title: Restorative justice : integrating theory, research, and practice /
  Aida Y. Hass-Wisecup and Caryn E. Saxon.
Description: Durham, North Carolina : Carolina Academic Press, LLC, [2018]
Identifiers: LCCN 2018023434 | ISBN 9781531003005 (alk. paper)
Subjects: LCSH: Restorative justice. | Reparation (Criminal justice) |
  Victims of crimes--Legal status, laws, etc. | Reparations for historical
  injustices.
Classification: LCC K970 .H37 2018 | DDC 364.6/8--dc23
LC record available at https://lccn.loc.gov/2018023434

e-ISBN 978-1-53100-735-5

Carolina Academic Press, LLC
700 Kent Street
Durham, North Carolina 27701
Telephone (919) 489-7486
Fax (919) 493-5668
www.cap-press.com

Printed in the United States of America
2020 Printing

Contents

Section Two • Restorative Processes and Practices in Action

Section Four • The Future of Restorative Justice

Acknowledgments

Aida Y. Hass-Wisecup—When I reflect on my personal values, goals, aspirations and successes, I can't help but recognize the important people in my life that have been the moral glue and foundation upon which I have built the ability to persevere. Without them, life and its meaning would not be defined by the perfect combination of strength and compassion that has always permeated my relationships. For that, I thank them, and dedicate this work to my new husband and best friend Jeff, my ever-loving father Edward, and my incredible kids, Natalie and Sofie.

Caryn E. Saxon—It is such an honor to write a book that will not only help educate people about restorative justice, but encourage others to reflect on what justice means to them and their community. That being said, an effort like this is a humbling endeavor that leaves me feeling an enormous amount of gratitude for those that have helped me along the way. I want to thank my students (past, present, and future) who give me joy, give me purpose, and stretch me as a person and as a teacher. I also want to thank my co-author, Aida, for her patience, positivity, and encouragement. I also owe so much to the many people I have met over the years in jails, prisons, and probation offices. I have never left an encounter with any of you that didn't teach me something about justice, community, love, gratitude, or responsibility. The most precious opportunities of my life have involved you and your paths toward accountability, healing, and restoration. Whether we met for five minutes or five years, thank you for letting me accompany you. Lastly, I want to thank my mother, Janet. Your love, guidance, and encouragement mean everything to me. You dedicate so much to me, and I dedicate this work to you.

Introduction

The potential for conflict is most universally seen as an intersection between an individual, other people, and their social environment. Without any reference to cause, we cannot help but articulate the resolution of such breakdowns in relationships as the defining epitome of restoring something that has been severed or broken. For this reason, we introduce here a paradigm of thought which has embraced this concept to form the foundation of processes involving dialog, inclusion, and the reparation of harm. While the imposition of criminal sanctions will continue to be the subject of much debate, we present here a journey which embarks on the exploration of the concepts of reconciliation and repair through a scientific understanding of theory, research, and its application to a variety of settings where conflict has permeated relationships in a manner that has led to breaches of trust, incidents of harm, and the breakdown of communication.

The material presented in this text is broken down into four sections. The first section provides an overview of restorative justice and its various historical, philosophical, and theoretical origins, which provides a framework within which we can further explore its application in diverse settings. The second section begins our navigation through the various processes and practices involved in the application of restorative justice in the real world of conflict and dispute resolution. In section three, we build on this knowledge by examining the interactive processes involved in the application of restorative justice processes in various systems, organizations, and communities. The final section of our text gives us a glimpse of the future of restorative justice as a field that continues to grow, expand, and explore further mechanisms of intervention involving its principled practices, guided by critique, research, and evaluation.

It is our hope and goal that, as we move forward with the presentation of this information, your mind will be challenged to greater heights of innovation and critical thinking that center upon a greater understanding of restorative justice and its various ways of bringing new and improved mechanisms of dialog to traditional methods of repairing harm and restoring relationships. And now let us begin our journey!

Section One

An Overview of Restorative Justice

As we embark on this exploration of restorative justice, we will begin by providing you with an overview of its defining values and characteristics, an in-depth look into its historical and theoretical origins, and an introduction to the principles and practices that sustain and propel its use in modern contexts such as schools, organizations, and the criminal justice system. The foundational knowledge you gain in this section will help us navigate, examine, and assess various applications of restorative justice as we progress through the book.

As you will see in the pages to come, restorative justice is a unique way of viewing crime and responding to the needs it creates in individuals and communities. Unlike retributive justice, which understands crime as a violation of law and seeks to maintain social order through punishment and deterrence, or rehabilitative justice, which seeks to prevent future crime by addressing criminogenic needs in the offender, restorative justice understands crime as the harm it causes in offenders, victims, and communities and seeks to both restore social order and address the needs that crime creates through meaningful and transformative social encounters.

Chapter 1

What Is Restorative Justice?

In this chapter, we will explore the following questions …

- *How do we define restorative justice?*
- *What are the key components of retributive justice?*
- *Where does rehabilitation fit into the practice of restorative justice?*
- *Does restorative justice align well with the concept of therapeutic jurisprudence?*
- *Are there aspects of restorative justice that are misunderstood?*

Defining Restorative Justice

As we embark upon this journey to better understand the concept of *restorative justice*, we must begin by exploring how it is defined and what sets it apart from other approaches to justice. Though we lack one unified definition of restorative justice, many theorists and practitioners have contributed to the ongoing conversation concerning what restorative justice is, what values best represent it, and what goals and outcomes restorative practices should aim to achieve.

Restorative Justice as Process

When trying to define restorative justice, the first thing that likely pops into most people's minds is process. There are five core processes or practice models that we most frequently connect with restorative justice. Those include:

- victim-offender mediation/dialog
- family group conferencing
- victim impact panels
- peacemaking circles
- sentencing/reparative boards

While these processes can help give definition to restorative justice, one thing we will explore further in this text is that restorative justice should not necessarily be limited to these core processes, and, indeed, sometimes does take on forms outside of these common models.

Restorative Justice as a Theory

Some feel that restorative justice is best described as a theory or philosophy.[1] As Howard Zehr states, for example, it is a "lens" through which we can view crime and justice.[2] When we define restorative justice in this way, it becomes less about the specific processes or practices that we associate with it, and more about articulating how we see crime, offenders, victims, communities, and even the experience of justice. As Van Ness & Strong write, for example, "Restorative justice is a theory of justice that emphasizes repairing the harm caused or revealed by criminal behavior. It is best accomplished through cooperative processes that include all stakeholders."[3]

Restorative Justice as a Social Movement

Stretching a bit beyond the idea that restorative justice is its own unique criminological theory, some see it as a social movement that seeks to significantly transform systems connected to crime and justice.[4] This view of restorative justice is closely aligned with our sense of social justice, and sees restorative justice, not just as a series of isolated practices, but the marriage of philosophy and process that seeks to change the way communities view, and respond to, crime, thereby changing important social systems associated with it.

Whether we see it as a theory, a process, or a social movement, it is commonly held that **restorative justice** refers to practices rooted in the idea that both the origins and outcomes of crime can be articulated as needs in communities, victims, and offenders. Restorative practices strive to acknowledge and address those needs as a way to create healing and transformative opportunities for those directly impacted by crime, in the hope that such opportunities will prevent future crime, strengthen communities, and socially reintegrate offenders and victims.

Restorative Justice as a Spectrum

As mentioned above, restorative process covers a wide range of practices. While some of these practices (such as victim-offender mediation) include both the offender and victim, some (such as sentencing/reparative boards) may not. While some practices (such as family-group conferencing) lend themselves better to juvenile delinquency cases, others (such as victim impact panels) are more often used in adult criminal cases. Due to the fact that restorative justice covers such a wide range of contexts and needs, any definition that we attempt to apply to its theory and practice needs to adequately represent that range. For this reason, some theorists prefer to see restorative justice as a spectrum or continuum rather than one static concept.[5] In other words, rather than seeing a process as "restorative" or "not restorative," we may instead view it as "partially restorative" or "mostly restorative" based on how well the process aligns with certain restorative values and principles, which we will explore more in Chapter 3.[6]

Despite the fact that we are still working to fully construct and articulate a definition for restorative justice, another way in which we can understand it is by examining other forms that justice can take. As we continue with this chapter, we will take a closer look at methods such as retributivism and rehabilitation in order to better understand the ways in which restorative justice is similar to, and different than, other practices we find in our own criminal justice system.

Characteristics of Retributive Justice

While the criminal justice system in the United States employs a variety of strategies when responding to crime (some of which we could classify as rehabilitative or restorative), it is most commonly associated with **retributive justice**. The driving motivation of a retributive philosophy towards justice is the application of reasonable and deserving compensation to victims, and punishment to offenders proportionate to the offense. The goals of retributive justice are to reinstate a moral balance within the community, as well as reinforce social and behavioral norms.

The Roots of Retributivism

While retributive justice can sometimes be confused with vengefulness, it is actually a very refined approach to discerning appropriate responses to criminal offending.[7] Rooted in the ancient Babylonian Code of Hammurabi, retribution as an expression of justice is intended to create a sense of equality between the impact of a criminal offense and our response to it. In other words, "eye for eye, tooth for tooth, hand for hand, foot for foot" as we see in the biblical mandate of Exodus 21:24.

Unlike vengeance, retributive justice refers to a society's public response to a crime, rather than a victim's private one. In a retributive system, punishment is distributed due to a violation of public law, rather than a personal response to one's own victimization or loss.[8] As mentioned above, retributive justice also requires that punishment be reasonable and proportionate in comparison to the crime committed. In other words, retributive justice, while punitive, should not be linked to practices, such as torture, that are cruel and reach beyond the scope or impact of the original crime.

Retributivism's notion that the concern of justice should be the violation of law and the sphere of justice should be a public, rather than private, one sets it distinctly apart from restorative justice. As we will see in our next chapter, restorative justice challenges these ideas by focusing on the harm created by crime rather than simply the violation of law, and by empowering victims and offenders to interact with one another rather than relying so heavily on formal intermediaries such as courts, arbitrators, judges, and lawyers.

Unilateral Decision Making

One thing that restorative and retributive processes of justice have in common is that sometimes their outcomes can be identical. For instance, a shoplifter going through a traditional court process may find herself doing 100 hours of community service, and that same offender going through a restorative process may also end up doing 100 hours of community service. Though the outcomes may be the same, the important distinction is in the process by which those decisions are determined. In a retributive system, decisions about justice are made unilaterally, meaning that, while following the demands of due process and individual rights, decisions concerning victims and offenders are imposed upon them. While restorative processes typically utilize inclusiveness and bilateral, consensus decision-making in order to directly involve offenders and victims in decisions concerning reparation, retributive processes of justice rely on the courts and the application of legal guidelines and precedents to determine and distribute compensation and punishment (see Box 1.1).

Box 1.1: Research in Restorative Justice — Beyond Retribution

In 2009, Okimoto, Wenzel, and Feather published an experimental study that sought to understand how bilateral versus unilateral decision-making affects our perception of fairness when responding to transgressions like deceit, rule-breaking, and minor crime. During their study, 217 undergraduate students from a university in Australia were asked to take the position of a victim when reading six different scenarios which were randomly paired with resolutions that ranged from unilaterally imposed punishments (retributive) to bilateral agreements (restorative).

After analyzing the data using a series of regression techniques, the researchers found that bilateral agreements were generally seen as more fair than unilateral decisions. Moreover, the connection between a bilateral response and one's sense of fairness increased when the participants reported strong feelings of loss in regard to the provided scenario. The researchers also found that punishment was seen as more fair when the transgression was presented as intentional and/or premeditated.

Though limited in their scope, the results of this study suggest that our sense of justice and fairness most likely has a strong connection to the processes we use to respond to relational transgressions, including crime, and that restorative processes may hold tremendous promise when it comes to our collective desire for personally satisfying and reparative paths toward justice.

Source: Okimoto, T. G., Wenzel, M., & Feather, N. T. (2009). Beyond retribution: Conceptualizing restorative justice and exploring its determinants. *Social Justice Research, 22,* 156–180.

Rehabilitation and Restorative Justice

While retributive justice seeks to respond to crime by punishing an offender, a rehabilitative approach to justice aims to understand and address the cause(s) of deviant behavior in order to reduce or eliminate the chance of recidivism.[9] This is the approach which programs such as MADD use when dealing with criminal offending (see Box 1.2).

Box 1.2: Restorative Justice in Action—
    Mothers Against Drunk Driving (MADD)
    Victim Impact Panels

One example of a restorative process working within a rehabilitative model is the use of victim impact panels by the non-profit organization Mothers Against Drunk Driving (MADD). Started in 1980, MADD works to increase awareness of problems related to impaired driving, as well as help and support victims harmed by intoxicated drivers. In counties throughout the U.S., MADD organizes victim impact panels which bring people directly impacted by impaired driving (such as victims, victim's families, law enforcement personnel, and first responders) together with individuals who have committed an impaired driving offense. Unlike victim-offender dialogs, which bring offenders into conversation with their own victim(s), victim impact panels allow a group of offenders to listen to the experiences of victims unassociated with their own crimes.

The goals of these panels are to help offenders understand how their actions directly impact other people, as well as provide victims with an opportunity to share their experiences in a way that may benefit others and prevent future offenses. For offenders working to understand their own substance abuse, as well as maintain sobriety, empathy-building processes, such as victim impact panels, have been shown to aid in the rehabilitation process and reduce recidivism; however, studies have also shown that the victim impact panel process has little to no effect on one's likelihood to commit an impaired driving offense in the future.

Though the recidivism research may be inconclusive, victim impact panels continue to be used by MADD, as well as other groups and agencies, to enhance the rehabilitation process of many different types of offenders.

Sources: You can read more about MADD's victim impact panels by visiting their website: http://www.madd.org/victim-impact-panels/.

Fors, S. W., & Rojek, D. G. (1999). The effect of victim impact panels on DUI/DWI rearrest rates: a twelve-month follow-up. *Journal of Studies on Alcohol, 60*(4), 514–520.

C'de Baca, J., Lapham, S. C., Liang, H. C., & Skipper, B. J. (2001). Victim impact panels: do they impact drunk drivers? A follow-up of female and male, first-time and repeat offenders. *Journal of Studies on Alcohol, 62*(5), 615–620.

While rehabilitation and restorative justice are distinct from one another, restorative practices lend themselves nicely to rehabilitative goals and programs. Since both approaches share an interest in the needs of the offender, and how those needs can be addressed in order to prevent future crime, we often see restorative practices utilized in rehabilitative settings or treatment plans. For example, if a lack of empathy is seen as a contributing factor to criminal behavior, a restorative process such as a victim impact panel may be utilized as a rehabilitative tool to correct that criminogenic deficiency in an offender.

While rehabilitation and restorative justice can complement one another, their main divergence lies in the way each one sees the role of the victim. While rehabilitative processes are almost entirely offender-focused, restorative processes seek to identify and address the needs of the victim with equal attention to those of the offender.

Therapeutic Jurisprudence: What Restorative Justice Is

A balance between traditional legal justice and therapeutic law permeates the ongoing search for justice. Put simply, how can we achieve legal justice while at the same time ensuring that justice processes are mutually beneficial for all parties involved? One important dynamic that is often neglected in the study of crime and criminal justice is the interaction between the legal values of due process and the psychosocial consequences of the law. Restorative justice attempts to reconcile the two through the approach of **therapeutic jurisprudence**, the study of how the law and the legal system affect human behavior and well-being, including emotions, psychological impact, and mental and physical health.[10] Therapeutic jurisprudence (TJ) "focuses attention on the ... law's impact on emotional life and psychological well-being" and "proposes ... [to] use the tools of the behavioral sciences to study the therapeutic and anti-therapeutic impact of the law."[11] This multidisciplinary approach underscores the connection between the processes underlying the resolution of legal matters and their ultimate impact on offender rehabilitation and correctional outcomes.

Origins of Therapeutic Jurisprudence

Therapeutic jurisprudence was developed in the late 1980s by Professors David Wexler and Bruce Winick in an effort to study the extent to which legal proceedings conducted within the courtroom by judges, lawyers, and prosecutors produce positive, therapeutic consequences, or negative, anti-therapeutic consequences for individuals.[12] Its origins are rooted in the application of mental health law in the treatment of psychiatric patients who were charged with a crime in both civil and criminal court proceedings. Traditional mental health law focused primarily on ensuring that the due process rights of mental health patients were protected. The framework of therapeutic jurisprudence, however, goes beyond the goal of structuring the boundaries of court proceedings to protect psychiatric patients. Therapeutic jurisprudence recognized the need to safeguard against the infringement of due process. In addition, this approach also attempted to envelope this safeguard through a wrap-around approach that relies on the use of multiple fields of knowledge, including psychology, criminology, and social work, to produce a holistic approach in the application of mental health court proceedings that optimize legal principles and therapeutic outcomes for offenders and victims.[13] Legal expert Bruce Winick summarizes this concept for us in a compelling way:

> Therapeutic jurisprudence is not only concerned with measuring the therapeutic impact of legal rules and procedures, but also of the way they are applied by various legal actors — judges, lawyers, police officers, and expert witnesses testifying in court, among others. Whether they know it or not, these legal actors are therapeutic agents, affecting the mental health and psychological wellbeing of the people they encounter in the legal setting. For example, how lawyers deal with their clients in the law office and the courtroom can have a significant impact on a client's emotional well-being, and therapeutic jurisprudence has spawned a growing literature concerning how attorneys should act in this regard.[14]

In the late 1990s, the concept of therapeutic jurisprudence emerged as the theoretical and practical foundation for a variety of solution-oriented courts, including drug courts, mental health courts, teen courts, and reentry courts. These courts were designed to be problem-solving courts that placed an emphasis on creative solutions and ethical care that took into consideration the psychological well-being of the accused as pivotal to their transformation. Practically, therapeutic jurisprudence encouraged the interaction between judges and offenders, the demonstration of empathy, and the development of mutual respect and agreement between the offender and courtroom officials, with the ultimate goal of encouraging trust, building confidence, and reducing stress within court proceedings.[15] This participatory nature of therapeutic jurisprudence is the cornerstone of restorative justice practice.

Restorative Justice as Therapeutic Jurisprudence

Restorative justice forces us to really examine the question, *what is the goal of the law*? We cannot doubt the implementation of law as a tool of achieving balance, fairness, and equity in the remedy of criminal offenses. However, in setting this as a goal, we must intuitively embrace and identify a framework for the application of legal principles from a humanistic, healing perspective. Restorative justice provides us with the intellectual structure for organizing various practices that mediate encounters between victims and offenders, that are informal and participatory. This approach engages participants to take on an active role in working out conflicts, placing great value on the role of individuals in dispute resolution. To this extent, restorative justice promotes therapeutic jurisprudence by empowering participants to become involved in problem-solving, rehabilitation, decision-making, and restoration.[16]

So, we go back to our original question: how can we achieve legal justice while at the same time, ensure that justice processes are mutually beneficial for all parties involved? To answer this question, we must first agree upon the goals of criminal law. While this task has been discussed and debated in various contexts, there are certain foundational components of criminal justice that define the role of criminal law.

Whether legal scholar, student of law, or average citizen, there appears to be an agreed upon goal of law as the arm of **retribution**, the means by which we seek to satisfy the desire for revenge upon an individual who has inflicted unfair harm upon someone else. This alone is not sufficient, however, and to imply so is a retrospective glimpse of a past society that we would not readily embrace. Another goal of law is therefore set, one which desires the **deterrence** of individuals from committing further acts of harm. The role of law in deterring individuals is to set forth a punishment that is harsh enough so as to prevent not just that individual from further offending but also as an example to society in general of what might befall an individual who breaks the law. Alongside retribution and deterrence as pillars of criminal law are the goals of **rehabilitation** and **incapacitation**. Ironically, these two goals seem to sit in opposite realms of justice, with one implying societal embrace and the other implying a total rejection. With rehabilitation, the intention of the law is to impose a punishment that has a value in changing an offender into a law-abiding member of the community by addressing the underlying issues that are causing the offending behavior. Incapacitation, on the other hand, aims at removing the offender from society, thereby protecting its citizens from their dangerous behaviors. What role, then, does restorative justice play in reconciling these goals and the role of therapeutic jurisprudence?

The interjection of restorative justice values, principles, and processes within criminal justice legal proceedings has added the goal of restoration within the application of law, ensuring that legal justice, balance, and equity are achieved while simultaneously seeking therapeutic jurisprudence (see Box 1.3). As agents of restorative justice, we seek to examine the potential healing role of the law as it manifests in the actions of the various agents of criminal justice. The fundamental concern behind restorative justice practices is achieving cooperation by increasing the opportunity for communication that builds positive relationships and a sense of community amongst individuals. To this extent, restorative justice aligns well with the core principles of therapeutic jurisprudence and has implications for the efficient and healing resolution of conflicts and disputes in a variety of contexts and settings within society, including workplace, schools, families, prisons, and even governments.

Box 1.3: Restorative Justice: Let's Take a Closer Look ...
Does Victim Impact Evidence Make Criminal
Hearings Unfair?

Since the Supreme Court's decision in the case of *Payne v. Tennessee* in 1991, as well as the Crime Victims' Rights Act of 2004, victims have been granted the right to share about the impact of a crime in court procedures that address the sentencing and release of offenders. Though they have this right, there exists much debate over whether the inclusion of evidence concerning the victim experience, especially the emotional, physical, and social impact of a crime, affects whether or not the offender is treated fairly during the court process due to concerns that this kind of evidence may influence the decisions of judges and juries.

Though it should not be confused with the victim advocacy movement, restorative justice does seek to empower victims to have a direct role in the justice process, and also strongly asserts that offenders should understand the impact of their actions.

What are your thoughts? Should the impact of a crime be left out of criminal court proceedings? Are the experiences of victims relevant to the decisions we make concerning what to do with an offender?

Source: Hoyle, C. (2011). Empowerment through emotion: The use and abuse of victim impact evidence. In E. Erez, M. Kilchling, & J. Wemmers (Eds.), *Therapeutic jurisprudence and victim participation in justice* (pp. 249–483). Durham, NC: Carolina Academic Press.

It can be argued, therefore, that restorative justice, as an instrument of therapeutic jurisprudence, is synonymous with creative justice. Throughout the remainder of this text, we will revisit this issue of creative justice, and continually cast it within the light of interjecting and fashioning responses to offending that are meaningful and effective; responses that are guided by the principles of legal tradition as well as procedural justice, with the ultimate goal of creating fairness, balance, and healing through an emphasis on mutual respect and constructive intervention. That is what restorative justice truly is! Before we move forward with that task, however, we turn to a brief discussion of what restorative justice is *not*.

What Restorative Justice Is *Not*

The focus on identifying outcomes within the domain of conflict resolution that are constructive can make a positive impact in changing an offender's behavior and assisting the victim in recovering from the injury of the offense. Restorative justice is therefore inherently supportive, and as such, the priority becomes addressing needs from the perspective of the victim, rather than focusing exclusively on remedies provided by the law. To this extent, restorative justice practices provide a different framework for addressing criminal events, one that is less concerned with punishment of the offender, and more concerned with accountability, reparation, and the rebuilding of relationships.

Restorative Justice Is Not Coercive

Rather than asking what law was broken, who broke that law, and how should the offender be punished, restorative justice focuses on what harm was done by the criminal act, who was harmed by the act, and what must the offender do to address the needs that have been created by this harm. Because of this focus, restorative justice processes are inherently non-coercive. Unlike traditional legal proceedings that have the rule of law as a primary focus, restorative justice processes rely on voluntary, informal mechanisms to identify needs of victims, as well as obligations of the offender, in order to bring healing to victims of crime and rebuild relationships that have been affected by the criminal event.[17]

In order for these processes to be successful, however, restorative justice relies on the offender's desire to hold himself or herself accountable, and to come up with ways to address the needs of the victim in repairing the harm. Restorative justice therefore seeks to increase dialog, encourage face-to-face encounters, and build up community support, rather than isolate criminal offenders and alienate them from the community through the symbolic rejection of formal court proceedings.

Restorative Justice Is Not Punitive

Restorative justice relies on our recognition that the goal of correctional intervention is not exclusively punitive. We must cease, therefore, to equate the concept of "justice" with the concept of "retribution." Restorative justice processes rely on cooperation, dialog, and agreement, and in order to work, the scales of balance in criminal justice must account for a more holistic reparation from criminal offending. By this, we exchange "an eye for an eye" account of balance for one that that fosters making amends that are achieved through mutual agreement between the victim and offender. Interpersonal acts of crime are acts against people, not states, governments, or the collective of humanity. Therefore, the repair should be personal, with the goal of addressing the harm done to the individual, and not some other entity that is seeking a generic form of a punitive goal based on the need to satisfy an elusive concept of justice.

Almost every act of harm can benefit from this type of approach.[18] Take, for example, an act of vandalism where a group of youth spray paint graffiti on a much-cherished public property. It is one thing to instill a fine, assign community service, and require probation as forms of correctional intervention. This alone, however, does not seek to repair the relationship between the youth and the community that was affected by their destructive actions. How much more effective would it be, how-ever, if the youth were required to actually participate in the repair of the public property that was destroyed, learn of the hard work that was put into making that structure, and identify its symbolic meaning to them and to the community in which they live through the organized facilitation of restorative justice practices?

Through this approach, acts of criminal offending are not merely punished but rather the process of repair takes on a transformative approach that builds relationships instead of tearing them down and furthering the divide between offenders and the communities in which they live.[19] Restorative justice therefore allows for processes that engage both the victim and the person who created the harm in identifying the needs created by the harm, and both become involved in the mechanisms of repair ... punitive mechanisms do not.

Restorative Justice Is Not Procedural Justice

The determination of guilt or innocence is a matter of great concern within the context of criminal offending. It must be noted, however, that restorative justice entails processes that begin intervention after a determination of guilt has been made. Thus, the denial of responsibility and the illusive admission of guilt during court proceedings hinder the progress of restorative justice goals, and therefore, restorative justice cannot be reeled into the process of fact finding and pursuit of justice for the offender. Effective dispute resolution hinges upon an offender's ownership of his or her own actions, and that ownership requires an admission of guilt and a dedication to resolution processes that aim at reconciliation and not legal fact finding.

A focus on repair and restoration as part of the remedy to criminal offending sets restorative justice apart from the adversarial legal system.[20] This separation lends a greater amount of strength and credibility to the diverse programs and practices that focus on bringing mutual healing to victims, offenders, and community. To this extent, there are no "sides," and the lines of accusation, investigation, and division become blurred in the face of healing and repair. This is not a bad thing, however, as we will see in chapters to come. For now, we must acknowledge that procedural justice is concerned with fairness in criminal justice *process*, and fairness of *outcome* therefore becomes the domain of restorative justice.[21]

Chapter Summary

How do we define restorative justice?

Whether we see it as theory, process, or social movement, restorative justice refers to practices rooted in the idea that both the origins and outcomes of crime can be articulated as needs in communities, victims, and offenders. Restorative practices strive to acknowledge and address those needs as a way to create healing and trans-formative opportunities for those directly impacted by crime.

What are the key components of retributive justice?

Retributive justice is distinct from vengeance and refers to a society's public response to a crime. Within a retributive system of justice, punishment is distributed due to a violation of public law, rather than a personal response to one's own victimization or loss. Retributivism's notion is that the concern of justice should be the violation of law and the sphere of justice should be a public, rather than private.

Where does rehabilitation fit into the practices of restorative justice?

While rehabilitation and restorative justice are distinct from one another, restorative practices lend themselves nicely to rehabilitative goals and programs. Since both approaches share an interest in the needs of the offender, and how those needs can be addressed in order to prevent future crime, we often see restorative practices utilized in rehabilitative settings.

Does restorative justice align well with the concept of therapeutic jurisprudence?

Restorative justice mediates various informal and participatory encounters between victims and offenders, engaging participants to take on an active role in working out conflicts, and placing great value on the role of individuals in dispute resolution. To this extent, restorative justice promotes therapeutic jurisprudence by empowering participants to become involved in problem-solving, rehabilitation, decision-making, and restoration.

Are there aspects of restorative justice that are misunderstood?

Restorative justice places priority on addressing needs from the perspective of the victim, rather than focusing exclusively on remedies provided by the law. Because of this focus, restorative justice processes are inherently non-coercive. In addition, restorative justice processes rely on voluntary, informal mechanisms to identify needs of victims, as well as obligations of offenders. Thus, acts of criminal offending are not merely punished but rather the process of repair takes on a transformative approach that builds relationships instead of tearing them down and furthering the divide between offenders and the communities in which they live. Finally, restorative justice processes rely on an offender's ownership of his or her own actions, and therefore, cannot be reeled into the process of legal fact finding and pursuit of justice for the offender.

Key Terms

Restorative Justice
Retributive Justice
Therapeutic Jurisprudence
Retribution
Deterrence
Rehabilitation
Incapacitation

Critical Thinking Questions

1. How do *you* define justice? Does your definition of justice connect more with retributivism, rehabilitation, or restorative justice?

2. You are an advocate of restorative justice theory and practice. How do you defend the implementation of a restorative justice model of dispute resolution within a school setting? What would this model look like?

3. Who ultimately benefits from restorative justice? Is therapeutic jurisprudence the right way of intervening within criminal justice? Are there cases that make more sense than others?

References

1. Van Ness, D. W., & Strong, K. II. (2015). *Restoring justice: An introduction to restorative justice* (5th ed.). Waltham, MA: Anderson Publishing.

2. Zehr, H. (1990). *Changing lenses: A new focus for crime and justice.* Harrisonburg, VA: Herald Press.

3. Ibid., see 1; page 44.

4. Umbreit, M., & Armour, M. P. (2010). *Restorative justice dialogue: An essential guide for research and practice.* New York, NY: Springer Publishing Company.

5. Bazemore, G., & Schiff, M. (2015*). Restorative community justice: Repairing harm and transforming communities.* Routledge.

6. Zehr, H. (2002). *The little book of restorative justice.* Intercourse, PA: Good Books.

7. Brooks, T. (2012). *Punishment.* New York, NY: Routledge.

8. Wenzel, M., & Okimoto, T. G. (2016). Retributive justice. In *Handbook of social justice theory and research* (pp. 237–256). New York: Springer.

9. Sung, H., & Gideon, L. (2011). Major rehabilitative approaches. In L. Gideon & H. Sung (Eds.), *Rethinking corrections: Rehabilitation, reentry, and reintegration* (pp. 71–95). Thousand Oaks, CA: Sage.

10. Kaiser, K. A., & Holtfreter, K. (2015). *An integrated theory of specialized court programs using procedural justice and therapeutic jurisprudence to promote offender compliance and rehabilitation. Criminal Justice and Behavior, 42*(1), 45–62. doi: 0093854815609642.

11. Winick, B. J., & Wexler, D. B. (Eds.). (2003). *Judging in a therapeutic key: Therapeutic jurisprudence and the courts.* Durham, NC: Carolina Academic Press.

12. Winick, B. J. (2013). Problem solving courts: Therapeutic jurisprudence in practice. In *Problem solving courts* (pp. 211–236). New York: Springer.

13. Babb, B. A., & Wexler, D. B. (2014). Therapeutic jurisprudence. In *Encyclopedia of criminology and criminal justice* (pp. 5202–5211). New York: Springer.

14. Winick, B. J. (2002). Therapeutic jurisprudence and problem solving courts. *Fordham Urban Law Journal, 30*(3), 1060.

15. Ibid., see 11.

16. Walgrave, L. (2016). Positive criminology, criminology of trust and restorative justice. *Restorative Justice, 4*(3), 424–434; Winick, B. J. (2013). "Problem solving courts: Therapeutic jurisprudence in practice." In *Problem solving courts* (pp. 211–236). New York: Springer.

17. Gal, T., & Wexler, D. B. (2015). Synergizing therapeutic jurisprudence and positive criminology. In N. Ronel & D. Segev (Eds.), *Positive criminology* (pp. 85–97). Routledge.

18. Bazemore, G., & Schiff, M. (2015). *Restorative community justice: Repairing harm and transforming communities.* Routledge.

19. Daly, K. (2016). What is restorative justice? Fresh answers to a vexed question. *Victims & Offenders, 11*(1), 9–29.

20. Gerkin, P., Walsh, J., Kuilema, J., & Borton, I. (2017). Implementing restorative justice under the retributive paradigm: A pilot program case study. *SAGE Open, 7*(1). doi: 2158244017691562.

21. Dekker, S. W., & Breakey, H. (2016). "Just culture:" Improving safety by achieving substantive, procedural and restorative justice. *Safety science, 85,* 187–193.

Chapter 2

Historical and Theoretical Framework of Restorative Justice

In this chapter, we will explore the following questions ...
- *How did the restorative justice movement begin?*
- *What is the theoretical grounding of restorative justice principles?*
- *How has restorative justice become integrated in the criminal justice system?*
- *In what ways is restorative justice used outside the criminal justice system?*

The Rise and Fall of Restorative Justice

The restoration of relationships has a long-standing tradition in the ideals of separating action from person. In traditional mechanisms of punishment, the goal is to punish individuals so that the behavior is not repeated. Restorative justice is a peacemaking process that helps offenders come to a realization that the actions that were committed are wrong. It is almost insignificant to pursue punishment alone without focusing on the instilling of a change in values, attitude, and ultimately action. One must go beyond proving that the elements of a crime are evidence of guilt and therefore the perpetrator is worthy of the punishment deemed necessary by the law. One must question why the action happened in the first place, the reason the harm was committed, and the best resolution to get to the bottom of the conflict. One must understand the historical significance of the restorative justice movement as the development of a better approach to conflict resolution, a mechanism of social action, and the clarification of conceptual ambiguity.

Historical Foundations of Restorative Principles

A significant body of literature suggests that the decade of the 1970s was a prominent time period for the introduction of restorative justice theory and practice. It was a time when criminologists around the world began to critically evaluate the criminal justice system, its mechanisms, and the outcomes of its proceedings.[1] While relevant to the contemporary evolution of restorative justice policy and practice, however, this understanding is incomplete. A full grasp of the evolution and development of restorative justice necessitates a more in-depth look at its ancient historical tradition.

Restorative justice ideology dates back to ancient societies that embraced the idea of making reparation to the victim of crime and not the State, which was believed to be a means of building interpersonal relationships and strengthening communities.[2] The connection between punishment and offending behavior within the context of a criminal justice system is a relatively recent dynamic. Historians and legal scholars have identified the earliest form of human social organization to be **acephalous societies**.[3] Anthropologists refer to these societies, dating back to prehistoric times, as "acephalous," meaning they were egalitarian societies, organized around tribes, with no central government or leadership.[4]

Within these primitive communities, members were concerned with creating close-knit relationships in order to sustain the integrity of the tribal structure. Consequently, conflicts between individuals were dealt with in a manner that lacked the type of institutional force characteristic of later types of State, centralized social structures. Rather, these early communities instilled a sense of belonging and obligation to the group, and discouraged deviance and potential deviants by encouraging collective responsibility and reducing the likelihood of selfish interests.[5] Errors against individuals were seen as disruptive to the balance of the group, and restoring that balance meant reaching a peaceful settlement between the victim and the offender that encouraged harmony, honor, and a sense of stability. This peaceful settlement most commonly revolved around some type of compensation or repayment to the victim. Since the relationship between the victim and offender was of utmost importance, the settlement was understood to be an effort at restoring that bond through the elements of repayment and forgiveness. Representatives of the community would serve as mediators in this process, with the understanding that deviant behavior was problematic for the community as a whole, and its elimination was dependent on dealing with the offense on a personal level, restoring the victim's sense of loss, and re-establishing the offender's relationship to the community.[6] Box 2.1 illustrates this process of mediation amongst the Ifugao of Northern Luzon in the Philippines.

Box 2.1: Restorative Justice in Action—
  The Ifugao Go-Between

One of the most important people found in Ifugao society is the **monkalun**. The monkalun is described as an entire entity that encompasses the role of judge, prosecutor, and defense attorney. Within Ifugao society, the goal of self-preservation is integral to the peaceful resolution of conflicts between individuals. On the one hand, the person who has been hurt or injured does not want to compromise his or her position in society by accepting anything less than the proper compensation for their loss, thereby avoiding being accused of weakness and disrespected by peers. On the other hand, the person who has committed the wrongdoing is reluctant to accept a punishment that is excessive or exorbitant for fear of being perceived as weak, as this is also looked down upon as a sign of indignity and powerlessness. The monkalun is the tribal mediator whose role is defined by the ability to reach a peaceful settlement between members of his tribe in a manner that epitomizes the art of diplomacy. Using the methods of persuasion, scolding, and influencing, the monkalun will not stop mediating until the opposing parties reach mutual agreement and listen to each other's arguments. As a neutral mediator, the monkalun should not be closely related to either party, nor have any personal interest in the matter in question. His role is defined amongst the Ifugao as a compelling leader whose only weapon is his tact and skill as a mediator. He is able to communicate each side's points to the other in a manner that is convincing, compelling both parties to reach a peaceful resolution based upon an empathetic understanding of the circumstances in question. Essentially, the role of the monkalun is linked to the preservation of the people, as without his effective guidance, the dangerous interplay of hurt and emotions can lead to the ultimate destructive forces of revenge and killing.

Source: Barton, B. F. (1919). Ifugao law. *American Archaeology and Ethnology*, *15*(1): 1–186.

The identification of restoration as a common mechanism of social control was recognized as essential in maintaining the integrity of primitive social structures. The concept of justice was equated with reconciliation between victims and offenders, and this act of reconciliation was seen as contributing to communal stability, peace, and progress. There was no clear classification of victim, offender, and State, but rather a mutual goal of resolving harms in a manner that would not contribute to the cycle of violence, hatred, animosity, and isolation. An emphasis on justice made forgiveness and communal help available to offenders, addressing wrongdoing with the goal of correcting their errors and acknowledging their feelings. At the same time, this emphasis on justice brought about balance and healing to victims, ensuring that their state of loss was made whole and any contempt for the offender was recognized and resolved.

Early societies indeed recognized the core principles of restorative justice. However, as their means of organization gave way to the complexities of emerging structures, the practices of restorative justice that were once embraced became diluted with the movement to a more State-like governance.

The Movement Away from Restorative Justice

Historians note that a significant decline in restorative justice principles and practices began during the Middle Ages, around the fifth century, with major shifts occurring around the ninth century.[7] What contributed to these changes? The transformation and movement of societies from simple, tribal communities, to more complex social structures, involves, over time, a transformation of social institutions, social groups, and social roles. Economic expansion and population growth created societies that were much larger and more heterogeneous, weakening social bonds between individuals, and creating a weaker sense of community. The common traditions that created unity and harmony amongst people dissolved as autonomy and individuality were brought about by changes in thinking, reasoning, and spirituality. Sociologist Emile Durkheim notes that modernization allows individuals more freedom, and that freedom encourages individuals to think for themselves and act in ways that reflect their own personal sense of right and wrong. This, in turn, decreases the personal nature of interactions between individuals, and hinders the normative effect of collective conscience and communal identity that inhibit acts of deviance.[8]

Moreover, a comparative historical analysis of the shift in civilization from acephalous societies into more complex, State structures, reveals that the variables of specialization, stratification, and centralization contributed to this change.[9] Historically, the development of complex societies was marked by an increase in **specialization**, whereby members of a social group who are most suited for a task, either by personal talent, skill, or other qualification, become responsible for that task, such as hunter, farmer, or artisan.[10] Specialization can lead to both competition and conflict. As differences begin to emerge over personal interests, the simplicity of communal living, with its emphasis on shared values, norms, and traditions, is replaced with a need for the development of a clearer definition of roles, systems of exchange, and guidelines for production, as people not only provide for their own family needs, but essentially fulfill the needs of others and also rely on others to meet their needs.

The inevitable outcome of the specialized production of goods and services is an increase in the diversity that exists between individuals. One aspect of this diversity is social **stratification**, the division of people into distinct groups based on personal traits such as wealth, status, occupation, and religion.[11] The concept of stratification creates a sense of fragmentation amongst the people of a society and differences in income, wealth, status, and power come to define the social position of individuals relative to one another. With these differences, cooperation amongst group members is compromised, as mutual interests disintegrate and the need to regulate the allocation of resources and maintain order in a centralized fashion becomes more apparent.

Governance within a simple, decentralized society relies on kinship bonds to maintain order and distribute resources to individuals within the group. Within complex social structures, however, a State system characterized by **centralization** is necessary, whereby a single, consolidated body of government or authority possesses the role of managing the allocation of resources, enforcing the rules, and protecting the common good of society.[12] The social order therefore becomes increasingly dependent upon the State's ability to provide a shared system of values and norms that legitimize the social order and validate the formal structure of law and social control. Tribal elders and leaders are replaced by government authorities and informal mechanisms of conflict resolution give way to formal processes. The common interests of the group, therefore, become the interests of the State, and formal leaders take on the administration of affairs for citizens.

Over time, however, the hierarchy of interests characteristic of State societies led to the resolution of conflicts in the interests of the leader—whether king, governor, or president; individuals who caused harm were held accountable to the leader, not the victim. Compensation meant repayment to the State, and by the twelfth century, the basis of conflict resolution as a mechanism of reconciliation between victim and offender eroded in the wake of a paradigm of formal criminal justice intervention. Historians Pollock and Maitland describe this new approach where, "the wrong done to an individual extends beyond her own family; it is a wrong done to the community of which she is a member; and thus the wrong-doer may be regarded as a public enemy."[13]

As acts of crime and delinquency became equated with a threat to the State, the hierarchical order of society continued to grow, widening the gap between those in power and the rest of the people. These dynamics ushered in an era of harsh punishments upon criminal offenders that were aimed at vengeance and retribution. During this time period, the church grew in power and became an arm of the law to secure power to its authority and the authority of rulers. Victim advocacy, reconciliation, and offender rehabilitation became a thing of the past, as crime and criminals were now regarded as enemies and a threat to the moral order. Legal scholars note that by the turn of the century, in the early 1200s, the concepts of restorative justice diminished as formal laws emerged to protect the interests of wealthy property owners, and State rights and interests took precedence over those of the victim.[14] Would the erosion of restorative justice become a permanent dynamic? History tells us no, and although decades, even centuries went by before it formally resurfaced, various forces were at work that demonstrate that its principles and practices were not forgotten, and scholars, political activists, and legal thinkers continued to advocate for various forms of informal community interventions as an alternative response to crime.[15]

The Rise of Restorative Justice

Correctional theory and criminal justice discourse during the 1960s and early 1970s set the stage for the modern restorative justice movement to begin its course. Psychologist Albert Eglash is credited with being one of the first documented writers to use the term "restorative justice."[16] Working with incarcerated offenders, Eglash recognized the rehabilitative value of holding offenders accountable for their harmful behavior. In his seminal paper "Beyond Restitution—Creative Restitution," Eglash describes **creative restitution**:

> A restorative approach of creative restitution accepts both free will and psychological determinism. It redefines past responsibility in terms of damage or harm done, and can therefore accept psychological determinism for our past behavior without destroying the concept of our being responsible for

what we have done. Similarly, it redefines present responsibility in terms of our ability or capacity for constructive, remedial action and can therefore accept free will for our present, ongoing behavior and for our future contemplated behavior, without destroying scientific explanations of past behavior. Only in legislative justice are determinations of past and present responsibility independent.[17]

For Eglash, the hallmark of change and transformation was a deliberate attempt on the part of the offender to repair the harm done to the victim. Eglash was careful to note that the goal of restorative justice is not to simply do away with the concept of retribution, but rather that the two can co-exist with the goal of remedy to actively involve the offender in restoring his or her relationship with the victim and not just merely to passively accept a criminal justice sanction.

In their 1977 book *Assessing the Criminal: Restitution, Retribution, and the Legal Process*, Randy Barnett and John Hagel called for a paradigm shift in criminal justice, one that moves away from current practices focusing on punishment, to one that incorporates the concept of restitution.[18] Similarly, Norwegian criminologist Nils Christie argued for a radical change in the criminal law and procedure that accounts for conflicts and resolutions as social problems that should be resolved through the interaction between society, victims, and offenders. "I don't like the term crime," notes Christie, "they are only unwanted acts. How we perceive them depends on our relationship with those who carry them out."[19] Martin Wright also called for a new penal philosophy that placed value on the need for offenders to make amends to the victim and the community. In his publication, *Nobody Came: Criminal Justice and the Needs of Victims* (1977), Wright proposed that we offer practical help to victims of crime, while at the same time intervening on behalf of the offender in a way that brings them back into society rather than advocates for their isolation.[20] He emphasized the importance for punishment philosophy to allow offenders to recognize the harm they have caused, rather than primarily focus on the punishment they can receive and how to circumvent or avoid its imposition. Wright believed that crime is a particular type of harm that is subject to criminal justice sanction and that restorative justice as a response to that act would be a creative approach that does not involve imposing more harm.

During the 1980s and early 1990s, criminologist Howard Zehr provided us with a framework for the restorative justice movement by articulating the difference between the traditional retributive model of justice and the restorative model of justice. In his prominent work, *Changing Lenses* (1990), Zehr laid the foundation for restorative justice theory and practice by calling for a transformation in the approach to criminal justice that is more focused on the harms surrounding criminal actions, rather than the punishment of criminal offenders.[21] For Zehr, the current retributive justice model was too concerned with allocating blame, guilt, and punishment in the name of criminal justice proceedings. This neglected the important aspects of restorative justice processes that focus on crime as a disruption of relationships between people and attempt to bring reconciliation and healing to victims and offenders. The criminal justice system needs to do more, according to Zehr, than find offenders guilty, impose punishment, and gain a victory against the criminal in the adversarial game of law. Rather, the administration of justice should focus on more than the criminal action, and ask such questions as *who has been hurt, what is the cause of their actions*, and *what remedies can bring healing in that situation*? Thus, because crime is seen as a conflict between individuals, there should be an active attempt to humanize the process of criminal justice by encouraging the restoration of bonds between individuals and uniting offenders with their communities.

The restorative justice movement continued to gain momentum throughout the 1990s. Policy makers began to see it as a means and hope of addressing the failure of the current criminal justice system to deal with offenders, victims, and communities in a holistic manner. The idea of bringing equity, justice, and healing to victims of crime, as well as addressing the problems brought about by criminal actions, resonated with the goals of crime control and prevention as a comprehensive approach that brought together various stakeholders. Restorative justice was seen as placing a greater burden on offenders to make things right, and in the process of making things right, to reevaluate the wrongfulness of their actions. The reintegrative goal brings about a transformation whereby offenders acknowledge the shame of their actions and seek the forgiveness of victims and their communities. As this goal took on a more definitive role, a theoretical understanding of restorative justice principles emerged to offer insight and guidance into its social and cultural validity. The theoretical constructs collectively reflect an evolving discussion regarding what restorative justice is and what practices and settings are most conducive to restorative encounters and outcomes.

Theoretical Grounding of Restorative Justice

While ideas and processes tied to restorative justice date back to ancient communities and civilizations, our contemporary practice of restorative justice is concerned with how these processes work within current societies, cultures, and systems.[22] While no single or unified theory exists that fully explains restorative justice, we can trace its evolution and rationale through several modern theoretical works important to understanding the development of its core values and assertions.[23] Let's turn now to an examination of the theoretical perspectives relevant to our understanding of community and restorative justice, emphasizing works or concepts that focus on their relationship to one another.

Albert Eglash and "Creative Restitution"

Many scholars attribute psychologist Albert Eglash with establishing ideas and processes that would eventually lead to modern conceptions of restorative justice.[24] Eglash's work with offenders in the 1950s led him to question how the concept of *making amends*, made relevant to many offenders by their participation in Alcoholics

Anonymous meetings, could be tied to restitution for criminal acts in a way that might make restitution more meaningful and socially significant for both offenders and victims. Eglash's thoughts evolved into what he later deemed "creative restitution," or acts of restoration that met certain criteria such as being driven by the offender, relating to the criminal offense, and contributing constructively to those directly affected by the crime.[25]

Important to Eglash is the need of offenders to reintegrate into the community, and in order to do so, he contends that offenders need the chance to make right their wrongs with the people most impacted by their behavior through opportunities for apology as well as reparative acts. In light of this, "creative restitution" is often generated through dialogs between victims and offenders, much like modern restorative processes such as victim offender mediation and family group conferencing.

In addition to concepts such as communication between victims and offenders, restorative restitution, and community integration of offenders, Eglash also challenges common cultural associations that link justice to acts of revenge and punishment. While Eglash does not dispute a victim's right to desire revenge, he asserts that society should not value or support vengeful responses to crime, an idea that would come to be a foundational tenet of contemporary restorative philosophy and practice.

Nils Christie: Crime, Conflict, and Community

The publication of Nils Christie's article "Conflicts as Property" (1977) is widely considered a seminal moment in restorative theory, thought, and practice.[26] Christie's thesis argues several points, including the idea that crime is a form of conflict between individuals; conflicts are vital to the health, vitality, and longevity of social systems, and conflicts are stolen within modern industrialized societies by the State, legal representatives, and other professionals, leading to the eventual erosion of empowered, viable communities.

In his article, Christie expresses faith in people and their communities to address crime and determine justice, and, as a criminologist, approaches the prevention of crime as secondary to the restoration of strong social systems capable of not only enduring conflict, but growing and strengthening through crime and conflict.

According to Christie, the criminal justice system leads to the re-victimization of victims who have a right to address their conflicts directly. In fact, he writes, "the one party that is represented by the state, namely the victim, is so thoroughly represented that she or he for most of the proceedings is … denied rights to full participation in what might have been one of the more important ritual encounters in life."[27] In other words, according to Christie, a justice system based upon representation and non-participation of victims and communities can create more harm and social destruction than crime itself.

In his article, Christie warns against the effects of industrialization, stating that the segmentation of social classes and increased mobility leads to the "depersonalization of social life" and the breakdown of community.[28] According to Christie, the community isn't merely an exercise in social control; it is instructive regarding many things, including behavior. When conflicts are resolved outside of those most directly involved in them, outside of the community, more is lost than just the conflict itself. Christie writes, "This is first and foremost a loss in opportunities for norm-clarification. It is a loss of pedagogical possibilities."[29]

Christie's ideas are important to consider, because, unlike other criminologists dedicated to explaining the phenomenon of crime and devising ways to prevent it, Christie proposes a process of justice less concerned with prevention or deterrence and more concerned with adherence to values and processes that will grow and sustain healthy communities capable of addressing crime. He writes, "we have not been able to invent any cure for crime.... We might as well react to crime according to what closely involved parties find is just and in accordance with general values in society."[30] In other words, rather than creating systems of justice focused on exerting state power and control, justice is found in our shared commitment to act in line with our social values and ideals even when confronting actions done in defiance of them.

As one of the few criminologists associated with setting the foundation of restorative justice, we can examine Christie's work and see that the theoretical roots of this movement place enormous importance on the power and vitality of the community and are profoundly critical of not only the paternalistic nature of the modern criminal justice and legal systems, but the professionalization of those systems which seek to prevent direct connection and communication between citizens in conflict.

John Braithwaite: Reintegrative Shaming

The theoretical construct most closely associated with restorative justice is found in John Braithwaite's **Reintegrative Shaming Theory**. In his formative work *Crime, Shame and Reintegration* (1989), Braithwaite argues that although the feelings associated with shame and remorse are key to crime control and the inhibition of offending, the current system of justice creates a form of shame that is stigmatizing and therefore counterproductive, as it breaks the bond between offenders and society.[31] Instead, Braithwaite argues that offenders should be given the chance to become law-abiding members of their community through the process of reintegrative shaming, which, according to Braithwaite, allows offenders to earn this as a right, by expressing remorse for their harmful actions, repairing the loss caused by the crime, and apologizing to their victim.

Reintegrative shaming theory contends that shaming, if coupled with community reintegration, can control crime rather than generate it and that criminal behaviors are criminal due to an offender's conscious choice to act in defiance to his/her community values and/or social code. Braithwaite's theory therefore hinges upon the reintegrative aspect of shaming. He writes, "Shaming is counterproductive when it pushes offenders into the clutches of criminal subcultures; shaming controls crime when it is at the same time powerful and bounded by ceremonies to reintegrate the offender back into the community of responsible citizens."[32] Reintegrative shaming, however, is dependent upon certain social conditions which Braithwaite describes as interdependency and communitarianism. Interdependency refers to the degree of inclusion and connection one feels in regard to social and familial relationships. In other words, "shame is more deterring when administered by persons who continue to be of importance to us; when we become outcasts we can reject our rejecters and the shame no longer matters to us."[33] Communitarianism is the "aggregation of individual interdependency."[34] In other words, it refers to societies with strong social bonds of mutual dependence and accountability. These two conditions, according to Braithwaite, are essential elements for successful reintegrative shaming as a method of crime control and effective criminal desistance. This would suggest that processes designed around this theory, as many restorative processes are, fail to be effective in communities with disintegrating or low levels of interdependency and mutuality unless those communities are transformed.

As alluded to above, Braithwaite's is an integrated theory, meaning it draws from many different theories of crime in order to more broadly explain general motivations to deviate and desist. In the following sections, we will summarize these theories and discuss how each contributes to Braithwaite's conclusions.

Subcultural Theories

Subcultural theories of crime attribute criminal delinquency to cultural norms and one's need or desire to behave in accordance with those norms. For example, one leading subcultural theorist, Walter Miller, purports the existence of competing values or focal concerns within lower-class communities, as opposed to middle and upper class communities, which, according to his theory, explain the prevalence of crime in these areas.[35] According to Miller, it is these cultural values, such as toughness and autonomy, which motivate individuals toward criminal behavior and causes these communities to be more conducive to crime than others. Regarding crime, he writes, "its principal motivational support, as in the case of any persisting cultural tradition, derives from a positive effort to achieve what is valued within that tradition, and to conform to its explicit and implicit norms."[36] In other words, the decision to behave criminally draws from one's desire to fulfill the cultural expectations of his/her family or group as a result of modeling and learning, and as an expression of cultural attachment and belonging.

Braithwaite's theory relies on subcultural theories of crime to explain why stigmatization, or shaming that fails to be reintegrative, can result in increased crime. He writes, "stigmatization tends to be criminogenic to the extent that those stigmatized find or are exposed to subcultures which provide social support for delinquency. Stigmatization itself is one of the variables which contribute to subculture formation."[37] Braithwaite also draws from subcultural theories a belief that criminal behavior can be suppressed by the degree to which one is attached to community values that emphasize pro-social attitudes and actions.

Labeling Theories

Labeling theorists, such as Frank Tannenbaum, assert that one's identity, and therefore behavior, is largely shaped by the "labels" attached to an individual by his/her community.[38] Tannenbaum describes the creation of a criminal as a gradual shift in how a community perceives an individual who commits delinquent acts or disassociates from the values of the collective. He writes that a society will typically move from labeling the acts themselves as deviant to eventually labeling the individual as deviant. This process can be perceived as a rejection by the labeled individual who is then more likely to become even more disassociated from the community and more deeply connected with other socially excluded persons or subcultural groups. This rejection, according to Tannenbaum, then acts as a way to rationalize future deviant and criminal activities. In other words, "the young delinquent becomes bad because he is defined as bad."[39]

Braithwaite accepts the assertions of labeling theories but extends their premise to suggest that while shaming labels can disconnect an offender further from his/her community and result in continued crime, these labels, if followed by offender integration back into the larger community, can also contribute to effective criminal desistance. For instance, he writes, "societies need to be interventionist in a communitarian sense, to be intolerant of crime in a way that is both spiteful and forgiving."[40]

Social Control Theories

Social Control theories, such as Travis Hirschi's **Social Bond Theory**, argue that people are less likely to commit crimes when bonded to social groups such as families and peers that act as social controls to criminal delinquency.[41] These bonds, according to Hirschi, are comprised of four interrelated elements: attachment, commitment, involvement, and belief.

Attachment refers to one's internalization of shared social norms as well as one's level of sensitivity to the opinions of others. Hirschi and Stark write, "If a person does not care about the wishes and expectations of other people, that is, if he is insensitive to the opinion of others, then he is to that extent not bound by the norms. He is free to deviate."[42] In other words, to the extent that we adopt social norms as our own and depend upon and desire the approval of, and connection with, those around us, our natural tendency toward deviance remains controlled.

A bond's second element, according to Hirschi's theory, is commitment. Commitment is described as one's willingness to conform to social norms due to an investment in any number of personal goals or ambitions, such as a job promotion or an educational degree. In other words, commitment restrains criminality through the threat of losses greater than the gains of deviance.

Regarding involvement, Hirschi and Stark write, "To the extent that he [man] is engrossed in conventional activities, he cannot even think about deviant acts, let alone act out his inclinations."[43] In other words, involvement simply refers to the idea that the more time one occupies with socially acceptable pursuits the less time remains to be tempted by deviant ones.

The final element of a bond is belief. Belief refers to one's faith in the shared values of the social group. Hirschi writes that criminality is not determined by one's mere agreement or disagreement with these values, nor the rejection of them for the adoption of others, but by the degree to which one trusts in the restrictions inherent in them.

Social Bond Theory assumes an interdependent relationship between the individual and the community. According to Hirschi's theory, society relies on individuals to behave in certain ways meant to ensure its own functionality and stability, and the individual, naturally inclined toward deviance, relies on his/her social bond to control or restrain his/her true nature. In short, it is the nature and health of the relationship itself that either unleashes criminality or successfully controls it — a relationship described by mutual dependence and the interrelated needs of both the individual and the community.

Braithwaite draws heavily from the premise these theories share regarding the interdependency of an individual and his/her community, and therefore the power the community holds in determining the escalation or de-escalation of criminal behavior.

Strain Theories

Theories regarding opportunity and social strain, such as Robert Merton's **Social Strain Theory**, argue that the degree of opportunity one has to meet goals shared and favored within one's community can determine one's likelihood to engage in deviant behavior.[44] Merton's theory sets forth the idea that while cultures contain specific values and shared goals, such as material wealth, groups within the culture have differing degrees of opportunity with which to meet those goals. The result of these inequities is social strain or pressure that compels some community members to use criminal or non-conformist means to achieve the desired goals.

In relation to the other theories we have examined, strain theories place a similar emphasis upon the relationship one has with one's culture or community in regard to individual behavior, a relationship also emphasized in Braithwaite's reintegrative shaming theory.

Differential Association Theory

Differential Association Theory presents crime as a learned behavior contingent upon the meanings or definitions we attach to the social conditions and cultural concerns or values that surround us.[45] As Sutherland and Cressey write, "When persons become criminal, they do so because of contacts with criminal patterns and also because of isolation from anti-criminal patterns."[46] According to this theory, differential association refers to one's exposure to the attitudes, motives, rationalizations, and techniques of criminal behavior, the impact of which is determined by the frequency and duration of the exposure, as well as its connection to one's physical, mental, and social development, and the meaning one attaches to the source of the exposure and/or the exposure itself.

Again, we see the decision to deviate determined, in part, by one's degree of exposure and attachment to social and cultural values. As Braithwaite writes, "my theory specifies how reintegrative shaming is the process that presents people with behavior patterns unfavorable to crime, and how stigmatization followed by subcultural learning is the process whereby behavior patterns favorable to crime are learned."[47]

Reintegrative shaming theory, as well as the many theories which it draws upon, builds a case for restorative justice that is embedded in an ideal model of justice that incorporates the power of community to correct and prevent deviant behavior. Likewise, the concept of community relies on the inclusion of people who will not only offer the offender support but will also effectively control crime and restoratively respond to harm in a non-confrontational, non-stigmatizing fashion.

By reviewing the theoretical foundations of restorative justice through the contributions of scholars like Eglash, Christie, and Braithwaite, the importance of theory in the implementation, function, and efficacy of restorative justice becomes apparent. With this theoretical foundation laid before us, we turn now to a discussion of how restorative theory is put into action.

Embedding Restorative Justice Principles in Criminal Justice

Restorative justice processes are designed to bring healing and closure to victims of a crime, as well as instill a sense of obligation upon offenders to contribute to that healing by making them confront the full effect of the trauma caused by their actions. Traditional mechanisms of criminal justice are not set up to facilitate encounters between victims of crime and their criminal offenders, and in fact, often do not provide a forum for victims to express the hurt and anxiety caused by the crime and especially not directly to the individual that caused that pain, their perpetrators (see Figure 2.1). This represents a significant gap in the use of restorative justice in the stages that emerge between the conviction of the offender and his or her sentencing. In this section, we will examine the application of restorative justice theory in the various stages of arrest, trial, court processing, and conviction. We will begin by developing a better understanding of this application as a plan of action that enhances the provision and delivery of restorative processes across various components of the criminal justice system.

Facilitating the Implementation of Restorative Justice

Assessing Need and Improving Access

There are several key considerations to account for in the administration of a programmatic initiative in order to ensure its successful implementation. Quite often, within the context of criminal offenses, it is sometimes difficult to comprehend the nature of further encounters between victims and offenders that will promote restora-

Figure 2.1: Restorative Justice v. Traditional Justice

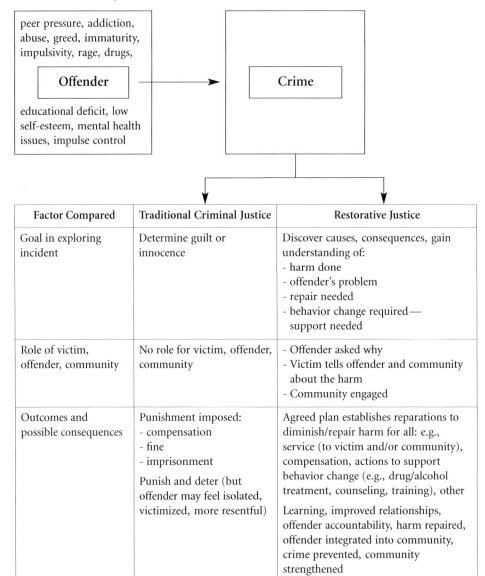

Factor Compared	Traditional Criminal Justice	Restorative Justice
Goal in exploring incident	Determine guilt or innocence	Discover causes, consequences, gain understanding of: - harm done - offender's problem - repair needed - behavior change required—support needed
Role of victim, offender, community	No role for victim, offender, community	- Offender asked why - Victim tells offender and community about the harm - Community engaged
Outcomes and possible consequences	Punishment imposed: - compensation - fine - imprisonment Punish and deter (but offender may feel isolated, victimized, more resentful)	Agreed plan establishes reparations to diminish/repair harm for all: e.g., service (to victim and/or community), compensation, actions to support behavior change (e.g., drug/alcohol treatment, counseling, training), other Learning, improved relationships, offender accountability, harm repaired, offender integrated into community, crime prevented, community strengthened

Source: Nicholl, C. G. (1999). Toolbox for implementing restorative justice and advancing community policing. Washington, DC: U.S. Department of Justice, Office of Community Oriented Policing Services.

tion and healing to the relationship. Consideration must be taken with regard to the need for this restoration, the seriousness of the offense, and the ability of the victim to reach out and embrace the mechanisms provided by restorative justice programs and practices.

For this reason, it is necessary to establish guidelines and protocols that ensure that victims of crime are aware of and can access or request to participate in restorative justice mechanisms when they feel it is beneficial for them. Research shows that for some victims of crime, access to restorative justice may be an immediate need after the incident, while others may not see the benefits until the post-sentencing stage.[48] Box 2.2 discusses research findings that address this issue. In any case, however, the need to integrate restorative justice programs and practice throughout the various stages of the criminal justice system is imperative.

Educating the Public and Practitioners

While restorative justice as a concept may be effective within the context of criminal justice administration, this doesn't necessarily mean that key stakeholders are aware of the various options available within their domain. The implementation of restorative justice within the criminal justice process presupposes the informative guidance of both the public and criminal justice professionals on the purpose and value of restorative justice as a mechanism of repair and healing. Communicating its ability to empower victims of crime, hold offenders accountable, and rebuild communities is an essential building block in educating individuals and raising awareness of restorative justice as a tool.

Box 2.2: Research in Restorative Justice —
A Comparative Analysis of Access to Restorative Justice
Programming

Empirical research into restorative justice has focused much attention on whether their implementation has had a transformational impact on offenders in terms of reducing crime and enhancing their experiences within the criminal justice system. This is arguably a necessary component of program evaluation where there is an emphasis on outcome and results in order to justify the continued financial support of a particular program or practice. Recently, however, a more comprehensive approach to studying restorative justice has directed attention on the impact it has on crime victims as well. The importance of assessing victim satisfaction with involvement in restorative justice programming is regarded as a critical piece of evidence to support the development and implementation of restorative justice approaches. After all, addressing victim needs is a pillar of restorative justice values and therefore should warrant attention in the literature, with a focus on evaluating the extent to which programs using restorative justice modules achieve the key goal of addressing victim needs and improving victim satisfaction with the justice process.

Researchers at the University of Delaware sought to explore satisfaction with post-conviction therapeutic restorative justice programs in both the United

States and Australia. Drawing upon interviews with program staff and facilitators engaged in these programs, their study focused on whether or not victim involvement created a sense of fairness and balance with regard to the procedural aspect of their experiences with the criminal justice system. Findings from their research suggest that the perception of victims about how they were treated during criminal justice proceedings is as important as the outcome of the proceedings itself. Specifically, they found that informal post-conviction restorative justice processes that are a victim-centered, inclusive approach not only provide victims with the opportunity to participate, share their feelings, and be heard, but also increase victim satisfaction with treatment by the legal process, as well as their belief and trust in the criminal justice system.

The long-term benefit of post-conviction restorative justice programming cannot be understated. Enhancing the procedural justice experienced by victims not only promotes their healing and increases their likelihood of relying on the formal criminal justice system for help in the future, but also reverses the long-term trend of focusing exclusively on the procedural rights of offenders, to a more balanced approach that elevates the needs of victims in the same manner.

Source: Miller, S. L., & Hefner, M. K. (2015). Procedural justice for victims and offenders? Exploring restorative justice processes in Australia and the US. *Justice Quarterly*, *32*(1), 142–167.

Outreach efforts directed at increasing awareness of the availability and benefits of restorative justice programs, as well as promoting a better understanding of the general principles upon which they are based, can take on several forms, including partnering with school systems, engaging community leaders through public forums, and utilizing civic volunteers to develop public education resources. The key to this outreach, however, is a more focused campaign to involve various form of media, whether traditional or social media, in promoting success stories, featuring educational workshops, and casting light on the success of restorative justice initiatives.[49]

Creating Program Accountability

Within the domain of criminal justice, the need for accountability in mandated programming has increased dramatically over the past several years. Federal, state, and county governments are requiring impact data that demonstrate how funds invested in programs and services are proving to be beneficial.[50] Evaluation strategies are developing to meet the needs of corrections agencies nationwide in an attempt to answer one question: "is this working?" The simplicity of this question is often overshadowed by the complexity of reaching an answer, and undoubtedly, no single strategy can be used to attempt to answer in all correctional settings. One important dynamic to consider, however, is that the key to understanding whether or not a particular intervention strategy or program works, is to assess its philosophical integrity and practical application in the setting where it is being used.

Thus, a major strength of restorative justice programming and its promise of continued success is to ensure that program evaluation is undertaken as programs are being designed and developed throughout various criminal justice agencies. The capacity to build knowledge which provides a good account of the specific restorative justice practice and its effect on victims, offenders, and community within the particular area it is being used can be achieved through the active engagement of research and scholarship. The recording of data and program monitoring should, therefore, be embedded components of program design from the inception of restorative justice models within the various stages of criminal justice processes. In the following sections, we will examine the importance of this process as restorative justice policies and practices emerge within the criminal justice system, beginning with policy, and throughout the mechanisms of law enforcement, courts, and corrections.

Restorative Justice and Public Policy

Restorative justice practices have the potential to transform criminal justice operations in how they enhance the ways in which victim needs are met while simultaneously ensuring that justice requires that offenders face the consequences of their actions upon others. Although the delivery of restorative justice services can be varied and have many different contextual elements, their benefit in reducing the frequency of reoffending is the hallmark pillar guiding the development of policies governing program design and implementation.[51] Thus, principles of restorative justice shaping the response of the criminal justice system to crime are guided by basic legal principles addressing the public policy dimensions of restorative justice processes and programs. While jurisdictions vary in their definitions and orientation of restorative principles and values, there are certain elements that define their legal basis.

Identifying Key Stakeholders

Policies governing program design and implementation of restorative justice practices should be guided by the principle that those who are most affected by the incidence of crime are victims, offenders, and their communities. Thus, in the pursuit of meaningful justice, it is their interests, and not the interests of professional authorities or state representatives, that should direct evolving legislation guiding programs. In doing so, the law should recognize that all human beings are equal, and regardless of their actions, should be treated with respect in restorative justice settings, as this engenders mutual trust on the part of all participants.

Promoting Accountability

The guidance and development of restorative justice policies relies on the basic premise that human beings are vulnerable and imperfect, and therefore, interventions designed to deal with criminal offenses should be designed around the concepts of mutual care and empathy. Establishing guilt may be a byproduct of criminal justice proceedings, but should not define the outcome of interventions that have the intended goal of repair and restoration. Thus, remedial actions that encourage open dialog and honesty should hold offenders accountable for their actions, while at the same time encourage their feelings of moral responsibility. In promoting moral obligation, the offender is more likely to accept responsibility for his or her actions.[52] Restorative justice policies must, therefore, provide opportunities for offenders to express remorse for their actions, seek forgiveness from their victims, and repair the harm that they have caused.

Meeting Needs of Crime Victims

Restorative justice recognizes that each criminal event is unique and creates conditions that must be addressed through meaningful interventions.[53] Therefore, policies are driven by reparative measures that are tailored to each circumstance involving a criminal offense, with the goal of meeting the specific needs of the victim of that crime. There is a general movement away from "umbrella" policies that cover a wide range of situations, to a more wrap-around approach that allows for the creative response according to the dynamics created by the harm. Integral to this aspect of restorative justice policy is the adoption of measures that call for a plan of repair that identifies all parties involved in this plan — both victims and offenders. This plan details specific actions that are to be taken to address the harm caused to the victim according to specific guidelines, including a timeline for completion and consequences for lack of compliance.

Empowering Communities

Restorative justice theory recognizes the inevitable connection that bonds victims and offenders within the context of community. Thus, policies governing the design and implementation of restorative justice practices acknowledge the need for society to share some of the responsibility for criminal behavior. By recognizing that the key to healing in many cases is to reconcile victims and offenders not just to each other but to their communities, restorative justice policies are built upon the ideals of empowering citizens by making the community itself an ideal setting to address the causes of the offense and its consequences and allow for the healing process to begin.[54] This creates a sense of personal autonomy and restores some of the power differential created by crime, giving communities affected by crime the opportunity to identify their needs and to have a say in how they are restored.

Ensuring Public Safety

The ultimate goal of any policy governing the intervention of criminal justice programs and practices is to reduce the risk of crime and ensure the public is protected from dangerous offenders. Restorative justice policies therefore take into account the need to balance reintegration with the goal of risk assessment.[55] An emphasis is placed on selecting offenders suitable for community supervision, highlighting the need for taking action to ensure offenders are appropriately assessed, treating and identifying other needs, and making available rehabilitative programs as well as employing community resources. While the nature and theoretical basis of restorative justice programming is built on the foundation of voluntary participation, policies guiding the implementation of such programming must nevertheless create mechanisms for oversight, with professional, responsible agents bearing the responsibility for monitoring compliance with terms of any court orders or conditions of probation.

Restorative Justice and Law Enforcement

The role of law enforcement within the criminal justice system necessitates that police invoke a certain set of criteria or standards when dealing with a criminal event. Essentially, they deal with harms that have been committed against individuals from the standpoint of legal guidelines that prohibit the commission of these harms. Restorative justice, on the contrary, compels us to understand the circumstances surrounding these harms, recognizing that a comprehensive response commands a focus that goes beyond the immediate harm itself to address the crime through a preventative approach. From the time a crime is reported and police are called on to respond, the steps taken are critical to the process of criminal justice in terms of evidence and procedure. During this time, police officers must not only think of their roles in this adversarial process, but also the requirements of restorative justice ideologies in terms of problem solving, victim protection, and creating the opportunity for safe dialog.

Some may wonder how it is possible to blend the non-coercive approach of restorative justice with the inherent coercive nature of law enforcement. However, restorative justice ideology and practice transcends the divide that exists between the enforcement role of police and their function as agents of community safety and protection. While the balance may be difficult to achieve, the implementation of restorative justice within law enforcement employs the tools of community-oriented policing, developing positive strategies to recognize harm, enhance problem solving, and build partnerships.[56]

Recognizing Harm

Police strategies centering upon restorative justice values recognize that the commission of a crime is more than a violation of the law. Thus, crime is redefined in a broader sense to take into account how the harm committed affects people. Restorative justice values challenge police to heighten their awareness and sensitivity to the personal and emotional nature of crime, where offenders and victims are seen as individuals and not just detached participants in a criminal event.

In order to effectively employ restorative justice within the context of law enforcement, therefore, police officers must understand the role that shame, fear, and isolation can play when encountering a criminal event, and approach a resolution that takes into account care and empathy over antagonism and vengeance. Likewise, victims of crime should be dealt with in a manner that displays respect and support without instilling a sense of guilt and despair. In recognizing harm, the restorative goal of law enforcement becomes transformed into one that alleviates suffering through the use of creative techniques that support, protect, and allow victims to heal.[57] At the same time, the goal is not to condemn the offender, but rather distinguish the offender from the offense in a pragmatic way, allowing the offender to take part in identifying the harm that was committed and developing a plan to repair that harm. In doing this, law enforcement becomes more about linking actions to meaningful consequences, thereby instilling a sense of empathy and a willingness to change.

Enhancing Problem-Solving

Integrating restorative justice theoretical principles in dealing with crime means responding to criminal offending in a manner that transcends the traditional role of law enforcement in the context of investigation and arrest. The involvement of police officers in restorative justice presupposes a challenge to prevailing views about fighting crime, enforcing the law, and dealing with criminal offenders in a forceful, combative way. Likewise, police officers who are held to strict guidelines governing adherence to procedures and practices must also transition into the role of effective, problem-solving mediators of conflicts that "think outside the box." How can this apparent paradox be resolved?

A major element of implementing restorative justice programming in the context of law enforcement procedures and practices involves the active attempt on the part of human resources and training personnel to enhance problem solving skills by creating the appropriate environment for restorative justice. Part of this effort needs to be driven by an emphasis on cultural sensitivity, an integral component of the restorative justice paradigm of thought. Very often, police departments rely on decision-making processes that are adversarial and steeped in hierarchical power distribution. This poses a great challenge to the mechanisms of restorative justice and the goals of promoting healing and conflict resolution through a competency building approach. Efforts dedicated to training and development are necessary to create a better awareness, understanding, and knowledge base of the problem-solving approach in restorative justice, one that emphasizes cultural sensitivity and the clear perception of a problem as well a comprehensive understanding of the information necessary to solve it (see Table 2.1).

Essentially, restorative justice gives law enforcement the most powerful tool for resolving the many conflicts encountered in their roles as first responders in criminal justice intervention: the tool of rational problem solving. Restorative justice therefore holds the greatest promise for promoting the essential building blocks of community confidence that police officers intuitively recognize is imperative to the success of their jobs. This is not a new approach in law enforcement, but rather, an attempt to shift weight to the integral role of problem-oriented policing, emphasizing new, more amicable and creative ways of resolving problems based on processes and mechanisms that strengthen communities and build emotional confidence in areas that are fragmented by crime and social problems.

Table 2.1: Building on the Paradigm of Problem Solving

Perceptual Blocks to Problem Solving	Effect of Block	Skills Necessary for Appropriate Resolution
• Seeing things from a single perspective due to stereotyping	• Placing little or no value on information that doesn't fit with stereotype	• Remove the effect of preconceptions when approaching a problem • Get the information based on fact alone
• Difficulty detaching the person from the problem	• Treating situations from one dimension alone as opposed to multiple components of a whole	• Adjust to situations based on the recognition that different people react differently in similar circumstances • Recognize the role that perception of individuals has on resolving the problem
• Tunnel vision	• Limiting opportunities for resolution that do not adhere to certain standards	• Learn to think in a manner that is creative and non-traditional • No two people are alike, so why are "solutions" "one size fits all"?
• Inability to identify with others	• Viewing solutions to a problem from your own perspective	• Be able to identify the resolution of a conflict from the perspective of the client • Try to see and hear things you are used to ignoring

Building Community Partnerships

Crime is very often seen as a crisis in communities that are most affected by its presence. Yet, ironically, the role of the criminal justice system in controlling the variable effects of crime can be considered to contribute to the problem rather than mediate its causes. A major source of this paradox is the lack of confidence the public has with regard to the criminal justice system as a whole and law enforcement in particular.[58] Part of the disconnect between law enforcement and the community is the lack of cohesion between the social realities of crime and the response to criminal offending. Legal rules, administrative procedures, and agency guidelines have obstructed the emphasis on community partnership and the mechanisms of community-oriented policing.

The role of restorative justice in law enforcement is most promising in offering alternative and creative strategies to enhance the partnership between police and the community in addressing various social problems that have a direct bearing on criminal behavior. The integration of restorative justice in policing alleviates the adversarial nature of law enforcement within communities, creating forums for dialog between community leaders and police officials to address concerns and mitigate social problems such as culture conflict, substance abuse, economic and social deprivation, and violence. The goal of building partnerships between law enforcement and community not only advances and sustains positive changes, but also reduces the social and moral cost of crime.[59] Restorative justice in law enforcement has the goal of administering justice through capacity building, offering protection and safety to communities by partnering with local agencies and area residents to identify common concerns and develop appropriate strategies to strengthen and improve neighborhoods and reduce conditions that foster fear, crime, and social disorder.

Restorative Justice and Courts

There is no greater forum for the advancement of human rights and due process than the court proceedings of a criminal trial where the role of justice takes on a transformative role in determining guilt, innocence, compensation, and punishment. While the concept of restorative justice within the context of courtroom dynamics and proceedings may seem obscure, there are compelling arguments for advocating a process that accounts for the restorative principles of victim advocacy, inclusion, and repair, as defining the roles of judges, prosecutors, and defense attorneys.

Judges

Within the courtroom, the judge has a tremendous role in affecting the interactions that take place between the defendant, the victim, the prosecutor, and the outcome of the trial. It is their role to ensure that procedures are followed according to the rule of law, as well as ensure that due process is achieved throughout the trial and adjudication. To this extent, judges can be seen as the gatekeepers of restorative justice within the courtroom.[60] We often can hear or imagine a judge referring to it as "my courtroom." This statement has tremendous meaning and signifies the influence a judge can exert in transforming the courtroom.

Within the domain of the courts, judges set the stage for the implementation of restorative justice values and procedures. From the very first contact with an offender, a judge has the authority and discretion to treat that person as an individual and to extend to them the role of a neutral arbitrator, where the punitive value of the criminal justice system is balanced with its contribution to forgiveness, repair, and healing. Judicial authority should be akin to one of leadership and respect and the deference that is commanded to a judge in the courtroom should be perceived as fair, deserved, and representative of the values of justice and equity. In order to create balance, therefore, the judge should adopt the principles of advocacy in addressing the needs of both offenders and victims of crime. There should be a strong emphasis on creating opportunities for informal dialog that support and accommodate the needs of victims in the court process, as well as provide offenders with the resources they need to make amends and reparation. As leaders, therefore, judges are able to endorse and advocate for processes that enhance the criminal justice court process for victims, offenders, and the community.

Prosecutors

Nowhere is the adversarial nature of the criminal justice system more apparent than the courtroom dynamics of prosecutors and defense attorneys. The very process of state v. offender or people v. offender implies a good v. evil mentality that permeates the trial process and makes retribution the root of fact finding and resolution. Taking on a restorative justice approach within the process of presenting evidence, examining witnesses, and determining facts would allow prosecutors to better address community safety, more readily account for the needs of victims, and possibly focus on the underlying reasons for the criminal behavior.[61] In doing this, punishment can go beyond the imposition of penalty and provide for interventions that focus on issues of substance abuse, mental health concerns, homelessness, or other issues. The role of the prosecutor allows for the immediate intervention by the court in a case of criminal offending, and therefore, the prosecutor has the ability to initiate restorative justice processes immediately upon first contact with the criminal justice system court process.

The role of the prosecutor within the paradigm of restorative justice transforms from one of an adversarial arm of criminal justice to more of a partner in a team of players whose goal is to serve the community in the best possible way by making it safer and ensuring that justice is served in a holistic manner. The ultimate goal of the prosecutor should therefore be to ensure that an offender rights the harms they committed against victims and the community, and that the proper interventions are implemented to address any underlying issues behind the criminal behavior. This focus will initiate the process of healing and reconciliation rather than add to the pain and suffering caused by crime, which will ultimately contribute to the goal of reducing criminal offending.

Defense Attorneys

With the role of defense attorney being defined as an advocate for the criminal offender, it is imperative that the domain of restorative justice programs and practices be sought out as the epitome of representation of interests for their client while not overstepping the needs and concerns of both victims and the community. Never has the need been more clear for defense attorneys to adopt the principles of restorative justice than in cases where the determination of guilt and innocence neglect the processes of repair, restoration, and healing.[62] While the identification of diversionary programs and treatment courts can be helpful in terms of meeting the needs of the defense attorney's clients, these courts focus almost entirely on the needs of the offender and do not provide a context where the victim and the offender can engage in encounters that are mutually beneficial.

By advocating for the implementation of restorative justice programming for their clients, defense attorneys can serve their clients in the best possible manner while playing a part in helping achieve justice for the victim through compensation and reparation. To this extent, the defense attorney becomes a bridge to restorative justice programming and practices rather than an obstacle that stands in opposition to the interests of the State as representative of victims and communities. The outcome of court proceedings therefore transitions from a focus on avoiding punishment or loss, to a focus on accepting responsibility, expressing remorse, and becoming reconciled to the victim and the community.

Restorative Justice and Corrections

At the heart of restorative justice theory is the implementation of policies and practices that allow for alternative mechanisms of dispute resolution within the context of the formal system of corrections. In Chapter 10, we will discuss at length the implementation of restorative justice practices within prisons and beyond prison walls to develop restorative reentry programs that are dedicated to helping offenders released from prison successfully transition into the community by allowing them to earn back the rights, privileges, and responsibilities of citizenship. In this section, we want to briefly discuss the application of restorative justice principles within corrections as an alternative means to incarceration which can provide cost-effective, innovative approaches, in a climate of correctional interventions that very often seem to "not be working." Restorative justice within the domain of corrections takes on a transformative, community-driven approach that encompasses a focus on repairing harm, neutralizing the effects of social stigma, and restoring the rights and privileges of a law-abiding citizen.[63]

Focusing on Harm

One very unique aspect of integrating restorative justice values within a correctional setting is recognizing that the harm caused by a criminal action cannot always be repaired by removing the offender from the community. By allowing for alternative sanctions that divert offenders away from incarceration, the process of reparation can be facilitated, and the needs of the victim can better be addressed.[64] Moreover, repairing harm also focuses on family and friends of the offender who can also be considered victims of the harm since they are also affected by the offender's actions, choices, and lifestyle. Restorative justice encourages those relationships to be repaired and does not add to the cycle of deprivation by severing ties between the offender and his or her family.

When appropriate, offenders under supervision and participating in restorative justice programming in the communities they have offended against can be held accountable in a way that their removal from that community does not allow. Within traditional criminal justice circles of dialog, we always talk of an offender doing time in prison as a means of "paying back their debt" to society. How ironic that this "debt" ends up costing society the financial burden of incarceration, as well as possibly the care and well-being of their families that have been left without their provider. Restorative justice challenges societies to remove punitive barriers that increase the failure of offender reintegration and contribute to already high rates of incarceration. In doing this, correctional programming becomes a mutual process between offenders and communities that accounts for the harm committed by the criminal action and focuses on the repair and restoration of relationships, as well as addressing the long-term needs of offenders and their families.

Neutralizing the Effects of Social Stigma

One of the most precarious aspects of criminal justice is the cycle of re-offending. The ultimate goal of correctional intervention is cessation of criminal behavior, and the hallmark of program success is measured by lower rates of recidivism. Completely absent from this goal, however, is a comprehensive understanding of the life-changing effects of legal and social stigma of criminal conviction and how this stigma can render any type of formal correctional intervention ineffective. The impact of arrest, trial, and conviction, and the process of applying the formal label of criminal, has a profound impact on conferring a deviant identity and self-concept upon individuals. The challenges created by criminal offending are therefore compounded by the reactions of family, friends, peers, and the community in general, creating a cycle of **deviance amplification**, where persistent involvement in criminal behavior is an outcome of isolation and the development of behavior patterns that reflect the values and beliefs of a deviant identity.[65]

Restorative justice is rooted in the principle that community-based social control agents such as family, friends, and coworkers are effective and positive forms of control that can increase the success of offenders under community supervision, while at the same time enabling them to avoid the stigma of incarceration and the application of formal labels. Community-driven correctional intervention that allows offenders to follow specific guidelines and make appropriate reparative amends increase the chances that offenders will become productive members of their communities and transform their perception of law and justice by allowing for their acceptance and a second chance at having a clean record. Accepting responsibility, developing respect, and taking on an active role in their reintegration changes the status of offenders from "convicts" to law-abiding citizens, impacting their own self-perceptions and driving them towards a life free of criminal offending against a community that has offered them forgiveness and acceptance.

Restoring Citizenship

The transformation of an offender's identity from that of criminal to a productive, law-abiding citizen is the cornerstone of the implementation of restorative justice within the domain of corrections. A focus on collaboration between the offender and the community reaffirms that identity by allowing the offender to see himself or herself in a new light in the public eye. By being given the chance to demonstrate remorse and show responsibility, offenders can experience acceptance instead of rejection and the hope of restoration of their full rights as citizens of their community.

Restorative justice practices therefore give offenders a chance at "shedding away" their cloak of criminal conviction. By participating in and successfully completing programs that divert them out of the formal criminal justice process, ex-offenders can be free from carrying their conviction throughout their lives and declaring it to potential friends, employers, and other officials. This allows a complete restoration of citizenship that renews the identity and reduces the likelihood of reoffending. Researcher Shadd Maruna explains, "convictions ... are merely labels given by the State in the name of punishment, and equally these can be taken away in the name of reintegration, along with a restoration of the full civil rights, liberties, and duties that all of us share."[66]

The ideas, principles, and practices of restorative justice align well with the goals of criminal justice policy and practice. Are there implications for the use of these same mechanisms outside the purview of criminal offending? We turn now to an exploration of the application of restorative justice principles and practices beyond the criminal justice system.

Restorative Practices Outside the Criminal Justice System

In section three of this textbook, we examine various contexts within which restorative justice models have been developed outside of the criminal justice system, including schools, work places, and community action groups. These practices have the collective effect of implementing peaceful alternatives to dispute resolution that address issues of discipline, disrespect, fear, and regulation. Throughout these practices, the integration of restorative values has created programmatic goals that emphasize informal social control, cultural awareness and sensitivity, and creative dialog.

Informal Social Control

The fundamental tenets of restorative justice place responsibility on all citizens for the goals of integration, crime control, and social order.[67] Restorative justice theory supports the notion that punishment alone does very little to promote responsibility and self-discipline.[68] The aim of creating a climate of discipline and regulation within various contexts such as school, workplaces, government agencies, and community organizations is best served by promoting the concepts of problem-solving and employing alternative sanctions that take into account the fact that behavior change has many different sources.

Very often, behavior that is viewed as disruptive, combative, and a threat to the peace and integrity of individuals is dealt with in a manner that fosters terminal actions such as suspension, expulsion, and termination. This punitive approach fails to recognize the signs and "symptoms" of conflict that lead to an escalation of disputes that ultimately could be prevented by addressing these signs and symptoms when they first appear. Social support mechanisms should be developed as a first line of defense approach to conflict resolution, where informal mechanisms of control are embedded in a more effective and efficient way that goes beyond administrative and legal disciplinary regimes to ones that embrace family engagement, therapeutic intervention, and community support.

The integration of restorative justice theory and practice in various community settings, therefore, requires a transformation of the approach to discipline and conflict resolution from one that relies on the formal mechanism of punishment to ones that are aimed at strengthening networks of informal control and social support. By connecting individuals with the ideas of reparation, reintegration, and stakeholder involvement, community settings involving the interaction between individuals will become revitalized and rely on the concept of relationship building, creating a new environment of resources that supports and encourages cooperation and mutual respect. This, in turn, will reduce the likelihood of escalating conflicts that can lead to violence and aggression, especially in school settings where an emphasis on repairing harm and restoring relationships gives students the opportunity to become reengaged with their classmates. This more positive approach to social control has proven to bring about better outcomes than the more punitive formal approach of **zero tolerance**, which emphasizes suspension from school, further isolating troubled teenagers and failing to address the underlying sources of the conflict.

Cultural Awareness and Sensitivity

Inherent to restorative justice theory and practice is the expansion of knowledge in conflict resolution to include an understanding of differences in worldview, social interactions, and the formulation of identity as defined through the lens of cultural diversity. The administration of justice within different contexts therefore must account for the fact that disputes and disagreements may be embedded in the type of environment in which an individual has been raised, and likewise, their resolution may rest upon a better comprehension of this environment. Thus, it is critical that schools, workplaces, community agencies, and religious organizations that come into contact with so many different people with different needs, views, and ideas, be equipped with an understanding of the role that cultural diversity plays in human interactions.

Restorative justice creates the opportunity for managers, administrators, and leaders to ensure that their role equips those around them with an awareness of cultural differences, in order to remove the presence of stereotypes that are barriers to conflict resolution and reconciliation. Sometimes, the most appropriate course of action in a resolution presupposes an understanding of the other's point of view. The integration of restorative justice in such settings promotes this understanding through its emphasis on developing empathy for others by removing barriers to reconciliation.[69] With such insight, the barriers created and reinforced by various stereotypes about people that are different from us are neutralized in the process of conflict resolution.

Enhancing cultural awareness and sensitivity can take on various forms and can include increasing access to diversity training, providing language interpreters when needed, creating programs that increase cultural proficiency, and increasing communication opportunities. Such techniques, programs, and interventions will encourage empathy and understanding and can have a positive impact on the resolution of conflicts and disputes.

Creative Dialog

When we think of dialog, we sometimes overlook the fact that it sometimes takes courage to talk about things that make us uncomfortable such as abuse, discrimination, anxiety, fear, and many other subjects that are at the heart of dissent and discord. The reparative actions of restorative justice in rebuilding relationships and creating mutual respect between citizens sustains the development of creative dialog that facilitates peaceful conversations that can avoid the escalation of further violence and hostility in certain situations (see Box 2.3). Relying on a participatory model of conflict resolution therefore allows all stakeholders to engage in constructive dialog to determine harms, needs, and obligations through peaceful collective action.[70]

Box 2.3: Restorative Justice: Let's Take a Closer Look...
How Restorative Is RJ? The Case of Ferguson, Missouri

On November 16, 2014, a grand jury of nine Whites and three Blacks acquitted police officer Darren Wilson from criminal charges related to the killing of Michael Brown, an unarmed Black youth, on a residential street in Ferguson, Missouri. The decision followed weeks of civil unrest and outrage throughout the St. Louis area over patterns of police brutality against young Black men. News of the decision caused hundreds of people gathered outside the Ferguson Police Department to take to the streets in an explosion of violence. Citizens and police clashed with one another as bottles were hurled at police, gunshots were exchanged, buildings were set on fire, and looting of businesses took place amidst the deploying of smoke and gas to control the crowds. What, if anything, could calm this apparent declaration of war between law enforcement and the community of citizens they are designed to serve and protect?

Restorative justice activists note that the only hope for rebuilding the trust between police and citizens in cases of extreme cynicism, fear, and hatred, is to bridge the divide that has been created through events such as those in Ferguson by acknowledging that injustice and oppression are not the answer nor are they the key to moving forward. From this perspective, reparation and peace can only restored by bringing together stakeholders with diverse interests and creating a forum for dialog and an expression of hurt, anger, and animosity in a manner that is productive and healing. This peaceful approach can better engage citizen representatives and members of law enforcement to create innovative solutions that acknowledge the harms that have been committed and that correct the wrongs that are experienced. Do you think this solution-oriented approach can better address injustice and show a genuine willingness on the part of both community and authority to work together to make things right?

Source: Rea, L. (2014, 19 August). Justice in Ferguson, Missouri: Can restorative justice apply here? *Restorative Justice International.* Retrieved from http://www.restorativejusticeinternational.com/2014/justice-in-ferguson-missouri-can-restorative-justice-apply-here/.

In chapters to come, we will discuss the specific types of creative dialog that are the foundations of restorative justice theory and practice. For now, we have laid the foundation and set the stage for the historical development of restorative justice, its theoretical roots, and the embedding of its principles and practices inside and outside the criminal justice system. In the next chapter, we will elaborate further on the standing pillars of restorative justice principles and practice.

Chapter Summary

How did the restorative justice movement begin?

Restorative justice ideology began with ancient societies that embraced the idea of making reparation to the victim of crime and not the State. Within these primitive communities, members were concerned with creating close-knit relationships in order to sustain the integrity of the tribal structure and, therefore, conflicts between individuals were dealt with in a manner that lacked the type of institutional force characteristic of later types of State, centralized social structures. These restorative ideologies declined significantly during the Middle Ages when simple, tribal communities transformed into more complex social structures. The key features of these societies—specialization and centralization—led to the emergence of stratification, whereby fragmentation amongst the people led to a decline in cooperation amongst group members. As acts of crime and delinquency became equated with a threat to the State, the hierarchical order of society continued to grow, widening the gap between those in power and the rest of the people. These dynamics ushered in an era of harsh punishments upon criminal offenders that were aimed at vengeance and retribution. However, during the 1960s and 1970s, correctional theory and criminal justice discourse set the stage for the modern restorative justice movement to begin its course. During the 1980s and early 1990s, criminologist Howard Zehr provided us with a framework for the restorative justice movement, laying the foundation for restorative justice theory and practice by calling for a transformation in the approach to criminal justice that is more focused on the harms surrounding criminal actions, rather than the punishment of criminal offenders.

What is the theoretical grounding of restorative justice principles?

The theoretical origins of restorative justice date back to the works of Eglash, who coined the term "creative restitution," or acts of restoration that met certain criteria such as being driven by the offender, relating to the criminal offense, and contributing constructively to those directly affected by the crime. Eglash also developed the ideas of communication between victims and offenders, restorative restitution, and community integration of offenders. Christie proposed a process of justice that was less concerned with prevention or deterrence and more concerned with adherence to values and processes that will grow and sustain healthy communities capable of addressing crime. Perhaps the most integral theorist that laid the theoretical foundation of restorative justice principles and practice is Braithwaite, who argued that offenders should be given the chance to become law-abiding members of their community through the process of reintegrative shaming, which, according to Braithwaite, allows offenders to earn this as a right, by expressing remorse for their harmful actions, repairing the loss caused by the crime, and apologizing to their victim.

How has restorative justice become integrated in the criminal justice system?

The application of restorative justice theory in the various stages of arrest, trial, court processing, and conviction is best described as a process which involves a plan of action that enhances the provision and delivery of restorative processes across various components of the criminal justice system. This includes assessing need and improving access, educating the public and practitioners, and creating program accountability. These dynamics become integral to the emergence of restorative justice policies and practices within the criminal justice system, beginning with policy, and throughout the mechanisms of law enforcement, courts, and corrections.

In what ways is restorative justice used outside the criminal justice system?

There are various contexts within which restorative justice models have been established outside of the criminal justice system. These settings include schools, workplaces, churches, government agencies, and community groups. While these contexts are discussed in great detail in upcoming chapters, we showed that the various practices of restorative justice established in these contexts are designed to emphasize informal social control, increase cultural awareness and sensitivity, and foster creative dialog.

Key Terms

Acephalous Societies
Monkalun
Specialization
Stratification
Centralization
Creative Restitution
Reintegrative Shaming Theory
Subcultural Theory
Labeling Theory
Social Bond Theory
Social Control Theory
Social Strain Theory
Differential Association Theory
Deviance Amplification
Zero Tolerance

Critical Thinking Questions

1. Consider the various historical stages of the rise and fall and rise again of restorative justice theory and practice. What obstacles exist in our society today that present a challenge to the continued evolution of restorative justice? How can these obstacles be overcome?

2. Is the concept of reintegrative shaming truly different from what we would consider disintegrative shaming? What clear example can you come up with that illustrates the difference in theory and practice between the two?

3. Which component of criminal justice do you find restorative justice to be most beneficial to? Why and how does the application of restorative justice within this component have long-term benefits to society in general?

4. With regard to restorative justice outside of the context of criminal offending, which social institutions and organizations would benefit most from creating programs and policies that advocate for informal dialog, conflict resolution, and a reintegrative approach?

References

1. Johnstone, G. (2013). *Restorative justice: Ideas, values, debates.* Routledge.

2. Bazemore, G., & Schiff, M. (2015). *Restorative community justice: Repairing harm and transforming communities.* Routledge.

3. Kradin, N. N. (2015). Nomadism, evolution and world-systems: Pastoral societies in theories of historical development. *Journal of World-Systems Research, 8*(3), 368–388.

4. Ibid.

5. Hames, R. (2014). Diversity in human behavioral ecology. *Human Nature, 25*(4), 443–447.

6. Sponsel, L. E. (2016). The anthropology of peace and nonviolence. *Diogenes, 61*(3–4), 30–45. doi: 0392192116648597.

7. Van Ness, D. W., & Strong, K. H. (2013). *Restoring justice: An introduction to restorative justice.* Routledge.

8. Durkheim, E. (2013). *Emile Durkheim on institutional analysis.* University of Chicago Press.

9. Hall, J. R. (Ed.). (2013). *Civil society: Theory, history, comparison.* John Wiley & Sons.

10. Durkheim, E. (2014). *The division of labor in society.* Simon and Schuster.

11. Kerbo, H. (2014). Social stratification: Trends and processes. *Contemporary Sociology: A Journal of Reviews, 43*(2), 225–226.

12. Gibson, D. B., & Geselowitz, M. N. (Eds.). (2013). *Tribe and polity in late prehistoric Europe: Demography, production, and exchange in the evolution of complex social systems.* Springer Science & Business Media.

13. Pollock, F., & Maitland, F. W. (1898). *The history of the English criminal law before the time of Edward I.* Cambridge: Cambridge University Press.

14. Michalowski, R. (1985). *Order, law and crime.* New York: Random House.

15. Sharpe, J. (1980). Enforcing the law in the seventeenth century English village. In V. Gatrell (Ed.), *Crime and the law.* London: Europa; More, T. S. (1990) [1515]. *Utopia.* New Haven, London: Yale University Press.

16. Bazemore, G. (1999). Restorative justice, earned redemption and a communitarian response to crime. *The communitarian network: Position papers and case studies,* 1–76.

17. Eglash, A. (1957). Creative restitution—A broader meaning for an old term. *J. Crim. L. Criminology & Police Sci., 48,* 619.

18. Barnett, R. E., & Hagel, J. (Eds.). (1977). *Assessing the criminal: Restitution, retribution, and the legal process* (p. 363). Cambridge, MA: Ballinger Publishing Company.

19. Beiser, V. (2009, September 21). Nils Christie: Empty the prisons. *Culture.* Retrieved from https://www.wired.com/2009/09/ff-smartlist-christie/.

20. Wright, M. (1977). Nobody came: Criminal justice and the needs of victims. *The Howard Journal of Criminal Justice, 16*(1), 22–31.

21. Zehr, H. J. (1990). *Changing lenses: A new focus for crime and justice.* Harrisonburg, VA: Herald Press.

22. Braithwaite, J. (2002). *Restorative justice and responsive regulation.* New York, NY: Oxford University Press.

23. MacRae, A., & Zehr, H. (2004). *The little book of family group conferences: New Zealand style: A hopeful approach when youth cause harm.* Intercourse, PA: Good Books.

24. Mirsky, L. (2003). Albert Eglash and creative restitution: A precursor to restorative practices. *International Institute for Restorative Practices.* Retrieved from http://www.iirp.edu/pdf/eglash.pdf.

25. Van Ness, D. W. (2007). Prisons and restorative justice. In G. Johnstone & D. W. Van Ness (Eds.), *Handbook of restorative justice* (pp. 312–324). Portland, OR: Willan Publishing.

26. Franko, K. (2010). Nils Christie. In K. Hayward, S. Maruna, & J. Mooney (Eds.), *Fifty great thinkers in criminology* (pp. 168–173). New York, NY: Routledge.

27. Christie, N. (1977). Conflicts as property. *The British Journal of Criminology, 17*(1), page 3.

28. Ibid., see 27, page 6.

29. Ibid., see 27, page 8.

30. Ibid., see 27, page 9.

31. Braithwaite, J. (1989). *Crime, shame and reintegration.* Cambridge University Press.

32. Ibid., see 31, page 4.

33. Ibid., see 31, page 55.

34. Ibid., see 31, page 85.

35. Miller, W. B. (1962). The impact of a 'total-community' delinquency control project. *Social Problems, 10*(2), 168–191.

36. Copes, H., Topalli, V., Copes, H., & Topalli, V. (2009). *Criminological theory.* McGraw-Hill Companies, page 191.

37. Ibid., see page 27.

38. Tannenbaum, F. (1938). *Crime and the community* (pp. 19–20). Boston: Ginn.

39. Ibid., see page 320.

40. Braithwaite, J. (1989). Crime, shame and reintegration. Cambridge University Press, page 21.

41. Hirschi, T., & Stark, R. (1969). Hellfire and delinquency. *Social Problems, 17*(2), 202–213.

42. Ibid., see page 264.

43. Ibid., see pages 265–266.

44. Merton, R. K. (1957). *Social theory and social structure* (rev). New York: Free Press.

45. Sutherland, E. H. (1947). *Principles of criminology: A sociological theory of criminal behavior.* New York: J.B. Lippincott Company.

46. Ibid., see page 225.

47. Braithwaite, J. (1989). Crime, shame and reintegration. Cambridge University Press, page 38.

48. Miller, S. L., & Hefner, M. K. (2015). Procedural justice for victims and offenders? Exploring restorative justice processes in Australia and the US. *Justice Quarterly, 32*(1), 142–167.

49. Johnsen, P., & Robertson, E. (2015). Protecting, restoring, improving: Incorporating therapeutic jurisprudence and restorative justice concepts into civil domestic violence cases. *U. Pa. L. Rev., 164*, 1557.

50. Miller, J. M., & Miller, H. V. (2015). Rethinking program fidelity for criminal justice. *Criminology & Public Policy, 14*(2), 339–349.

51. Bouffard, J., Cooper, M., & Bergseth, K. (2016). The effectiveness of various restorative justice interventions on recidivism outcomes among juvenile offenders. *Youth Violence and Juvenile Justice, 15*(4), 465–480. doi: 1541204016647428.

52. Bazemore, G., & Schiff, M. (2015). *Restorative community justice: Repairing harm and transforming communities.* Routledge.

53. Flynn, A. (2015). Sexual violence and innovative responses to justice. In *Rape justice* (pp. 92–111). Palgrave Macmillan UK.

54. Gonzalez, T. (2015). Reorienting restorative justice: Initiating a new dialogue of rights consciousness, community empowerment and politicization. *Cardozo Journal of Conflict Resolution, 16*.

55. Mercer, V., & Sten Madesen, K. (2015). *Doing restorative justice in cases of sexual violence: A practice guide.* Edited by M. Keenan & E. Zinsstag. Leuven Institute of Criminology.

56. Normore, A. H., Ellis, B., Clamp, K., & Paterson, C. (2015). Cross-cultural collaboration for community-oriented policing and restorative justice. In N. D. Erbe & A. H. Normore (Eds.), *Cross-Cultural Collaboration and Leadership in Modern Organizations* (pp. 255–272). IGI Global.

57. Hoyle, C., & Willis, R. (2016). The challenge of integrating restorative justice into the "deep-end" of criminal justice. In T. G. Blomberg, J. M. Brancale, K. M. Beaver, & W. D. Bales (Eds.), *Advancing criminology and criminal justice policy* (pp. 324–336). London: Routledge.

58. Cao, L. (2015). Differentiating confidence in the police, trust in the police, and satisfaction with the police. *Policing: An International Journal of Police Strategies & Management, 38*(2), 239–249.

59. Boateng, F. D., Lee, H. D., & Abess, G. (2016). Analyzing citizens' reported levels of confidence in the police: A cross-national study of public attitudes toward the police in the United States and South Korea. *Asian Journal of Criminology,* 1–20.

60. Hernández, C. A. M., Solís, L. M. C., Fernández, M. A. M., & Cisneros-Cohernour, E. (2016). Alternative dispute settlement mechanisms: Towards restorative justice in Yucatán, Mexico. *US-China Education Review, 6*(2), 118–124.

61. Wong, D. S. (2016). Restorative justice at different levels of the criminal justice system in China: Challenges and paths forward. *Restorative Justice, 4*(1), 10–26.

62. Szabo, A. (2016, June). Bringing justice back into the community: The case of Vermont, US. European Forum for Restorative Justice.

63. Rocque, M., Posick, C., & Paternoster, R. (2016). Identities through time: An exploration of identity change as a cause of desistance. *Justice Quarterly*, *33*(1), 45–72.

64. Glynn, L. H., Kendra, M. S., Timko, C., Finlay, A. K., Blodgett, J. C., Maisel, N. C., ... & Blonigen, D. M. (2016). Facilitating treatment access and engagement for justice-involved veterans with substance use disorders. *Criminal Justice Policy Review*, *27*(2), 138–163.

65. Bouffard, J., Cooper, M., & Bergseth, K. (2016). The effectiveness of various restorative justice interventions on recidivism outcomes among juvenile offenders. *Youth Violence and Juvenile Justice*, *15*(4), 465–480. doi: 1541204016647428.

66. Maruna, S. (2006). Who owns resettlement? Towards restorative reintegration. *British Journal of Community Justice*, *4*(2), 23–33, see page 31.

67. Gal, T. (2016). "The conflict is ours": Community involvement in restorative justice. *Contemporary Justice Review*, *19*(3), 289–306.

68. Vincent, C. G., Inglish, J., Girvan, E. J., Sprague, J. R., & McCabe, T. M. (2016). School-wide positive and restorative discipline (SWPRD): Integrating school-wide positive behavior interventions and supports and restorative discipline. In R. J. Skiba, K. Mediratta, & M. K. Rausch (Eds.), *Inequality in school discipline* (pp. 115–134). Palgrave Macmillan US.

69. Parsons, A. R. (2015). Understanding restorative justice—How empathy can close the gap created by crime. *British Journal of Community Justice*, *13*(1), 114–116.

70. Ortega, L., Lyubansky, M., Nettles, S., & Espelage, D. L. (2016). Outcomes of a restorative circles program in a high school setting. *Psychology of Violence*, *6*(3), 459.

Chapter 3

The Pillars of Restorative Values

In this chapter, we will explore the following questions …
- *What are the various types of harms that people can experience?*
- *Are there specific needs created by the harms that individuals go through?*
- *How do we hold offenders accountable for the wrongs that are committed?*
- *In what ways is community engaged in restorative justice processes?*

Redefining the Concept of Harm

We have seen thus far that restorative justice addresses crime as conflict with the goal of restoring autonomy to victims and offenders by engaging them directly in the process of determining just responses to criminal offenses.[1] Rather than imposing punishment on the offender for a violation of law, restorative processes acknowledge the needs of victims, offenders, and communities after crime by focusing on repairing the harm of the offense and allowing those involved and impacted to mutually agree upon that repair, thereby encouraging the process of reconciliation to begin.

As restorative processes become increasingly accepted as worthwhile and effective, we continue to strive to understand the very mechanism by which we hope to achieve such outcomes as victim satisfaction and offender transformation and desistance. Additionally, we continue to explore the motivations, experiences, and perceptions of key participants in restorative processes and how their experiences can better inform those who are the practitioners and purveyors of restorative opportunities within the criminal justice system. Moreover, as restorative processes become more and more legitimized, they inevitably expand into more contexts and are offered to a greater number of offenders and victims. As this occurs, we are seeing some restorative programs expanding into institutions such as schools and correctional facilities. As we move forward towards the institutionalization of restorative processes, however, we must first take a step back and look at the very pillars upon which restorative justice programs and practices rest. In doing this, we can better understand what it will take to maintain the integrity of restorative justice policy and fulfill its established goals and desired outcomes.

What Is Harm?

Understanding the harm that has been done is the first defining pillar of restorative justice values and principles. Likewise, the rehabilitative value of restorative justice is tangible only to the extent that the offender acknowledges the harm caused to their victim and to the community and begins making amends. Of utmost importance, however, is that the offender has a full awareness of the diverse meaning of harm in order to begin taking responsibility for their actions. The defining character of restorative justice, therefore, hinges upon a comprehensive understanding of the concept of harm, its nature, consequences, and remedy in various different contexts and circumstances.

Following a criminal act, victims experience a variety of consequences that begin with an immediate disruption of their lives and continue through various stages that may include long-term trauma. Understanding the impact that crime has on victims has been the subject of criminal justice literature for quite some time.[2] The expanding field of **victimology** focuses on a scientific study of the physical, emotional, and social harm that victims experience from crime.[3] Victimologists include experts such as researchers, academics, and investigators who study victimization in order to gain a better perspective of the relationship between victims, offenders, and their interactions with the criminal justice system. In fact, it is the study of victimology that first established the often-neglected relationship between victimization and offending (see Box 3.1). Through the expansive understanding this field has provided us, we are able to approach the concept of victimization in a holistic manner that includes a variety of meanings depending on the context of its use. Victimization is indeed a complex phenomenon that is subject to a multitude of broad social-cultural and micro-situational influences. This complexity, in turn, necessitates a more concise theoretical approach to the defining character of the experience of harm.

Box 3.1: Restorative Justice: Let's Take a Closer Look ...
Victimology: A Restorative Justice Paradigm?

Central to the restorative justice paradigm's focus on identifying victim needs and emphasis on reparation of harm is a better understanding of crime victimization and its potential overlap with criminal offending. The concept of a victim-offender overlap can be traced back to Hans Von Hentig, whose formidable work, *The Criminal and His Victim* (1948), was the first major criminological publication to explicitly recognize the phenomenon and provide us with a theoretical understanding. Von Hentig argued that there are two categories of crime victims: individuals who passively become recipients of violence and those who through their own actions contribute to their unfortunate circumstances. It was this latter class of victims that many criminologists and other legal professionals overlooked within their research studies. Von Hentig notes that the idea of the victim-offender overlap by the law's criterion includes "perpetrators and victims as being distinguished ... [but] it may happen that the two distinct categories merge … and in the course of causative forces the victim assumes the role of a determinant." Additionally, Von Hentig speculated that this overlap among both victims and offenders could also arise from potential perpetrators pursuing victims who have some type of involvement in crime as a result of their reluctance to contact the police. Finally, Von Hentig recognized the plethora of research literature revealing multiple shared characteristics between criminal offending and victimization in several dynamic ways, including age, gender, socioeconomic status, and other demographic traits.

While Von Hentig did not actually articulate a particular theoretical explanation of the victim-offender overlap, his work marked the beginning of studies identifying the significance of victimization research for criminological knowledge. Through his efforts and contributions, Von Hentig drew attention to the relationship between crime victimization and criminal offending, setting the stage for the development of decades of research designed to explain the nature, cause, and extent of this relationship. What is your view on the relationship between criminal victimization and criminal offending?

Source: Hass, A., & Hannis, C. (2016, July). In their words: A qualitative analysis of the victim-offender overlap. *International Victimology Review.* doi: 10.1177/0269758016654238.

Restorative justice processes utilize a victim-centered approach that is designed to empower victims of crime. This empowerment is seen as key to healing and is often neglected during traditional criminal justice proceedings that fail to fully acknowledge and address the trauma experienced by victims. Victimization creates a sense of imbalance, as the sudden experience of harm can lead to stigmatization, isolation, and self-blame. These variables, in turn, compound the experience of harm that they have already suffered from the criminal act.[4] Responding to crime as more than just a violation of law changes the way people think about crime as a mere act of rebellion against the State. A focus on the harms that resulted from the criminal action takes on a preventative approach that not only helps victims recover from their loss, but also allow offenders to deal more effectively with their actions and promote care and responsibility for their victims and their communities. The task of repairing harm, however, necessities a better understanding of the harm that was committed. Table 3.1 provides an overview with the various types of harm associated with criminal offending.

What then do we need to know about how to better address harm through the implementation of restorative justice programs and practices? Let's take a closer look at the necessary elements of effective harm reparation.

Table 3.1: The Experience of Harm

Physical/Material Harm	Emotional/ Psychological Harm	Social Harm
Property damage	Loss of confidence	Disconnected from people
Bodily injury	Feeling humiliated/ashamed	Relationship interruption
Loss of tangible memories	Emotional trauma	Reduced mobility/autonomy
Loss of life	Depression	Loss of control
Missing work	Anxiety/fear	Feeling alone and isolated
Loss of income	Feeling helpless/weak	Unable to relate to people
Identity theft	Betrayal	Loss of social networks
Physical pain	Loss of control	Lack of interest in activities
Loss of sleep	Loss of safety and security	Cannot concentrate at job
Hospital bills	Feelings of anger and revenge	Incapable of trusting others

A Restorative Approach to Repairing Harms

From the perspective of traditional criminal justice intervention, court proceedings that establish guilt and exact punishment are equated with "making things right," restoring balance, and bringing justice to the victim of crime. However, studies show that many victims of crime who go to court, follow the trial of their offenders, and sit through the sentencing process, still do not feel that the harms they experienced and the resulting needs have been taken care of in a manner that promotes healing and repair.[5] In fact, this process negates the very premise upon which children are raised to become responsible, empathetic individuals who are able to identify the wrongfulness of their actions by reflecting on the harm and expressing remorse.

Consider, for example, Kohlberg's theory of moral development (see Figure 3.1). According to Kohlberg, the earliest, most primitive state of moral development involves the avoidance of punishment, while the highest state of moral development implies an abstract understanding of standards of right and wrong. The message that punishment alone sends to offenders, therefore, does nothing to promote a higher level of moral reasoning but rather equates the outcome of their actions with a consequence that is desired to be avoided in the future.[6] While deterrence of criminal behavior is necessary, the traditional criminal justice system does not force us to think of the impact of crime beyond court proceedings and sentencing outcomes. Restorative justice values take us a step further by outlining standards by which we should approach the reparation process from a more meaningful perspective that redefines justice and punishment beyond conviction and sentencing to appropriately addressing harm and promoting the victim's needs for healing. What exactly are these standards of repairing harm that are advocated by restorative justice?

Figure 3.1: Kohlberg's Theory of Moral Development

LEVEL 3	POSTCONVENTIONAL (shared standards, rights, duties)	Stage 6: self-selection of universal principles Stage 5: sense of democracy and relativity of rules
LEVEL 2	CONVENTIONAL (performing right roles)	Stage 4: fulfilling duties and upholding laws Stage 3: meeting expectations of others
LEVEL 1	PRECONVENTIONAL (values in external events)	Stage 2: "getting what you want" by trade-off Stage 1: punishment avoidance

Source: Kohlberg, L. (1973). The claim to moral adequacy of a highest stage of moral judgment. *The Journal of Philosophy, 70*(18): 630–646. Used by permission.

Let Victims Tell Their Story

The experience of being able to verbally express a hurt is seen as one of the most significant steps towards healing.[7] Being able to communicate to offenders the emotions, feelings, and anxieties felt by the experience of harm is paramount to the process of reparation. It allows those feelings to become transferred to the offender, who would then feel a sense of obligation to right the wrong and properly address the harm that has been committed by their actions. A simple statement of the pain during the sentencing phase of formal court proceedings does little to include the victim as a key player in determining what should be done in response to a crime, whereas the ability to fully express their feelings and tell their story becomes a symbolic gesture that helps create healing.

Treat Each Harm as Unique

In recent years, **reentry** programming aimed at reintegrating offenders back into the community after a period of incarceration, has focused on a wrap-around approach that accounts for the unique risks, needs, and abilities presented by a single offender.[8] These programs are based on the ideology that crime and its solutions are not a "one size fits all," and the best approach to reduce recidivism is one that accounts for the variable dynamics that exist from offender to offender. Likewise, when dealing with the reparation of harm from a criminal offense, there should be an understanding, as we have seen, that harms come in many different forms and therefore the reparation of harm should be dealt with through a creative mixture of methods that exercise care and empathy.

Alleviate Suffering

Since material reparation is not possible in many cases, a restorative approach to the reparation of harm must have at its core value the alleviation of suffering. Feelings of despair, sadness, and grief often accompany the experience of crime victimization, especially when the loss is permanent, such as in the case of homicide. Such severe emotions cannot be effectively dealt with through the process of dealing with the criminal act as a violation of law. There should be a significant focus on reparation that mediates the pain associated with the loss as part of the process of addressing this harm. As part of alleviating suffering, a restorative approach promotes healing by empowering crime victims through an approach that increases trust, reduces fear, and fosters healing.

Moreover, victims of crime often experience another form of victimization, the psychological stress, trauma, and re-victimization of living the crime once again, that is associated with trial proceedings.[9] While the goal of the criminal court is to restore justice to the victim of the crime, that justice is neither restorative nor healing, and can actually further the trauma experienced by victims. The goal of restorative repair is therefore to intervene in a manner that makes the victim's suffering more tolerable, provide support during trial procedures, and prevent any further emotional and psychological pain to the victim.

Acknowledge Secondary Victims

When a crime occurs, it is usually pretty easy to identify the **primary victim**, the individual who was directly impacted by the crime ... a child is the victim of abuse, a neighbor's car is vandalized, a police officer is shot, a department store experiences theft, and so on. There are other victims, however, that are sometimes forgotten, individuals who are indirectly impacted by a criminal act, but are not acknowledged as **secondary victims** of crime (see Box 3.2).[10] These individuals can include families, coworkers, friends, and the community at large. Consider, for example, when a school shooting takes place. There are, of course, individuals who are the direct victims of the shooting—students, teachers, administrators—but there are also other victims of such tragedies. The parents and friends of those who are killed, coworkers and students that witness the shooting, and even the community where the shooting takes place, where other parents experience fear, anger, and anxiety about their own kids. Restorative justice addresses needs and seeks reparative solutions that take into account all those who have suffered from the experience of harm, encouraging those who have been impacted to speak out about their victimizations and making sure that actions to repair the harms are extended to them.

Repairing harm based upon the founding principles of restorative justice is imperative to the healing and restoration of offenders in a manner that cannot be reached through traditional mechanisms of criminal justice. In a similar fashion, restorative justice principles are best utilized when identifying the needs of victims and ensuring the proper stages of victim recovery are taking place.

Box 3.2: Research in Restorative Justice —
   The Non-Offending Parent ... A Secondary Victim of
   Child Sexual Abuse

Criminologists refer to the experience of trauma caused by witnessing the victimization of another person as **vicarious victimization**. It can occur within the context of various forms of criminal events, from a purse snatching, to a robbery, homicide, mass shooting, or an act of terrorism. The psychological impact of such experiences can have long-term negative effects if not properly addressed. Moreover, the emotional reactions of the secondary victims who experience vicarious victimization can be intense, especially if those individuals themselves have experienced direct victimization, increasing their sense of fear, anxiety, and feelings of helplessness. The outlook of these dynamics can lead to despair without the proper intervention mechanism to target secondary victims of crime.

Researchers note that the experience of child sexual abuse has a significant impact on the non-offending parent. The feelings of denial, anger, and disbelief are compounded by the emotional reaction of sadness, grief, guilt, and shame at not being able to protect their child from harm. Moreover, the non-offending parent has to deal with the burden of hurt and betrayal that accompany such a violation of trust on the part of the offending parent, as well as the possibility of divorce, financial worries, and the long-term impact of the crime on their relationship with the injured child.

In a pilot program designed to treat non-offending parents of sexually abused children, an integrated approach was used to combine components of trauma-focused cognitive-based therapy with educational and supportive interventions. Researchers found a significant decrease in posttraumatic stress and family dysfunction by parents who completed the program, with participants reporting satisfaction with this type of family-centered intervention to help cope with the psychosocial trauma of being the non-offending parent of a child abuse victim. Implications from these findings suggest an urgent need for the extension of restorative justice focused settings to help secondary victims of crime cope with their feelings and emotions and better integrate these individuals into programming that engages them in a dialog that promotes their healing and restoration.

Sources: Fuller, G. (2016). Non-offending parents as secondary victims of child sexual assault. *Trends and Issues in Crime and Criminal Justice*, (500), 1. Hernandez, A., Ruble, C., Rockmore, L., McKay, M., Messam, T., Harris, M., & Hope, S. (2009). An integrated approach to treating non-offending parents affected by sexual abuse. *Social Work in Mental Health*, *7*(6), 533–555.

Identifying Victim Needs through Restorative Justice

A hallmark of restorative justice programming and practices hinges upon the involvement of victims as key players in the process of recovery and healing.[11] Thus, the identification of victims' needs through restorative justice is the second major pillar upon which building opportunities for victims of crime to become engaged in the justice process rests. This includes developing, implementing, and operating restorative justice programs that account for the various stages of victim recovery (see Figure 3.2) and that provide a chance for victims to become involved in the

Figure 3.2: Recovering from Crime: Key Stages

Establishing safety

↓

Reconstructing the crime—ventilation

↓

Acknowledgment from others—validation

↓

Supporting the victim—words of empathy or "I'm sorry"

↓

Providing information

↓

Maintaining good communication

↓

Reconnecting with people

↓

Help in reconstructing life to make sense of what happened after a crime

↓

Giving victims a role in making decisions for the justice process

Source: Nicholl, C. G. (1999). *Toolbox for implementing restorative justice and advancing community policing*. Washington, DC: U.S. Department of Justice, Office of Community Oriented Policing Services.

process of addressing their needs. How can we then best meet the needs of crime victims using the approach of restorative justice?

Restorative Justice Lets Victims Regain Control

Criminal behavior is a form of harm that involves the exercise of control against the will of another. Whether it is a sexual assault, robbery, a theft, or embezzlement, victims are not active participants with a choice in the action that was committed. Thus, crime not only creates a significant physical and emotional harm that disrupts the lives of victims, but it also creates a sense of powerlessness that leaves individuals with a total loss of control.[12] The need to regain control over their lives is therefore an essential component of victim services and victim advocacy. Unfortunately, the formal mechanism of criminal justice does very little to help victims reclaim the power that was diminished through their experience of victimization, by focusing on fact finding, determination of guilt, and sentencing.

Restorative justice processes help victims restore their sense of autonomy by allowing them the opportunity to voice their feelings and recognize the legitimacy of their emotions. The values, principles, and core concepts of restorative justice interventions optimize the ability to address victims' needs for healing from the coercive actions of harm caused by crime by making victims feel safe.[13] By acknowledging their hurt and rebuilding their sense of confidence through open dialog, an expression of empathy, and the opportunity to engage in meaningful interactions, restorative justice processes can reduce the fear and anxiety experienced by crime victims and allow them to reclaim the power that was disrupted.

Restorative Justice Provides a Safe Environment

We have seen that criminal victimization creates a sense of fear and psychological trauma that requires a need for the expression of emotion in a safe environment that accounts for the past victimization as well as the potential for the fear of future victimization. While victims long for justice through the punishment of offenders for their criminal acts, they also have an urgent need to feel safe and secure, knowing that they can relive their trauma for the purpose of therapeutic healing in order to express their fear, anger, shame, and grief over what has happened to them.

Restorative justice acknowledges that every victimization experience is unique and can therefore offer various contexts within which victims can safely and securely engage in programs and interactions that can help them synthesize their cognitive reactions with their emotional manifestations.[14] Victims' perspectives on their needs can only be felt and articulated through their own stories, and this can only be accomplished through the dialogs created by restorative justice interventions that offer them the opportunity to organize their thoughts and feelings in an environment that promotes safety and mutual respect and that is free of judgement. The voluntary, non-coercive nature of restorative justice principles and practices optimizes feelings of safety and security and are best suited to address the need of crime victims to heal from the emotional trauma of crime.[15]

Moreover, restorative justice encounters are highly personal, allowing individuals to express deep-rooted feelings of anxiety, pain, and fear. For this reason, the need for victims to heal and positively integrate their negative experience into their lives allows for recovery in a manner that restores safety, a sense of dignity, and creates a fairness that goes beyond the punishment of offenders, which can often leave empty feelings of "hollow" justice.[16]

Restorative Justice Allows Victims to Define Their Needs

Restorative justice policies and practices are founded upon the principle that victim support should involve experiences that allow crime victims to become actively involved in dialog that makes them partners in addressing the harms they experienced. Thus, the recovery from harm hinges upon a victim's definition and articulation of their own needs, and an understanding of which forms of restoration are most integral to their healing.[17] Sometimes, it is difficult to establish a tangible construction of the loss a crime victim experiences. Thus, for example, while a court can establish some form of monetary compensation, this addresses that particular need for financial restoration. However, it doesn't account for the pain and hurt experienced by the loss of trust, feelings of betrayal, and the fear and anger that are associated with the experience of crime. No one who has not walked in the same shoes of a victim of crime can come to fully understand what they went through and how to go about helping meet their needs. By giving victims the opportunity to speak through the restorative justice methods of dialog, we can learn more about victim needs for reparation and be able to properly address those needs.

In such a case, a letter of apology to the victim or a personal act of restoration involving service to the community, may become a critical element in the healing process. These acts of **symbolic reparation** can have great meaning to the victim, beyond the scope of punishment and retribution.[18] The goal of restorative justice is transformation, and this ideal is often the key to healing from the harms caused by crime. Transformation also means that the needs of victims are properly met through processes and encounters that allow them to be heard and communicate their needs. Once victims of crime are able to express their needs in a safe, intimate, restorative setting, the proper resources can be mobilized to include formal and informal social networks of support that are tailored to the specific victim and their stated difficulties.

Restorative Justice Re-Establishes Trust

The experience of harm resulting from crime creates a sense of powerlessness and imbalance that permeates the sense of trust that individuals have for one another.[19]

An employer places his financial integrity in the hands of his accountant and ends of losing large sums of money due to embezzlement. A parent places their valuable baby in the care of a day care center where the innocent child experiences sexual abuse. An elderly man donates a portion of his meager income to a charity that uses the money to serve their own fraudulent purpose. These crime scenarios are but a tiny glimpse of the obvious breach of trust that occurs when an individual is betrayed by such violations. How can this broken trust be restored in order to optimize the healing process for victims of crime?

Restorative justice processes focus on a key component of building trust, which recognizes that a relationship has been broken. The reparation of harm, often the first step in the goal of imposing sanctions within criminal justice, frequently neglects the need to build trust as a predecessor to that reparation.[20] Consider, for example, a child who is learning how to ride a bicycle. As the parent is holding on to them, they are building that trust. Once the parent lets go, and the child falls for the first time, that trust is broken. While the immediate attention may be on caring for possible injuries, the only way to heal completely from that experience and have the courage to try once again, is to rebuild that trust that has been broken due to the parent letting go and the child falling off the bicycle.

In a similar fashion, a holistic approach to healing from crime victimization through restorative justice interventions accounts for the need to rebuild relationships that have been broken through direct or symbolic trust-building experiences and exercises. Since the trust that has been broken can often vary from victim to victim, the capacity of restorative justice to identify victim needs and intervene on behalf of the victim creates the greatest chance for rebuilding relationships. Moreover, the focus on forgiveness as a central component of restorative justice is not only important for the transformation of offenders but is also key to giving victims the opportunity to enjoy the sense of power experienced by the liberating effect of giving forgiveness. In essence, this forgiveness allows the victim to acknowledge the breach of trust and at the same time let go of it through the poignant experience of restorative healing.[21]

Crime is personal. It hurts. We have established the various harms that result from crime and understand the need to make reparations that are not defined merely by the outcome of punishment. In the next section, we would like to explore the third pillar of restorative justice, which is to address the crime that has been committed by taking the appropriate action to repair the harm that was created through offender accountability.

Meeting Needs and Repairing Harm through Accountability

While traditional forms of criminal justice focus on the concept of "paying for one's crime," there is often a disconnect between the idea of repayment and restoration. In fact, the two terms, often used synonymously, can have very different meanings.[22]

Repayment implies that there is a fixed, known loss, that can be returned through some type of monetary or tangible compensation. So, for example, an offender steals some items from a neighbor and pawns them at a pawn shop. While the items cannot be found or returned, the offender is ordered to make payments to the neighbor for the value of the items that were lost. So, with this type of repayment, loss is restored … right? Wrong! Very often, there are losses that cannot be repaid and require a different type of compensation in order to allow a victim to feel somewhat restored, whole, and to begin the path to healing (see Box 3.3). The concept of restoration involves an active attempt to hold offenders accountable in a way that promotes responsibility and creates a sense of healing for the victim. We turn now to a discussion of this type of restorative accountability.

Box 3.3: Restorative Justice in Action—
A Tale of Remorse, a Tale of Healing

Strain and frustration can create hurt and disappointment in some, while others become angry and resentful. Feelings of injustice can lead to a desire for revenge, which some may use to rationalize criminal activities. Studies show that individuals who blame others for their own misfortunes may turn to delinquency and crime. Consider the following events in the life of a teenager:

A 14-year-old boy lives with his mother and her alcoholic boyfriend; his father left them several years earlier. His mother is diagnosed with cancer and spends her last days in great pain in the hospital. One Saturday morning, the hospital calls and tells the boy to rush over, as his mother is dying. On the way, the mother's boyfriend insists on stopping at the liquor store to buy some alcohol. The boy begs him not to, but he does so anyway; his mother dies 10 minutes before they arrive, and he never says goodbye. The boyfriend is uncaring, and the boy runs away from home. He spends a year or so moving from one foster home to another. He becomes angry, hurt, and resentful. He turns to drugs and alcohol to find some relief from his pain. He begins to steal to support his habits. One day, the young teenager breaks into a neighbor's house with a friend of his. The neighbor is an elderly woman who was out grocery shopping for the afternoon. When she returns, she finds that her house has been ransacked, and some items are missing. She reports the incident to the police. A few days later, the two boys are arrested. They are both sentenced to participate in the Greene County Missouri Restorative Justice Program.

These events in the life of the teenager in this story are not totally unique and can reflect many similar circumstances amongst young people involved in juvenile delinquency. However, the participation in restorative justice programming changed his life completely. As part of his obligation to successfully complete the program, the offender was given the opportunity to hear the victim tell her story about how she experienced a deep sense of loss and violation due to the crime that happened to her. She shared her story on a *Victim Impact Panel*, where the two teenagers were sitting in the audience amongst other offenders and listening. The young teenager who committed the theft began to sob as she told of a ring that was stolen, a ring that had little value in terms of money but that was given to her by her late husband over 50 years ago. She talked about how much that ring reminded her of her love for her husband and how when it was taken away from her that it felt like he was taken away from her all over again. The young boy, appearing a week later before the Restorative Justice Board, described this story in great detail, and how much it burdened him with a sense of responsibility to change and that it was not fair to create such a loss for this poor woman, and that her feeling of loss reminded him of the loss and injustice that happened to him with his stepdad and mom. He wrote her a heartfelt letter of apology that he described as a most healing experience that changed his entire outlook on the crime he committed. He felt a sense of peace and a healing from his own hurt and anger over the loss of his mother. He said he began to care again … about himself, about people, about everything.

Source: Hass, A. Maloney, C., & Chambliss, W. J. (2017). *Criminology: Connecting theory, research, and practice*. Routledge: New York. Used by permission.

Creating Balance Through Restorative Accountability

In our quest for solutions to criminal offending, there is a general tendency to focus on controlling the behavior of individuals though deterrence strategies that create a fear of punishment. In doing this, however, we neglect the powerful mechanism of instilling within that individual a sense of self control.[23] Neither the fear of punishment nor following rules and guidelines of behavior involve taking full responsibility for actions. Rather, according to criminologist Walter Reckless, our greatest hope for criminal desistance is the development of *containment*.[24] Reckless studied juvenile delinquency and the cycle of involvement in law-breaking behavior among juvenile offenders. He proposed a **containment theory** of crime, which argued that there are internal and external forces of restraint that keep individuals from breaking the law. **External containment** is developed through forces such as effective supervision, parental disapproval, and sanctioning. **Internal containment**, a more powerful mechanism of inhibition, comes from a sense of right and wrong that develops through personal conviction, moral reasoning, and a sense of responsibility to others.

Thus, the progression of internal containment as a mechanism of social control hinges upon developing accountability for one's actions by accepting full responsibility for the wrong and taking on the personal goal of making it right.[25] This is the premise, belief, and foundation of restorative accountability. We have seen before that the core principles of the traditional criminal justice system rest upon an adversarial approach to the resolution of crime. As a matter of fact, in the pursuit of justice, individuals are encouraged to remain silent, are told to deny guilt, and typically strive to escape the reality of their involvement in the crime by somehow reaching an artificial agreement of facts that portrays some version of the individual's involvement.[26] This distortion of the justice process neglects the importance of embracing one's actions, accepting responsibility, and becoming actively involved in the reparation process.

Contemporary attitudes about crime and criminals embrace the idea of separation. Crime fighting is "us" versus "them," with law breakers and law abiders being on the opposite side of the spectrum and public safety becoming equated with this dichotomous relationship. However, restorative accountability seeks to blur this distinction in an effort to restore harmony by seeking more than punishment, holding offenders accountable for their behavior in ways that are meaningful for both the offender and the victim, as well as the community to which they belong. What, then, is meaningful accountability?

Meaningful accountability seeks to strike a balance between the shaming outcome of punishment that condemns crime as wrongdoing and the inhibitory effect of feeling shame as an outcome of accepting responsibility.[27] Restorative justice processes epitomize this balance by making a clear distinction between the criminal behavior and the offending criminal. On the one hand, the behavior deserves to be condemned in a manner that exercises fairness, justice, and equity for the victim. One the other hand, however, there is an exploration of the reasons why the offender committed the harmful action, and an opportunity to find an explanation. In doing this, the offender is held accountable and given the chance to identify their problems or shortcomings and become part of the solutions towards resolution and reparation.

Shaming and humiliation create a sense of self-rejection that prompts individuals to not only reject their negative status, but to deny it altogether. This denial has the net effect of escaping responsibility for their behavior, and even seeking to justify or neutralize their feelings of guilt. These are referred to as **techniques of neutralization**, and according to criminologists Sykes and Matza, these are used by individuals to redefine their actions in a way that escapes the negative and shaming status of being immoral, a social wrongdoer who has erred against the values and norms of society.[28] Table 3.2 outlines these various rationales used by individuals to escape responsibility from their wrongful actions and separate themselves from feelings of guilt, shame, and remorse.

Thus, punishment and humiliation alone are counterproductive and make accepting responsibility almost impossible. However, treating offenders with dignity and respect allows them to become a part of the process of transformation into a law-abiding cit-

Table 3.2: Techniques of Neutralization

Ways to Avoid Accepting Responsibility	What Does This Mean?
Denial of responsibility	We acknowledge doing the behavior considered wrong, but we claim that we had no choice — that we had to do so, or we were forced to do so.
Denial of injury	We acknowledge doing the wrong action, but we claim that no one was harmed by what we did, so it really shouldn't be a problem.
Blaming the victim	We acknowledge that people were hurt by our actions, but we claim that though we did the action, it was really the victim's fault — they brought about or otherwise deserved our behavior.
Condemn the condemners	We abdicate all responsibility for our behavior, and instead we point to the people condemning us. They are the problem, not us. What they have done wrong excuses our behavior.
Appealing to higher loyalties	We claim that while we violated some social norms, we're actually adhering to other norms and loyalties, and these higher principles justify our behavior.

Source: Wright, B. (2008, October 26). Techniques of neutralization. *Everyday Sociology*. Retrieved from http://www.everydaysociologyblog.com/2008/10/techniques-of-n.html.

izen. By holding offenders accountable for their actions in a restorative way, the outcome of this approach will encourage offenders to understand the impact of their wrongful actions, accept responsibility for it, and seek to repair the harm that has been caused. This will avoid the process of denial associated with feelings of shame and guilt and play a crucial role in rebuilding the broken relationship and developing positive social bonds instead of succumbing to the effects of rejection and isolation. This theoretical approach to restorative accountability can better inform an understanding of what exactly this concept entails and how it can work to restore balance and justice to victims while creating a sense of acceptance and instilling responsibility within the offender.

Characteristics of Restorative Accountability

As we have said, punishment alone and adherence to guidelines and rules does not instill a sense of moral obligation to accept responsibility for one's behavior, a necessary requisite for making reparations and experiencing true remorse. The experience of restorative justice processes that allow for face-to-face encounters between offenders and victims of crime, and the process of community integration involved in restorative circles and dialogs, constitute significant means of accountability that allow for the transformation of the offender from avoiding responsibility to fully embracing it.[29] The characteristics of restorative accountability involve a series of actions that make it possible for an individual to take full responsibility for their behavior.

Restorative Accountability Requires Understanding

Developing accountability involves a process whereby an offender is allowed to answer to the individuals who have been affected by their actions.[30] In order for this type of encounter to be effective, however, the offender must have a full understanding of how their harmful actions have impacted the lives of others. This understanding requires a meaningful opportunity to take responsibility for actions through an emerging perception of the role of choice and free will in determining their behavior. In a famous line from the 1994 movie *The Shawshank Redemption*, Andy Dufresne, a clever banker convicted of murdering his wife and her lover, yet maintaining innocence, asks another inmate, "Red," if he is guilty of his crimes. Red answers him, "only guilty man in Shawshank," implying that the overwhelming majority of inmates in Shawshank prison deny their guilt. What a simple yet poignant statement on the process of justice whereby a convicted offender serving serious time in prison is the only one who seemingly has accepted responsibility for their actions amongst the hundreds of others similarly tried and convicted.[31]

The implication of this statement is a lack of understanding on the part of offenders as to their role in the predicament of criminal offending and its consequences. Without the understanding that crime is a choice, that conviction is a consequence of that choice, and that the first step in the road to healing and transformation is an understanding of this process, offenders will continue to deny their guilt, make excuses for the behavior, and fail to be held accountable for their actions. The victim-centered approach of restorative accountability provides a forum in which this type of understanding can develop and flourish. Giving offenders a chance to experience their own actions as impacting victims, their families, the community and themselves instills remorse and responsibility by creating a better comprehension of the depth of pain and suffering they have caused through the choices they have made.[32]

Restorative Accountability Requires Acknowledging

A paramount concern within restorative justice principle and practice is the restoration of victims from the harms committed against them. Accepting responsibility for one's actions is often a required component of formal court proceedings. A judge may, prior to sentencing or during the plea agreement stage, ask a defendant if they acknowledge their guilt and accept responsibility for their actions. Upon advice from legal counsel, the defendant will agree to these statements, without truly experiencing the genuine feeling of remorse and empathy associated with taking responsibility for the harm that was done to the victim. Restorative justice processes create an opportunity for the offender to not only understand the wrongfulness of their choice to commit the crime, but to also acknowledge the harm that was done to the victim in a very personal way. Part of this acknowledgment involves taking responsibility for the harm by experiencing, in an indirect way, the pain that was experienced by the victim. Fully acknowledging responsibility for the harm to others through written apologies or face-to-face encounters can be a painful experience for an individual, yet it has a transforming impact that opens up the opportunity for offenders to recognize the error in their thinking and actions and the recognition that this choice could have been made differently.[33] The processes involved in restorative dialog can bring closure to both victims and offenders by mending the adversarial nature of justice and forcing the offender to realize the human costs of their actions. This, in turn, has a greater impact on changing the life of the offender from focusing entirely on how to go about reducing the costs and penalties associated with their actions to focusing on the process of reparation, gaining acceptance, and experiencing forgiveness and healing.[34]

Restorative Accountability Requires Taking Action

Once an offender understands their role in engaging in wrongful behavior and acknowledges the harm of their actions, restorative accountability requires that offenders take on an active role in repairing the harm committed. This includes providing a process for making amends to the victim and their families who were impacted by the crime, as well as making amends to the community for violating its norms and values of law-abiding behavior. Moreover, restorative accountability calls for a focus on making changes in erroneous thinking that leads to such harmful behavior in the future.[35] With traditional methods of criminal justice intervention, the punishment is the final outcome or goal of proceedings, and rehabilitation becomes a matter of choice within the context of punishment.

However, a major goal of restorative accountability involves taking on an active role in the process of change to avoid the harms caused by criminal actions. By actively engaging offenders in reparation, restorative accountability provides a sense of hope and personal responsibility to change. Controlling the behavior of criminal offenders so that they don't repeat their crimes can be accomplished either directly through punishment and incapacitation or indirectly by equipping offenders with the mechanisms to control themselves. Restorative accountability instills within offenders a desire to desist from re-offending by teaching them to live in a manner that does not violate the rights of others as well as giving them a stake in their own communities by creating a greater respect for others, themselves, and the law.

Transforming the meaning of past negative behavior by creating an active desire to develop accountability and taking the necessary action to repair the harm and make personal changes is a step in the direction of moving forward, letting go of the past, and making constructive progress that impacts criminal thinking through a self-actualized commitment to change.[36] Once offenders experience this type of transformation and they unequivocally understand, acknowledge, and take action to correct their behaviors, the process of restoring a sense of justice and healing for victims takes on new meaning.

When examining the dynamic restorative justice pillars of understanding harm, defining needs, and developing restorative accountability, the importance of community in the implementation, function, and efficacy of restorative justice becomes apparent. Without community, the ideas and processes they present are weakened if not made completely ineffective. We turn now to an exploration of the transformative role of community in restorative justice processes.

The Role of Community in Restorative Justice

Restorative justice principles and values challenge us to not only utilize restorative justice processes as ways to address crime, but to see them as vehicles by which we can potentially strengthen community connections. Indeed, restorative justice has been linked to such outcomes as social transformation, enhanced civility, community building, and the reinforcement of behavioral norms.[37] The pivotal inclusion of community is therefore the fourth pillar upon which restorative justice policy and practice is founded, and thus, it is essential that we better understand what community means in our contemporary culture and how it is represented in restorative justice processes.

What Is Community?

Community is a difficult concept to define in that we use the term to express tangible things such as neighborhoods or social groups, as well as experiences and feelings of belonging and connectedness to others.[38] In this section, we would like to explore in greater depth how this term is used and understood, particularly within the restorative paradigm, as well as explore our understanding of community as it relates to theoretical perspectives relevant to the rationale of restorative justice.

The meaning of community can encapsulate anything from groups and associations to feelings and experiences of connection.[39] Within the context of restorative justice, there are four core conceptualizations of community: *community as the context, outside of official systems, professions, and institutions, within which restorative processes occur*; *community as networks of care and support for key stakeholders such as victims and offenders*; *community as an additional victim of crime*; and, lastly, *community as a potential outcome of restorative practice*.[40] We will take a closer at each of these concepts individually.

Community as Context for Restorative Justice

Pertinent to our understanding is the fact that most restorative justice programs operate outside of the traditional criminal justice system. Typically based in community organizations, trained volunteers commonly function as the facilitators of these processes, leaving official justice agencies and professionals on the periphery as supporting collaborators in, and observers of, restorative justice. Community, therefore, becomes a way of describing the social sphere in which processes of restorative justice take place. This distinction between community and professionalization is significant in restorative justice, as, in many ways, restorative processes are crafted around the exclusion of a justice system dependent upon representation rather than direct social encounter, as well as focused on punitive, rather than reparative, responses to crime.[41] Of the four available interpretations of community within restorative justice, this is the only conceptualization that appears to directly relate itself to the presence of community volunteer facilitators; however, as previously stated, with the advancement of restorative inroads into the criminal justice system, we are seeing restorative processes removed from the domain of community and enacted as institutionalized imitations of community-based restorative practice.

Community as Network of Care and Support

Community is also identified in restorative processes as networks of support and care that operate on behalf of victims and offenders.[42] Often members of these communities have been personally impacted by the offense due to their relationship with at least one of the key stakeholders involved, and so, when at all possible, these individuals are invited as participants into restorative processes such as mediations, peacemaking circles, and family group conferences.[43] Communities of care and support can also emerge from restorative processes if bonds and connections are reestablished within the restorative encounter.

Community as a Victim of Crime

Within restorative justice, community is also identified as a victim to the criminal offense, a participant in the restorative process with distinct needs, as well as its own experience of harm.[44] The community can also take on certain responsibilities in restorative processes. For instance, many advocates of restorative justice point to the need for both victims and offenders to reintegrate, or assimilate, into the community after crime, and particularly in regard to offenders, this is often ritualized through the commonplace inclusion of community service into reparation agreements drafted within restorative processes like victim offender mediation. By encouraging reparation to the community, this acknowledges that crime impacts individuals more broadly and immediate victims are part of a larger community of citizens that also experience fear, anxiety, and material harm from criminal offending.

Community as an Outcome of Restorative Processes

Finally, community is also understood as a potential outcome of restorative processes.[45] Many contemporary scholars have identified a breakdown, or weakening, of community in our contemporary culture, particularly as it relates to social bonds and connections within geographic frames such as neighborhoods, towns, and cities.[46] For instance, a majority of Americans, when asked, indicate that our culture focuses more on the individual than the collective and identify this as a social problem.[47] Relatable to restorative theorists like Christie, social critics, such as McKnight and Block, connect this degradation of community bonds, in part, to the consumerist nature of our society and its elevation of the professional above community systems and relationships.[48] If we accept this analysis, restorative processes, if community-based and facilitated by volunteers, can become an exercise in community-building, rather than socially isolating processes of justice.

This breakdown in social ties and networks is extremely relevant to the field of criminology because of the generally acknowledged relationship between community attachment and criminogenic tendencies.[49] In this light, the potential for community as a restorative outcome becomes even more compelling; it becomes a possible tool in crime prevention. For this kind of community enhancement to occur, theorists agree that the restorative paradigm must permeate more than just the criminal justice system; its values and principles must stretch into other social institutions and networks, such as schools, associations, and workplaces, as well as become embedded into our daily lives and personal relationships.[50]

The literature is very clear and compelling with regard to community being a key element in restorative justice, an element, as outlined above, that we can interpret in at least four different ways. Each conceptualization of community's role in restorative justice is vital to its function and efficacy, as well as decisions regarding its implementation. The role of volunteer facilitators as key stakeholders in restorative processes is very often neglected in our discussion of community as it relates to restorative justice. While we can connect volunteers to the social context of community-based practices, we have yet to fully define the meaning of their role and examine their place, if any, within our other interpretations of community. This lack of attention to the community volunteer can affect new implementations and models of restorative justice and may have deep implications regarding the ability of restorative processes to function effectively without the presence of community-based volunteer facilitators. We turn now to a thorough examination of the concept of volunteerism as it pertains to restorative justice policy and practice.

Community and Volunteerism

Our conceptualization of volunteerism is often understood simply as one's decision to offer his/her services to another without receiving financial compensation; however, defining the community volunteer also brings up questions regarding planning and commitment.[51] Commitment is often an element that distinguishes volunteerism from spontaneous, short-term helping behaviors such as coming to the aid of a stranded motorist or opening a door for someone in need.[52] In other words, volunteerism is, in part, made distinct from other service roles by the planning involved in one's decision to serve, as well as the commitment to do so for a sustained period of time appropriate to the type of service. For our purpose, the community volunteer is defined as a person who commits to, is trained in, and participates in a planned or scheduled activity that benefits a person, organization, and/or social movement, and for which s/he receives no financial payment.

Studies show that volunteer facilitators view the voluntary nature of their role as important to the efficacy of the restorative process, as well as the perceptions of process participants.[53] Moreover, they view their identity as a volunteer facilitator as building rapport and trust with the participants, as well as modeling restorative values and principles such as voluntary participation and community service. This voluntary role enhances the quality of the restorative process, allowing opportunities for transformation in regard to professionalized systems such as law enforcement and juvenile justice through the adoption of restorative processes and principles, as well as the transformation of participants' perceptions concerning these systems.

Moreover, the use of volunteer facilitators is seen as increasing trust and openness on the part of process participants, with less pressure on the part of the facilitator to "perform" well and produce certain outcomes, while increasing community presence within the restorative process.[54] In addition, the role of volunteer facilitators increases the ease participants feel after learning about their role as a volunteer and their separation from the criminal justice system, an ease which leads to greater openness and willingness to engage in restorative justice on the part of victims and offenders.

A major connection between community and volunteerism lies within the role of community as part of the criminal justice process in its identification as an additional victim of crime. With this role of community, the concept of its representation in the restorative justice process becomes an integral component of reparation, healing, and acceptance. Studies show that volunteer facilitators view it as important for community members to hold a place within the restorative process, and that the use of volunteer facilitators may be a practical and effective way of including community representation within restorative justice. This is seen as increasing feelings of unity, the discovery of connections, and the building of social capital on the part of process participants.[55]

Volunteer participation within various social service, health industry, and community agencies has a long-standing history. While the tasks and roles volunteers play in these various settings may change, a remaining constant is the role of altruism and the desire to "give back" to society something of value. In addition to this dynamic of volunteerism, the role of community volunteers takes on an additional meaning in a restorative justice correctional setting whereby volunteers are representative of community in a manner that connects offenders with their victims and allows volunteers to become symbolic networks of support and healing.[56] Volunteers therefore contribute not only their time, energy, and personal knowledge and experience to the restorative process, but also become agents of informal social control within the community, as well as provide offenders with a context for change and accountability, thereby encouraging dialog, building community capacity, and enhancing social justice.

Chapter Summary

What are the various types of harms that people can experience?

We have seen in this chapter that criminal actions impact victims in many ways, and that victims of crime experience a variety of consequences that begin with an immediate disruption of their lives and continue through various stages that may include long-term trauma. Victimology focuses on a scientific study of the physical, emotional, and social harm that victims experience from crime, and has allowed us to better understand the role of restorative justice in addressing victim needs. Restorative justice values outline standards by which we should approach the reparation process from a more meaningful perspective that redefines justice and punishment beyond conviction and sentencing to appropriately addressing harm and promoting the victim's needs for healing.

Are there specific needs created by the harms that individuals go through?

Identifying victims' needs through restorative justice is the second major pillar upon which building opportunities for victims of crime to become engaged in the justice process rests. This includes developing, implementing, and operating restorative justice programs that account for the various stages of victim recovery and that provide a chance for victims to become involved in the process of addressing their needs. These programs are designed to meet the specific needs created by the harms of crime by helping victims restore their sense of autonomy through voicing their feelings and recognizing the legitimacy of their emotions; acknowledging that every victimization experience is unique and can therefore offer various contexts within which victims can safely and securely engage in programs and interactions that can help them synthesize their cognitive reactions with their emotional manifestations; giving victims the opportunity to speak through the restorative justice methods of dialog; and focusing on a key component of building trust which recognizes that a relationship has been broken.

How do we hold offenders accountable for the wrongs that are committed?

The concept of restoration involves an active attempt to hold offenders accountable in a way that promotes responsibility and creates a sense of healing for the victim. The goal is to instill a sense of internal containment as a mechanism of social control. We have seen that doing this hinges upon developing accountability for one's actions by accepting full responsibility for the wrong and taking on as a personal goal making it right. Thus, this is the premise, belief, and foundation of restorative accountability. Meaningful accountability seeks to strike a balance between the shaming outcome of punishment that condemns crime as wrongdoing and the inhibitory effect of feeling shame as an outcome of accepting responsibility. Restorative justice processes epitomize this balance by making a clear distinction between the criminal behavior and the offending criminal by encouraging steps towards understanding, acknowledging, and taking action.

In what ways is community engaged in restorative justice processes?

Restorative justice has been linked to such outcomes as social transformation, enhanced civility, community building, and the reinforcement of behavioral norms, and therefore, the inclusion of community is a foundation upon which restorative justice policy and practice is built. Within the context of restorative justice, there are four core conceptualizations of community: community as the context, outside of official systems, professions, and institutions, within which restorative processes occur; community as networks of care and support for key stakeholders such as victims and offenders; community as an additional victim of crime; and, lastly, community as a potential outcome of restorative practice. Each conceptualization of community's role in restorative justice is vital to its function and efficacy, as well as decisions regarding its implementation. Moreover, the role of volunteer facilitators as key stakeholders in restorative processes is imperative to our discussion of community as it relates to restorative justice. We defined the community volunteer as a person who commits to, is trained in, and participates in a planned or scheduled activity that benefits a person, organization, and/or social movement, and for which s/he receives no financial payment. The role of volunteerism in restorative justice processes is seen as intensifying feelings of unity, increasing the discovery of connections, and the building of social capitol.

Key Terms

Victimology
Reentry
Primary Victim
Secondary Victim
Vicarious Victimization
Symbolic Reparation
Containment Theory
Internal Containment
External Containment
Techniques of Neutralization

Critical Thinking Questions

1. How does restorative justice transform our understanding of harm? How does a holistic understanding of harm contribute to reparation and healing for both victims and offenders as well as the community in general?

2. What do you think of the concept of victim-offender overlap? Can you think of examples of particular types of crimes or categories of offenders to which this

concept most applies? In what ways does the theoretical understanding of this concept have implications for the implementation of restorative justice policies and practices?

3. Do you agree that symbolic reparation is as important to victims of crime as punishment and retribution? Why or why not? Are there situations where symbolic reparation is more meaningful? If so, what are they?

4. When does internal containment develop in the life cycle? How is restorative justice consistent with the theoretical basis of this concept? In what ways does the development of internal containment increase restorative accountability?

5. How do you perceive the role of volunteerism as adding value to formal processes and organizations? Have you ever been a volunteer? In what ways did your volunteerism affect you and the people you served?

References

1. Gal, T. (2016). "The conflict is ours": Community involvement in restorative justice. *Contemporary Justice Review, 19*(3), 289–306.

2. Møller, V. (2004). Living with crime: Does crime affect victims' perceived quality of life? *South African Crime Quarterly*, (9).

3. Ballinger, A., Chakraborti, N., Condry, R., Elias, R., Gallo, C., Katz, R., ... & Miers, D. (2016). *Reconceptualizing critical victimology: Interventions and possibilities.* Lexington Books.

4. Aguilar, M. E. (2016). The effects of shame and self-blame on disclosure in survivors of sexual assault. *Psychology Student Research Journal*, 74.

5. Haney, K. R. (2016). *Increasing victim satisfaction with traditional criminal justice systems: Lessons learned from restorative justice.* Master's thesis, University of Oregon.

6. Mulvey, K. L., Hitti, A., Smetana, J. G., & Killen, M. (2016). Morality, context, and development. In L. Balter & C. Tamis-LaMonda (Eds.), *Child psychology: A handbook of contemporary issues*, 3rd edition (pp. 285–304). NY: Psychology Press.

7. Bandes, S. A. (2016). Share your grief but not your anger: Victims and the expression of emotion in criminal justice. In J. Smith & C. Abell, (Eds.), *Emotional expression: Philosophical, psychological, and legal perspectives.* Cambridge University Press.

8. Visher, C. A., Lattimore, P. K., Barrick, K., & Tueller, S. (2016). Evaluating the long-term effects of prisoner reentry services on recidivism: What types of services matter? *Justice Quarterly, 34*(1), 136–165.

9. Wemmers, J. A., & Cyr, K. (2016). Gender and victims' expectations regarding their role in the criminal justice system: Towards victim-centered prosecutorial policies. In H. Kury, S. Redo, & E. Shea (Eds.), *Women and Children as Victims and Offenders: Background, Prevention, Reintegration* (pp. 233–248). Springer International Publishing.

10. Lundström, R. (2016). Secondary victimization and the collective identity of crime victims: A qualitative analysis of Swedish crime news discourse. *Journal of Scandinavian Studies in Criminology and Crime Prevention, 17*(1), 36–52.

11. Graham, L. K. (2016). Inside victim support groups. In L. Graham (Ed.), *Beyond social capital: The role of leadership, trust and government policy in Northern Ireland's victim support groups* (pp. 45–75). Palgrave Macmillan UK.

12. Ceccato, V., & Bamzar, R. (2016). Elderly victimization and fear of crime in public spaces. *International Criminal Justice Review, 26*(2), 115–133.

13. Walker, P. (2016). Acting together to disrupt cycles of violence: Performance and social healing. In P. Gobodo-Madikizela (Ed.), *Breaking Intergenerational Cycles of Repetition: A Global Dialogue on Historical Trauma and Memory* (pp. 325–342). Barbara Budrich Publishers.

14. Dekker, S. W., & Breakey, H. (2016). "Just culture": Improving safety by achieving substantive, procedural and restorative justice. *Safety Science, 85*, 187–193.

15. Maglione, G. (2016). Embodied victims: An archaeology of the "ideal victim" of restorative justice. *Criminology and Criminal Justice, 17*(4), 401–417. doi: 1748895816677172.

16. Fattah, E. A. (Ed.). (2016). *From crime policy to victim policy: Reorienting the justice system.* Springer.

17. Robinson, J., & Hudson, J. (2016). Restorative justice: A typology and critical appraisal. *Willamette J. Int'l L. & Dispute Res., 23*, 335–367.

18. Cramer, S. W. (2016). Restorative resources: A new theory in juvenile offender control: Examining the successes of restorative resources in Sonoma County and the impact it had on one police sergeant's journey. *The International Undergraduate Journal for Service-Learning, Leadership, and Social Change, 3*(1), 1–12.

19. Dearden, T. E. (2016). Trust: The unwritten cost of white-collar crime. *Journal of Financial Crime, 23*(1), 87–101.

20. Stubbs, J. (2016). Gendered violence and restorative justice. In A. Hayden, L. Gelsthorpe, & A. Morris, (Eds.), *A restorative approach to family violence: Changing tack* (pp. 199–210). Routledge.

21. Weitekamp, E. G. M., & Parmentier, S. (2016). Restorative justice as healing justice: Looking back to the future of the concept. *Restorative Justice, 4*(2), 141–147.

22. Robinson, J., & Hudson, J. (2016). Restorative justice: A typology and critical appraisal. *Willamette J. Int'l L. & Dispute Res.*, *23*, 335–367.

23. Pogarsky, G., & Loughran, T. A. (2016). The policy-to-perceptions link in deterrence. *Crim inology & Public Policy*, *15*(3), 777–790.

24. Schroeder, R. D. (2016). Social bond theory. *The encyclopedia of crime & punishment*. doi: 10.1002/9781118519639.wbecpx121.

25. Gottfredson, M. R., & Hirschi, T. (2016). The criminal career perspective as an explanation of crime and a guide to crime control policy: The view from general theories of crime. *Journal of Research in Crime and Delinquency*, *53*(3), 406–419.

26. Bibas, S. (2016). Designing plea bargaining from the ground up: Accuracy and fairness without trials as backstops. *William & Mary Law Review*, *57*, 1055.

27. Bouffard, J., Cooper, M., & Bergseth, K. (2016). The effectiveness of various restorative justice interventions on recidivism outcomes among juvenile offenders. *Youth Violence and Juvenile Justice*, *15*(4), 465–480. doi: 1541204016647428.

28. Boyle, K. M., & Walker, L. S. (2016). The neutralization and denial of sexual violence in college party subcultures. *Deviant Behavior*, *37*(12), 1392–1410.

29. Roche, D. (2003). *Accountability in restorative justice*. Oxford University Press on Demand.

30. Bohmert, M. N., Duwe, G., & Hipple, N. K. (2016). Evaluating restorative justice circles of support and accountability: Can social support overcome structural barriers? *International Journal of Offender Therapy and Comparative Criminology*, *62*(3), 739–758. doi: 0306624X16652627.

31. Grady, M., & Magistrale, T. (2016). In the belly of the beast: Ohio State Reformatory and *The Shawshank Redemption*. In M. Grady & T. Magistrale (Eds.), *The Shawshank Experience* (pp. 27–85). Palgrave Macmillan US.

32. Chapman, T., & Chapman, A. (2016). Forgiveness in restorative justice: Experienced but not heard? *Oxford Journal of Law and Religion*, *5*(1), 135–152. doi: rwv066.

33. Cohen, R. L. (2016). Restorative justice. In C. Sabbagh & M. Schmitt (Eds.), *Handbook of social justice theory and research* (pp. 257–272). Springer New York.

34. Bandes, S. A. (2016). Remorse and criminal justice. *Emotion Review*, *8*(1), 14–19.

35. Paul, G. D. (2016). But does it work? The influence of presumed goal attainment effectiveness on willingness to use legalistic and restorative responses to offensive behavior. *Communication Studies*, *67*(2), 239–258.

36. Bazemore, G., & Schiff, M. (2015). *Restorative community justice: Repairing harm and transforming communities*. Routledge.

37. Pointer, L. C. (2016). Understanding transformational space: An analysis of restorative justice conferences through religious studies theoretical lenses. *Restorative Justice*, *4*(2), 148–167.

38. Wagar, W. W. (2015). Toward a praxis of world integration. *Journal of World-Systems Research*, *2*(1), 36–48.

39. Irwin, M. D. (2016). The concept of community as theoretical ground: Contention and compatibility across levels of analysis and standpoints of social processes. In S. Abrutyn (Ed.), *Handbook of contemporary sociological theory* (pp. 247–268). Springer International Publishing.

40. Gonzalez, T. (2015). Reorienting restorative justice: Initiating a new dialogue of rights consciousness, community empowerment and politicization. *Cardozo Journal of Conflict Resolution*, *16*.

41. Barnes, G. C., Hyatt, J. M., Angel, C. M., Strang, H., & Sherman, L. W. (2015). Are restorative justice conferences more fair than criminal courts? Comparing levels of observed procedural justice in the reintegrative shaming experiments (RISE). *Criminal Justice Policy Review*, *26*(2), 103–130.

42. Van de Vyver, J., Travaglino, G. A., Vasiljevic, M., & Abrams, D. (2015). The group and cultural context of restorative justice: A social psychological perspective. In T. Gavrielides (Ed.), *The psychology of restorative justice: Managing the power within* (pp. 29–48). Routledge.

43. Quigley, M., Martynowicz, A., & Gardner, C. (2015). Building bridges: An independent evaluation of Le Chéile's Restorative Justice Project. Research findings. *Irish Probation Journal*, *12*.

44. Burks, A. C., Cramer, R. J., Henderson, C. E., Stroud, C. H., Crosby, J. W., & Graham, J. (2015). Frequency, nature, and correlates of hate crime victimization experiences in an urban sample of lesbian, gay, and bisexual community members. *Journal of Interpersonal Violence*. doi: 0886260515605298.

45. Bazemore, G., & Schiff, M. (2015). *Restorative community justice: Repairing harm and transforming communities*. Routledge.

46. Allen, D. F., Carroll, M. A., Allen, V. S., Bethell, K. Y., & Manganello, J. A. (2015). Community resocialization via instillation of family values through a novel group therapy approach: A pilot study. *Journal of Psychotherapy Integration*, *25*(4), 289.

47. Putnam, R. D. (2000). Bowling alone: America's declining social capital. In L. Crothers & C. Lockhart (Eds.), *Culture and politics: A reader* (pp. 223–234). Palgrave Macmillan US.

48. Block, P., & McKnight, J. (2010). The abundant community: Awakening the power of families and neighborhoods. Berrett-Koehler Publishers.

49. Craig, J. M., Baglivio, M. T., Wolff, K. T., Piquero, A. R., & Epps, N. (2016). Do social bonds buffer the impact of adverse childhood experiences on reoffending? *Youth Violence and Juvenile Justice*. doi: 1541204016630033. Donner, C., Maskaly, J., & Fridell, L. (2016). Social bonds and police misconduct: An examination of social control theory and its relationship to workplace deviance among police supervisors. *Policing: An International Journal of Police Strategies & Management*, *39*(2), 416–431.

50. Bouffard, J., Cooper, M., & Bergseth, K. (2016). The effectiveness of various restorative justice interventions on recidivism outcomes among juvenile offenders. *Youth Violence and Juvenile Justice*. doi: 1541204016647428. Dzur, A. W. (2015). Public restorative justice: The participatory democratic dimensions of institutional reform. *Raisons politiques*, (3), 51–71.

51. Jain, A. K. (2016). Volunteerism, affective commitment and citizenship behavior: An empirical study in India. *Journal of Managerial Psychology*, *31*(3), 657–671.

52. Romaioli, D., Nencini, A., & Meneghini, A. M. (2016). How to foster commitment among volunteers: A social constructionist study in Italian nonprofit organizations. *Journal of Social Service Research*, *42*(5), 718–728.

53. Maruna, S., & LeBel, T. P. (2015). 5 Strengths-based restorative approaches to reentry. *Positive Criminology*, *23*, 65; Crocker, D. (2016). Balancing justice goals: Restorative justice practitioners' views. *Contemporary Justice Review*, *19*(4), 462–478.

54. Claes, E., & Van Daele, E. (2015). Restorative justice and volunteering in a secular age. In L. Hustinx, J. von Essen, J. Haers, & S. Mels (Eds.), *Religion and Volunteering* (pp. 191–215). Springer International Publishing.

55. McDonald, Y. H. V. (2016). *Restorative justice: Transformation Project Prison Ministry's reason for growth and motivation of the volunteers* (Doctoral dissertation, Asbury Theological Seminary).

56. Cornelius, L. J. (2016). Reflections on engaging in social action against social injustice, while developing a survey to study it: Restorative social justice as a lived experience. *Reflections: Narratives of Professional Helping*, *21*(3), 26–33.

Section Two

Restorative Processes and Practices in Action

Now that we have examined the historical, theoretical, and philosophical roots of restorative justice, and understand its unique approach to crime and conflict, it is time to learn more about the core practices most associated with its application in the real world. As we will see in the following chapters, there are five practices that we often affiliate with a restorative approach to criminal justice and conflict transformation. These include: victim-offender mediations or dialogs, family group conferences, victim impact panels, peacemaking circles, and reparative boards.

In the chapters that follow, we will dive into each of these models, examining their historical origins, their defining elements and characteristics, and empirical research results concerning their efficacy. As we will see, the successful application of restorative justice often lies in its faithfulness to restorative values and principles rather than its fidelity to any one model. While the models we will explore are frequently replicated in various communities and contexts, the strength of restorative justice lies in its ability to be easily adapted to meet the needs of different cultures, groups, and situations.

Chapter 4

Victim-Offender Mediation

In this chapter, we will explore the following questions …
- *From where do we get the concept of victim-offender mediation?*
- *How do we apply mediation programs in various contexts?*
- *Can the mediation of conflicts bring about restoration and healing?*
- *What does the research literature say about the success of this type of practice?*

The Origins of Victim-Offender Mediation in Restorative Justice

The core concepts of restorative justice have brought about an understanding of reparation that takes on a victim-centered approach, whereby there is an emphasis on forgiveness and healing as well as offender accountability and reintegration into the community. The various forums for dialog and communication that we will discuss in this section of the book will bring us closer to the application of the values and principles of restorative justice in a practical way. Here, we begin this discussion by describing the closest encounters between victims and offenders, those that take place within the practice of *victim-offender mediation* programs.

The term **mediation** is used to describe a process whereby two or more parties come together with a neutral facilitator to discuss, and attempt to resolve, shared issues and conflicts.[1] Thus, **victim-offender mediation** (VOM) is a process whereby victims are given the opportunity to meet with their offender to engage in a facilitated discussion, in a structured and safe environment.[2] How did this practice come to evolve as a process within restorative justice? Let's begin by examining the historical origins of victim-offender mediation as an anchor for reparation and healing in early Aboriginal cultures.

Responsibility and Healing: The Aboriginal People of Canada

For our purposes, **Aboriginal** is a term used to describe the original peoples of North America in what is known today as Canada. There are three distinct groups, each with their own unique cultures, traditions, beliefs, and value systems. These groups are Indians, also referred to as **First Nations**, **Métis**, and **Inuit**.[3] The history of the Aboriginal indigenous population predates the arrival of European settlers in North America, and, although colonial forces threatened their extinction, the Aboriginal system of norms, values, and social organization significantly shaped the development of Canada.

Aboriginal culture is collectively built upon the notion of mutual respect between tribal leaders or elders and the members of a community. Within this structure, it is the role of elders to transmit knowledge, culture, and history to children. Moreover, child rearing is seen as a cooperative effort between families, and conflicts that arise are dealt with by elders whose main focus is to use their faith and piety to restore relationships and preserve the sense of order and community. Thus, authority is driven by a strong emphasis on traditions that integrate the concepts of healing and spirituality.[4]

Historically, the Aboriginal system of justice developed its distinct character based upon an understanding of criminal offending as a harm against the entire community and something that has a direct or indirect effect on everyone. Elders play an integral role in the process of conflict resolution, identifying what needs have been created by the act of harm. These needs include both the victim and the offender. These needs are acknowledged in healing circles, where traditions and spirituality are used to express remorse, forgiveness, and the need for reparation. Within these healing circles, offenders' needs are also addressed, and a mechanism for reintegration back into the community becomes the central focus, as opposed to being driven out in shame. This process provides both victims and offenders a sense of empowerment, taking on an active role in fixing the wrongdoing.[5]

Throughout the period of North American colonization, the structure of Aboriginal society was compromised as the process of domination and control by European settlers. Suffering hundreds of years of oppression and forced assimilation, the First Nations, Métis, and Inuit became increasingly displaced and marginalized, as their system of beliefs and traditions, so embedded in nature and spirituality, dissipated in the wake of European imposition of their own mechanisms of social control.[6] The Aboriginal heritage became one of strife and struggle to regain self-control and identity. With this effort came a strong awareness of the injustices of formal government and a heightened search for fairness and equity, especially in the treatment of offenders and victims of crime. It is within this context that a joint project between criminal justice authorities and a local church organization renewed the concept of reconciliation between victims and offenders.

During the early 1990s, in the midst of increasingly disproportionate representation of Aboriginal people as both victims of crime and criminal offenders and mounting tensions between them and the criminal justice system, the Canadian government began to recognize the need for reform. Aboriginal grassroots leaders advocated for a system of intervention that was less intrusive and that allowed for more opportunities for their communities to intervene in matters of criminal offending. Despite disagreement on how to best come to a resolution, it was clear to Canadian government reformers that the answer to Aboriginal autonomy in the domain of justice was to resurrect some of their ideals of restorative justice.[7]

The promise of restorative justice as a means of integrating Aboriginal cultural beliefs and traditions into the application of law was reflected in Canada's 1994 **Sentencing Reform Bill**, which focused on a more unified and equitable system of sanctioning criminal offenders. This bill, which became law in 1995, was the first formal attempt at incorporating principles of restorative justice into the Canadian criminal justice system.[8] Aboriginal values and cultural principles of forgiveness and healing were promoted by expanding the traditional goals of sentencing, which focus exclusively on punishment, deterrence, and separation, to include provisions for the reparation of harm done to the victims or the community, as well as promote a sense of personality responsibility on the part of the offender. A new emphasis in sentencing came to light, one which included a better understanding of the needs of the offender, as well as one that brought about efforts at change and reconciliation through open dialog and meaningful encounters between victims and offenders. In doing this, the specific customs and rituals of Aboriginal culture, with their emphasis on healing and responsibility, became the hallmark ideals of evolving restorative mediation practices in Canada and across the world.

Soon, practices focusing on peacemaking, reconciliation, and mediated forgiveness found their way into the criminal justice systems throughout the United States and in many countries following in the programmatic footsteps established in Canada and New Zealand. Since the 1990s, concepts of restorative justice were embraced by criminal justice systems as an alternative way of dealing with offenders, victims, and communities in a holistic manner. The goal of bringing equity, justice, and healing to all individuals impacted by the criminal act, while holding offenders accountable for their behavior, was seen as a step to alleviate some of the conditions associated with crime and formal criminal justice intervention.[9] We turn now to a closer look at the development of victim-offender mediation strategies within the formal system of criminal justice administration and its potential for dealing with harms between individuals and within the community in a manner that promotes mutual respect, accountability, and healing.

The Kitchener Experiment

In 1974 in a well-publicized case in the Waterloo Region of Ontario, two young offenders pleaded guilty to 22 different charges when they went on a drunken vandalism spree involving significant damage to several vehicles, stores, and churches within the local community. In their case, the sentencing judge asked probation officer Mark Yantzi to prepare a pre-sentence investigation report for the two teenagers. Yantzi, a Mennonite Christian, partnered with the **Mennonite Central Committee (MCC)**, a local chapter of a national and international social service agency of the Mennonite and Brethren in Christ Churches to try something different with this case.[10]

Yantzi, along with Dave Worth of the MCC, was convinced that the anger and frustration experienced by the various community members victimized by these two young offenders could best be alleviated through efforts at reconciliation between them and the offenders. They persuaded Judge McConnell that this would be the perfect case to test this concept of reconciliation through a mediated face-to-face encounter between the offenders and their victims. The judge somewhat reluctantly sentenced the teens to probation and required that they make restitution through a face-to-face meeting with their victims. Subsequently, the two young offenders met with each one of their twenty-two victims in a conference involving their listening to the hurt and anger of the victim, a formal apology for their actions, and agreement over how to make things right.[11] The sentencing judge was so impressed with the value of this unique sentencing experience as well as the positive outcomes of the meetings, that this experiment, commonly referred to as the **Kitchener Experiment**, marked the beginning of Canada's **Victim Offender Reconciliation Project (VORP)**, a program that has since been replicated and implemented in various provinces throughout Canada.[12]

From Canada to the United States: Elkhart, Indiana and VORP

It didn't take long for the widespread use of reconciliation and mediation programs between victims and offenders throughout Canada to catch on in the United States, and in 1978, the efforts of probation officers and the Mennonite Church in Elkhart County, Indiana led to the development of the first VORP. As advocates of reconciliation between victims and offenders, the program founder and two local probation officers partnered with **Howard Zehr**, a pioneer in restorative justice theory and practice and a member of the MCC, to establish a process for implementing a program modeled after the Kitchener Experiment.[13]

Elkhart County Judge William Bontrager implemented the first VORP project in his court, testing the waters with a limited number of cases, and the results, like those in Kitchener, seemed to yield positive outcomes in terms of successful reconciliation between victims and their offenders.[14] The fledgling program soon flourished and moved from the confines of the probation office into the community to take on a truly restorative approach. Program advocate Zehr as well probation staff recognized the need for transforming this process into one that incorporated members of the community as citizen activists in the mediation process and program oversight. Searching for a community-based organization to sponsor the program, grow it, and help make it reach its greatest potential, they found **Prisoner and Community Together** (**PACT**), an organization based in Michigan City, Indiana that strongly advocated for, developed, and administered several community-based correctional programs to enhance the reentry process.[15] Through the leadership, organization, and fundraising efforts of PACT as well as the local Mennonite Church, the Elkhart County VORP grew into a solid, highly organized programmatic initiative, marking the first large-scale VORP in the United States, to be modeled after and replicated in many jurisdictions in the decades to come, and to evolve into what we now refer to as victim-offender mediation within restorative justice.[16] We turn now to a discussion of the application of this mediation process within the context of criminal justice policy and practice.

The Application of Victim-Offender Mediation Programs

As we navigate through the diverse features of restorative justice policy and practice, we can't help but wonder if the common threads of theory and principles that underlie the various programs allow for a diversity of encounters that are tailored to the specific needs for reparation and healing and the restoration of relationships. Earlier in this chapter, we saw how the need for the Aboriginal population to return to their cultural roots for conflict resolution led to a search for practices that centered upon healing, forgiveness, and the development of mutual trust and respect. It is in this direction that victim-offender mediation takes us, and it is in this direction that we hope to develop a better understanding of the significance of applying this type of encounter between victims and offenders in order to mediate conflicts and disputes in a direction that brings about restoration and healing.

Victim and Offender Face to Face: What Does That Mean?

In a very general sense, the term mediation describes a process whereby a neutral, third-party arbiter intervenes between two disputants.[17] So, for example, two neighbors cannot agree on what to do with a tree that is on the property of one but creating a nuisance for the other. Tempers can flare, and the dispute can escalate if the two cannot reach an agreement. Mediation within the context of a civil dispute implies a sense of equity and balance, whereby each party has an equal and valid claim to their side of the issue. With victim-offender mediation programs, however, the balance in status is unclear in the least, and at most tipped in favor of the victim as there is no room for making excuses, minimizing the offender's action, or taking the victim's side for granted. Advocates of conflict resolution through a face-to-face encounter recognize the potentially emotional, intense dialog that can stem from feelings of anger, frustration, and hurt.[18] Box 4.1 illustrates the use of these types of encounters in an office setting. Thus, this method of restorative justice brings some unique dynamics to the table that warrant further investigation.

The mediation of conflict between victims and offenders recognizes the essential process of restoration in balance that occurs when victims are given a chance to express their anger and hurt in a very personal and impactful way by directly addressing the behavior of the offender through a face-to-face encounter. This dialog leaves no room for the offender to escape accountability. Their actions are brought to the surface in a manner that is empowering to victims, as the contact is made in a safe, structured environment. This is in direct contrast to the depersonalization of justice within traditional courtroom proceedings where offenders, even when spoken to directly, can turn away to avoid the shame and guilt associated with direct eye contact. Within this context, the dialog is mutual, and offenders must engage in a reaction to the anger and hurt and not merely be passive receptors of the statements made by their victims.[19]

This process recognizes the fundamental principle of restorative justice that criminal behavior involves actions against individual people and not just merely the State or government. Thus, rather than advocate for an adversarial system of justice, victim-offender mediation reinforces the need for the mending of relationships, opening dialog between individuals, and in essence teaching individuals the skills necessary to restore relationships, resolve conflict, and reach mutual agreement and respect for the point of view of others while creating psychological closure for the victim as well as responsibility on the part of the offender. This, of course, implies that the application of victim-offender mediation cannot be used in all circumstances, especially ones where victims and offenders have little or no direct relationship with one another. As most restorative justice practices imply, victim-offender mediation, perhaps more so than any other practice, can only work when the participants are completely willing to become engaged as participants. As such, victim-offender mediation programs are unique within criminal justice, representing a mechanism that places both victim and offenders on the same side towards resolution.[20]

Box 4.1: Restorative Justice: Let's Take a Closer Look ...
A Dramatic Portrayal of Restorative Justice

What do budget cuts, an Australian film, and restorative justice have in common? One can ponder this question and upon quick glance dismiss the idea that they have anything at all in common. However, upon a closer examination, the 2011 film, *Face to Face* was adapted from playwright David Williamson's portrayal of conflict resolution sessions transcribed from true life disputes in an office setting. The film dispels myths about guilt and blame as events leading up to a young construction worker charged with assaulting his boss unfold. When tensions mount and emotions erupt into outward actions of hostility, the dynamics of a formal courtroom resolution, especially considering budget cuts that encourage reaching agreements in the quickest and least costly manner, often leave individuals dissatisfied, uneasy, and with nowhere to "move on." In this film, conflicts are described as layers of emotion that can only be addressed and resolved if disputants are given the opportunity to face one another where more than the ultimate consequence of the emotions—usually the action itself under question—come to surface. In *Face to Face*, the angry construction worker who slams his hot rod into the back of his boss's Jaguar, destroying his car and injuring him, is given a chance to avoid court proceedings and rather explain his actions in a community setting through a controlled, guided, and mediated face-to-face conference with his boss, his boss's wife, co-workers, and his best friend as well as his own mother. This encounter surfaces a swell of emotional events as a toxic workplace environment of harassment, lies, bullying, betrayal, and racism, has pushed several individuals to an emotional breaking point.

As the events of this drama unfold, we can't help but recognize the hidden yet obvious message about the powerful effect of the restorative justice art of mediation, where the release of emotion is allowed in an open, yet constructive way, and anger and frustration are used to diffuse but not excuse the outcome of the emotion. This in turn leads to a resolution that is mutually beneficial for all parties involved, a resolution that transcends the closed-door environment of courtroom agreements to involve a translucent dialog that revolves around multiple issues that affect more than just the direct disputants. The potential for long-term satisfaction and creating a more peaceful work environment are clear, and relationships are restored. Here, the outcome is not only more cost effective, it is more swift, practical, and has a more positive impact on both the victim and the defendant … which, speaking of the defendant, what do you think his fate was in this case?

Source: Burke, K. (2011, September 19). Coming face to face with emotion behind office conflict. *The Sydney Morning Herald*. Retrieved from http://www.smh.com.au/national/coming-face-to-face-with-emotion-behind-office-conflict-20110918-1kfuz.html.

Dispelling Misconceptions and Finding the Truth … The Art of Mediation

The concept seems to be simple enough. Two or more individuals are in a dispute over a matter; bring them together, and through the help of a mediator, resolution is reached. This might be simple if we are talking about two small children in a classroom arguing over who gets a certain toy or resolving a complaint in a grocery store where a sale price is not ringing up correctly in a register. However, in a world of complicated social settings, structural contradictions, inconsistencies in expectations, personal disappointments, and wide-scale lack of civility, conflicts can either escalate or diffuse depending on the mechanisms of intervention that are employed. In the end, however, the ultimate goal is an exercise in fact finding that clarifies, implores, and appeals to the search for truth, understanding, and justice.[21] Within this search, the very mechanisms of mediation rise to the challenge of conflict resolution, addressing a wide range of interpersonal conflicts within a variety of settings involving neighborhood disputes, school infractions, and workplace disagreements.

Table 4.1 Number and Percent Distribution of Incidents, by Type of Crime and Victim-Offender Relationship

| Type of crime | All incidents | | Percent of incidents | | | |
| | | | Involving strangers | | Involving nonstrangers | |
	Number	Percent	Number	Percent	Number	Percent
Crimes of violence	**8,316,180**	**100 %**	**4,242,050**	**51.0 %**	**4,074,130**	**49.0 %**
Completed violence	2,437,260	100	1,164,660	47.8	1,272,600	52.2
Attempted/threatened violence	5,878,920	100	3,077,390	52.3	2,801,530	47.7
Rape/Sexual assault	291,820	100	99,760	34.2	192,060	65.8
Rape/Attempted rape	181,390	100	56,730	31.3	124,660	68.7
Rape	96,110	100	22,690 *	23.6 *	73,420	76.4
Attempted rape/a	85,270	100	34,040	39.9	51,230	60.1
Sexual assault/b	110,430	100	43,030	39.0	67,400	61.0
Robbery	1,040,480	100	792,500	76.2	247,980	23.8
Completed/property taken	690,220	100	533,460	77.3	156,760	22.7
With injury	240,750	100	182,720	75.9	58,040	24.1
Without injury	449,470	100	350,740	78.0	98,730	22.0
Attempted to take property	350,260	100	259,040	74.0	91,210	26.0
With injury	75,460	100	41,150	54.5	34,310	45.5
Without injury	274,800	100	217,890	79.3	56,910	20.7
Assault	6,983,880	100	3,349,790	48.0	3,634,090	52.0
Aggravated	1,678,720	100	892,220	53.1	786,500	46.9
With injury	441,110	100	155,510	35.3	285,600	64.7
Threatened with weapon	1,237,610	100	736,710	59.5	500,900	40.5
Simple	5,305,160	100	2,457,580	46.3	2,847,590	53.7
With minor injury	1,117,920	100	422,050	37.8	695,870	62.2
Without injury	4,187,240	100	2,035,530	48.6	2,151,710	51.4

Note: Detail may not add to total shown because of rounding.
*Estimate is based on about 10 or fewer sample cases.
a/Includes verbal threats of rape.
b/Includes threats.

Available at https://www.bjs.gov/content/pub/pdf/cvus/previous/cvus27.pdf.

When a crime has been formally committed, however, mediation and the face-to-face encounter between victims and offenders takes on a new meaning. This meaning becomes essential to the restoration of relationships, as statistics show that crime victimization is as likely to occur between individuals who are non-strangers, including friends, family, neighbors, coworkers, and intimate partners, as individuals who are strangers (see Table 4.1).[22] Thus, various considerations in the implementation of this restorative justice practice must take place, including establishing common ground, targeting appropriate cases, and defining contact between victims and offenders.

Establishing Common Ground

Inherent to the concept of mediation is that there are two sides with opposing viewpoints that are more than likely to have opposite goals in mind when coming to resolution. To avoid confusion and ensure the integrity of the process of mediation, therefore, it is essential to establish common ground.[23] What exactly does this mean? First and foremost, this means that the goal of reconciliation based on finding the truth from a variety of perspectives is placed as the number one priority. This not only places emphasis on the processes of dialog and communication, but it also recognizes that our central focus after crime should be its inherent disruption of relationships.

The goal of reconciliation will ultimately lead to provisions for resolving the conflict, preventing future criminal actions, providing appropriate remedy to the victim, and holding the offender accountable. For this to occur, however, reconciliation must be guided by principles and practices that consider the material and emotional needs of both the victim and the offender.[24] This includes a recognition of the humanity of the victim, rather than the objectified label of "victim," and likewise, removing the label of "criminal" and recognizing the offender as a person. Moreover, the mediation of disputes between victims and offenders towards the goal of reconciliation involves a mutual need for honesty and understanding of the feelings, hurts, frustrations, and motivations of one another. Through this process, the expression of remorse on the part of the offender can be met with a genuine forgiveness from the victim, as well as an agreeable outcome for restitution and restoration.[25]

Targeting Appropriate Cases

Another consideration in the effective implementation of victim-offender mediation programs and processes is case selection. While this consideration has an operational side, there are also major elements of selection that need to follow appropriate theoretical guidelines and principles. Within the formal criminal justice system, case referral is often made by sentencing judges, probation officers, prosecutors, and even law enforcement personnel. While not automatically excluded from mediation referral criteria, violent crime cases must be very carefully selected to ensure that the appropriate mechanisms of formal intervention are not compromised. Most case referrals are therefore for property crime cases such as vandalism, burglary, and theft. Cases referred can be diversions from formal court proceedings or in conjunction with a formal court disposition.[26]

Case screening also includes elements of consideration that are necessary for the effective outcome of reconciliation to occur. Notably, the offender must accept responsibility for their role in the criminal offense, while at the same time, the victim recognizes that resolution and restoration are negotiable outcomes of the mediation process. Moreover, the nature of the offense creates an imbalance so that there is an actual need for negotiation and dialog, meaning, there must be room for making things right through the actions of the offender. It is this criterion that often excludes the inclusion of violent felony offenses, where any amount of financial restoration is outweighed by the need for punishment through formal sanctioning. Even when considering cases involving property offenses, there needs to be a clear understanding that there is no potential for violence or interpersonal hostility between victim and offender and that both parties are willing participants.[27] Without these considerations, compromising the mediation process is inevitable.

Defining Contact between Victims and Offenders

Reconnecting a victim with their offender through a face-to-face encounter is a difficult task. Once a case is identified for victim-offender mediation, the facilitator must contact each party separately to let them know of this option as an intervention that can help all parties involved. This is usually done through an individual phone call or a direct contact interview which explains the benefits that can be reaped through participation in mediation.[28] During this initial phase, the program facilitator gets more information from each party about their experiences of the offense and the aftermath of what happened, as well as gains some perspective on attitudes towards one another. Victims are never pressured to participate and are given time to think and reflect on the process in a very respectful and sensitive manner. Likewise, offenders are made aware of their participation within the context of a supportive environment that is designed to promote healing, accountability, and reconciliation. Thus, an environment for dialog is created that is built on contact and interactions that are defined by mutual trust, respect, and rapport.[29]

Once both parties, victim and offender, agree to participate in the victim-offender mediation program, a face-to-face meeting is scheduled. During that encounter, the mediator explains the important dynamics of interaction in a respectful, safe manner, lays the various ground rules of the meeting, and identifies the different goals of the process. This is followed by a brief discussion of the factual elements of the crime and the opportunity for each party to express their feelings towards the offense. During this time, victims are afforded the rare opportunity to share with the offender the emotional outcome of their criminal actions, as well as ask the often lingering, unanswered questions that give way to a cathartic experience of healing and forgiveness (see Box 4.2). This sense of peace and forgiveness is also encouraged by listening to the offender's story, experiencing their vulnerability, and getting to know their "human" side, as the offender is also afforded the rare opportunity to express guilt and remorse in a very personal, intimate manner.[30] The defining nature of the face-to-face encounters between victims and offenders within the context of mediation is therefore designed to reshape human interactions in a way that dispels stereotypes, demystifies reconciliation, and allows individuals to deal with one another as people rather than objects. This optimizes the chances for restoration and healing and allows for offender accountability in the effort to reach an agreement for restitution and reconciliation. Once agreement is reached, a written contract is made which is signed by both parties and sent to the referring court or agency for approval, monitoring, and enforcement.

Box 4.2: Restorative Justice in Action —
Why ...? Searching for Answers and Finding Healing

Elizabeth Menkin suffered a tragic loss when a drunk driver took the life of her sister, Elaine. However, through the use of victim-offender mediation, Menkin found a place where justice actually prevailed. After her sister's death, Menkin experienced the first of the four steps that most victims undergo. Menkin initially felt shock, grief, and an upwelling, vengeful anger. Menkin strived to overcome her loss and grief, yet she was left feeling helpless, frustrated, and angry. Menkin concentrated all her thoughts on the 25-year-old offender and the fact that the offender might plead not guilty. Menkin's father, Peter, handled his grief over the tragedy differently. Although tormented by his daughter's death, he focused on the prevention of further tragedy and suffering to his and the offender's families. Peter contacted Marty Price, the director of the Victim-Offender Mediation Reconciliation Program in Clacksman County, Oregon, about his situation. Price agreed to conduct a victim-offender mediation between the offender and Peter, but encouraged Peter to get the other members of his family involved in the process as well. Although his family members were initially reluctant to participate in the mediation, as Peter shared his experiences many members of the family decided to become involved in the meditation.

Menkin wondered what the drunken driver who killed her sister would have to do to earn her forgiveness. Menkin realized that she needed the offender to recognize her wrongdoing and to express remorse for the consequences of her criminal behavior; only then would Menkin believe she could stop hating her. In addition, Menkin wanted the offender to feel regret, shame, suffering, and humility. Once Menkin was able to recognize what she needed from the offender, she was able to imagine facing her in mediation. Even before the actual meeting, Menkin and her family began to feel the benefits of the process. Menkin acknowledged that the greatest benefit for the family was to feel that we were trying to make something positive out of a very negative situation, as Elaine would have wanted. The actual mediation proceeded as the victim's family members and the offender intended, and by all accounts, the parties' experience served as a success story for using this process in the context of serious and violent crimes. The entire family had the opportunity to individually address their feelings and desires to the offender, the offender listened and expressed feelings of sincere remorse, and the parties collectively created a restitution agreement that incorporated all the family members' needs.

The family noted the immediate emotional healing from the mediation. Menkin reported that the day after the mediation she noticed her tension had disappeared and she felt relief as she let go of feelings of vengeance and despair. Elaine's husband noted how his brightness and vigor were restored. The offender also benefited from the process. She completed the provisions of the restitution agreement and has since remained sober and used her experience as a way to better her life.

Source: *Wellikoff, I. (2003).* Victim-offender mediation and violent crimes: On the way to justice. *Benjamin N. Cardozo School of Law Journal of Conflict Resolution, 5.1.* Used by permission. Retrieved from http://cardozojcr.com/issues/volume-5-1/note-1/.

Restoration through Mediation between Victims and Offenders

By now, we have a clear understanding of the passive role victims play within the formal criminal justice system. The sharing of information is limited, opportunities to express feelings of anger and hurt, as well as any chance of confronting offenders in a constructive manner, are faced with obstacles and barriers that make it difficult to heal effectively from the experience of crime. Likewise, offenders do not get the opportunity to experience the human side of their victim, feeling their pain and suffering and allowing themselves to express their remorse in a real, heartfelt manner. Rather than placing the victim and the offender in such a passive, impersonal role, victim-offender mediation reduces the adversarial dynamic of formal justice, allowing for emotional closure for the victim and calling for direct accountability by the offender. In doing so, victim-offender mediation represents a mechanism of restorative justice that achieves justice and brings about transformation.[31]

Mediating Disputes Effectively to Achieve Justice

What constitutes "effective" mediation? Is it the outcome? What about the process itself? How do we measure participant satisfaction? The answers to these questions

Table 4.2: Mediating Disputes: The Art of Dialog

Mediation Technique ...	The Outcome ...
Listening	Listening intently and sincerely builds trust between all parties, encouraging dialog in a safe, neutral context
Motivating	Motivating both sides to share their feelings openly and honestly results in a balancing of power between victim and offender
Facilitating	Facilitating allows for input from the mediator regarding the process, not the outcome, thereby placing ownership of resolution in the hands of the disputants
Regulating	Regulating a mediation meeting clarifies the ground rules, sets goals, and calls for sticking to an agenda, which maximizes the opportunity for effective dialog by monitoring verbal and nonverbal communication and avoiding one side dominating the discussion
Instilling	Instilling ownership in the conflict resolution creates a sense of balance whereby the victim feels strengthened and empowered, and the offender accepts responsibility and feels obligated to make things right with the ultimate goal of reconciliation at the heart of resolution

can be gauged through a better understanding of the delivery of quality mediation techniques. As we have alluded to before, mediation is truly an art, an element that is rarely if at all contained in any other correctional intervention. It is one thing to resolve a dispute; however, it is a totally different matter to resolve a dispute in a manner that leaves both parties that were once on opposite sides, on the same side of agreement. This, therefore, is the true measure of victim-offender mediation as exemplifying restorative principles and theory, for its outcome redefines justice.

Bringing two opposing viewpoints to the same side of agreement requires significant skills in negotiation and communication. These skills require a mediator that is neither too flexible or too rigid.[32] An individual who wants to please everyone will keep the arguments going around in circles to avoid the discomfort of leaving one side dissatisfied. This, of course, achieves nothing in the long run. On the other hand, an individual who is too authoritative can take charge and through personal bias or opinion, sway the scale of balanced discussion towards one side or the other. Again, this defeats the goal and purpose of mediation. Thus, being assertive and collaborative are personality qualities of a mediator that are most likely to balance the needs of both victims and offenders while at the same time ensuring that justice is clearly defined by that balance.

Moreover, a unique feature of victim-offender mediation is the ability to achieve justice while avoiding the process of arbitration. The process of arbitration, which is characteristic of most dispute resolution alternatives, involves mechanisms whereby a final judgment is reached by a neutral third-party individual designated to listen to both sides and make a final, binding decision based on arguments made. With mediation, however, the outcome is reached through a process of communication, negotiation, and agreement … not agreement based on a decision made by the third-party facilitator, but actual agreement between the victim and the offender. If agreement cannot be reached, the case is not decided by the mediator but rather referred back to the court for further action.[33] This process not only optimizes the potential for justice, but in many cases, it transforms the ability of disputants to rely on their own communication skills to reach a peaceful, equitable resolution. To this effect, mediation serves as a learning tool for future disputes that might arise, allowing victims and offenders to further the reconciliation process by relying on their better understanding of justice, fairness, and equity.[34] Table 4.2 summarizes the role of a mediator in facilitating judicious outcomes that achieve justice and accountability. In the section to come, we will examine the role of these techniques in creating a transformative process of restoration and balance.

Transformation Through the Resolution of Conflicts in a Positive Way

As a philosophic approach, restorative justice challenges traditional responses to wrong doing where justice is equated with making things "even" by exacting some form of negative reaction upon the errant person or wrongdoer. Within a restorative approach the goal is to make things "even" by balancing power and creating restoration through the reparation of relationships. This represents the concept of rewards and punishments as mechanisms of reinforcement that can be used in a positive way to instill a sense of responsibility and shared accountability.[35]

Victim-offender mediation transforms the process of dispute resolution from one that focuses on a punitive approach, to one that recognizes the harm as inappropriate and thoughtless but does not confine its resolution by those parameters. In doing so, victim-offender mediation calls for reflection rather than hostility and resentment, and conceptualizes fairness and balance as mutually beneficial outcomes for all parties involved.[36] This process leaves wrongdoers with a sense of responsibility to take corrective action while freeing them from the sense of alienation that comes with the inability to have an active role in the process of justice and restoration.

The term "empty justice" reminds us of the failure of punishment alone to bring healing and resolution to the victims of crime. While sometimes it is difficult to gauge what exactly constitutes a transformation for victims to heal from the pain and loss of crime, efforts at mediation can at least facilitate this process by allowing victims to be heard, while at the same time giving them the chance to better understand how the situation came about, how it can be avoided in the future, and how this negative experience can be used as a mechanism of learning, retrieving balance and control over their lives, and placing a face on the fear caused by their victimization. By giving both victims and offenders the responsibility of finding their own resolution to the conflict, restorative mediation creates a positive outcome whereby needs are met through a process that treats both sides respectfully, allows both sides to be heard, emphasizes listening as much as speaking, builds responsibility and trust, and encourages the development of empathy in making choices in future situations.[37] Victim-offender mediation is therefore a cohesive approach that seeks to build communities by instilling the ideals of collaboration, compassion, and mutual well-being through positive intervention that builds and restores relationships. In the final section of this chapter, we will take a closer look at the success of these processes in achieving restorative justice outcomes.

Evaluating the Success of Victim-Offender Mediation

When considering the research literature on restorative justice, we see major gaps in the outcome evaluation of specific programs and practices. With regard to victim-offender mediation programs, however, their long history of integrated practices in juvenile and adult court systems has given us a somewhat better glimpse of their success in achieving restorative outcomes. Within the literature, this success has been measured in terms of client satisfaction and perception of fairness, and specific outcomes for victims and offenders such as healing and reducing recidivism (see Box 4.3).

Box 4.3: Research in Restorative Justice —
   A Cross-Site Evaluation of Victim-Offender
   Mediation Programs

   The first large-scale evaluation study of victim-offender mediation took place in 1992. The study was conducted by researchers Mark Umbreit and Robert Coates, a research team from the Citizens Council Mediation Services in Minneapolis, MN. The team examined four program sites that were integrated into the juvenile court systems in Albuquerque, NM; Austin, TX; Minneapolis and St. Paul, MN; and the East Bay area of California. Researchers collected a significant amount of both quantitative and qualitative data through 1,153 interviews with victims and offenders, a content analysis of program and court records, as well as interviews with court officials and program staff and the observation of 28 mediation sessions. The following is a summary of their findings:

   • With regard to client satisfaction with the victim-offender process, 87% of offenders and 79% of victims reported high levels of satisfaction with the outcome

- Regarding the perception of fairness, 89% of offenders and 83% of victims found the mediation process to be fair
- Both victims and offenders found the face-to-face encounter through the mediation process to be an important feature of the program
- Participants in the mediation process found it to have a strong humanizing effect in contrast to traditional mechanisms of the juvenile justice system
- When examining a comparison group of non-participants, the victim-offender mediation process had a more significant positive effect on crime victims in terms of their satisfaction with the outcome
- Victim-offender mediation reduced the anxiety and fear of being revictimized by 15% among victim participants
- As an intervention technique, victim-offender mediation was found to be a useful response in working with a variety of juvenile offenders for both serious and less serious crimes and holding them accountable for their actions
- Within a one-year follow-up period, fewer and less serious crimes were committed by offenders participating in the victim-offender mediation programs, when compared to a similar group of non-participants.
- Regarding program obligations, 81% of juvenile offenders participating in victim-offender mediation completed their restitution obligation to the victim as compared to 58% of similar offender non-participants completing their restitution obligation to the victim

Source: Umbreit, M. S., Coates, R. B., & Roberts, A. W. (2000). The impact of victim offender mediation: A cross national perspective. *Conflict Resolution Quarterly*, *17*(3), 215–229.

While the research highlighted in the box above may not be generalizable to all victim-offender mediation programs, the data provide us with compelling evidence of the potential for this type of restorative justice intervention to increase accountability on the part of offenders while at the same time providing victims of crime a positive outlet for engaging in dialog that promotes healing and empowerment. Moreover, researchers note that long-term evaluation studies spanning decades of research on the benefit of victim-offender mediation programs over traditional criminal justice dispute resolution mechanisms indicate the potential for great benefit to both victims and offenders, enhancing victim satisfaction and their perception of fairness, increasing offender accountability, reducing recidivism, diverting offenders away from formal criminal charges, and being cost effective.[38]

From our standpoint, we need no further evidence other than the recognition and critical understanding that victim-offender mediation as a restorative justice intervention, represents a radical break from criminal justice alternatives, where the focus is on unilateral justice that is unclearly defined at best. With a critical eye of justice, we move forward in our exploration of restorative justice theory and practice with the recognition of the tremendous value in promoting programs that focus on dialog, communication, and the transformation of victims and offenders through reconciliation and reparation.

Chapter Summary

From where do we get the concept of victim-offender mediation?

The concept of victim-offender mediation is rooted in early Aboriginal cultures, which understood criminal offending as a harm against the entire community and something that affects everyone. Their process of conflict resolution emphasized that victims and offenders take on an active role in fixing the wrongdoing. This process was compromised during the period of North American colonization, and the structure of Aboriginal society, dominated and controlled by European settlers, led to a rise in the representation of Aboriginal people as both victims of crime and criminal offenders. Recognizing the need for reform, the Canadian government began to integrate restorative justice as a means of resurrecting Aboriginal cultural beliefs and traditions into the application of law.

In 1974, in the Waterloo Region of Ontario, two young offenders pleaded guilty to 22 different charges when they went on a drunken vandalism spree. The probation officer assigned to the case was convinced that the anger and frustration experienced by the various community members victimized by these two young offenders could best be alleviated through efforts at reconciliation between them and the offenders, and persuaded the presiding judge that this would be the perfect case to test the concept of reconciliation through a mediated face-to-face encounter between the offenders and their victims. This case became known as the Kitchener Experiment, and marked the beginning of Canada's Victim Offender Reconciliation Project (VORP). Shortly thereafter, the use of reconciliation and mediation programs between victims and offenders caught on in the United States, and in 1978, the efforts of probation officers and the Mennonite Church in Elkhart County, Indiana led to the development of the first VORP.

How do we apply mediation programs in various contexts?

The application of mediation within the context of criminal justice sanctioning recognizes that criminal behavior involves actions against individuals and not just merely the State or government. Thus, rather than advocate for an adversarial system of justice, victim-offender mediation reinforces the need for the mending of relationships. It allows for open dialog between individuals, teaching them the skills necessary to restore relationships, resolve conflict, and reach agreement. This builds trust and creates respect for the point of view of others while providing a psychological closure for the victim as well as instilling responsibility on the part of the offender. Victim-offender mediation therefore can only work when the participants are completely willing to become engaged as participants. As such, victim-offender mediation programs are unique within criminal justice, representing a mechanism that places both victim and offender on the same side of resolution. The goal of this process is to clarify facts, persuade opinion, and search for truth, understanding, and justice in the attempt to address a wide range of interpersonal conflicts. Moreover, various considerations in the implementation of this restorative justice practice must take place, including establishing common ground, targeting appropriate cases, and defining contact between victims and offenders.

Can the mediation of conflicts bring about restoration and healing?

A unique feature of victim-offender mediation is the ability to achieve justice while avoiding the process of arbitration, a process that characterizes most dispute resolution alternatives and involves mechanisms whereby a final judgment is reached by a neutral third-party individual designated to listen to both sides and make a final, binding decision based on arguments made. Contrary to this process, mediation reaches an outcome through a process of communication, negotiation, and agreement between the victim and the offender. If agreement cannot be reached, the case is referred to the court for further action. This process optimizes the potential for justice and transforms the ability of disputants to rely on their own communication skills to reach a peaceful, equitable resolution, serving as a learning tool for future disputes that might arise. This restorative approach balances power and creates restoration through the reparation of relationships. By instilling a sense of responsibility and shared accountability in a positive way, victim-offender mediation transforms the process of dispute resolution from one that focuses on a punitive approach, to one that recognizes the harm as inappropriate and thoughtless but does not confine its resolution by those parameters.

What does the research literature say about the success of this type of practice?

The empirical literature evaluating the success of victim-offender mediation services provides ample evidence that this mechanism of intervention gives victims of crime a positive outlet for engaging in dialog that provides healing and empowerment. Moreover, researchers note that long-term evaluation studies on the benefit of victim-offender mediation programs over traditional criminal justice dispute resolution mechanisms indicate the potential for great benefit to both victims and offenders, enhancing victim satisfaction and their perception of fairness, increasing offender accountability, reducing recidivism, diverting offenders away from formal criminal charges, and being a cost-effective alternative.

Key Terms

Mediation
Victim-Offender Mediation (VOM)
Aboriginal
First Nations
Métis
Inuit
Sentencing Reform Bill
Mennonite Central Committee (MCC)
Kitchener Experiment
Victim Offender Reconciliation Project (VORP)
Howard Zehr
Prisoner and Community Together (PACT)

Critical Thinking Questions

1. Critics of restorative justice intervention might regard programs advocating for mediation as "getting soft" on crime and criminal offenders. What would you say to that? Do you feel victim-offender mediation is a less rigorous intervention than traditional forms of criminal justice? Why or why not?

2. How does victim-offender mediation represent the core ideals of restorative justice? What aspects of this process would you advocate for the most? Is there room for change/improvement?

3. Are there particular types of criminal cases that would be most suitable for victim-offender mediation intervention? If so, what are these cases and what makes them most suitable?

4. Do you think victim-offender mediation as an intervention is appropriate for violent crime cases where the victim is amenable to this approach? What precautions would you as a mediator want to take to ensure the dialog is safe for both parties?

References

1. Pepinsky, H. (2015). 8 Peacemaking. *Positive Criminology, 23,* 109.

2. Mullane, R., Burrell, N. A., Allen, M., & Timmerman, L. (2014). Victim-offender mediation. In N. A. Burrell, M. Allen, B. M. Gayle, & R. W. Preiss (Eds.), *Managing interpersonal conflict: Advances through meta-analysis* (pp. 106–124). Routledge.

3. Miller, S. L., & Hefner, M. K. (2015). Procedural justice for victims and offenders? Exploring restorative justice processes in Australia and the US. *Justice Quarterly, 32*(1), 142–167.

4. Fox, D. (2016). Canada: Community, reintegration, restoration and Aboriginal responses. In E. Arnull & D. Fox (Eds.), *Cultural perspectives on youth justice: Connecting theory, policy and international practice* (pp. 111–130). Palgrave Macmillan UK.

5. Rudin, J. (2011). Aboriginal justice and restorative justice. In E. Elliott & R. M. Gordon (Eds.), *New directions in restorative justice* (pp. 89–114). Routledge.

6. Porter, A. J. (2014). *Decolonising juvenile justice: Aboriginal patrols, safety and the policing of indigenous communities* (Doctoral thesis). University of Sydney.

7. Rudin, J. (2016). *Aboriginal peoples and the criminal justice system.* Retrieved from https://www.attorneygeneral.jus.gov.on.ca/inquiries/ipperwash/policy_part/research/pdf/Rudin.pdf.

8. Doob, A. N., & Webster, C. M. (2016). Weathering the storm? Testing long-standing Canadian sentencing policy in the twenty-first century. *Crime and Justice, 45*(1), 359–418.

9. Van Ness, D. W., & Strong, K. H. (2014). *Restoring justice: An introduction to restorative justice.* Routledge.

10. Bright, C. (n.d.). Victim-offender mediation. Center for Justice and Reconciliation. Retrieved from http://restorativejustice.org/restorative-justice/about-restorative-justice/tutorial-intro-to-restorative-justice/lesson-3-programs/victim-offender-mediation/.

11. A comparison of four restorative conference models: Victim-offender mediation. (2001, February). *Juvenile Justice Bulletin.* National Criminal Justice Reference Service. Retrieved from https://www.ncjrs.gov/html/ojjdp/2001_2_1/page1.html.

12. Fox, D. (2016). Canada: Community, reintegration, restoration and Aboriginal responses. In E. Arnull & D. Fox (Eds.), *Cultural perspectives on youth justice: Connecting theory, policy and international practice* (pp. 111–130). Palgrave Macmillan UK.

13. Van Ness, D. W., & Strong, K. H. (2014). *Restoring justice: An introduction to restorative justice.* Routledge.

14. Messmer, H., & Otto, H. U. (Eds.). (2013). *Behavioural and Social Sciences Series: Vol. 64. Restorative justice on trial: Pitfalls and potentials of victim-offender mediation — International Research Perspectives.* — Springer Science & Business Media.

15. PACT. *Prisoner and Community Together.* Retrieved from https://www.linkedin.com/company-beta/3194615/.

16. Center for Community Justice. Retrieved from http://www.centerforcommunityjustice.org/.

17. Roberts, M. M. (2014). *Mediation in family disputes: Principles of practice.* Ashgate Publishing, Ltd.

18. Lederach, J. (2015). *Little book of conflict transformation: Clear articulation of the guiding principles by a pioneer in the field.* Skyhorse Publishing, Inc.

19. Hagen, T. (2013, July). Forgiveness, peace and conflict resolution in the Balkans: A survey of Albanian students. International Balkan Annual Conference.

20. Pepinsky, H. (2015). 8 Peacemaking. *Positive Criminology, 23,* 109.

21. Wood, D. (2014). Civilizing criminal justice: An international restorative agenda for penal reform. *Probation Journal, 61*(2), 211–212.

22. McQuade, K. M. (2014). Victim-offender relationship. *The encyclopedia of criminology and criminal justice.* Retrieved from http://onlinelibrary.wiley.com/doi/10.1002/9781118517383.wbeccj131/full.

23. Moore, C. W. (2014). *The mediation process: Practical strategies for resolving conflict.* John Wiley & Sons.

24. Umbreit, M. S., Bradshaw, W., & Coates, R. B. (1999). Victims of severe violence meet the offender: Restorative justice through dialogue. *International Review of Victimology, 6*(4), 321–343.

25. Mullane, R., Burrell, N. A., Allen, M., & Timmerman, L. (2014). Victim-offender mediation. In N. A. Burrell, M. Allen, B. M. Gayle, & R. W. Preiss (Eds.), *Managing interpersonal conflict: Advances through meta-analysis* (pp. 106–124). Routledge.

26. Álvarez, C., Baig, M., Casado, C., Gómez, A., Llenas, M., Martínez, M., & Rodríguez, A. (2015). Making the balanced approach between victim and offender a reality: Integrating a proactive approach towards the victim. *Ljetopis Socijalnog Rada/Annual of Social Work*, *22*(1).

27. Bachinger, L. M., & Pelikan, C. (2015). Victims' experiences in victim-offender mediation in Austria: The "real" story. In I. Vanfraechem, D. Bolívar, & I. Aertsen (Eds.), *Victims and restorative justice* (pp. 83–106). Routledge.

28. Victim-offender mediation: A national perspective. (2000, April). guidelines for victim-sensitive victim-offender mediation: Restorative justice through dialogue. Office for Victims of Crime. Retrieved from https://www.ncjrs.gov/ovc_archives/reports/96517-gdlines_victims-sens/guide4.html.

29. Lewis, T., & Umbreit, M. (2015). A humanistic approach to mediation and dialogue: An evolving transformative practice. *Conflict Resolution Quarterly*, *33*(1), 3–17.

30. Strelan, P., Karremans, J. C., & Krieg, J. (2016). What determines forgiveness in close relationships? The role of post transgression trust. *British Journal of Social Psychology*, *56*(1), 161–180.

31. Tamarit, J., & Luque, E. (2016). Can restorative justice satisfy victims' needs? Evaluation of the Catalan victim-offender mediation programme. *Restorative Justice*, *4*(1), 68–85.

32. Miles, S. (n.d.). Winning at mediation: The strategies for effective dispute resolution. American Bar Association, Young Lawyers Association. Retrieved from https://www.americanbar.org/groups/young_lawyers/publications/the_101_201_practice_series/winning_at_mediation_the_strategies_for_effective_dispute_resolution.html.

33. Moore, C. W. (2014). *The mediation process: Practical strategies for resolving conflict.* John Wiley & Sons.

34. Miller, S. L., & Hefner, M. K. (2015). Procedural justice for victims and offenders? Exploring restorative justice processes in Australia and the US. *Justice Quarterly*, *32*(1), 142–167.

35. Belsky, J. (2008, September 25). Rewards are better than punishments: Here's why. *Psychology Today*. Retrieved from https://www.psychologytoday.com/blog/family-affair/200809/rewards-are-better-punishment-here-s-why.

36. Tamarit, J., & Luque, E. (2016). Can restorative justice satisfy victims' needs? Evaluation of the Catalan victim-offender mediation programme. *Restorative Justice*, *4*(1), 68–85.

37. Normore, A. H., & Jarrett, B. (2017). Implementing restorative processes to mediate conflict and transform urban schools. In S. Singh & N. D. Erbe (Eds.), *Creating a sustainable vision of non-violence in schools and society* (pp. 222–237). IGI Global.

38. Umbriet, M. S., Coates, R. B., & Vos, B. (2000). The impact of victim-offender mediation: Two decades of research. *Fed. Probation*, *65*, 29. Strelan, P., McKee, I., & Feather, N. T. (2015). When and how forgiving benefits victims: Post transgression offender effort and the mediating role of deservingness judgements. *European Journal of Social Psychology*, *46*(3), 308–322; Mullane, R., Burrell, N. A., Allen, M., & Timmerman, L. (2014). Victim-offender mediation. In N. A. Burrell, M. Allen, B. M. Gayle, & R. W. Preiss (Eds.), *Managing interpersonal conflict: Advances through meta-analysis* (pp. 106–124). Routledge; Keeton, R. B. (2015). Crime victims and offenders face to face: An overview of the Texas Department of Criminal Justice Victim Offender Mediation/Dialogue Program. *Resolved: J. Alternative Disp. Resol.*, *5*, 26.

Chapter 5

Family Group Conferencing

In this chapter, we will explore the following questions ...
- *Where did the concept of family group conferencing originate?*
- *What are the basic elements of this restorative justice process?*
- *How does family group conferencing work?*
- *Is this an effective approach?*

Early Origins of Family Group Conferencing— The Maori

The inception of restorative justice processes has a history and tradition with long-standing roots in conflict resolution, and with significant implications for multiple contexts, including workplaces, schools, families, and corrections. These processes have developed around the goal of improving the overall quality of interactions between individuals in a manner that brings healing and restoration. One of the earliest restorative justice processes, *family group conferencing*, can be traced to the Maori people of New Zealand.

The Maori of New Zealand

The **Maori** are the indigenous Polynesian people of New Zealand. They are a people with a rich culture, history, and tradition. Historical records and archaeological finds trace the arrival of Maori in New Zealand in about the thirteenth century.[1] Although facing centuries of struggles common to indigenous populations, the Maori culture continues to persist and thrive, experiencing a rebirth in New Zealand during the early 1980s.[2]

A cornerstone foundation of the Maori culture is the concept of balance. A balanced community is seen as one where each person strives to achieve physical health, spiritual wellness, a healthy mind or conscience, and educational wellbeing.[3] When a particular member of the community experiences a disruption in one of these cornerstone aspects of balance, the community as a whole is required to intervene to restore that person to health and bring them back into the collective. Likewise, criminal offending is regarded as action that compromises or causes a harm to the wellbeing and integrity of persons or things. The only right thing to do under such circumstances, therefore, is to rectify the disruption in balance that has occurred. During this process, the goal is not to find fault or establish liability but rather to achieve a rebalance and restoration of the relationships of the parties involved.

Contrary to the warrior tradition captured in various accounts of Maori culture, researchers and anthropologists note that the Maori had a tribal history closely rooted in peaceful dispute resolution and community dialog, even for the most serious criminal acts, including violent crimes such as rape and murder.[4] The following excerpt from an oral history of the Maori captures this in great detail:

> If a dispute arose or a crime [was] committed in a village which involved or impacted on many members of the village a **hui** (meeting) would be called and all those who wished to be, or should be involved, gathered at the hui. No time frame was set for the duration of the hui but all those involved knew it would keep going until a consensus was reached, no matter how long that took. The key to the process was the method of dialog (the process can probably best be described as dialog) and how "issues" are spoken about. When all were gathered the **korero** (talk) would begin. The speakers would speak one at a time and each would know that their opportunity to speak a second time might wait until all others had had the opportunity to speak. The first speaker, knowing full well what the issue, which had caused the need for the hui, would be careful to avoid talking directly, or even indirectly, about the "issue." Each speaker in turn would first accept what has gone before still avoiding talking directly about the issue would ensure in his/her korero he/she would add to what the previous speaker has said. Already you can see that this is completely at odds with how matters are dealt with today (even in much of Maori society), and many will say this would be completely hopeless. However, in this process, where speakers do not stand to contradict the previous speaker and avoid speaking directly about the issue, that as the dialog goes around the group commonalities are found rather than enhancements of the original conflict. In this process speakers need to listen very carefully to all previous speakers, rather than jumping up to counter points throughout the discussion. In this process a speaker must be able to capture their thoughts and then try to add something to the total dialog. Their opportunity to speak in the dialog may only come once and the opportunity needs to be carefully taken. Respect is given for those who could remember the entire discussion and the very best speaker would wait for the end to demonstrate their prowess, not only at oratory but also, at being able to recall all of what has gone before. One must remember that Maori was an oral culture and the society put high value on those whose oral and memory skills were well honed. In Maori society a leader of people was called a **rangatira**. This is a word made of two parts with its root being "tira" meaning to knit together and "ranga" meaning to uplift. Combined then a rangatira is someone who can uplift the people, while binding them together. This is a difficult combination of skills to attain and use. Rangatira could lose their

status if they failed in their skills. Ariki on the other hand would be born to that status and would maintain it no matter what—lineage was everything for them and not their ability in leadership skills.[5]

The Maori system of justice was therefore premised on the notion that responsibility and accountability were not individual but rather based on a collective need to restore balance not only to the victim but also the victim's family. This also included an understanding of why an individual offended and not just an attempt to create an outcome rooted in revenge and punishment. For the Maori, it was important to understand the offender's behavior, as the criminal act was seen as a product of imbalance in the offender's social environment. This imbalance had to be addressed in a collective manner and had to be restored for both the offender and the victim. Inclusion of parents, children, and other close kin in this process was paramount to the successful restoration of balance and harmony to all those involved in the dispute or harmful outcome of criminal action.

The ideas of balance and restoration within the Maori culture create a sense of punishment and conflict resolution that are "future oriented," taking the stance that correcting past wrongs can only be achieved by reconnecting and repairing relationships and thereby creating harmony and balance. This idea became an integral component during the 1980s when New Zealand began to experience a crisis in the juvenile justice system, with the incarceration rate for young offenders being one of the highest worldwide.[6]

Let Shame Be the Punishment

Amongst juveniles involved in the criminal justice system, the minority Maori youth were disproportionately represented. Child welfare authorities began to question this dynamic in light of the culture's strong value on family and kinship as mechanisms of social support and control. Observations led to the conclusion that the Maori family structure and cultural norms of kinship were fractured, with young people experiencing broken bonds and increasingly becoming fragmented and alienated from their families, leading to their involvement with State authorities.[7] This was compounded by a system of justice that created further separation and violated the Maori goal of restoring communal harmony. Maori people viewed the New Zealand criminal justice system as counterproductive and inappropriate. A Maori citizen describes its outcome in the following excerpt:

> Very cold, unnatural ... you go in alone, you stand alone. If you're lucky you get to say what you want, but usually not the way you want to ... if you're the victim you seem to get no say. The lawyers, judges, police, they rule everything that goes on ... only those with degrees can talk. It mishandles Maori offenders. [In what way?] It relies too much on prison, on sending them away. Their families suffer, you know, loss of money; it just makes

things worse … the young guys go in and learn crime off the older ones … prisons cause a vicious cycle.[8]

The New Zealand juvenile justice system focused almost entirely on punishing offenders and correcting their erring ways, with very little attention given to repairing the harm they had caused. Maori leaders emerged to advocate for a return to their system of justice and conflict resolution and begin involving the community as a whole to find the cause of crime as part of finding the resolution. They maintained that the shame of getting caught and being held accountable was far more productive in terms of problem-solving and healing than punishment alone.[9]

Alternative models of decision making were sought, ones that made provision for including families and communities, and that were consistent with the kinship values of the Maori culture. Criminal offenses, according to Maori tradition, were believed to be past actions that were predictive of future events, and therefore could not be dealt with in a reactive manner alone. Their unique, traditional way of handling disputes was neglected by the criminal justice system that failed to account for the restoration of **mana**, or the honor and prestige that is derived from birth and throughout a lifetime of good deeds and peaceful association with community members. They believed that the key to conflict resolution and crime and the lawless behavior of youth was a reaffirmation of the value of **tapu**, the sacred spiritual and moral code that affirmed the collective-based, family-centered culture of the Maori.[10]

As an outcome of the government's attempt to integrate Maori recommendations to restore the involvement of family and community to address juvenile delinquency, the New Zealand legislature enacted the 1989 **Children, Young Persons and Their Families Act**. This act revamped the juvenile justice system in New Zealand, creating a process that focused on repair of harm and creating dialog between victims, offenders, family, and community.[11] Over time, this process gave New Zealand the global recognition for being the first legal system to institutionalize what became known as the *family group conference*. In the sections to come, we will discuss this concept in great detail. For now, we will identify it here as a major form of restorative justice that is intended to help youth involved in the juvenile justice system, as well as their victims, to come up with creative solutions through the guidance of their families, as well as the help of coordinating professionals. The development and implementation of the family group conferences in New Zealand marked the beginning of an unprecedented growth in restorative justice policy and practice. Let's take a closer look at the restorative practice of family group conferencing by identifying its various elements of design and implementation.

Design and Implementation

Within the domain of restorative justice practices, the **family group conference** (**FGC**) involves bringing together victims, offenders, family, friends, and other supporters to discuss the resolution of a criminal incident.[12] These affected parties are brought together by a trained facilitator to talk about the crime that was committed

Table 5.1: Participants in the Family Group Conference

Offenders and Family	*Courts mandate that the offender and their immediate family attend the conference, but extended family who are mechanisms of social support are also encouraged to participate*
Victims and Victim Supporters	*While not required to attend, victims are encouraged to participate in the FGC process*
Coordinator	*Moderates all dialog and communication during the FGC*
Professional and Lay Advocates	*These are individuals that can be appointed to advise on legal matters, serve as cultural moderators, religious advocates, and language translators*
Social Workers	*Professional social workers are often consulted in matters of custody, placement, community referrals, and other matters pertaining to child and family welfare*
Community Representatives	*When relevant and beneficial, members of the community such as employers, teachers, counselors, etc., who can provide helpful information, are invited*

Source: MacRae, A. & Zehr, H. (2004). *Little book of family group conferences New Zealand style: A hopeful approach when youth cause harm.* Good Books.

and how it has impacted all those involved in the incident, as well as develop a plan for reparation. Family group conferencing is a restorative process designed for group dialog and decision making.[13] Family group conferencing allows families and groups to come together to privately discuss their issues and concerns, as well as generate a shared plan of action to help move them forward. Trained coordinators help the group plan the conference and get it started; however, an important element to group conferencing is the opportunity for families and communities to work without the aid of a service provider to communicate, share, and make decisions.[14]

Family group conferences are designed to encourage open dialog and create a restorative plan of action; they are a unique practice in that they welcome more people into the process, such as family members and friends, and focus not only on repairing the harm of the offense but preventing future offenses by identifying criminogenic concerns and providing support for the offender in his/her effort to desist and transform the effects of the crime.[15] Like mediation, these processes are commonly utilized to divert offenders and victims from the court; however, family group conferencing is also widely used to prepare offenders, their families, and communities for prisoner reentry after incarceration.[16]

Key Features of the Family Group Conference

Family group conferences involve a gathering of family members, relatives, friends, and community specialists, as well as victims and other key stakeholders who join together to develop a plan of action where the community is central to decision making and the formal court system safeguards the process through oversight.[17] Table 5.1 provides a summary of the various individuals that can be involved in this process. The format of FGC is modeled after the natural and nurturing way in which families are a helping system that provides care and meets the needs of its members. Thus, this format allows parents, caretakers, and children to take ownership of any wrongdoing and take it upon themselves to develop family-centered corrective action that addresses multiple deficits that could exist.

Family group conferences allow for greater flexibility in decision-making, providing families with a neutral context that is non-threatening and non-adversarial, adapting to the needs of the parties involved and the issues that are being discussed.[18] These conferences take place in a community setting and take into consideration multiple views when developing a plan of action. They are facilitated by a neutral third party who has the primary role of encouraging the family to work together to reach an agreement on a course of action that improves the safety and wellbeing of the offender while addressing the reparative needs of the victim.[19] The facilitator also has the role of making sure that parties speak to each other in a positive and respectful manner.

Operating Framework

Selecting cases suitable for resolution through family group conferencing is the identifying feature within which this restorative justice mechanism operates. The referral of matters to FGC is usually provided for according to operating procedures of either the juvenile or adult court systems as part of diversion, alternative dispute resolution, and restorative justice programs.[20] Guidance is provided relative to case selection, review, assessment, referral, and factors to be considered in the identification of appropriate cases. While programs may vary in this guidance process, a general flow of events and information seems to be consistent within the operating framework of family group conferences. Figure 5.1 provides an overview of how the FGC flow of events takes place within the context of the juvenile justice system.

Stakeholder Support for the Family Group Conferencing Approach

As a practice, the successful implementation of family group conferencing relies on community support for its guiding principles.[21] Thus, the FGC approach is embedded in norms and values that promote the overall wellbeing of the community (see Box 5.1). Getting community buy-in can be a daunting task when promoting practices that might appear to be diverting formal criminal justice intervention. However, the FGC as an intervention is an easy "sell" given its overall mission of building healthy, resilient communities. While most widely used as diversion from formal court processing for juveniles, family group conferencing processes have also been implemented in a variety of contexts, such as schools, residential treatment programs, community mediation avenues, and police departments, to address conflicts and

Figure 5.1: How Cases Might Enter the Family Group Conference Setting

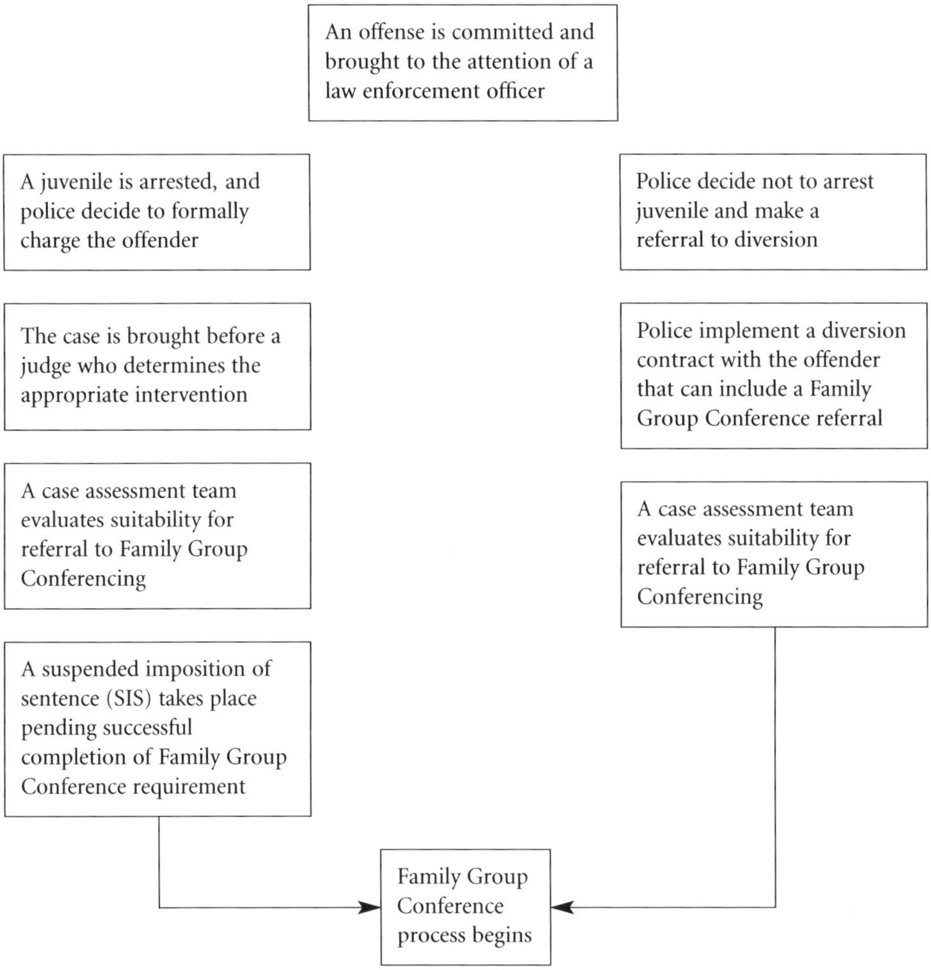

An offense is committed and brought to the attention of a law enforcement officer

A juvenile is arrested, and police decide to formally charge the offender

Police decide not to arrest juvenile and make a referral to diversion

The case is brought before a judge who determines the appropriate intervention

Police implement a diversion contract with the offender that can include a Family Group Conference referral

A case assessment team evaluates suitability for referral to Family Group Conferencing

A case assessment team evaluates suitability for referral to Family Group Conferencing

A suspended imposition of sentence (SIS) takes place pending successful completion of Family Group Conference requirement

Family Group Conference process begins

other matters of adjudication. We will discuss this in greater detail in sections to come. However, within these diverse contexts, the important role of family in the life of an individual is emphasized, with family empowerment seen as a central component of strengthening accountability and restoring balance and healing.

Box 5.1: Restorative Justice: Let's Take a Closer Look ...
Restoring Communities in Wagga Wagga?

A major impetus behind the development of the Wagga Wagga model of family group conferencing in New Zealand in the early 1990s was to create a mechanism whereby communities can become involved in the resolution of their own problems. The goal was to improve the process whereby citizen complaints made to the police were handled so that overall satisfaction with the mechanism of resolution would be achieved. family group conferencing was seen as an innovative mechanism by which police can use their cautionary discretion to give a young offender a warning rather than formally processing the offence by the court.

The first case implementing this practice involved four teenage boys who stole a motorcycle. Although the motorcycle was found, they had caused $1,000 in damages. The offenders and their families, as well as the victim, were brought together in a conference setting where the offenders talked about what happened, their thought process during the crime, and how their behavior affected the victim. The victim and victim's supporters also expressed their sentiments, and input was also made by the offenders' families and supporters. With the help of a facilitator, all parties involved came to a mutually satisfying agreement to restore the damage done to the victim, as well as discuss the various motives, problems, and issues leading up to the criminal behavior, and future goals in preventing such behavior from occurring to other members of the community.

The guided discussions of the Wagga Wagga model were seen to provide an informal, non-threatening opportunity to create restoration and healing not only to the victim, but to the community as a whole. An emphasis on setting limits to behavior while still providing support and guidance was achieved through the dialog between the various stakeholders. The conference setting allowed the parties to look beyond the single action of violation to emphasize and articulate the values and norms of the community as a whole. Do you think this process of establishing collective accountability for the behavior of erring youth, and creating a sense of community responsibility for the reconciliation of offenders, is truly restorative?

Sources: Langdon, J. J. (2016). Talk it out: Toward a narrative theory of community conferencing. *Contemporary Justice Review*, *19*(1), 19–30. Moore, D. B., & O'Connell, T. (1994). Family conferencing in Wagga Wagga: A communitarian model of justice. In C. Alder & J. Wundersitz (Eds.), *Family conferencing and juvenile justice: The way forward or misplaced optimism?* (pp. 45–86). Canberra: Australian Institute of Criminology.

Thus, FGC is seen as significantly contributing to the empowerment of the community as a whole, as its very structure widens the net of community involvement by allowing a broader range of individuals who are affected by a crime to discuss the offense as well as its detrimental effects, and how to go about finding a remedy and

Table 5.2: FGC Principles as Restorative Justice

Family Group Conferencing ...	*This Is Restorative Because ...*
Limits formal criminal justice intervention	Offenders often commit crimes as a symptom of larger interpersonal and social conflicts; FGC, when appropriate, brings about healing and resolution in a manner that accounts for offending within a context of community and avoids the stigma of formal labeling processes
Strengthens families	Families are the primary unit of care for juvenile offenders, as well as support mechanisms for adult offenders; empowering families to become part of the resolution of conflict within their own domain is a step in the direction of building trust and increasing commitment to making things right and holding one another accountable
Reintegrates offenders into the community	Involving multiple stakeholders as part of the FGC process increases the role of community in understanding offending behavior, and embracing offenders and accepting them back into society while at the same time coupling efforts at reintegration with accountability and reparation
Protects the interests of victims	Protecting the interests of victims not only ensures their restoration and healing, but also creates a sense of responsibility within the offender by increasing their awareness of the impact of their actions and allowing them to develop empathy

resolution to the harm that was committed. In doing this, a wider circle of people is seen as being victimized by the offense, with the FGC dynamic allowing these individuals to express the full impact of their victimization.[22] By engaging collective responsibility for making amends and shaping the future of the offender, a greater number of citizens become direct stakeholders in the process of creating fairness and equity when a crime is committed through their active participation in the process of achieving justice.

Consistency with Restorative Justice Principles

The cornerstone of the family group conference mechanism of restorative justice rests upon the foundation of principled practices that aim at limiting formal criminal justice intervention, strengthening families, reintegrating offenders into the community, and protecting the interests of victims. To this extent, the family group conference process is guided by restorative justice principles. Table 5.2 gives us a glimpse of the building blocks of FGC and how these various elements advance the goals of restorative justice principles and practices.

A major goal in developing a protocol for family group conferencing is therefore to reflect the basic ideological components of restorative justice theory and practice. How does the FGC process create flexibility in terms of conflict resolution and reconciliation? How do facilitators become culturally sensitive, impartial arbiters of justice? Does the dialog involved in a FGC address safety concerns and provide adequate opportunity to express feelings in a safe, neutral environment? Are the proper support services being delivered when needed? Is family group conferencing truly restorative? Let's take a closer look.

Family Group Conferencing in Action

The FGC model is structured around the idea that the family unit should be the first line of defense when becoming involved in the resolution of conflicts and in the planning of restoration to erring members.[23] This includes families intervening in systems involving juvenile justice, child protection, education, and corrections. The FGC model involves implementing a process whereby the role of family enhances the decision making and development of interventions that would sustain and support family preservation while meeting the goals of justice and reparation. In the sections to come, we will examine the family group conferencing process in greater detail, beginning first with the goals of the FGC model.

What Are the Goals of the Conference?

The overarching goal of the FGC model is to develop and implement plans that involve the creative integration of family as well as the mobilization of formal and informal resources within the context of a conference setting. In order to achieve this goal, the FGC model is guided by a set of criteria that advance the principle values of restorative justice, reparation, and healing. These criteria revolve around the goals of diversion, accountability, victim involvement, strengthening family, developing consensus, cultural sensitivity, and due process:

- *Diversion:* Individuals who become involved in activities that are harmful, errant, or detrimental to the wellbeing of society are in many ways alienated from the normative structure and expectations of their surrounding environment.[24] The goal of utilizing the FGC model is therefore to put in place mechanisms that bring back the individuals into the folds of acceptance in a manner that avoids further alienation through formal intervention and labeling as a delinquent, criminal offender, and outcast. Reconnecting delinquents and offenders to their families by keeping them away from formal criminal justice processing sends them a message of acceptance and gives them hope for turning from their criminal ways and rejoining the fold of society.[25]

- *Accountability:* By bringing offenders face to face with the people they are closest to, a sense of reintegrative shaming develops around the notion of accountability. The FGC model places offenders in a position whereby they understand how their actions not only affected their direct victim, but also the members of their family who also suffer the pain of embarrassment, financial burden, and loss of time, energy, and effort due to the criminal action. This accountability goal is also enhanced by the involvement of victims in the process of articulating loss and the need for healing and recovery from the harmful action.

- *Strengthening Family:* A central component of the FGC model revolves around the notion that families are most readily equipped with the knowledge and understanding of how to improve the quality of life of their members and therefore, if properly directed, have the greatest potential in resolving conflicts and solving problems. Thus, a major goal of the FGC is to strengthen a family's capacity to provide its members with the resources to make good decisions and to encourage, support, and guide young ones in the proper direction.[26]

- *Consensus, Agreement, and Due Process:* A final criterion that dictates the structure and operation of the FGC involves the goal of achieving consensus through open, fair, and non-threatening dialog that both takes into account an awareness of cultural diversity and ensures that an offender's due process rights are protected.[27] The FGC structure shies away from decision making as a process that involves the imposition of sanctions from a higher authority. Rather, the goal is to ensure that there is agreement amongst all key stakeholders and that the agreement is reached through a process that balances the rights of the offender with the need to achieve justice and restoration to the victim. Thus, there is a discussion of needs from the perspective of all members attending the FGC meeting so that nobody feels left out, neglected, or unheard.[28]

How Do Conferences Take Place?

The family group conferencing process has been implemented in a variety of contexts, including police stations, probation offices, juvenile justice centers, residential treatment facilities, mediation outlets, and neighborhood groups.[29] The FGC process begins when a referral is made. Referrals to FGC can be made as part of a formal court sentencing plan, used as diversion from formal charges being filed or part of alternative dispute resolution in collaborating agencies. A referral is made based on the decision of an agency representative or formal authority that the welfare of a child, young adult, or other individual involved in a dispute, as well as the interests of any victims affected, will be best served and protected using the FGC model of resolution. The FGC is based on the premise of volunteerism, so in order to move forward, the family has to come to an agreement that this method of intervention is best for them.

Once the referral is made, and the approach is embraced voluntarily by a family, a coordinator is assigned to the case and begins preparing for the meeting. This involves informing the direct child, youth, or offender about the program, what it offers, and how he/she, as well as their family, can benefit from utilizing a family group conference. The coordinator also collaborates with all family members involved to discuss the various services that could help them, as well as address any practical concerns over the process. A time, date, and venue for the conference is also discussed and agreed upon. Once that agreement is reached, planning begins for the conference

Figure 5.2: The Family Group Conference Process

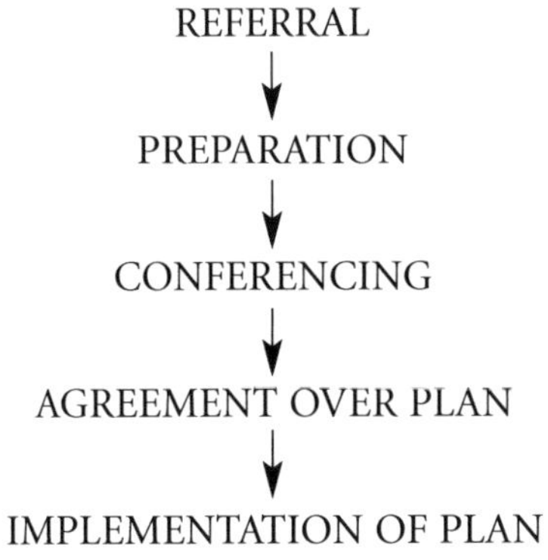

REFERRAL

↓

PREPARATION

↓

CONFERENCING

↓

AGREEMENT OVER PLAN

↓

IMPLEMENTATION OF PLAN

phase, as well as developing a long-term plan for implementing any resolutions that are reached (see Figure 5.2).

What Goes on During a FGC?

While each FGC experience is unique to its own dynamics of interaction, there are general components of this experience that define the structure of the meeting. Most FGC meetings last between 1 and 2 hours and follow along these guidelines:

- *Icebreaker*—Sessions begin with everyone present having the opportunity to introduce themselves and tell everybody why they are there, and what they hope to get out of this process. The coordinator assigned to the particular FGC talks a little about the goals of the meeting and expectations and explains the process to all that are there. The purpose of the opening part of the FGC is to set everyone's mind at ease, in order that they feel comfortable talking and sharing their feelings.[30]

- *Getting the facts*—During this time, all parties gathered at the FGC will have the opportunity to review the facts of the case as described in official documents such as a police report, school record, or agency file. The specific child, youth, or adult involved in the matter will have an opportunity to agree with, disagree with, or clarify any discrepancies they may have. Agreement on the facts of the case or incident must be reached in order to move forward with further discussions. Thus, it is important that individuals involved in the dispute, disagreement, or offense, understand the facts as they are recorded.

- *Discussion time*—The FGC is built around dialog and discussion and therefore, there is a significant amount of time dedicated to discussing the particular incident from the perspective of what wrong was committed, the resulting harm caused by the action, and what needs to be done to make things right. During this time, the offender is given the opportunity to explain their motive, state of mind, and reasoning for acting the way they did. During this time, the coordinator can ask questions in order to bring about more informative dialog

and communication that will help those listening better understand the behavior of the offender.[31] Family members and advocates for the offender are
also given the opportunity to ask questions or make statements about how
they perceive the incident and its impact on their lives. Once the offender is
through with their story, the victim is given an opportunity to describe their
feelings of hurt and anger about the harm they experienced. They can speak
directly to the offender and to family members. All parties involved discuss
and suggest ways that reparation can be made, relationships restored, and healing be achieved.

- *Planning and implementation*—During this part of the FGC session, the family
  discusses a plan to put into place to get things right. This means developing
  concrete goals to help the individual offender learn from their mistakes, as well
  as necessary actions that need to be taken to restore any loss and repair any
  harm caused to the victim. The family is usually given the opportunity to
  discuss this in private, without the presence of either the coordinator, formal
  authorities, outside stakeholders, or the victim. Once a plan is developed and
  agreed upon, it is brought back and presented to the larger group for review
  and discussion. The key "ingredients" of this plan must include admission on
  the part of the offender to their wrongdoing, steps towards reparation to the
  victim, guidelines by which the family can support the offender in making
  positive choices in the future, and mechanisms of reintegrating the offender
  back into their community. Plans cannot be vague statements reflecting ideals,
  but rather must be based on specific action items that involve key individuals
  in the lives of the offender who will ensure the plan is followed, as well as a
  timeframe for completing the goals that are set. Very often, the plan becomes
  a formal document that not only ensures accountability but is legally binding
  and enforceable within the context of a mediating authority such as a court,
  juvenile office, probation, social service agency, or school authority. The coordinator will continue checking with the responsible family members to ensure
  that the plan is being followed and executed as agreed upon, reinforcing their
  role of empowerment and authority in moving the offender, victim, and all
  those involved, in the right direction towards restoration and healing.[32] Box
  5.2 describes the effective power of family conferencing as a mechanism of
  support in a variety of contexts.

Since the inception of the FGC as a restorative justice practice, the literature on
its successful implementation in various settings has been compelling in terms of
producing positive outcomes for families as well as victims of crime.[33] In the section
to come, we will critically evaluate the FGC approach in terms of its value in advancing
restorative justice principles and values.

Box 5.2: Restorative Justice in Action—
      How Family Group Conferences Have the Power to
      Change Lives

The following is an excerpt from an article by Catherine Hasted:

An FGC is a very simple, immediate, and common-sense solution to a range of problems, most commonly used to safeguard children. Rather than facing a lonely battle, parents, their parents, wider family, friends, and most importantly, the child or children, come together to make a joint decision about their future. Instead of visiting austere council buildings, family and professionals come together in a more comfortable, neutral venue. Professionals present the bottom line; often a child will have to enter the care system if a safe plan can't be agreed. Then the family come together, the door is closed, and professionals wait outside until they're invited back to hear the proposed plan of action. If it is safe, it is agreed upon there and then.

Last year 89.5% of children referred to Daybreak FGC by social services found a safe home within their extended family. That means hundreds of children avoided facing a life in the care system. The results are rapid; from start to finish, the whole process takes a maximum of four weeks. Sitting in the middle of a family group conference, for the first time, felt like gate crashing a family party. It was noisy, children were chatting and playing, and there was a constant flow of tea and coffee. As chaotic as it sounds, there was magic at work. The family reconnected, ready to come together to tackle the serious concerns expressed by baby Jake's social worker. The bottom line was clear: Jake's older sibling had been taken into care from birth, and if a safe plan could not be found for Jake then history would repeat itself. But the referring social worker could see that mum was back on track; she loved her child, had the support of her family, and wanted to make it work. Both sides of the family came together, although many of them had never even met each other before, but they shared a joint purpose and a feeling of responsibility towards this little boy. Gradually I saw a change in body language; the family were animated and engaged. Jake took centre stage; you could feel his mum bursting with pride at the fuss being made of her son. Then we were asked to leave the room and leave the family to it. What went on during those two hours will only ever be known by the family; they shared private information and deep family history and were more open and honest than they could ever hope to be in front of professionals. When the family presented the plan to Jake's social worker, it was mum who stood at the front with a flip chart, standing her ground to answer questions and defend the plan. What a change from the hunched teenager, hiding behind her mobile phone at the beginning of the day.

Two hours later Jake left the room with his mum, her family, and a safe plan of action agreed to there and then by the social worker. I left that first meeting with admiration for the family and the professionals. Through our learning and experiences with families, Daybreak has moved on to apply FGCs to an ever-increasing range of issues, from preparing for terminal illness, to planning the release of prisoners. A single thread runs through each and every circumstance: the compelling message that families have the power to change their own lives.

Source: Hasted, C. (2012, October 12). How family group conferences have the power to change lives. *The Guardian*. Used by permission. Retrieved from https://www.theguardian.com/social-care-network/2012/oct/10/family-group-conferences-change-lives.

Evaluating Family Group Conferences

There are several questions to ask when determining the long-term impact of programmatic implementation in order to define its success. Ultimately, within the context of criminal behavior, the goal is desistance. However, there are intermediate variables that must be taken into account in order to better inform the process of desistance as an outcome of a particular intervention. The theoretical grounding of the FGC as a restorative justice practice allows us to better understand its value in promoting conflict resolution, increasing family cohesiveness, restoring balance, and ultimately reducing delinquent behavior.[34]

The power of the FGC approach lies in its ability to represent a radical break from traditional criminal justice interventions. Family group conferencing epitomizes the values of acceptance, reintegration, and healing by its key focus on dealing with problems in a collective manner rather than targeting conflict as an isolated incident.[35] Moreover, FGCs get at the heart of problems by allowing for the expression of feelings and emotions instead of just dealing with disputes in a rational or confrontational manner. Despite procedural differences, scholars generally agree that the FGC model has been successful in the following important ways:

- *FGCs engage families*—The driving force behind the FGC model hinges on the ability of the conference coordinator to engage family members in resolving problems.[36] To this effect, the central role of the conference coordinator focuses on developing a productive dialog between family members in order to allow each individual to have the opportunity to have a voice in the conference. Very often, formal interventions neglect this aspect of reparation that involves developing long-term communication skills that continue to reinforce goals that are set and established. The structure of family conferences maximizes this opportunity by providing a safe, non-judgmental environment wherein issues can be discussed in an open manner that allows for mutual respect, sensitivity, and the development of trust. Box 5.3 provides an illustration of an evaluation study demonstrating how families are a key resource in the planning and successful outcome of interventions in child welfare.

Box 5.3: Research in Restorative Justice —
The Family Unit: An Obvious Yet Underutilized Resource

While there is no doubt that family dysfunction is at the heart of many conflicts involving juvenile delinquents and at-risk children, the literature is also compelling in terms of the family being a key component in the successful planning and implementation of long-term care plans that reintegrate children and their families with one another and also with their communities in a positive manner. As a matter of fact, family-based interventions are seen as one of the most cost-effective and successful programmatic features aimed at reducing recidivism and reversing the behavioral aspects of juvenile delinquency. Moreover, a recent interest in family involvement within juvenile justice has resurfaced in the criminal justice literature.

In a recent study, researchers propose developing a framework for involving family that is based on a theoretical analysis of current arguments for the effective use of family in juvenile justice. In their literary analysis of outcome-based arguments pertaining to the involvement of parents in juvenile justice, the authors conducted a conventional content analysis utilizing an inductive, non-theoretical approach to identify various themes revolving around parental support and engagement in the juvenile justice process. Findings from that study suggests that an increase in reliance on family as a resource has beneficial outcomes in juvenile court cases at many different levels. Multiple studies find support for family intervention as providing both instrumental and emotional support to youth, increasing the likelihood of their cooperation. Moreover, the involvement of family as a key resource in the juvenile justice process was found to improve the functioning of the court system itself, including increasing the efficiency of the process as well as increasing the likelihood of success in the rehabilitation goals set by the court. Finally, findings suggest that the family as a central focus in the juvenile justice process is found to create significant improvements in the behavior of youth offenders, including increased follow-through with treatment plans, less reliance on the use of transitional settings, and an overall reduction in recidivism.

Source: Walker, S. C., Bishop, A. S., Pullmann, M. D., & Bauer, G. (2015). A research framework for understanding the practical impact of family involvement in the juvenile justice system: The juvenile justice family involvement model. *American Journal of Community Psychology*, *56*(3–4), 408–421.

- *FGCs use collaboration to solve problems*—When a crisis happens, whether it be an act of delinquency, a threatening incident in a workplace, or a case of child welfare, the outcome of that event depends largely on the response efforts that come into place to bring about resolution. FGCs offer a collaborative approach that solicits the input and help of multiple stakeholders, those that are closest to the issue at hand, to work together to seek the most positive outcome possible. This collaboration allows families to avoid the need for formal interventions that essentially divert responsibility away from family-centered conflict resolution and deal with matters from an external focus instead of a family-centered focus.[37] The unique approach of the FGC model allows for decision making to take place with the help, aid, and advice of professional services, while at the same time enabling families and their community to take ownership of problem solving, planning, and decision making. Evaluation studies have shown that this approach not only empowers families but mobilizes the greatest and most immediate formal and informal support structures that provide care and protection in difficult situations and produce the most favorable outcomes in circumstances of conflict.[38]

- *FGCs provide constructive shaming*—A key dynamic that is absent from formal mechanisms of intervention is the emotional connection between accountability, shame, and remorse.[39] The concept of **constructive shaming** is quite akin to that of *reintegrative shaming*, discussed in Chapter 2. Constructive shaming relies on the bonds that connect family members with one another to bring about a genuine, emotional desire to seek approval by correcting action that has brought about shame and humiliation not only to the individual actor but to their entire family. Very often, when a young person or a persistent delinquent fails to recognize their errors, we speak of "getting through" to them. The FGC targets intervention from a teaching perspective, relying on family intuition and feelings of personal belonging and self-worth as mechanisms of reintegrative shaming, rather than assigning blame and dealing with offending in a public manner. Sitting face to face with individuals that matter the most and having those individuals express their contempt in a manner that elicits accountability, provides support, and seeks healing, the FGC approach creates a sense of shame that is paired with a desire to make things right.

The development of family group conferencing as an informal decision-making forum represents a step in the direction of bettering the lives of individuals by approaching conflict from the standpoint of empowerment and engagement rather than rendering individuals helpless and disengaged. In this chapter, we have seen that the dialog created in a family group conference setting provides key stakeholders with a tremendous opportunity for change, social support, healing, and restoration. In the next chapter, we will discuss an equally powerful but very different approach within restorative justice practice, the victim impact panel.

Chapter Summary

Where did the concept of family group conferencing originate?

Family group conferencing originated with the Maori system of justice, which was premised on the notion that responsibility and accountability were not individual but rather based on a collective need to restore balance not only to the victim but also the victim's family. In the late 1980s, the New Zealand legislature enacted the Children, Young Persons and Their Families Act to revamp the juvenile justice system in New Zealand and create a process that focused on creating dialog between victims, offenders, family, and community by integrating Maori recommendations to restore the involvement of family and community to address juvenile delinquency. This gave New Zealand global recognition for being the first legal system to institutionalize what became known as the family group conference.

What are the basic elements of this restorative justice process?

Family group conferences involve a gathering of family members, relatives, friends, and community specialists, as well as victims and other key stakeholders who join together to develop a plan of action involving the settlement of a dispute or the reparation of a harm. These gatherings are facilitated by a neutral third party and take place in a community setting. The referral of matters to FGC is usually provided for according to operating procedures of either the juvenile or adult court systems as part of diversion, alternative dispute resolution, and restorative justice programs. The FGC approach is embedded in norms and values that promote the overall wellbeing of the community, with restorative justice principles and values serving as the foundation. Their aim is to limit formal criminal justice intervention, strengthen families, reintegrate offenders into the community, and protect the interests of victims.

How does family group conferencing work?

The FGC model is guided criteria that revolve around the goals of diversion, accountability, victim involvement, strengthening family, developing consensus, cultural sensitivity, and due process. The goal is to reconnect delinquents and offenders to their families by keeping them away from formal criminal justice processing, thereby sending them a message of acceptance. In addition, the FGC model allows offenders to understand how their actions not only affect their direct victim, but also the members of their family who also suffer due to their criminal action. This accountability goal is also enhanced by the involvement of victims in the process. Moreover, the FGC strengthens a family's capacity to provide its members with the resources to make good decisions and to encourage, support, and guide family members in the proper direction. Ultimately, the goal is to achieve consensus through open, fair, and non-threatening communication that takes into account an awareness of cultural diversity and ensures that an offender's due process rights are protected.

Is this an effective approach?

The success of the FGC approach lies in its ability to represent a significant break from traditional criminal justice interventions by implementing the values of acceptance, reintegration, and healing and dealing with problems in a collective manner rather than targeting conflict as an isolated incident. An examination of the FGC model finds that it has been able to successfully engage family members in resolving problems, offer a collaborative approach that solicits the input and help of multiple stakeholders, and rebuild the bonds that connect family members with one another through constructive shaming.

Key Terms

Maori
Hui
Korero
Rangatira
Mana
Tapu
Children, Young Persons and Their Families Act
Family Group Conference (FGC)
Constructive Shaming

Critical Thinking Questions

1. What do you see as the most positive aspects of the family group conferencing approach? Are there any cons to this type of restorative justice model? If so, what are they and how would they be resolved?

2. Let us say that you are a coordinator of a family group conference involving a domestic dispute where a single mom is having recurrent problems with her teenage girl running away from home and skipping school. The case was referred to you by a family court. How would you handle this particular case?

3. Are there certain components of the family group conference method of restorative justice that you find most useful? If so, what are they and why do you think these components are more effective than others?

References

1. Mokuau, N., & Mataira, P. J. (2016). *From trauma to triumph: Perspectives for Native Hawaiian and Maori peoples.* In M. Grey, J. Coates, M. Yellow Bird, & T. Hetherington (Eds.), *Decolonizing social work* (pp.145–164). Routledge.

2. Jones, A. (2016). *A mark on paper: The matter of indigenous-settler history.* In C. A. Taylor & C. Hughes (Eds.), *Posthuman research practices in education* (pp. 75–92). Palgrave Macmillan UK.

3. Reid, J., Varona, G., Fisher, M., & Smith, C. (2016). Understanding Maori "lived" culture to determine cultural connectedness and wellbeing. *Journal of Population Research*, 33(1), 31–49.

4. Walsh, T. G. (2016). *Justice, faith, and interfaith: The relevance of faith and interfaith relations to crime prevention.* In H. Kury, S. Redo, & E. Shea (Eds.), *Women and children as victims and offenders: Background, prevention, reintegration* (pp. 369–393). Springer International Publishing.

5. Love, M. T. W. (2007). A traditional Maori form of dispute resolution. Raukura Consultants. Retrieved from http://www.iiirm.org/publications/Articles%20Reports%20Papers/Cultural%20 Resources%20Management/dispute_res.pdf.

6. Shepherd, S. M., & Ilalio, T. (2016). Maori and Pacific Islander overrepresentation in the Australian criminal justice system—What are the determinants? *Journal of Offender Rehabilitation*, 55(2), 113–128.

7. Barretto, C., Miers, S., & Lambie, I. (2016). The views of the public on youth offenders and the New Zealand criminal justice system. *International Journal of Offender Therapy and Comparative Criminology*, 62(1), 129–149. doi: 0306624X16644500.

8. Tauri, J., & Morris, A. (1997). Re-forming justice: The potential of Maori processes. *Australian & New Zealand Journal of Criminology*, 30(2), 149–167.

9. Moyle, P., & Tauri, J. M. (2016). Maori, family group conferencing and the mystifications of restorative justice. *Victims & Offenders*, 11(1), 87–106.

10. Eketone, A. (2016). Maori parenting, from deficit to strength. *Aotearoa New Zealand Social Work*, 24(3–4), 75–80.

11. Cleland, A. (2016). Portrait of the accused as a young man: New Zealand's harsh treatment of young people who commit serious crimes. *The Round Table*, 105(4), 377–387.

12. Robinson, J., & Hudson, J. (2016). Restorative justice: A typology and critical appraisal. *Willamette J. Int'l L. & Dispute Res.*, 23, 335–367.

13. Moyle, P., & Tauri, J. M. (2016). Maori, family group conferencing and the mystifications of restorative justice. *Victims & Offenders*, 11(1), 87–106.

14. MacRae, A. (2004). Little book of family group conferences New Zealand style: A hopeful approach when youth cause harm. Skyhorse Publishing, Inc.

15. Jones, A. D., Jemmott, E. T., Da Breao, H., & Maharaj, P. E. (2016). Working with young people with harmful sexual behaviour. In Treating child sexual abuse in family, group and clinical settings (pp. 139–217). Palgrave Macmillan UK.

16. Johnstone, P. (2016, March). Emerging developments in juvenile justice: The use of intervention, diversion and rehabilitation to break the cycle and prevent juvenile offending. In Judicial review: Selected conference papers: *Journal of the Judicial Commission of New South Wales*, 12(4), 455. Judicial Commission of NSW.

17. Szabo, A. (2016, June). Bringing justice back into the community: The case of Vermont, US. Presentation at the 9th international conference of the European Forum for Restorative Justice, Realising restorative justice: Human rights and personal realities. Leiden, Netherlands, 24th June 2016.

18. Dijkstra, S., Creemers, H. E., Asscher, J. J., Dekovi , M., & Stams, G. J. J. (2016). The effectiveness of family group conferencing in youth care: A meta-analysis. *Child Abuse & Neglect*, 62, 100–110.

19. Langdon, J. J. (2016). Talk it out: Toward a narrative theory of community conferencing. *Contemporary Justice Review*, 19(1), 19–30.

20. Kim, J., Pierce, B. J., Jaggers, J. W., Imburgia, T. M., & Hall, J. A. (2016). Improving child welfare services with family team meetings: A mixed methods analysis of caseworkers' perceived challenges. *Children and Youth Services Review*, 70, 261–268.

21. Gal, T. (2016). "The conflict is ours": Community involvement in restorative justice. *Contemporary Justice Review*, 19(3), 289–306.

22. Abbamonte, L., & Cavaliere, F. (2016). Restorative justice, a comparative analysis of discursive practices: Dialogistic exchanges in the USA and Italy. In C. Williams & G. Tessuto (Eds.), *Language in the negotiation of justice: Contexts, issues and applications* (pp. 121–145). Ashgate.

23. Metze, R. N., Abma, T. A., & Kwekkeboom, R. H. (2015). Family group conferencing: A theoretical underpinning. *Health Care Analysis*, 23(2), 165–180.

24. Johnstone, P. (2016, March). Emerging developments in juvenile justice: The use of intervention, diversion and rehabilitation to break the cycle and prevent juvenile offending. In Judicial review: Selected conference papers: *Journal of the Judicial Commission of New South Wales*, 12(4), 455. Judicial Commission of NSW.

25. Hamilton, C., & Yarrow, E. (2016). Preventing and addressing youth offending: Restorative justice and family focused programming. In H. Kury, S. Redo, & E. Shea (Eds.), *Women and children as victims and offenders: background, prevention, reintegration* (pp. 301–339). Springer International Publishing.

26. LaBrenz, C. A., & Fong, R. (2016). Outcomes of family centered meetings for families referred to Child Protective Services. *Children and Youth Services Review*, 71, 93–102.

27. McGrath, J. (2016). Family group conferencing. Involving the wider family in child protection decision making. MINORI GIUSTIZIA.

28. MacRae, A. (2004). Little book of family group conferences New Zealand style: A hopeful approach when youth cause harm. Skyhorse Publishing, Inc.

29. Dijkstra, S., Creemers, H. E., Asscher, J. J., Dekovi , M., & Stams, G. J. J. (2016). The effectiveness of family group conferencing in youth care: A meta-analysis. *Child Abuse & Neglect*, 62, 100–110.

30. Moyle, P., & Tauri, J. M. (2016). M ori, family group conferencing and the mystifications of restorative justice. *Victims & Offenders*, 11(1), 87–106.

31. Anyon, Y., Gregory, A., Stone, S., Farrar, J., Jenson, J. M., McQueen, J., . . . & Simmons, J. (2016). Restorative interventions and school discipline sanctions in a large urban school district. *American Educational Research Journal*, 53(6), 1663–1697.

32. Pleysier, S., Vanfraechem, I., & Walgrave, L. (2017). Restorative justice and adolescent health. In A. L. Cherry, V. Baltag, & M. E. Dillon (Eds.), International handbook on adolescent health and development (pp. 115–142). Springer International Publishing.

33. Zillmann, D., Bryant, J., & Huston, A. C. (2013). Media, children, and the family: Social scientific, psychodynamic, and clinical perspectives. Routledge; Paul, G. D., & Schenck Hamlin, W. J. (2017). Beliefs about victim offender conferences: Factors influencing victim offender engagement. *Conflict Resolution Quarterly*, 35(1), 47–72; How effective are family group conferences at reducing re-offending? Evidence Network.

34. Johnstone, G. (2013). *Restorative justice: Ideas, values, debates.* Routledge.

35. Crawford, A., & Newburn, T. (2013). *Youth offending and restorative justice.* Routledge.

36. National Institute of Justice. Office of Justice Programs. Family group conferencing. Retrieved from https://nij.gov/topics/courts/restorative-justice/promising-practices/Pages/family-group-conferencing.aspx.

37. de Jong, G., Schout, G., Meijer, E., Mulder, C. L., & Abma, T. (2016). Enabling social support and resilience: Outcomes of family group conferencing in public mental health care. *European Journal of Social Work*, 19(5), 731–748.

38. Sherman, L. W., Strang, H., Mayo-Wilson, E., Woods, D. J., & Ariel, B. (2015). Are restorative justice conferences effective in reducing repeat offending? Findings from a Campbell systematic review. *Journal of Quantitative Criminology*, 31(1), 1–24.

39. Barnes, G. C., Hyatt, J. M., Angel, C. M., Strang, H., & Sherman, L. W. (2015). Are restorative justice conferences more fair than criminal courts? Comparing levels of observed procedural justice in the reintegrative shaming experiments (RISE). *Criminal Justice Policy Review, 26*(2), 103–130.

Chapter 6

Victim Impact Panels

In this chapter, we will explore the following questions …

- *Where did the concept of victim impact panels originate?*
- *How are these types of panels put in place?*
- *Are the basic elements of victim impact panels restorative?*
- *What research has been done to evaluate the success of this type of practice?*

The Emergence of Victim Impact Panels in Restorative Justice

We have seen so far that there are a variety of restorative justice practices that can differ in process and function yet share the common goals of reconciliation, community reintegration, offender accountability, and victim healing. Moreover, the common characteristics shared by the various processes defining these practices place value on the integration of community within criminal justice as well as the inclusion of victims in the response to criminal offending. In this chapter, we turn to a discussion of a practice that uniquely combines those components in a manner that is not only restorative but has long-term implications for crime desistance and cessation.

Giving Victims a Voice: MADD

On an ordinary day in Fair Oaks, California, a 13-year-old little girl named Cari Lightner was walking on a fairly quiet road in her neighborhood going to a church carnival. That day, May 3, 1980, became nothing but ordinary when a car swerved out of control and struck that little girl, killing her. The man driving that car, 46-year-old Clarence Busch, fled the scene and left Cari's body on the road. He was later arrested by police and found to have had a record of numerous arrests for DUI as well as an arrest for another hit and run accident related to drunk driving.[1]

The tragic death of Cari Lightner marked the beginning of her mother's campaign to end drunk driving and to raise public awareness of its devastating consequences. Outraged by the reluctance of law enforcement to put an end to this type of behavior as well as lack of aggressive pursuit in terms of criminal prosecution, Candace Lightner (Cari's mother) began her own social movement to bring about change and give victims of drunk driving as well as their families a say and voice in the expression of

Table 6.1: A MADD Campaign Strategy

What Needs to Be Done?	How Are We Going to Do It?
Support our heroes	• Support high-visibility law enforcement to catch drunk drivers and discourage others from driving drunk
Sober to start	• Require ignition interlock devices, or in-car breathalyzers, for all drunk drivers, to prove they are sober before their car will start
Secure the future	• Support the development of technology to determine automatically whether or not the driver is above the legal limit of .08 and failing to operate if the driver is drunk

Source: MADD's Campaign to Eliminate Drunk Driving, *MADD: No More Victims*. Retrieved from http://www.madd.org/the-solution/drunk-driving/.

their hurt and anger. On September 5, 1980, in California, Candace Lightner founded an organization known as MADD, Mothers Against Drunk Drivers. The organization became the face and voice of victims throughout the country to unite against the senseless acts of violence that are the product of drinking and driving under the influence of alcohol and drugs.[2] Their activities included candlelight vigils for victims of drunk driving accidents, holding meetings and rallies to share stories, increasing education in schools about this social problem, and lobbying for tougher penalties for drunk driving, as well as legislation to raise the drinking age.

At the time the organization was first incorporated, the stated mission was "to aid the victims of crimes performed by individuals driving under the influence of alcohol or drugs, to aid the families of such victims and to increase public awareness of the problem of drinking and drugged driving."[3] In July of 1984 the organization changed its name to **Mothers Against Drunk Driving** in a conscious effort to emphasize their focus on changing a pattern of destructive behavior and not wage a war against individuals. As part of their goal to bolster national attention to the tragic effects of drunk driving, MADD successfully campaigned to raise the drinking age to 21 in all states, and on July 17, 1984, the legal age of drinking became 21 under federal law.

In 2006, MADD extended its efforts to further reduce driving under the influence of alcohol and drugs by launching the **National Campaign to Eliminate Drunk Driving**. The campaign promoted three important and creative steps in reducing the tragic and senseless act of drunk driving (see Table 6.1).

In 2016, MADD's board of directors revised its mission to better align with its priorities, stating, "The mission of Mothers Against Drunk Driving is to end drunk driving, help fight drugged driving, support the victims of these violent crimes and prevent underage drinking."[4] Today, MADD is one of the most influential nonprofit organizations in the United States, with at least one office headquarters in each state. The organization continues to promote the healing and restoration of victims of the violent crime of driving under the influence through various methods of support and intervention. It is within this context that *victim impact panels* emerged as a tool by which victims experiencing the tragedy of losing a loved one to a senseless act of crime and negligence had a chance to speak

VIPs: What Are They and Why Do We Use Them?

Victim impact panels (VIPs) emerged in 1982 as part of the mission and goal of MADD to change the common misconception of injuries and deaths caused by drunk driving as mere accidents. By making public the devastation of these actions on victims and on society, it was hoped that the view of impaired driving would become transformed into a behavior considered to be a crime.[5] This was best achieved by allowing victims of drunk driving crashes to confront drunk drivers with their own first-hand testimony of how their lives were impacted by the negligent actions of others. For the very first time, a context for putting a face rather than a statistic on victims of impaired driving emerged. VIPs provided a forum for these victims to tell their story to a group of offenders and share the impact that the incident had on their lives and the lives of their families and friends. For the very first time, a context emerged which allowed offenders to understand the devastating financial, physical, and psychological trauma that is caused by the consequences of impaired driving.

Over time, the use of VIPs received tremendous positive feedback from both victims and offenders participating in a panel, with studies showing this process helped victims heal and recover as well as better inform and educate offenders and change their attitudes and perception of their actions, reducing rates of reoffending in the long run (see Box 6.1).[6] The opportunity to expose offenders to the pain and suffering caused by their actions was seen as an effective tool in changing the attitudes of individuals by appealing to their emotions. This represented a divergent strategy to traditional criminal justice interventions, where victims of crime did not have a voice and through this silence offenders were actually protected from facing the violent and devastating consequences of their actions.

Box 6.1: Research in Restorative Justice—
   The Greene County, Missouri, Victim Impact
   Panel Program

In March of 2007, the CDR (Center for Dispute Resolution) at Missouri State University partnered with the Greene County Juvenile Justice Office in Springfield, Missouri, to launch the first VOM (Victim-Offender Mediation) program. Offenders participating in the VIP do not meet with their direct victims, but rather are part of an audience of offenders who listen to the stories of "surrogate" victim presenters who recall their stories of how crime has affected them. The VIP program currently also services youth who are direct referrals

---

from Juvenile Court. The Greene County Juvenile Justice VIP program provides youth offenders with a vivid glimpse of the impact of crime on its victims. The goal is to provide a safe environment that creates a context which encourages youth offenders to reflect on their actions and become more empathetic towards crime victims by "seeing" the long-term consequences of their behavior.

VIPs are held every other month at the CDR. They run about 20 to 30 minutes per victim-presenter and there are typically two presenters on each panel. On average, about 10 to 15 juvenile offenders are referred to each VIP program. Following the VIP meeting, youth participants are required to reflect on what they have seen and learned through this experience in a written essay describing their participation in the panel. This post-participation analysis of the written essays served as an empirical inquiry within a real-life context that allowed us to examine the juvenile offenders' reaction to the VIP, and to compare their thoughts and feelings after that experience, with their thoughts and feelings prior to participating in the VIP. The pre-test questionnaire used for this study was designed to evaluate the juvenile offenders' trait emotions of remorse and empathy prior to participating in the VIP program. The structure of the questionnaire focused on whether the juvenile was currently experiencing feelings of personal wrongdoing as reflected in measures of guilt, shame, and empathy. The instrument was distributed in a group setting by the researchers to 8 juvenile offenders at the Greene County Juvenile Academy, a 90-day residential program for juvenile offenders who are involved with the Greene County Juvenile Court. To assess post-VIP participation changes in offender attitudes and perceptions regarding crime, victimization, and perceptions of remorse and empathy, we analyzed the written reaction essay that is a requirement of each juvenile participant.

The pre-test questionnaire was designed to measure the offender's self-conscious emotions by conceptualizing self-oriented feelings of guilt and shame. The distribution of responses indicates that the overwhelming majority of juvenile offenders scored low on the various trait measures of shame, while items measuring guilt seemed to paint a different picture, with findings suggesting that most of the juveniles in our study do indicate feelings of regret. However, with regard to items measuring feelings of guilt and shame based on the perception of treatment by others, responses suggest that whatever feelings of guilt juveniles are experiencing did not impact their feelings of how others will treat them, indicating a discrepancy in the moral evaluation of their behavior. Respondents' reflection on questionnaire items measuring empathy indicates that their evaluation of self includes an understanding of how their actions can affect other people; with reference to their particular crime, however, over 36% of juvenile respondents indicated that they did not feel that "their offense hurt someone," reflecting a distinction between the presence of cognitive empathy and the development of affective empathy.

The findings from this case study of juvenile participants in a VIP program suggest that this method of criminal justice intervention has the potential to enhance the offender's understanding of the concept of empathy and help develop their moral evaluation of offending behavior. An examination of the pre-test questionnaire indicated that the majority of juvenile respondents scored low on items measuring the emotional feelings of shame, indicating a lack of moral self-judgment in the evaluation of their behavior. On the contrary, a significant number of the juveniles indicated a sense of apology and regret, reflecting some emotional feeling of guilt towards their actions. In this study, juveniles indicated a negative evaluation when focusing on their particular "bad" behavior. However, when reflecting on themselves as individuals, there was no indication of a negative judgment of self. From this perspective, the differential evaluation indicates that the juvenile offenders are detaching their behavior from themselves so that they are not the object of judgment, in order to protect their core identity. According to the emerging themes in the post-VIP participation reaction essays, however, juvenile participants indicated an increase in their scrutiny of self, and the potential for actions to produce cognitive states of humiliation and embarrassment, and the negative evaluation by others as reflected in their disapproval and disappointment. This finding is consistent with the development of shame as more linked to the public exposure of disapproving others.

An examination of the reaction essays of the juvenile participants indicated a recurrent theme of regret whereby the majority of offenders expressed a desire to apologize and make up for their wrongful behavior towards their victims. With regard to the effect of participation in the VIP program on offender perception of empathy, emerging themes within the juvenile respondents' reaction essays indicate a better articulation of affective empathy. Of significance, prior to listening to, observing, and interacting with the victims of crime on the VIP, a third of the juvenile offenders in the study indicated that they did not feel that their criminal actions actually hurt anyone, despite the fact that all of the offenders in the study communicated an indicates an awareness of another's emotions as a mechanism of perspective taking. This is akin to putting yourself in someone else's shoes and being able to identify with their emotional state, without actually experiencing those emotional states. Affective empathy, on the contrary, is the ability to not only recognize the emotions by imagining oneself in that situation, but to actually feel the emotional state of another human being while recognizing that they are not your own.

Source: Hass, A. Y., & Lucas, S. (2013). The impact of the Greene County Juvenile Justice VIP (Victim Impact Panel) on offender development of remorse and empathy. *Psychology Research*, *3*(9), 529. Used by permission.

The emotional appeal of VIPs found its way and became mainstreamed into the criminal justice system as a mechanism of intervention designed to provide offenders with the opportunity to empathize with the pain and suffering caused by their criminal actions. It became a strategy used within the juvenile and adult court systems to deal with crimes such as domestic violence, theft, sexual assault, and homicide to help offenders understand the magnitude and scope of victimization and its traumatic effects on individuals. We turn now to a discussion of the design and implementation of victim impact panels within the context of restorative justice theory and practice.

Victim Impact Panels: Design and Implementation

Victim impact panels represent an opportunity for both crime victims as well is offenders to participate in a process that revolves around the trauma of victimization. From the perspective of the victim of crime, this experience allows them to tell their stories and share with others their hurt and loss with the intent of creating a common understanding of the impact of crime on the lives of individuals. With regard to offenders, they are afforded a chance to become an audience and listen intently to the experiences of crime victims with the hope of developing a sense of empathy for their loss. Within this context, the role of VIPs as a restorative justice process becomes more apparent and the interplay between repair, healing, and accountability become intertwined within the concepts of remorse and empathy. We will discuss these dynamics in greater detail in sections to come. First, however, we must develop a better understanding of how VIPs are designed and implemented within the context of criminal justice policy and practice.

Creating a "Captive" Audience

Very often, offenders are court ordered to participate in a victim impact panel as part of a probation or diversion sentence within the juvenile and adult criminal court.[7] VIPs are also used as part of restorative justice programming in a prison setting. The panels are usually operated by a victim service organization that works in collaboration with the criminal justice system. This is the best possible set up, as victims who participate on these panels must be sufficiently healed from the trauma of their victimization experience in order to avoid the detrimental effects of re-victimization as well as ensure that the VIP encounter is productive in its outcome. Moderators who run the program must prepare the victim participants, moderate the panels, and obtain participant feedback, as well as coordinate this feedback with the court.

The ideological basis behind this process is that formal court proceedings neglect a very important dynamic in the process of creating accountability and promoting positive citizenship and community reintegration. Notably, the formal criminal justice procedures of arrest, prosecution, sentencing, and punishment in no way provide a chance for the necessary type of encounters between crime victims and offenders that would promote the reparation and healing that could only come from developing a better understanding of the hurt and pain caused by criminal offending.[8] Thus, the focus of VIPs is to help offenders think about the impact their crimes have had on both their victims and their families as well as the communities in which they live, while providing victims of crime with a positive and structured outlet to share and communicate their personal experiences in a constructive manner.

Structure and Format of a Victim Impact Panel

The typical victim impact panel consists of a group of three or four speakers who have each in some way been the direct victims of crime. They are rarely if ever the direct victims of the offenders who are there as part of a court order or sentencing agreement. The number of offenders present can vary anywhere from 10 to 15 members in the audience. When juvenile offenders are involved, they are usually accompanied by a parent or guardian. Victim impact panels are considered community meetings and therefore take place in schools, libraries, social service agencies, courts, and probation and parole offices. Panels are held in a conference room, auditorium, or similar type of environment that allows for an audience to face the speakers. This set up sends the message that this is a time for listening and learning, where there is an expectation of respect and attentiveness to the speakers. A moderator or program coordinator is usually present to ensure that these dynamics are understood and to also ensure the proper flow of the panel as well as introduce panel members to the audience.

VIPs are structured around the concept of using **surrogate victims** who have not been directly involved with the offenders to whom they are speaking. This allows for a more neutral dialog to emerge that is free of judgment and emotion.[9] Each victim speaks one at a time explaining their story and describing in vivid detail the nature of their victimization as well as the resulting trauma it caused. The goal is to tell their story in a non-blaming manner that focuses on communicating to offenders and educating them about the harmful consequences of their criminal actions on their victims. Each panelist spends about 15 minutes speaking and when all panelists have been given the opportunity to share their story, there is usually some time for an open dialog that allows for questions and answers. Victims who become involved in these types of panels often do so out of a genuine desire to assist in the fight against criminal offending and out of a need for healing through the process of restoration that comes from telling their personal encounters and stories.[10]

The rationale behind using the VIP approach is that this process provides a unique opportunity for offenders to perceive their actions from the perspective of their victim and not simply focus on their own actions and entanglement with law enforcement and the criminal justice system. In contrast to the outcome of arrest, prosecution, finding of guilt, and sentencing, VIPs make an emotional appeal that emphasizes changing the attitudes and behaviors of individuals by focusing their attention on the pain and suffering caused by criminal behavior. This exposure is more likely to have a profound impact in modifying behavior then the more rational/cognitive appeal of punishment.[11] With this in mind, we turn now to a discussion of the restorative aspect of VIPs.

Victim Impact Panels as Anchors of Restorative Justice

So far, we have seen that victim impact panels emerged out of a desire on the part of victims of drunk driving accidents to help offenders understand the impact their behavior had on their victims and the communities in which they live. This grew into a practice utilized by agents of criminal justice to provide victims of crime with a positive outlet that is structured around the idea of sharing their personal experiences in order to educate offenders about the emotional, psychological, physical, and financial consequences of crime. This captive audience format seems to diverge from the traditional practices of restorative justice that allow for direct dialog and encounters between victims, offenders, and the communities in which they live. However, upon closer examination, we will see how and why VIPs are considered anchors of restorative justice theory and practice.

Transforming a Victim's Identity

We have seen in previous chapters that the experience of crime victimization creates a transformation in the identity of an individual, which includes feelings of despair, powerlessness, fear, and anxiety. Moreover, victims of crime report feelings of stigma not only by the criminal justice system but by members of their own families, leading to feelings of guilt, shame, self-blame, and embarrassment.[12] Under these circumstances, victims are left without a voice, without a forum to be heard beyond their own personal encounters with counselors or psychologists, and the intimidating and awkward dynamic of making a statement in court prior to sentencing. While these outlets may represent positive encounters, at the best they are not inclusive of the very essential and restorative elements of transformation that are necessary for the victim to regain their identity prior to becoming victimized.

Victim impact panels therefore represent one of the most useful and effective means for victims to communicate their thoughts, feelings, and experiences in a constructive manner that allows them to be heard by the very group of individuals responsible for creating similar types of harms on others. This communication not only represents a personal release of the trauma caused by their victimization but also represents an encounter that allows for this release to work as a mechanism and tool of education and prevention of further criminal offending. This provides victims with a sense of empowerment that their experiences and suffering may not be in vain but rather may serve as an opportunity to prevent someone else from experiencing the same type of trauma.[13] Researchers note that VIPs help bring closure to victims of crime by allowing victims the opportunity to engage criminal offenders in a process that allows them to actively witness the human suffering and damage caused by their actions, where the goal and outcome is the positive release of emotions and the healing effect of forgiveness.[14] Box 6.2 provides us with a powerful example of these dynamics.

Box 6.2: Restorative Justice: Let's Take a Closer Look—
Does Forgiveness Heal the Heart?

On March 26, 2014, 59-year-old Jeffrey Ferguson was put to death by lethal injection in a St. Louis, Missouri, prison. This came 25 years after his conviction of kidnapping, raping, and killing 17-year-old Kelli Hall. Jim Hall, the father of the victim, was present and witnessed his execution. At a press conference following the execution Hall expressed relief at Ferguson's death stating, "Hopefully, now we can move forward.... Kelli can rest now." The Hall family however did not find that sense of rest and a few years later, something changed, and the anger and hatred for Ferguson which were thought to be expressed in his execution no longer seemed to be the case.

While the Hall family thought their pain would subside, thinking "it's finally over," they found neither comfort nor healing in the execution of Ferguson. In the weeks following, the road to recovery began when members of the Hall family viewed a documentary called "Potosi: God in Death Row." The documentary featured prisoners who have found spiritual guidance through the intervention of a Christian prison ministry. One of the featured prisoners was Ferguson. During this documentary, Ferguson expressed a strong sense of remorse for the pain and suffering that he caused to the victim's family as well as to his own family. It is during this time that the Hall family was able to find healing through the act of forgiveness that they extended to Ferguson upon viewing his sense of regret. In an interview, the Hall family expressed a deep regret for the execution of Ferguson after learning of his participation in restorative justice programming inside the prison, where he was an active participant in a victim impact program. Moreover, Jim Hall expressed the extent to which the remorse of an offender as well as their understanding of the devastating impact of their crime can provide the comfort and relief that are necessary for broken hearts to heal.

Jim Hall referred to the mechanisms of revenge and capital punishment as forms of healing for emotional wounds as a "myth," advocating an approach that fosters repair and healing through the expression of remorse and the dynamic act of forgiveness. Jim Hall has now become an advocate for commuting death sentences, maintaining that the opportunity to encounter offenders face-to-face as an expression of reparation is far more healing ... *what do you think?*

Source: Hall, J. (2016, December 27). Commute all death sentences: Governor should have mercy on 25 inmates. *Columbia Daily Tribune*. Retrieved from http://www.columbiatribune.com/opinion/oped/commute-all-death-sentences/

article_045535e0-f4a0-59d4-90bb-405fc0ceaaaa.html. *St. Louis Post-Dispatch.* (2014, March 26). *Law and order.* Missouri executes St. Louis-area man who raped, killed teen girl. Retrieved from http://www.stltoday.com/news/local/crime-and-courts/missouri-executes-st-louis-area-man-who-raped-killed-teen/article_25e7fa3d-6a02-5868-9825-ddfbcc9d97d3.html.

Feeling Remorse by Experiencing Empathy

In addition to transforming the identity of victims from fearful and stigmatized individuals to empowered advocates of justice that can play an active role in making positive change, victim impact panels also have a profound influence on the perception of offenders about their own actions and their participation in criminal behavior.

Let us recall our discussion of John Braithwaite's theory of reintegrative shaming in Chapter 2, which argued that the process of shaming, if coupled with community reintegration, will serve to control crime because of its impact on an offender's choice to act in direct violation of his or her community's norms and values. Thus, according to Braithwaite, the concepts of guilt and shame are embedded in the emotional feeling of remorse and the development of empathy and therefore play a very important role in the desistance of criminal behavior.[15] The experience of disapproval that takes place as part of the VIP process is regarded as having an inhibiting force that tugs at the offender's internal conscience as guilt and shame initiate the emergence of remorse and empathy for the hurt and pain that has been inflicted upon the victim panelists.

In a setting where offenders are face to face with the victims of crime, the exposure of their behavior in such a public manner allows them to not only reflect on their harmful behavior but to also understand its impact on their victims with the hope of relating to their suffering. This reflection enhances the experience of remorse and repentance and will encourage the offender to repair the harm that they have caused and to ensure that they will think through their actions before offending again, knowing firsthand its devastating results. This will in turn create feelings of remorse and repentance that will encourage the offender to repair the harm they have caused and desist from future offending behavior, by morally and cognitively understanding the extent of harm they have caused.[16]

The research literature validates the idea that the development of remorse and empathy serve as the foundation for the success of VIPs in reducing criminal offending.[17] The ability to fully understand and experience the emotional state of another human being is the cornerstone of empathy.[18] Moreover, scholars note that empathy consists of multiple dimensions, including cognition, affect, and behavior (see Table 6.2).[19] **Cognitive empathy** involves an understanding of another person's feelings, while **affective empathy** involves the sharing of another's emotional state. **Behavioral empathy** involves a conscious decision to alter one's response patterns as a direct result of experiencing cognitive and affective empathy, which create a responsive distress upon

Table 6.2: The Dimensions of Empathy

Type of Empathy	Dimension Involved	How It Works
Cognitive Empathy	Understanding	*When I see someone who is sad or crying, I understand those types of feelings, what they mean, and where they come from. I recognize the concepts of pain and hurt.*
Affective Empathy	Sharing	*When someone is sad or crying, I not only understand what they are experiencing but I also to some extent share in that experience and their pain and hurt is transferred on to me … I can actually feel it.*
Behavioral Empathy	Acting	*Understanding and sharing in the hurt of another makes me feel a deep sense of regret that causes me to alter the way I act so as to avoid causing that type of hurt to others.*

hearing of the suffering and hurt of another individual and the subsequent desire to relieve that stress by taking corrective action.[20] Jackson et al. (2011) note that "through guilt, the transgressor is able to self-reflect and empathize with the victim. This also allows the transgressor to understand his or her role in the causing of harm, which may reduce his or her chances of placing blame on the victim or society at large. Individuals who are guilt-prone are more likely to experience empathy and can begin to understand the true extent of the harm."[21]

Thus, feeling remorse by experiencing empathy is seen as an essential part of the process of restoration and reconciliation as it is a gateway towards accepting responsibility and accounting for harm from within as opposed to the process of blaming external controls. By participating on a victim impact panel, offenders may experience a sense of guilt towards their behavior and may make the conscious attempt in the future to ensure that the behavior does not happen again, as they are now able to relate to their victim on an emotional level.

Raising Community Awareness

A final component of victim impact panels that render this practice an anchor of restorative justice is built upon the concept of raising community awareness. A major task of restorative justice programming is building partnerships that transcend typical connections that may exist between members of the community and various social service agencies as well as the criminal justice system.[22] The implementation of VIPs within the context of criminal desistance and offender reintegration also has the additional reverse effect of integrating the community into the problem of crime and delinquency. By building a partnership between victim service providers and agencies of criminal justice, this approach raises the awareness of the impact of crime at both an individual and community level.

The approach and task of VIPs make victims of crime the central focus. It is a dynamic of interaction that makes the personal experiences of crime victims the heart of the dialog, sending a clear message to criminal offenders that victims have a right to be heard, respected, and protected. This enhances the effect of healing and transformation for victims as well as provides an informative forum for members of the community to understand the experience of crime within their own domain, raise their awareness of their own potential for victimization, and recognize the need to provide victims of crimes with both direct and indirect mechanisms of compensation and restoration.[23] With this potential for success, we turn now to a better look at the outcome of VIPs in terms of successful implementation in a restorative justice context.

Outcome Evaluation of Victim Impact Panels as an Intervention

Facilitating dialog, encouraging reconciliation, and increasing accountability are hallmark components of restorative justice theory and practice that have been consistently found to have a positive impact in reducing recidivism and enhancing the process of community reintegration.[24] To this extent, there is a compelling argument that victim impact panels as anchors of restorative justice theory and practice also have a positive impact in terms of offender behavior and the desistance of criminal offending, with the empirical literature confirming the conclusion that the development of remorse and empathy in offenders participating in the VIP programming is largely responsible for their acceptance of responsibility and desire to make things right as well as change their actions.[25]

Some of the earliest studies evaluating the effects of victim impact panels on the behavior of participating offenders come to us from studies of drunk driving panels. In a hallmark study by the Rutgers Center of Alcohol Studies, researchers set out to assess the effectiveness of the VIP in reducing the rate of re-arrest for drinking and driving. The study was conducted in a southeastern county of the United States where offenders attended a VIP presentation as part of their sentence for a drunk driving charge. The study sample of 404 participants was compared to a group of 431 non-participants. Statistical analyses were conducted, and researchers found that the re-arrest rate was significantly lower for the group participating in the VIP as compared to nonparticipants, controlling for multiple independent variables.[26] Another study examined 103 VIP attendees who had been convicted of a drunk driving offense. Researchers administered a pre- and post-test to this group as well as a comparison group of nonparticipants to determine attitudes about drinking and driving as well as potential for re-arrest. Statistical testing revealed significant changes in attitudes towards drinking and driving as well as lower recidivism rates for offenders participating in the VIP program as opposed to subjects in the comparison group.[27]

More recent studies have looked at the effects of VIP programs on the development of guilt and remorse in offenders. In a 2006 study of the Missouri Department of Corrections Restorative Justice **Victim Impact Training** (**VIT**) program, researchers using a regression analysis design found a significant relationship between the development of guilt, shame, and empathy amongst participants in the VIT program. In addition, VIT participants had lower rates of recidivism than the comparison group of non-participants.[28] Similar findings were noted in a 2008 study on the effect of VIPs on DWI offenders, where an analysis of pre-and post-test questionnaires found a significant increase in empathy scores amongst 61 participating offenders after attending a victim impact panel.[29] Likewise, a 2011 study by Kim and Gerber examining data on juvenile offenders participating in Australia's **RISE** (**Re-integrative Shaming Experiments**) found a positive change in the attitudes of offenders with regard to their desire to make things right with their victim, as well as society, and also with regard to their feelings of remorse and repentance.[30]

Finally, in a formidable study of the Le Chéile Justice Project in Limerick, Ireland, researchers developed a long-term analysis of the impact and outcome of this restorative justice intervention program for youth offenders. Findings from their study suggested a strong impact on youth in terms of changing their attitudes and behaviors. With regard to VIPs as a particular component of this program, qualitative interviews and focus groups with youth participants indicated that they reported increased levels of empathy towards their victims as well as their families. Moreover, the young offenders indicated that meeting victims face to face and hearing their stories helped them understand the impact of their previous behavior and what it does to disrupt the lives of individuals. The following excerpts are direct quotes from youth speaking about how powerful it was to experience the VIP:

> I was glad I did it. It was good for me to meet the victim and understand how my actions affect others. I think it was good for the victim as well, to see that I didn't plan any of the crime; that it was just random, like. (Youth Participant)

> You know more how the victim felt. If I was thinking about how the victims were feeling before then I probably wouldn't have done it [the crime]. (Youth Participant)[31]

The restorative impact of VIPs has thus been well noted in the research literature. Its potential for changing offenders by instilling not only feelings of remorse but a sense of responsibility towards the victim, thereby reducing the chances of recidivism, is a compelling argument for the implementation of this programming in a correctional and therapeutic setting. Box 6.3 highlights this type of programming in action, as the **Sycamore Tree Project** strives to put simple words into real action.

Box 6.3: Restorative Justice in Action—

    Saying Sorry versus Acting Sorry . . . The Sycamore Tree Project

The Sycamore Tree Project is a 5- to 8-week program that is run inside prisons in various parts of England. This program was developed by Prison Fellowship International as a victim awareness program designed to teach inmates to take responsibility for their actions in order to direct them on the path of remorse and empathy. The program, which brings groups of crime victims inside the prison to meet with groups of unrelated offenders, aims at achieving four main goals: creating reconciliation, reparation of harm, transformation of victims and offenders, and reducing reoffending. An average of 20 prisoners participate in each cycle of the program. During this time, prisoners discuss with educators and facilitators the devastating effects of crime and the importance of taking responsibility as well as taking personal action to make reparation. They also have the opportunity to engage in face-to-face encounters with victims of crime as they come to learn the powerful effect of bearing witness to the devastating impact of crime on its victims and the community as a whole. Offenders also have the opportunity during a final session to express their feelings of remorse by putting their feelings into action through symbolic acts of verbal apologies, letters, short poems, or creative works of arts and crafts. Community members are also invited to the sessions in order to support both victims and offenders through this process.

Various evaluation studies conducted by Sheffield Hallam University in England show that the Sycamore Tree Project has had a tremendously positive impact on the attitudes of offenders participating in the program. In 2009, a study evaluating 5,000 prisoners completing the program between 2005 and 2009 found statistically significant positive attitudinal changes associated with completion of the program. Notably, amongst the sample, there was significant improvement in victim empathy, changes in attitude toward offending, an increase in awareness of the impact of their actions, as well as a reduction in the anticipation of reoffending. The following quotes capture the sentiments of both offenders and victims participating in the program:

> "The Sycamore Tree Project® really makes you think. It's not like any other course I've been on. It makes you think about feelings. It's about what's inside. It changes how you feel about victims and that. . . . STP is different because it's about what's in here." —Offender from England and Wales

> "I witnessed a man murdering my father. I have been carrying this hatred and hurt for more than 25 years. For the first time, I can truly say that I have forgiven the man that murdered my father. The feeling is something I can't describe." —Crime victim from New Zealand

Source: Center for Justice and Reconciliation. Sycamore Tree Project. Retrieved from http://restorativejustice.org/we-do/sycamore-tree-project/. Prison Fellowship. Sycamore Tree. Retrieved from http://www.prisonfellowship.org.uk/what-we-do/sycamore-tree/.

We have seen in this chapter the application of restorative justice theory within the context of victim impact panels, and the long-term impact of this type of intervention in terms of offender attitude and behavior by providing offenders with a "live," vivid glimpse of the impact of crime on its victims. In the chapter to come, we will further explore restorative encounters between victims and offenders through the mechanism of restorative peacemaking circles.

Chapter Summary

Where did the concept of victim impact panels originate?

Victim impact panels (VIPs) emerged in 1982 as part of the mission and goal of MADD to change the common misconception of injuries and deaths caused by drunk driving as mere accidents. By making public the devastation of these actions on victims and on society, it was hoped that the view of impaired driving would become transformed into a behavior considered to be a crime. Victim impact panels found their way into the criminal justice system as a mechanism of intervention designed to provide offenders with the opportunity to empathize with the pain and suffering caused by their criminal actions. It became a strategy used within the juvenile and adult court systems to deal with crimes such as domestic violence, theft, sexual assault, and homicide.

How are these types of panels put in place?

Offenders can be court ordered to participate in a victim impact panel as part of a probation or diversion sentence within the juvenile and adult criminal court. VIPs are also used as part of restorative justice programming in a prison setting. The panels are usually operated by a victim service organization that works in collaboration with the criminal justice system. The typical victim impact panel consists of a group of three or four speakers who have each in some way been the direct victims of crime. VIPs use surrogate victims that have not been directly involved with the offenders to whom they are speaking.

Are the basic elements of victim impact panels restorative?

Victim impact panels are described as anchors of restorative justice as they are an effective means of empowering crime victims by allowing them to communicate their thoughts, feelings, and experiences in a constructive manner. Moreover, VIPs also have a profound influence on the perception of offenders about their own actions and their participation in criminal behavior. By allowing offenders to come face-to-face with the victims of crime, offenders can not only reflect on their harmful behavior but also understand its impact on their victims. This reflection enhances the experience of remorse and repentance and will encourage offenders to repair the harm that they have caused and to ensure that they will think through their actions before offending again, knowing firsthand its devastating results.

What research has been done to evaluate the success of this type of practice?

The research literature in criminal justice has provided us with ample evidence on the successful application of victim impact panels, with evidence that this approach has had a positive impact on offender attitudes towards crime and their potential for reoffending. Participation in a VIP encourages the acceptance of responsibility and the desire to make things right as well as change their actions.

Key Terms

Mothers Against Drunk Driving
National Campaign to Eliminate Drunk Driving
Victim Impact Panels (VIPs)
Surrogate Victims
Cognitive Empathy
Affective Empathy
Behavioral Empathy
Victim Impact Training (VIT)
RISE (Re-integrative Shaming Experiments)

Critical Thinking Questions

1. What features of a victim impact panel do you find the most consistent with restorative justice theory and principle? Are there aspects of this practice that are more restorative than others, and if so, what are they?

2. Do you think the use of "surrogate victims" is an effective tool? How can offenders relate to the pain and suffering of individuals they have not directly victimized? Would the use of direct crime victims and offenders be more productive?

3. How are the concepts of remorse and empathy considered components of restorative justice? Are there ways that we can apply these concepts in different formats besides the use of victim impact panels?

4. Have you or has anyone you know ever been the victim of a crime? Do you personally feel that participating in this type of restorative justice programming brings healing and closure to crime victims? Why or why not?

References

1. Alcohol Problems and Solutions. (n.d.) *Candy Lightner (Candace Lightner): Founder of MADD.* Retrieved from https://www.alcoholproblemsandsolutions.org/candy-lightner/.

2. *MADD: No More Victims.* (n.d.) Retrieved from http://www.madd.org/.

3. Mission Statement. (n.d.). *MADD: No More Victims.* Retrieved from http://www.madd.org/about-us/mission/.

4. Ibid.

5. Center for Justice and Reconciliation. (n.d.). *Victim impact panels.* Retrieved from http://restorativejustice.org/restorative-justice/rj-in-the-criminal-justice-system/victim-support-and-restorative-justice/victim-impact-panels/.

6. Fors, S. W., & Rojek, D. G. (1999). The effect of victim impact panels on DUI/DWI rearrest rates: A twelve-month follow-up. *Journal of Studies on Alcohol, 60*(4), 514–520; Keeton, R. B. (2015). Crime victims and offenders face to face: An overview of the Texas Department of Criminal Justice Victim Offender Mediation/Dialogue Program. *Resolved: J. Alternative Disp. Resol., 5*, 26.

7. Zehr, H. (2015). *The little book of restorative justice: Revised and updated.* Skyhorse Publishing, Inc.

8. Chenault, S., Martin, J., & Matusiak, R. E. (2016). The ripple effect: Empathy statements of participants of an impact of crime on victims class. *Corrections, 1*(3), 196–214.

9. Walshe, B., & Geske, J. (2014). Dialogical progress examined: A victim offender dialogue case study. *Journal of Mediation & Applied Conflict Analysis, 1*(1).

10. Dawson Edwards, C. (2016). Restorative justice. *The encyclopedia of crime & punishment.*

11. Ptacek, J. (2014). Restorative justice as an alternative to criminalization?

12. Kunst, M. J. J., & Koster, N. N. (2016). Psychological distress following crime victimization: An exploratory study from an agency perspective. *Stress and Health, 33*(4), 405–414.

13. Klaus, W., Buczkowski, K., & Wiktorska, P. (2015). Empowering the victims of crime: A real goal of the criminal justice system or no more than a pipe dream? In G. Mesko & J. Tankebe (Eds.), *Trust and legitimacy in criminal justice* (pp. 65–91). Springer International Publishing.

14. Quigley, M., Martynowicz, A., & Gardner, C. (2015). Building bridges: An independent evaluation of Le Chéile's Restorative Justice Project. Research findings. *Irish Probation Journal, 12.*

15. Braithwaite, J. B. (2016). *Restorative justice and responsive regulation: The question of evidence.* RegNet Working Paper No. 51, School of Regulation and Global Governance.

16. Braithwaite, J. (2003). Principles of restorative justice. In A. von Hirsch, J. V. Roberts, A. E. Bottoms, K. Roach, & M. Schiff (Eds.), *Restorative justice and criminal justice: Competing or reconcilable paradigms?* (pp. 1–20). Oxford: Hart Publishing.

17. Sprang, G., & Compton, R. (1998). Victim impact panels: An examination of the effectiveness of this program on lowering recidivism and changing offenders' attitudes about drinking and driving. *Journal of Social Service Research, 22*, 73–84. Gilligan, J. (2003). Shame, guilt, and violence. *Social Research, 70*, 1149–1180. Jolliffe, D., & Farrington, D. P. (2007). Examining the relationship between low empathy and self reported offending. *Legal and Criminological Psychology, 12*(2), 265–286. Harris, N., Walgrave, L., & Braithwaite, J. (2004). Emotional dynamics in restorative conferences. *Theoretical Criminology, 8*, 191–210. Palermo, G. B. (2012). Moral reasoning and recidivism in young sex offenders. *International Journal of Offender Therapy and Comparative Criminology, 56*(7), 983–985.

18. Cohen, D., & Strayer, J. (1996). Empathy in conduct-disordered and comparison youth. *Developmental Psychology, 32*(6), 988.

19. Wallis, P., Aldington, C., & Liebmann, M. (2009). *What have I done? A victim empathy programme for young people.* Jessica Kingsley Publishers.

20. Hass, A. Y., & Lucas, S. (2013). The impact of the Greene County Juvenile Justice VIP (Victim Impact Panel) on offender development of remorse and empathy. *Psychology Research*, *3*(9), 529.

21. Jackson, A. L., Blackburn, A. G., Tobolowsky, P., & Baer, D. (2011). An examination of guilt, shame, empathy and blaming among a sample of incarcerated male and female offenders. *The Southwest Journal of Criminal Justice*, *8*(1): 1–29.

22. Bazemore, G., & Schiff, M. (2015). *Restorative community justice: Repairing harm and transforming communities*. Routledge.

23. Burrows, J. (2014). Victim awareness. *Probation Journal*, *61*(2), 113–116.

24. Braithwaite, J. B. (2016). Restorative justice and responsive regulation: The question of evidence. RegNet Working Paper No. 51, School of Regulation and Global Governance.

25. Miller, P. G., Curtis, A., Sønderlund, A., Day, A., & Droste, N. (2015). Effectiveness of interventions for convicted DUI offenders in reducing recidivism: A systematic review of the peer-reviewed scientific literature. *The American Journal of Drug and Alcohol Abuse*, *41*(1), 16–29.

26. Fors, S. W., & Rojek, D. G. (1999). The effect of victim impact panels on DUI/DWI rearrest rates: A twelve-month follow-up. *Journal of Studies on Alcohol*, *60*(4), 514–520.

27. Sprang, G. (1997). Victim impact panels: An examination of the effectiveness of this program on lowering recidivism and changing offenders' attitudes about drinking and driving. *Journal of Social Service Research*, *22*(3), 73–84.

28. Jackson, A. L., & Bonacker, N. (2006). The effect of victim impact training programs on the development of guilt, shame and empathy among offenders. *International Review of Victimology*, *13*(3), 301–324.

29. Schaaf, K. (2008). Empathy: Victim impact panels and DWI offenders. *UW-L Journal of Undergraduate Research*, *XI*.

30. Kim, H. J., & Gerber, J. (2012). The effectiveness of reintegrative shaming and restorative justice conferences: Focusing on juvenile offenders' perceptions in Australian reintegrative shaming experiments. *International Journal of Offender Therapy and Comparative Criminology*, *56*(7), 1063–1079.

31. Quigley, M., Martynowicz, A., & Gardner, C. (2015). Building bridges: An independent evaluation of Le Chéile's Restorative Justice Project. Research findings. *Irish Probation Journal*, *12*.

Chapter 7

Peacemaking Circles

In this chapter, we will explore the following questions …

- *What were the early origins of peacemaking circles?*
- *What are the six different types of peacemaking circles related to crime and justice?*
- *What are the common characteristics, principles, and challenges of peacemaking circles?*
- *What do we know from the research on peacemaking circles?*

The Early Origins of Peacemaking Circles

Much like the restorative processes we have examined up to this point, a **peacemaking circle** (also referred to as a circle) is a dialog process that brings members of a community or group together to facilitate mutual understanding, discuss important issues, and/or make decisions.[1] As we will explore in this chapter, there are many different types of peacemaking circles, making it a highly adaptable process that can be utilized in a variety of ways both inside and outside of the criminal justice system. Much like victim-offender mediations and family group conferences, peacemaking circles can include the full spectrum of stakeholders (including victims, offenders, and community members), and can easily accommodate both large and small groups.

Circles can be convened to address a variety of needs in a diverse range of contexts. For example, while a sentencing circle may be used, much like a victim-offender mediation, to discuss the impact of an offense and create a plan to repair the harm, circles can also be used to prevent crime and violence (talking circles) or to help an offender reintegrate into society after serving time in prison (reintegration circles). Circles can be especially useful when there is a need to gather a large group of people to discuss a specific incident or issue, and, much like family group conferences, can be customized to meet the cultural needs of a particular group or community.

While circles have deep historical roots in native cultures, the first use of a circle process in a criminal justice proceeding took place in 1982 in Yukon, Canada.[2] In 1982, Philip Moses was a 26-year-old member of the Na-cho-Ny'ak Dun First Nation with 43 prior criminal convictions. Facing new convictions for theft, violating probation, and carrying a weapon with the intent of assaulting a police officer, the judge presiding over his case decided that traditional sentencing options were proving ineffective for Moses.[3] Before sentencing, the judge therefore decided to convene Moses, his family, his probation officer, members of the First Nation, and law enforcement officers to discuss the case and brainstorm ways to break the cycle of chronic offending in which Moses was engaged.[4]

During the gathering, the courtroom was rearranged in order to place everyone in a circle.[5] This was done to encourage everyone to participate and share responsibility, to honor the values and customs of the First Nation, and to communicate the equality of all the participants.[6] During the circle process, the participants discussed circumstances that may have contributed to the offenses committed by Moses. For example, Moses was relatively uneducated, had suffered physical and sexual abuse during his childhood, abused alcohol, and had difficulty finding employment.[7] The circle participants agreed that a more rehabilitative approach was necessary in his case if there was to be any hope of preventing Moses from committing future offenses and further escalating his violence.[8] Following the recommendation of the circle, the judge ordered Moses to two years of continued probation and treatment for his alcoholism, a sentence which worked successfully for Moses, his family, and his community.[9]

While the circle in this case was used to support the sentencing process for Moses, circles are now used in many different ways to address conflict and prevent crime, to facilitate community responses to crime and acts of delinquency, and to provide support to victims and offenders.

Six Types of Peacemaking Circles

As mentioned above, peacemaking circles are highly adaptable to almost any situation, group, and culture. While peacemaking circles do share certain characteristics and values, which we will explore later in this chapter, there is no one set reason or way to organize a circle. Unlike most of the other restorative justice processes we are exploring in this book, peacemaking circles are often organized outside of the realm of crime and criminal justice. For instance, as we will explore in Chapter 12, circles are often used by schools, as well as other institutions and organizations, to discuss sensitive issues or make important decisions. While peacemaking circles can be organized for almost any purpose, when we consider how circles are used in relation to crime and criminal justice, we find six different models that merit more understanding and exploration. Those are: sentencing circles, circles of understanding, talking circles, healing circles, support circles, and reintegration circles.[10] While this is not a comprehensive accounting of circles, exploring these six models will give us a thorough understanding of how circles are used in the context of restorative justice.

Sentencing Circles

The circle process used in the case of Philip Moses, which we explored above, is an example of a sentencing circle. **Sentencing circles** work with formal institutions of justice, such as the juvenile justice system or the criminal justice system, to bring together those most affected by an offense in order to create a sentencing plan that is not only reasonable and proportionate, but meets the needs of the victim, the offender, and the community.[11] Much like a mediation agreement written during a victim-offender mediation, a **sentencing plan** is simply a written plan created during the circle process that details what an offender agrees to do in an effort to repair the harm experienced by the victim and community. Unlike a victim-offender mediation, it is not uncommon for criminal justice professionals, such as judges, police officers, and probation officers to be active participants in a sentencing circle.[12] Though sentencing circles typically work in conjunction with formal courts, it is important to note that in order for a sentencing circle to take place the offender must acknowledge guilt.[13] In other words, sentencing circles are not used to determine the guilt or innocence of a defendant, but rather bring important stakeholders together to discuss an offense and create a community-driven sentencing plan.

Circles of Understanding

While the main purpose of a sentencing circle is to make a decision concerning a community's response to an offense, a circle of understanding does not necessarily aim for such a concrete outcome. **Circles of understanding** are organized in order to discuss a specific incident in the hopes of coming to a better understanding of how and why it occurred.[14] For example, let's imagine a neighborhood in which a young child is abducted while playing in their front yard. Such a traumatic incident would surely leave the neighborhood, and larger community, with a lot of unresolved feelings and questions. In this situation, we could organize a circle of understanding in order to piece together how the incident happened and how we might prevent it from happening again.

An offender could also convene a circle of understanding with friends, family, and support persons in order to discuss their behavior and seek input on what led to their offense and how they can prevent future criminal offending. Generally speaking, circles of understanding are community-based and do not work within the criminal justice system. They can, however, be a unique and effective way of creating space for a community to have important discussions about crime and crime prevention, as well as process their experiences and emotions in a safe and supportive environment after a crime has occurred.

Talking Circles

Much like circles of understanding, talking circles do not require that a group make any decisions together or arrive at any unified conclusions about a particular issue. Instead, **talking circles** are typically initiated so that members of a community or group can discuss an issue that concerns them, as well as share their experiences, thoughts, and feelings with each other. A talking circle can be focused on something specific such as a new school policy, or it could target a broader issue such as racism or transphobia within a city, agency, or organization.[15] Though it is possible, talking circles are not necessarily organized in response to a specific crime. Instead, their relationship to crime is often preventative in nature (see Box 7.1 for an example). For instance, if we were to organize a talking circle about racism within a local university, we might be responding to racial tensions or even incidents of racial discrimination, but our purpose would likely be to prevent those tensions from escalating rather than addressing a specific crime.

Talking circles allow participants to share their stories, feelings, thoughts, and opinions openly and without interruption. They are as much about speaking as they are about listening. Again, talking circles do not necessarily conclude with the group making any formal decisions or recommendations (though this could, indeed, happen); they are instead a practice that encourages deep listening and personal reflection about an issue that matters to a community or group.[16]

Box 7.1: Restorative Justice in Action — Cherokee Talking Circle

The Cherokee Talking Circle program was designed to prevent and reduce substance abuse among Native American teens. It is a 10-week, school-based program that is rooted in values, such as self-reliance and confidence, that are integral in Keetoowah-Cherokee culture. In response to data showing that Native American teens are at increased risk for issues such as substance use, depression, and anxiety, the Cherokee Talking Circle program uses talking circles to address the needs of its adolescent participants in a restorative way.

Using Cherokee high school students in Oklahoma, an evaluation of the program compared outcomes from the Cherokee Talking Circle and another, more traditional, substance abuse educational program. Findings from the evaluation showed that the Cherokee Talking Circle program was significantly more effective at reducing substance abuse and positively affecting other behavioral issues among the Cherokee youth. This would indicate that culturally sensitive, restorative programming is a promising way to address the needs of marginalized teens and prevent the abuse of alcohol and drugs.

Source: Lowe, J., Liang, H., Riggs, C., & Henson, J. (2012). Community partnership to affect substance abuse among Native American adolescents. *The American Journal of Drug and Alcohol Abuse, 38*(5), 450–455.

Healing Circles

Like talking circles, healing circles can certainly exist outside of the scope of crime and criminal justice, but, considering that our exploration is focused on restorative justice, we will center our attention on how these circles are used after a crime. **Healing circles** are typically organized for the purpose of providing support and care for someone who has been victimized by crime. While we often discuss the way in which offenders become isolated or estranged from the community after committing a crime, we need to remember that victims can often experience social isolation as well. While victims may receive support from various people in their lives, a healing circle brings those people together to give a victim collective and unified support, encouragement, and comfort while they are processing and recovering from their experience of victimization.[17]

While a healing circle is not organized for the sole purpose of making group decisions or resolutions, they can sometimes result in plans of support.[18] A **plan of support** may include commitments made by members of the circle to provide specific forms of support to the victim in direct response to the victim's expressed needs and concerns. For instance, a plan of support may include a circle participant offering to accompany a victim to court proceedings or provide needed services such as meals or transportation while the victim adjusts emotionally, physically, and financially after the crime.

Due to the fact that a healing circle does not require the offender's participation (in fact, in most cases it would explicitly not include the offender), this kind of circle process is unique in relation to most restorative justice processes in that a healing circle can take place even if an offender is not identified, apprehended, willing to participate, or able to participate. A common criticism of restorative justice from a victim advocacy perspective is that even though restorative justice is more inclusive of victims than traditional models, most restorative processes are still dependent upon offender participation.[19] Healing circles stand as an exception to this rule, opening restorative justice up to victims and communities affected by crime regardless of the offender's involvement or status.

Support Circles

In essence, support circles function much like healing circles in that the intention behind the circle process is to provide support for someone impacted by crime. What makes these two models different is that while healing circles tend to be organized on behalf of victims, support circles can be held for victims or offenders. Simply put, a **support circle** is a gathering of individuals committed to supporting someone through a particularly difficult or challenging time in their life.[20] While many types of circles may convene more than once around a particular issue or individual, support circles will commonly gather multiple times on a regular basis until the need for such intensive support comes to an end.

Though not necessary, it is common in support circles to create a **plan of support**[21] which, as we discussed above in the case of healing circles, is a plan that details specific ways in which members of the support circle commit to providing aid, consolation, and/or help to the person at the heart of the circle process.

One increasingly popular use of the support circle model is found in offender reintegration programs that use **Circles of Support and Accountability** to provide sex offenders coming out of prison with community supervision and support as they work to find housing, employment, and treatment.[22] We will focus on this program model in greater depth in Box 7.2 (below) and in Chapter 10.

Box 7.2: Restorative Justice: Let's Take a Closer Look …
    Can Circles Help Restore Trust When
    Sex Offenders Leave Prison?

Circles of Support and Accountability (COSA) were first developed and implemented in Canada in the 1990s (Hannem & Petrunik, 2007). The model was created by a group of community chaplains who wanted to find a way to apply the values and principles of restorative justice to sex offenders at high risk of recidivism (Hannem & Petrunik, 2007). The model was then implemented in the United Kingdom in 2002 (Bates, Macrae, Williams, & Webb, 2012), and eventually in the United States (Duwe, 2012).

In a nutshell, the COSA model brings together a high-risk sex offender with a group of community volunteers willing and capable of providing the offender with various forms of social support and accountability (Bates, Macrae, Williams, & Webb, 2012). The offender must volunteer for the COSA program and demonstrate his/her commitment to social reintegration and criminal desistance (Hannem & Petrunik, 2007). The community volunteers must be equally committed to aiding the offender with practical needs, such as housing, employment, and companionship, while also confronting the offender if they suspect s/he might be struggling in their commitment to abstain from sexual offending (Hannem & Petrunik, 2007). As part of the circle process, a "covenant" is forged between the offender and the community volunteers, each making clear commitments in support of their shared goal of the offender's safe and successful reintegration into the community (Hannem & Petrunik, 2007). Circles typically occur weekly for a minimum of one year, and at least one circle member is available to the offender for emergency support on a daily basis (Hannem & Petrunik, 2007).

The COSA model was not only developed to provide support to offenders, but to also alleviate community fears upon a sex offender's release from prison (Hannem & Petrunik, 2007). Since sex offenders tend to face enormous social stigma upon their release, the founders of COSA developed the model, in part, to addresses these fears and assure the community that these offenders were under intense and supportive community supervision (Hannem & Petrunik, 2007).

What are your thoughts? Do you support the use of circles to help a sex offender reintegrate socially and build trust with his/her community? How would you feel if a COSA program were implemented in your community?

Sources: Bates, A., Macrae, R., Williams, D., & Webb, C. (2012). Ever-increasing circles: A descriptive study of Hampshire and Thames Valley circles of support and accountability 2002–09. *Journal of Sexual Aggression, 18*(3), 355–373. Duwe, G. (2012). Can circles of support and accountability (COSA) work in the United States? Preliminary results from a randomized experiment in Minnesota. *Sexual Abuse: A Journal of Research and Treatment, 25*(2), 143–165. Hannem, S., & Petrunik, M. (2007). Circles of support and accountability: A community justice initiative for the reintegration of high-risk sex offenders. *Contemporary Justice Review, 10*(2), 153–171.

Reintegration Circles

Circles of Support and Accountability are interesting in many ways, but one thing that makes them noteworthy is that they are essentially a hybrid model that draws upon elements of support circles as well as reintegration circles. In the context of crime and criminal justice, **reintegration circles** are used to foster reconciliation and the social reintegration of an offender after crime and/or after a period of separation due to detention or incarceration.[23] As we know, crime breaks trust between an offender and the community, but it can also weaken bonds within an offender's more intimate circles such as family, friends, worship groups, and coworkers. If a crime also results in some form of incapacitation, such as imprisonment, juvenile detention, or residential drug or mental health treatment, an offender is faced with the need to reenter his/her community and social groups after a period of detachment and disassociation. In these cases, reintegration circles can be used to provide the opportunity for intentional dialogs concerning what an offender needs from the community and what the community needs from the offender in order to build renewed trust and provide a clear pathway for the offender to successfully reconnect to the community after a crime.[24] For example, let's imagine a 36-year-old father who has been incarcerated for five years due to a drug conviction. A reintegration circle might meet several times in order to give his children, spouse, family members, and friends a chance to share how his crime and incarceration have impacted their lives, as well as explore everyone's needs concerning his reentry into the community and their family. The reintegration circle could even convene before his release from prison in order to begin the work of reconciliation and reentry planning before he reenters the family home.

Unlike some circle models that may not result in group decisions or plans of support, reintegration circles frequently include the drafting of action plans or agreements that detail the needs and commitments of circle members concerning common goals such as reconciliation, reintegration, and the prevention of future criminal offending.[25] As we will explore in Chapter 10, successful prisoner reentry is vitally important when considering the needs of children and families, as well as community safety, and reintegration circles are a promising way of using restorative justice to facilitate offender reintegration and lower rates of recidivism.

Common Characteristics, Principles, and Challenges

While there is not one set type of circle process, circles do share some common characteristics, principles, and challenges. Unlike victim-offender mediations, which are organized after a crime in order to meet very specific goals, circles can be utilized by families, communities, organizations, and groups to discuss any issue of importance, make decisions, and/or address shared problems.

Due to the fact that circles have the potential to gather such a large number of people, they are a prime example of a reintegration process which, as we discussed in Chapter 2, is a critical component of John Braithwaite's theory of Reintegrative Shaming.[26] In the context of crime and criminal justice, circles are uniquely capable of bringing a community or group together to reinforce the dignity and worth of the offender, heal social bonds broken through crime, and create new avenues toward trust and reconciliation.[27]

Common Characteristics

In this section, we will focus on five elements common to any circle process. While circles can convene for a variety of different purposes, we will identify and explore some core elements that they all share, including: ceremony and rituals, circle keepers, a talking piece, shared behavioral guidelines, and consensus decision-making.[28]

Ceremony and Rituals

Regardless of the participants, size, or function, circles all share some form of ceremony or ritual.[29] Drawing from their roots in native cultures, circles are intended to be ceremonial. In other words, they are distinct from the routine and mundane, they signify that something important is taking place, and they call upon a community's most sacred values and principles. In essence, the very act of forming a circle together is symbolic of a community bringing itself back into relationship in the midst of tension, conflict, and even crime.[30] When community members seat themselves in a circle, they are making a statement about the importance of relationship, the importance of listening to one another, and the value they place on all members of the group.

As a way to mark the ceremonial nature of circling, peacemaking circles include **opening and closing rituals**.[31] These rituals bring attention to the group's collective transition into and out of the circle process,[32] reinforcing the idea that the act of engaging in a circle is a sacred or otherwise special practice. These rituals are unique to each circle, but in a general sense opening and closing rituals should support and convey the group's shared values, affirm the intentions of the circle process, and be culturally meaningful to the group members (see Box 7.3).[33]

Box 7.3: Peacemaking Circles —
     Opening and Closing Rituals

According to Pranis, Stuart, and Wedge (2003), opening and closing rituals should:

- Demonstrate respect for everyone
- Convey inclusion and connection
- Call upon personal values and intentions important to the circle process
- Establish safety within the circle

Source: Adapted from Pranis, K., Stuart, B., & Wedge, M. (2003). *Peacemaking circles: From crime to community.* St. Paul, MN: Living Justice Press, p. 118.

Circle Keeper

As we know from previous chapters, restorative justice processes require some kind of facilitator tasked with organizing the process, preparing participants, and keeping the dialog moving forward in a safe and respectful way. These individuals are frequently community volunteers, but can also be paid professionals such as counselors, social workers, or police officers. In the case of peacemaking circles, we identify these facilitators as circle keepers. **Circle keepers** are referred to as "servant leaders"[34] due to the fact that their role is to support the circle process and its participants, rather than exert authority or control over it. Peacemaking circles are commonly facilitated by two circle keepers;[35] however, the role can also be filled by one person or even a small group. While the exact nature of the role can change due to situational factors and the type of circle being held, circle keepers are typically responsible for discerning whether a case is appropriate for a circle process, identifying and preparing circle participants, facilitating group sharing and dialog, and following up with the group concerning sentencing, reparation, and/or support plans when applicable.[36]

Talking Piece

An important practice that the circle keeper will introduce to the group is the use of a talking piece. A **talking piece** simply refers to an object that is passed around a circle, allowing the participant holding it to speak without being interrupted.[37] Circle participants agree that no one will speak within the circle unless they are holding the talking piece. The only exception to this agreement is the circle keeper, who may need to speak when someone else is sharing in order to effectively support and facilitate the circle process.[38] The talking piece may have significance to the group (such as a totem or a sacred object), but it can also be neutral (such as a keychain or a plush toy). When choosing a talking piece, it is important not to select something that might make some participants feel uncomfortable, nor something that reinforces one participant's power over another.[39]

Using a talking piece can have several positive effects within a circle. Considering the fact that most circles convene to discuss an issue that might be sensitive and/or emotionally difficult for some participants, using a talking piece can slow things down and give everyone time to reflect and focus before speaking.[40] It can also prevent one-on-one debates or arguments from erupting within the circle. The talking piece also helps to reinforce values that are critical to the circle process, such as shared responsibility and the equality of all participants.[41]

Shared Guidelines

As mentioned above, an important function of the circle keeper is to facilitate the collective creation of behavioral guidelines for the circle process. While the circle keeper may encourage the participants to adopt certain guidelines such as *treating one another with respect* or *not interrupting someone who is speaking*, participants in the circle process are asked to contribute to the creation of **shared guidelines** as a way of demonstrating important values and principles such as equality and shared responsibility,[42] which we will explore later in this chapter.

Creating shared guidelines can be done during the preparation phase or in the very beginning of the circle process. As noted by Carolyn Boyes-Watson[43] in her research on the use of peacemaking circles with marginalized, urban youth (see Box 7.4 for more information):

> It is not unusual for a Circle with young people to spend hours or even days discussing guidelines. In a series of Circle for thirty young people at Youth Star (an AmeriCorps program at Roca), the group spent two whole days— four to six hours each day—*just talking about guidelines*. In talking Circles with gang members, the guidelines discussion often focuses on the meaning of a few core values: What does respect mean to you? What does love mean to you? What does confidentiality mean? Agreeing on a Circle's guidelines involves a deep discussion about the meaning of these values and the concrete implications of acting on them.[44]

While most circles would never devote 8–12 hours for a discussion on shared guidelines, this observation by Boyes-Watson[45] certainly emphasizes the importance of this part of the circle process regardless of whether the circle will convene multiple times or just once.

Box 7.4: Research in Restorative Justice —
Peacemaking Circles and Urban Youth

In 2008, Carolyn Boyes-Watson, Ph.D., published an extensive, qualitative evaluation, titled *Peacemaking Circles & Urban Youth: Bringing Justice Home*, which examined the use of peacemaking circles in Roca, a community-based organization near Boston. Roca carries out its mission to prevent poverty and incarceration by developing and implementing programs in the Boston area that focus on needs such as education and employment skills for marginalized youth.

Boyes-Watson conducted multiple, intensive interviews with forty-three people from Roca in order to gain a better understanding of the impact of peacemaking circles on the organization and its members. What she found is that peacemaking circles not only supported the organization's overall mission, but provided opportunities and space for empowerment, accountability, and healing among youth in the Boston area.

You can find out more about Roca by exploring their website at www.rocainc.org.

Source: Boyes-Watson, C. (2008). *Peacemaking circles & urban youth: Bringing justice home*. St. Paul, MN: Living Justice Press.

Consensus Decision Making

The final characteristic common to all circles has to do with how the group makes decisions. Even if a circle doesn't convene in order to create a formal plan for reparation or support, the group will inevitably make some decisions together. Examples may include their list of shared guidelines, whether or not to gather in the future, and/or how and when to close the circle. So, what is **consensus decision making**? When we make decisions by consensus we take everyone's needs and opinions into consideration and try to arrive at a decision that reflects the group as a whole rather than one person or one part of the group.[46] While group decision making often relies on a voting process which then supports the majority, peacemaking circles take a more integrated approach and allow participants to continue discussing important issues until a unified decision can be reached.[47] Due to the fact that consensus decision making requires unity rather than a majority, decisions can take longer to finalize; however, participants usually feel more satisfied with, and committed to, decisions generated through consensus.[48]

Common Principles

While common elements such as a talking piece and a circle keeper help to distinguish a peacemaking circle from other restorative practices, a circle is most clearly defined by the principles and values that guide its facilitation and function. While circles are often rooted in the cultural norms of a community or group, and certainly one's personal values play a role in the decision of each member concerning their participation in the process, there are at least five core principles that are fundamental to understanding the practice of peacemaking circles. These principles are as follows:

- Peacemaking circles are **inclusive**
- Peacemaking circles are **voluntary**
- Peacemaking circles support the **equality and dignity of all persons**
- Peacemaking circles encourage **shared responsibility**
- Peacemaking circles promote **collective efficacy**

In this section we will explore each of these principles and discuss the ways in which they are expressed, symbolized, and reinforced within a circle.

Peacemaking Circles Are Inclusive

In order for peacemaking circles to function as processes that restore relationships, reintegrate estranged group members, and give voice to the community, it is important that the necessary people be a part of them. Unlike more intimate processes, such as victim-offender mediations, circles can accommodate large numbers of people and thereby enable us to welcome more individuals into the restorative dialog. While it is important that people not be forced to participate, it is equally important that certain individuals who might have something to contribute or receive from the circle are not excluded from it.[49] Therefore, an essential part of facilitating a circle is identifying who needs to be invited into the process and making sure those individuals are thoroughly prepared for their involvement.[50]

Peacemaking Circles Are Voluntary

In Chapter 1 we discussed the idea that restorative justice is best measured using a spectrum rather than one single definition.[51] While it is true that people can be compelled to participate in some restorative justice programs, such as victim impact panels, a truly restorative process will be vigilant in ensuring voluntary participation by everyone involved, including criminal offenders.

Requiring someone to participate in a peacemaking circle can violate other core principles of circles (such as equality and shared responsibility) and can also lead to an unsatisfying experience and even failed outcomes. It is important to note that if a key stakeholder (such as an offender) decides not to participate in a circle process this does not mean that a circle cannot take place. The circle's goals and intentions may need to be adjusted and what might have been a sentencing circle may need to become a support circle.[52] As is the case in family group conferences, a stakeholder (such as a victim) may also choose to modify their involvement in a circle by only attending a portion of the circle or sending someone to share their story or otherwise represent them during the circle process.[53]

Ensuring the voluntary nature and possible modification of stakeholder involvement in a circle is an important function of the circle keeper. As a keeper prepares individuals to participate in a circle, it is important that they take the time to explore each person's understanding and level of consent to the process.[54] While it is normal and natural for some people to feel anxious and unsure about participating in a circle, it is critical that no one feels coerced or compelled to participate.[55]

Peacemaking Circles Support the Equality and Dignity of All Persons

Throughout the world, systems of criminal justice use power, authority, and even force to control social behavior and administer justice. Peacemaking circles subvert typical power dynamics by supporting the principle of equality and asserting that the dignity of every group member should be valued and protected, even if a member has caused harm to others or broken the law.[56] Circles reinforce the principle of equality through many of the common characteristics we explored above, such as sitting in a circle, the role of the circle keeper, the use of a talking piece, and the commitment to consensus decision making.

The act of sitting in a circle together is a potent physical reminder that no one group member holds more power in the circle than another. When participants form a circle, they are demonstrating that regardless of someone's age, race, gender identity, profession, wealth, or education everyone has a place and a voice within the circle process, as well as equal input into any decisions the group makes.

As we explored earlier, even the facilitator of a peacemaking circle does not hold a position of leadership that elevates their status above others in the group. In fact, most circle keepers participate fully in the circle while also fulfilling their organizational and facilitative role.[57]

Similarly, the way circle participants share experiences, discuss issues, and make decisions all embrace the principle of equality. For example, the use of a talking piece helps ensure that every participant is given an equal opportunity to speak within the circle, and consensus decision making is rooted in the fundamental principle that equality, collaboration, and unity lead to better, more creative, and more sustainable group decisions.

Peacemaking Circles Encourage Shared Responsibility

As is the case with any restorative justice process, peacemaking circles operate from a belief in the interconnection and interdependence of all people.[58] In other words, while it is certainly the case that individuals make choices when they break the law or harm others, restorative justice is not only interested in addressing one's personal responsibility for such actions, but the community's shared responsibility as well. In other words, while punitive forms of justice seek to isolate an individual and disassociate him/her from the community, restorative justice seeks to identify and address the harm while embracing victims and offenders as vital members of the group.[59] In a peacemaking circle, common elements such as the creation of shared guidelines and consensus decision making support the principle of shared responsibility by ensuring that nothing is imposed upon the group, but rather the culture, process, and outcomes of the circle routinely promote collaboration and the under-standing that every member of the circle must work together if they are to be successful in reaching their shared goals and intentions.

Peacemaking Circles Promote Collective Efficacy

Collective efficacy is a term that refers to a community's sense of shared respon-sibility. In the context of crime, communities with high levels of efficacy have a desire to intervene when something goes wrong and express an interest in correcting social deviance and repairing harm. In other words, collective efficacy is, in part, the measure of a community's social bonds, sense of mutuality and support, and interest in re-inforcing behavioral norms.[60] As we explored in Chapter 2, in John Braithwaite's theory of Reintegrative Shaming he contends that processes, such as circles, rely on the communities that practice them to have strong social bonds and a developed sense of mutual accountability and interdependence.[61] In this light, not only do peace-making circles require a high level of collective efficacy in order to be effective, but the practice can promote and strengthen collective efficacy as well.[62] In other words, we can use circles to enhance collective efficacy within our communities or groups by designing them with the values, principles, and practices we've just examined.

Common Challenges

While different circles share common values and characteristics, they can also face similar challenges. The issues that can occur during the implementation of peace-making circles are common to almost any restorative justice process, including vic-tim-offender mediations and family group conferences. While each circle process can come with its own unique difficulties, such as scheduling problems or intragroup conflicts, we will focus our attention on three common challenges that can arise when peacemaking circles are used in conjunction with the criminal justice system. These include:

- Time Constraints
- Community Partnerships
- Finding Appropriate Cases

Time Constraints

As you are probably starting to realize, restorative justice takes time. Though the outcomes may often be more satisfying, restorative justice can be extremely inefficient. It is much easier to simply impose a punishment than it is to organize a gathering of stakeholders, discuss the impact of an offense, collaborate on a plan to respond to the offense, and then follow up until the case is resolved. Not only does all of this take time, but it can also require a great deal of emotional energy and personal in-vestment on behalf of everyone involved.[63]

It is clear that restorative justice and the criminal justice system operate on two very different timetables. Yet, restorative justice is often trying to function alongside, or in relation to, the criminal justice system, and so tensions concerning time can inevitably begin to arise. For instance, let's imagine a juvenile offender who has been placed on informal probation for one year and referred to a community-based organization for a sentencing circle. By the time the referral is received and the circle is organized, that juvenile may only have a few months before they need to complete their sentencing plan and successfully conclude their probation. If the circle process had not been utilized in order to create a collaborative sentencing plan, a juvenile probation officer would have likely imposed their own sentencing plan on the juvenile very quickly, thereby giving them much more time to complete reparative activities like community service, letters of apology, and restitution.

Time constraints can also be an issue for circle participants. Peacemaking circles can often be held more than one time, making ongoing circle processes such as reintegration circles and support circles extremely time intensive for their members. One way that the traditional criminal justice system functions in a community is that, for the most part, it transfers the responsibility of responding to a crime into the hands of specific institutions and professionals. When a process like a sentencing circle places that responsibility back into the community, it requires community members to invest their time and energy into a process that would normally be handled without their direct involvement.

Community Partnerships

While some peacemaking circles, such as healing circles and talking circles, often operate outside of the criminal justice system, circle processes often require collaboration between community-based organizations that facilitate circles and referring agencies and institutions such as the courts, juvenile justice agencies, and offices of probation and parole. While these partnerships are common in the criminal justice system, they also come with their own unique challenges. Criminal justice agencies and community-based organizations may operate from different values and/or have competing interests and needs. For example, while circle members may love the idea of an offender providing direct service to a victim in order to repair damage done to the victim's property during the offense, a referring agency may have policies against this kind of sentencing plan due to liability concerns. It is therefore common practice for referring agencies to provide suggestions and/or restrictions to circle participants convening to create a sentencing plan; however, this practice can begin to detract from the restorative nature of the circle process.[64]

Finding Appropriate Cases

One final challenge that can be common when considering the use of peacemaking circles within a particular community or group is the process of discerning when cases are appropriate, or not appropriate, for a circle process. According to Pranis, Stuart, and Wedge,[65] concerns about lack of time, safety, and resources can indicate that a peacemaking circle may not be the best model to use when addressing a particular issue or offense.

As we discussed earlier, peacemaking circles require a lot of time and energy. Especially in the case of sentencing circles, if a referral comes with a deadline that makes it incompatible with a circle process or would require a circle keeper to compromise or eliminate important practices such as the preparation of participants, then a circle process may not be the best fit for that case.[66] A lack of critical resources such as an available circle keeper, a safe and neutral location for the circle process, or participants willing and able to engage in the circle can also signal the need to address a situation in another way.[67]

Emotional and physical safety can be additional concerns, especially when a victim and offender are being brought together.[68] While a sentencing circle may require that a victim and offender meet fairly quickly after the offense, this may not be appropriate in all cases. A victim may need more time and preparation before directly encountering the offender, and the offender may also have concerns about their safety when participating in a circle. In cases like this, the circle process may not need to be abandoned altogether. For instance, rather than convening a sentencing circle, support circles could be organized separately for both the victim and offender while the sentencing plan is imposed through the courts. These concerns emphasize the importance of voluntary participation and adequate preparation as part of the circle process. If a peacemaking circle were to be compulsory for participants or be convened without first preparing participants for their involvement, circles could easily exacerbate the conflicts, tensions, and harm they seek to repair.

Research and Evaluation on Peacemaking Circles

Research focused on the exploration and evaluation of peacemaking circles is fairly limited. For the most part this research is comprised of impact and process evaluations that each describe a specific application of peacemaking circles and measure outcomes such as participant satisfaction and offender recidivism.

For the most part, the evaluative research on peacemaking circles is very positive. Research consistently shows that victims, offenders, and community members feel high levels of satisfaction[69] and a sense of fairness[70] regarding their participation in a circle. Other promising outcomes suggest that circles can lead to reduced conflict outside of the circle process,[71] as well as feelings of community empowerment.[72] Research comparing the costs and benefits of circles to more traditional, retributive sentencing models indicates that circles may also reduce offender recidivism, as well as decrease criminal justice related costs within a community.[73]

Research findings also caution against the use of circles in some contexts, as well as provide information concerning what participants find least satisfying about the process. For instance, in one evaluation of a peacemaking circle program in Canada, participants indicated that when a circle was dissatisfying it often had to do with the requisite time commitment and/or the decision of certain stakeholders not to participate.[74] An evaluation of sentencing circles used in cases of intimate partner violence concluded that circles were ill-equipped to address issues of inequality and provide adequate support and safety for victims of abuse and relationship violence.[75] These findings suggest that not only do circles become less effective when important stakeholders are not present, but that certain types of cases may not be appropriate for the circle process. This latter issue is one we will examine further in Chapter 11 when we explore restorative justice in cases involving relationship abuse and sexual assault.

Due to the fact that there are so many types of circles, we need to be careful about assuming that results from one study can be applied to any circle process. For instance, just because one research study indicates that sentencing circles are highly effective in juvenile justice cases in Canada, we cannot assume that a reintegration circle for adult sex offenders in the U.S. will be as successful. As we explored earlier, circles are not only adaptable to different cultures, but different circles are designed around different goals. In other words, what works in one community for one type of case, may not work quite the same way in another community dealing with a different type of case. This issue is not unique to peacemaking circles and can be equally as important to keep in mind when we examine any of the research literature on restorative justice. For example, in our next chapter we will examine reparative boards, which is another restorative model that can function differently depending on the community in which it is used and the needs it is designed to address.

Chapter Summary

What were the early origins of peacemaking circles?

While the practice of circling together in order to discuss issues and make important decisions can be traced back to early tribal societies, a peacemaking circle was first used in a criminal justice proceeding in 1982. This occurred in the case of Philip Moses, who had already accrued multiple criminal convictions by the age of 26. Upon facing even more charges, the presiding judge decided to gather important stakeholders in the case including Moses, his family, members of the Na-cho-Ny'ak Dun First Nation (of which Moses belonged), and various criminal justice professionals. Together the members of the circle discussed the needs of Moses, his victims, and his community and created a sentencing plan that the judge adopted on behalf of the court. The case of Philip Moses took place in Yukon, Canada, and stands as our first known example of what would later come to be called a sentencing circle.

What are the six different types of peacemaking circles related to crime and justice?

While a circle was first used in the context of criminal justice in order to facilitate the creation of a collaborative sentencing plan, peacemaking circles have since been used to meet a variety of needs in relation to crime and criminal justice. Peacemaking circles are unique among restorative justice processes in that they are frequently used outside of the context of crime to address conflict, facilitate group decision-making, and provide supportive spaces for individuals in need. Though not a comprehensive accounting of circles, we identified six different types of circles that can be used in cases involving crime, including: sentencing circles, circles of understanding, talking circles, healing circles, support circles, and reintegration circles. These models are distinct from one another in regard to their intended function, as well as who is invited to participate.

What are the common characteristics, principles, and challenges of peacemaking circles?

While we explored what makes certain circles different from one another, we also explored what they have in common. Regardless of important variables such as the driving purpose of a circle, how many people are involved, where it is taking place, or how often the circle will convene, all circles share at least five common elements. These are: ceremony and ritual, circle keepers, a talking piece, shared behavioral guidelines, and consensus decision making.

In this section, we discussed the ceremonial nature of circles and the importance of including opening and closing rituals in the circle process. We also explored the role of the circle keeper as both a participant and a facilitator who supports the circle but does not control it. We were introduced to the concept of a talking piece, which is an object used within circles to give everyone an equal chance to speak. Lastly, we discussed the fact that participants in a circle take the time to create their own shared guidelines concerning behavioral norms and values important to the circle process, and also use consensus decision making when creating agreements or making decisions within the group.

We also identified and explored five core principles that help guide the design and implementation of peacemaking circles. Those principles are inclusivity, voluntary participation, equality, shared responsibility, and collective efficacy. We concluded this section by discussing common challenges faced during the implementation of circles, including time constraints, community partnerships, and finding appropriate cases.

What do we know from the research on peacemaking circles?

Though research on peacemaking circles is fairly limited, empirical findings suggest that circles can result in favorable outcomes such as participant satisfaction, criminal desistance, and decreased costs for the criminal justice system. Not all evaluations on peacemaking circles are positive, however, suggesting that certain situations (such as cases involving intimate partner violence) may not be a safe and effective fit for circles.

Key Terms

Peacemaking Circle
Sentencing Circle
Sentencing Plan
Circle of Understanding
Talking Circle
Healing Circle
Plan of Support
Support Circle
Circles of Support and Accountability
Reintegration Circle
Opening and Closing Rituals
Circle Keeper
Talking Piece
Shared Guidelines
Consensus Decision Making
Collective Efficacy

Critical Thinking Questions

1. What is one problem in your campus community that could be addressed through the use of a talking circle? Why do you think a talking circle might be a good way to open dialog around the issue?

2. What are some reasons why it might be a good idea to convene a reintegration circle before an offender leaves prison, rather than waiting until the offender is released?

3. Try to imagine that you are organizing a peacemaking circle within your family, school, or worship group. What might be a good opening and closing ritual that would fulfill the recommendations outlined in Box 7.3 while also being meaningful to you and your group members?

4. Do you think it is important for each circle to make their own behavioral guidelines or would a common set of guidelines work just as well? Be sure to explain your answer.

References

1. Pranis, K. (2005). *The little book of circle processes: A new/old approach to peacemaking.* Intercourse, PA: Good Books.

2. Umbreit, M., & Peterson Armour, M. (2010). *Restorative justice dialogue: An essential guide for research and practice.* New York, NY: Springer Publishing Company.

3. Regina v. Moses, (1992) 3 C.N.L.R. 116.

4. Ibid.

5. Ibid., see 3.

6. Ibid., see 3.

7. Ibid., see 3.

8. Ibid., see 3.

9. Umbreit, M., & Peterson Armour, M. (2010). *Restorative justice dialogue: An essential guide for research and practice.* New York, NY: Springer Publishing Company.

10. Pranis, K. (2005). *The little book of circle processes: A new/old approach to peacemaking.* Intercourse, PA: Good Books.

11. Ibid.

12. Umbreit, M., & Peterson Armour, M. (2010). *Restorative justice dialogue: An essential guide for research and practice.* New York, NY: Springer Publishing Company.

13. Ibid.

14. Pranis, K. (2005). *The little book of circle processes: A new/old approach to peacemaking.* Intercourse, PA: Good Books.

15. Umbreit, M., & Peterson Armour, M. (2010). *Restorative justice dialogue: An essential guide for research and practice.* New York, NY: Springer Publishing Company.

16. Pranis, K. (2005). *The little book of circle processes: A new/old approach to peacemaking.* Intercourse, PA: Good Books.

17. Umbreit, M., & Peterson Armour, M. (2010). *Restorative justice dialogue: An essential guide for research and practice.* New York, NY: Springer Publishing Company.

18. Pranis, K. (2005). *The little book of circle processes: A new/old approach to peacemaking.* Intercourse, PA: Good Books.

19. Herman, S. (2010). *Parallel justice for victims of crime.* Washington, DC: The National Center for Victims of Crime.

20. Pranis, K. (2005). *The little book of circle processes: A new/old approach to peacemaking.* Intercourse, PA: Good Books.

21. Ibid.

22. Duwe, G. (2012). Can circles of support and accountability (COSA) work in the United States? Preliminary results from a randomized experiment in Minnesota. *Sexual Abuse: A Journal of Research and Treatment, 25*(2), 143–165.

23. Pranis, K. (2005). *The little book of circle processes: A new/old approach to peacemaking.* Intercourse, PA: Good Books.

24. Ibid.

25. Ibid., see 23.

26. Braithwaite, J. (1989). *Crime, shame and reintegration.* New York, NY: Cambridge University Press.

27. Pranis, K., Stuart, B., & Wedge, M. (2003). *Peacemaking circles: From crime to community.* St. Paul, MN: Living Justice Press.

28. Umbreit, M., & Peterson Armour, M. (2010). *Restorative justice dialogue: An essential guide for research and practice.* New York, NY: Springer Publishing Company.

29. Ibid.

30. Pranis, K., Stuart, B., & Wedge, M. (2003). *Peacemaking circles: From crime to community.* St. Paul, MN: Living Justice Press.

31. Ibid.

32. Baldwin, C. (1998). *Calling the circle: The first and future culture.* New York, NY: Bantam Books.

33. Umbreit, M., & Peterson Armour, M. (2010). *Restorative justice dialogue: An essential guide for research and practice.* New York, NY: Springer Publishing Company.

34. Ibid.

35. Pranis, K., Stuart, B., & Wedge, M. (2003). *Peacemaking circles: From crime to community.* St. Paul, MN: Living Justice Press.

36. Umbreit, M., & Peterson Armour, M. (2010). *Restorative justice dialogue: An essential guide for research and practice.* New York, NY: Springer Publishing Company.

37. Pranis, K. (2005). *The little book of circle processes: A new/old approach to peacemaking.* Intercourse, PA: Good Books.

38. Ibid.

39. Pranis, K., Stuart, B., & Wedge, M. (2003). *Peacemaking circles: From crime to community.* St. Paul, MN: Living Justice Press.

40. Ibid.

41. Ibid., see 39.

42. Ibid., see 39.

43. Boyes-Watson, C. (2008). *Peacemaking circles & urban youth: Bringing justice home.* St. Paul, MN: Living Justice Press.

44. Boyes-Watson, C. (2008). *Peacemaking circles & urban youth: Bringing justice home.* St. Paul, MN: Living Justice Press, p. 116.

45. Ibid.

46. Umbreit, M., & Peterson Armour, M. (2010). *Restorative justice dialogue: An essential guide for research and practice.* New York, NY: Springer Publishing Company.

47. Ibid.

48. Ibid., see 46.

49. Stuart, B. (2001). Guiding principles for peacemaking circles. In G. Bazemore & M. Schiff (Eds.), *Restorative community justice* (pp. 219–241). Cincinnati, OH: Anderson Publishing Company.

50. Pranis, K., Stuart, B., & Wedge, M. (2003). *Peacemaking circles: From crime to community.* St. Paul, MN: Living Justice Press.

51. Zehr, H. (2002). *The little book of restorative justice.* Intercourse, PA: Good Books.

52. Pranis, K. (2005). *The little book of circle processes: A new/old approach to peacemaking.* Intercourse, PA: Good Books.

53. Stuart, B. (2001). Guiding principles for peacemaking circles. In G. Bazemore & M. Schiff (Eds.), *Restorative community justice* (pp. 219–241). Cincinnati, OH: Anderson Publishing Company.

54. Umbreit, M., & Peterson Armour, M. (2010). *Restorative justice dialogue: An essential guide for research and practice.* New York, NY: Springer Publishing Company.

55. Van Ness, D., & Strong, K. H. (2015). *Restoring justice: An introduction to restorative justice* (5th ed.). Waltham, MA: Anderson Publishing.

56. Pranis, K. (2005). *The little book of circle processes: A new/old approach to peacemaking.* Intercourse, PA: Good Books.

57. Pranis, K., Stuart, B., & Wedge, M. (2003). *Peacemaking circles: From crime to community.* St. Paul, MN: Living Justice Press.

58. Umbreit, M., & Peterson Armour, M. (2010). *Restorative justice dialogue: An essential guide for research and practice.* New York, NY: Springer Publishing Company.

59. Zehr, H. (2002). *The little book of restorative justice.* Intercourse, PA: Good Books.

60. Higgins, B., & Hunt. J. (2016). Collective efficacy: Taking action to improve neighborhoods. NIJ Journal, 277.

61. Braithwaite, J. (1989). *Crime, shame and reintegration.* New York, NY: Cambridge University Press.

62. Bazemore, G. (2000). *Community justice and a vision of collective efficacy: The case for restorative conferencing.* Retrieved from https://www.ncjrs.gov/criminal_justice2000/vol_3/03f.pdf.

63. Stuart, B. (2001). Guiding principles for peacemaking circles. In G. Bazemore & M. Schiff (Eds.), *Restorative community justice* (pp. 219–241). Cincinnati, OH: Anderson Publishing Company.

64. Saxon, C. (2013). *Consistency and proportionality in victim-offender mediation agreements.* Retrieved from http://www.mediate.com/articles/SaxonC1.cfm.

65. Pranis, K., Stuart, B., & Wedge, M. (2003). *Peacemaking circles: From crime to community.* St. Paul, MN: Living Justice Press.

66. Ibid.

67. Ibid., see 65.

68. Ibid., see 65.

69. Potas, I., Smart, J., & Brignell, G. (2003). *Circle sentencing in New South Wales: A review and evaluation.* Retrieved from https://www.judcom.nsw.gov.au/wp-content/uploads/2016/07/research-monograph-22.pdf.

70. Coates, R. B., Umbreit, M., & Vos, B. (2003). Restorative justice circles: An exploratory study. *Contemporary Justice Review, 6*(3), 265–278.

71. Paiement, R. (2006). *Peacemaking circles pilot project in St. James Town and Regent Park (Toronto, Canada) Phase two: January 30, 2005–June 30, 2006.* Retrieved from http://www.peace-buildersinternational.com/RelatedFiles/1/FINAL%20Evaluation%20Report.pdf.

72. Potas, I., Smart, J., & Brignell, G. (2003). *Circle sentencing in New South Wales: A review and evaluation.* Retrieved from https://www.judcom.nsw.gov.au/wp-content/uploads/2016/07/research-monograph-22.pdf.

73. Buller, E. (2004). A cost-benefit analysis of Hollow Water First Nation's community holistic healing process. *Aboriginal Policy Research Consortium International.* Retrieved from http://ir.lib.uwo.ca/cgi/viewcontent.cgi?article=1310&context=aprci.

74. Paiement, R. (2006). *Peacemaking circles pilot project in St. James Town and Regent Park (Toronto, Canada) Phase two: January 30, 2005–June 30, 2006.* Retrieved from http://www.peace-buildersinternational.com/RelatedFiles/1/FINAL%20Evaluation%20Report.pdf.

75. Cameron, A. (2006). Sentencing circles and intimate violence: A Canadian feminist perspective. *Canadian Journal of Women and the Law, 18,* 479–512.

Chapter 8

Reparative Boards

In this chapter, we will explore the following questions ...

- *Where did the concept of reparative boards originate?*
- *What are the basic elements of this restorative justice component?*
- *How do reparative boards work?*
- *Is this restorative justice practice an effective approach?*

Origins of Reparative Boards: Adoption in Vermont

Community reparative boards are yet another mechanism of restorative justice that have similar ideological foundations as the ones we have discussed in previous chapters. It is a non-adversarial approach designed to be more inclusive of community members in the justice process. While its origins do not have a strong historical foundation such as that of family group conferencing and the Maori, there is no doubt that the concept of a community reparative board is rooted in various contexts where community justice is the primary mechanism of social control.[1] Community reparative boards originated in and are exemplified by the Vermont model.

Probation in Vermont

Within the Vermont Department of Corrections, standard probation involves a suspension of an imposition of a sentence contingent upon the offender abiding by a set of rules, standards, and criteria that become conditions which are binding, legally, and which require strict adherence. These conditions include such rules as undergoing psychiatric assessment, participating in specific treatment programs, refraining from the use of alcohol, restrictions on living arrangements, obtaining employment, and other conditions as deemed appropriate in the particular case.[2] Essentially, the offender must agree to abide by these rules, and therefore, probation supervision becomes a contract between the offender and the sentencing court.

Within the broad category of probation, the Vermont Department of Corrections has divided, practically, community supervision caseloads into three groups depending on the risk presented by the offender as well as the complexity of the supervision conditions. The largest population of offenders is under what is called **standard pro-**

165

bation. These offenders are on a suspended sentence with a general or standard set of criteria for their period of supervision, by which they have to abide or their probation will be terminated. A second type of caseload within the Vermont Department of Corrections is **risk management probation**, which includes offenders that present multiple management issues, risk factors, or are a particular category of offenders such as sex offenders and domestic violence offenders.[3] The third category of probation offenders is what is referred to as **reparative probation**, which includes offenders with minimal supervision requirements and conditions aside from a contract that is signed between them and the restorative justice board members. It is this category of probation that has given rise to the Vermont model of community justice, to which we now turn for a closer look.

The Vermont Model of Community Justice

The concept of a community reparative board began with the implementation of the reparative probation condition in Vermont in 1995. The motivation of this approach was largely in response to rising rates of incarceration across the state. The goal was to develop a process that would address the needs of crime victims, encourage offenders to take responsibility for their actions, and at the same time involve communities in the restoration process. The commitment to this emerging process was consistent with Vermont's longstanding history of collaborative practices between criminal justice, corrections, and human services agencies.[4] Moreover, the Vermont Department of Corrections is recognized as being a leader and an innovator in founding the use of volunteer community boards, epitomizing the example of restorative justice and serving offenders through this reparative approach. In 1998, the Vermont Department of Corrections was recognized for their efforts by winning the very prestigious Ford Foundation Innovations in Government Award in recognition of their work and advancement of restorative justice within corrections.[5]

Vermont's reparative probation program was designed to allow offenders who are convicted of a generally minor, nonviolent crime, to be sentenced to probation with the primary condition that they participate in the community reparative board process. These are offenders who would have normally been sentenced to standard probation or jail time. The participation consists of a series of meetings between the offender and a reparative board of trained citizen volunteers. Other members affected by the crime, including the victim, are also invited to attend should they choose to do so. The offender and reparative board members will discuss and agree upon a variety of tasks and conditions that the offender must complete to be successful in the program during the period of their probation supervision. This can include things such as community service, a letter of apology to the victim, payment of restitution, drug and alcohol screening, and other required interventions aimed at targeting certain needs or deficits of the offender on supervision. The goal of the meetings is to help the offender understand their actions, hold them accountable for what they agreed to do to repair the harm, and keep them on track to their restoration as law-abiding members of the community.[6] Offenders have 90 days to abide by the rules of the program and fulfill the obligations of the reparative contract agreement. If the offender does not abide by the conditions of the agreement reached, they will be considered in violation of their probation and will return to the court for further action.

Over the last several decades, community reparative boards have evolved within departments of correction across the United States, developed after the approach exemplified by the Vermont model. These boards, existing now in almost all states in one form or another, serve both adult and juvenile offenders, and are known by a variety of names, including community conference boards, diversion boards, restorative justice boards, and neighborhood accountability boards.[7] While variations undoubtedly exist in the structure and operation of these boards, the overarching purpose of the community board model is to involve citizens in the justice process, enhance social control, and work with offenders at the local level to resolve problems caused by criminal actions. In the sections to come, we will further elaborate on the design and implementation of community reparative boards as a model of restorative justice theory and practice.

Designing and Implementing a Reparative Board

The concept of a community reparative board, while fairly new within the context of restorative justice programming, dates back to the juvenile justice system in the 1920s, when youth panels, citizen diversion boards, and neighborhood boards were used as an informal response to youth offending. Since the implementation of the Vermont model in the 1990s, reparative boards have taken on an integral role in restorative justice program and practice.

Citizen Engagement: The Foundation of Reparative Boards

Community reparative boards are built on the notion of citizen engagement and a growing trend among criminal justice and social service agencies nationwide to involve members of the community in the administration of justice.[8] This ideology is reflected in various practices throughout criminal justice, such as teen courts and youth offender panels, where volunteers become engaged in the process of determining sanctions for youth offenders.[9] Moreover, the notion of justice as embracing the participation of citizens has embedded normative and historic roots in our system of government and deliberation. This is true in our political process as reflected in our democratic system of government as well as in the process of determining guilt and innocence by a jury panel of citizens during a criminal trial.

The involvement of citizen volunteers in the justice process represents a constructive format in which to address the offending behavior of individuals by bringing forth multiple perspectives, soliciting input from a variety of individuals with different experiences, and finding creative solutions that parallel the goals of justice, reintegration, and accountability. This not only builds the capacity of criminal justice agencies as a form of bureaucratic and managerial support, but it also enhances the restorative justice process by modeling the principles of volunteerism and dialog.

The principle of engaging citizens enhances the justice process in a transformative way by giving formal proceedings a personal side that allows for the emotional and expressive aspects of responding to criminal offending. Moreover, studies show that the facilitated dialog between volunteers and offenders allows for the expression of values, encourages responsivity, and helps to build a rapport that is difficult to attain on a professional level.[10] This in turn engenders a stronger sense of trust between offenders, formal agents of criminal justice, and the community as a whole. It bridges the divide that often exists between criminal justice agencies and the population of offenders, which is often a barrier and hindrance to the process of reintegration and restoration. Box 8.1 gives us a glimpse of how ordinary citizens can impact the lives of offenders in a positive way.

Box 8.1: Restorative Justice: Let's Take a Closer Look …
Restoring Lives in Greene County, Missouri?

As a citizen volunteer on the Greene County, Missouri, restorative justice board, I have had the opportunity to participate in this program for nearly 10 years. Without a doubt I have seen numerous clients come through the program and, while each represents a unique individual with their own story, there are some that have made an impact on me personally because of the significance of the change that I observed during their year of supervision.

One such individual was a shy, quiet young man who was barely 18 years old. When he first came before the restorative justice board it was quite obvious that he was lost, broken hearted, and on the path to drug addiction and chronic criminal offending. While his story was not unique, his manners and demeanor certainly were. He was unusually polite while at the same time seemingly uncaring and unmotivated not just about the program but about anything in life. After several weeks of interaction with this offender, it was clear to me that he had the desire to change and get on the right path towards success, education, and a substance abuse-free life; however, what he clearly lacked was a support system.

Once we picked up on this, we decided to work together as a group of concerned citizens to help this young man become successful and complete all components of his program. I guess you can say we somewhat teamed up to become his "cheerleaders." Once we embraced this approach and explained to him how much we wanted to see him succeed, how sincere he was in his desire to become better, that we would be behind him 100%, and that we understood the hardships that he had gone through and how this led to his state of apathy, his entire demeanor changed. He could see that we took on a personal interest in his goals and aspirations and he began to avidly pursue completing his GED, and seeking out different junior-college programs to enroll in. He began attending treatment groups regularly and stopped hanging around the group of individuals that were bringing him down and influencing his behavior in a negative way. He obtained a part-time job at the YMCA, and it is there that this particular case stood out in my mind and became ingrained in my memory as a profound success.

As very often occurs in a fairly small town, I ran into this young man at the YMCA, where my kids and I would regularly go to exercise and participate in other programs. He had completed the restorative justice program successfully about six months earlier and that evening when I ran into him I could barely recognize who he was. That shy, broken, scruffy young man who I had met about a year and a half earlier was now smiling, upbeat, well-kept, and working in various parts of the YMCA. He recognized me immediately and said hello and asked if he could give me a hug, to which of course I said yes. He told me how wonderful he was doing and how happy he was and how he owed that to his interaction with the "ladies of the board," as he said it. He indicated to me with tears beginning to well up in his eyes how supportive we were and how much he appreciated that as it made him feel that people cared about him during a time when he had nobody. He thanked me ardently and all I could do was look at him and thank him too! If you had this experience, wouldn't you thank him too?

Source: Aida Y. Hass, reflection journal from an encounter with an offender at a Greene County, Missouri, Restorative Justice Board meeting.

Dynamics of Interaction

Community justice restorative boards are usually comprised of a fairly small group of citizen volunteers that are solicited from different avenues. They can be university professors, teachers, social service agency providers, executive directors of companies, businessmen and women, college students, retired members of the community, and even ex-offenders who are exemplary citizens that are trying to help individuals who are heading down the wrong path. These individuals must go through an intensive training period that prepares them for their role as board members. They are instructed in the basic ideals of restorative justice, their role as participants in this process, and the various limitations of their interactions with offenders appearing before them. Very often this training session includes an instructional video, or a classroom type lecture by a training facilitator. Information regarding offender confidentiality is also discussed, as well as safety issues that might arise as an outcome of their interaction and encounter with the offenders. Board members are not always knowledgeable in matters of criminal justice, so basic terminologies such as sanctioning, probation conditions, community service, and other matters that might become relevant, are reviewed.[11]

Many jurisdictions that have implemented the reparative board process within restorative justice programming have both day boards and evening boards, to accommodate the time needs of citizen volunteers. Board meetings are typically held once a month and entail face-to-face meetings with offenders who have been referred by the court to participate and complete a restorative justice program. During these meetings, the board members discuss with the offender the conditions and obligations of their sentencing agreement, as well as review their progress from month to month in completing various tasks and determining their compliance with certain requirements. Meetings can last anywhere from 15 minutes to half an hour, depending on the complexity of the case and the dialog that ensues between the offender and the board members. Caseloads can vary, with board members meeting with anywhere from two or three offenders to 10 or 15 offenders in a given session.[12]

A great deal of the successful dynamics of interaction between board members and offenders rests upon the commitment and organization of the supervising probation restorative justice caseload manager.[13] This includes having a positive rapport with judges, prosecutors, and defense attorneys to ensure that referrals are made according to set guidelines and in a timely manner. This keeps the flow of clients in the program steady as well as ensures that risk management guidelines are appropriately followed. Moreover, the caseload supervisor must work hand-in-hand with community service agencies, social service providers, treatment facilitators, and victim organizations in order to coordinate the various components of the offender's supervision plan and restorative justice agreement. They must also take the time to explain each case to the community board members in a manner that is efficient and understandable, as well as make sure that the environment in which the meetings takes place is adequate and comfortable.

Goals and Tasks of Board Meetings

While the literature abounds with information about various restorative justice programs and practices, it is interesting to note that information on reparative citizen boards is rather limited and fragmented across various different forms. What makes our task easy here however is that while we as authors are restorative justice advocates, researchers, and practitioners, we also both participate as citizen volunteers with the Greene County, Missouri, Restorative Justice Program. Thus, many of our understandings and observations about this particular restorative justice practice come from a combined decade of direct experience with this process.

From the inception of our participation with the Greene County restorative justice program, we have come to understand the various goals and tasks that are part of this process. Reparative boards, consistent with the restorative justice literature, are designed around the ideals of dialog, accountability, and the reintegration of offenders into society as law-abiding citizens that are free of the negative effects of criminal labels.[14] Thus a primary goal is to make sure that offenders understand that this program, as well as making board members satisfied with their progress, represents a last chance for offenders to continue with their lives as law-abiding members of their community. This is a sentiment that is repeated many times to offenders who appear to be taking the conditions of their agreement lightly. At the same time, however, board members highlight to offenders their voluntary role in this process as a testimony to their concern for the wellbeing of their community as well as the wellbeing of the offender and their desire to see them succeed.

Another major task that reparative boards are designed to do is to promote a sense of ownership to ordinary citizens whereby their direct involvement in the justice process creates a vested interest in the success of offenders under supervision within the restorative justice program. This not only encourages participation but enables a genuine concern for members of their community that translates to offenders a feeling that people care and that it is not an "us versus them" dynamic where they feel alienated from the justice process. This type of interaction is regarded as integral in increasing the chances for success while under community supervision.[15] The reparative board process therefore exemplifies the ideals of **community justice** as described by researchers Clear and Karp:

> community justice refers to all variants of crime prevention and justice activities that explicitly include the community in their processes and set the enhancement of community quality of life as an explicit goal. Community justice is rooted in the actions that citizens, community organizations, and the criminal justice system can take to control crime and social disorder. Its central focus is community-level outcomes, shifting the emphasis from individual incidents to systemic patterns, from individual conscience to social mores, and from individual goods to the common good.[16]

To this extent, reparative boards share the common goal of enhancing community building by identifying problematic behaviors and finding resolutions that involve social participation and the integration of offenders into the values and ideals of citizenship.

Consistent with the ideals of building community, reparative boards also represent an attempt to decentralize the criminal justice system to make it less formal and more accessible to members of the community.[17] This creates greater flexibility within the justice process, which in turn allows for the creative implementation of programming that is more suitable for individuals with their own unique needs and concerns. They offer a unique interaction between the goals of formal justice and the goals of informal restorative practices that enhance the quality of supervision by providing the maximum benefits of informal social control. The following dialog between a board member and an offender illustrates this point:

> *Board member*: So, how did you do this month in the various goals that you set?

> *Offender*: I completed most of my community service hours but did not get a chance to contact the treatment provider.

Board member: What you mean you "didn't get a chance"?

Offender: Work was really busy, and I had several personal problems. My car broke down for one, my dog got really sick, and my roommate had a lot of health problems.

Board member: I understand that life happens, and we are in no way trying to be insensitive to your personal circumstances. But you have to understand the importance of your obligations to this board. When we go to work every day we are expected to complete certain tasks, regardless of how busy we are in other areas of our lives. You do realize that if you do not complete your obligations you will run out of time and will not successfully complete this board?

Offender: Yes, I do; I really do want to complete this program and I do appreciate it and your time, it's just been a rough month, but I promise I will get things done and make you proud next board meeting.

Board member: Well, we will just have to see, and decide if we want to sanction you this time or not. We are not trying to make you more miserable, but it seems that you might not be aware of this being your last chance at wiping your record clean.

Offender: I understand, and will work harder, I promise.[18]

Community reparative boards therefore provide informal social control by their ability to negotiate with offenders, creating correctional actions that are independent of the formal authority of probation officers, prosecutors, and judges in a manner that instills a sense of obligation upon the offender while giving them a role in the negotiation process. Table 8.1 provides you with a contrast between the goals of formal supervision and the flexibility of terms offered by the dialog created between board members and offenders.

Because of the integral role of community in this process, community reparative boards are also a mechanism of accountability for offenders. From our own experience as restorative justice board members in Greene County, we are able to understand the potential impact we have on offenders that come before us from month to month. Through the dialog and rapport that is built in our discussions with offenders about their personal circumstances, the progress they have made, and possible areas that they need to work on, the reparative board has taken on a form of accountability whereby offenders feel a personal responsibility to fulfill the obligations of their supervision. There have been numerous times that offenders report to us their progress and state that they completed a task for the simple reason that they did not want to disappoint us.

Thus, a major goal of the reparative board process is to create meaningful relationships between board members and "clients" that transcend that of the formal relationship of criminal justice agents and offenders. This relationship becomes integral to the restorative process as it instills in offenders the idea of success and reparation as a personal endeavor to be reached for their own wellbeing and to seek the approval

Table 8.1: Formal Versus Creative Alternatives

Formal Supervision Obligation	Creative Correctional Action
Write a letter of apology	• letters of apology are read by each board member to ensure that they are adequate in terms of grammar and context • letters of apology must be sincere, personal, and not have any undertones of making excuses but rather reflecting a genuine attitude of remorse • offenders are commended for writing exceptional letters of high quality
Write a respect essay	• the respect essay is reviewed for content, length, and coherence by each board member • essays that fall short are required to be redone, and offenders have a chance to understand why the essay is not acceptable • the essay can become a point of discussion to ensure that the offender understands why it is important to respect others as well as their property
Complete 100 hours of community service	• the concept of community service is discussed with offenders to make sure that it is not perceived as a task or punishment but rather as a way to give back to their community and do something positive and meaningful • community service hours are set as a goal during each board meeting and this is used as a method of teaching offenders time management skills and holding them accountable
Maintain employment	• offenders without employment are pointed in the proper direction and given adequate resources to search for a job because board members are from the same area as offenders their knowledge of various community agencies is often used as a tool to link offenders to the proper resource • offenders are instructed in the value of meaningful work and are encouraged to contribute financially to their families as a means of personal integrity
Attend substance abuse treatment	• board members discuss with offenders their obligation to follow through on referrals for treatment • because of the informal and intimate setting of a board meeting, an offender is more likely and more willing to be forthcoming on their feelings about obtaining substance abuse treatment as well as their desire to get help • the interaction between board members and offenders allows the provision of treatment to be enhanced through encouragement, and through the ability of board members to see the progress or lack of progress and offender is making from month to month • suggestions for alternative treatment programs as well as ways to optimize the treatment experience can also be made
Do not leave the county	• during a given period of supervision, it is very natural that certain events may arise that require an offender to leave the county; this can be attending a concert, a graduation, a wedding, or a reunion • board members discuss requests to leave the county and can make exceptions based on circumstances as well as how meaningful the event is to the client, it's possibility to be detrimental, as well as use approval to travel as an incentive to gain compliance

of others, as opposed to a series of tasks that need to be completed in order to avoid further punishment.[19] In the sections to come we will discuss how this type of relationship evolves through the interactions that take place during the reparative board process.

Reparative Boards in Action

Community reparative boards are indeed one of the most innovative concepts within restorative justice theory and practice. They represent the core elements of restoration as their central focus is the involvement of community in repairing the harm done to one of its citizens as well as reintegrating the offending member and promoting their success as a law-abiding citizen. In this section, we will explore in some detail the dynamics of interaction that take place during reparative board meetings.

In the Beginning: Setting the Stage

The changing aspects of restorative justice board meetings depend largely on the various personalities of the different board members. We are constantly reminded that these are regular members of the community that may or may not have any experience with criminal justice administration. While this may be perceived as a disadvantage, the literature is compelling in noting that this actually produces a more positive outcome in terms of enhancing dialog, establishing trust, and increasing the chances of success.[20] Prior to the commencement of a board meeting, the probation officer will engage in a brief dialog with board members about any changes that have occurred since the prior board meeting. This can include updates on current offenders that are both positive and negative such as obtaining a new job, completing a task, incurring a violation for failing to report to a probation meeting, or having a positive drug test. It can also include updates on new offenders that have been added to the board's caseload.

Board meetings are usually held in a conference-style room where everyone sits in a circle either around a table or just in chairs. This format immediately encourages face-to-face contact as well as establishes a sense of ease that diffuses the possibility of anxiety and intimidation.[21] The tone of a board meeting is set in the early stages of meeting an offender who has been directed to participate in restorative justice programming, for the very first time. As a newly assigned offender enters the meeting session, they are greeted by the board members and instructed by the supervising probation officer where to sit. Each board member will introduce themselves, indicating their first name as well as a brief description of their background. A board member will then ask the offender to give everyone a brief overview of what happened, including the events that brought them to where they are, as well as what they hope to get out of this experience. To set the offender at ease and build trust as well as optimize dialog, it is reiterated that board members are volunteers who represent the interests of the community and that their role is not to put the offender on trial, judge their past actions, or scrutinize their behavior, but rather it is to help them through the program, make sure they stay on task, and encourage their successful completion. The goal here is to shatter the adversarial nature of the criminal justice process and to make *community* a central aspect of the offender's goal in fulfilling the obligations of the program.

Somewhere in Between: Balancing Power

A primary function of the restorative justice reparative board process is to create a sense of accountability. Notably, accountability is very often connected to the concepts of punishment and sanctioning and implies that an entity has the power of enforcement and coercion.[22] Within the context of restorative justice, however, this is counterproductive and detrimental to the structure and design of board meetings.

To enhance the reparative board process, board members must therefore create a balance between gaining compliance and ensuring that offenders are held accountable for completing their tasks and staying on target. For this reason, accountability is defined as a personal obligation on the part of the offender to ensure that they make amends to the both the victim and the community for the damages caused by their criminal actions. The central component of discussions between board members and the offender at any given meeting focuses on the identification of behavior patterns, lifestyle, interactions, and thought processes that not only are detrimental to the offender's successful completion of the program but also serve as obstacles to the goal of reparation. This restorative focus provides a model of justice that is neither punitive nor rehabilitative but rather a model that places a burden and obligation on the offender to feel a sense of responsibility in making amends to the victim and to the community in which they belong.

Thus, balancing power essentially involves empowering offenders to feel that they have a stake in their own actions and not that they are simply meeting requirements to avoid sanctions and getting into trouble. This is the hallmark contribution that the reparative board process contributes to the restoration of offenders and their reintegration into the community. The following table illustrates how obligations of supervision can become more meaningful when cast in the light of a personal sense of accountability.

Board members indeed have a unique relationship with the offenders that appear before them. Without any formal authority, they nevertheless represent agents of justice who are backed by formal mechanisms of social control. Under these circumstances, compliance and cooperation rests upon the ability of board members to gain power and authority through respect, and balance that power by also allowing offenders to realize their own role in making reparation to the victim, recognizing the empowerment they will gain by reintegrating themselves into the law-abiding community.[23] By clarifying expectations and redefining for the offender the normative standards of society that are shared collectively, the reparative board process elicits a sense of commitment from the offender that emanates from a feeling of responsibility and mutual trust and respect.

Table 8.2: Fulfilling Tasks through Meaningful Accountability

Writing a respect essay	*I broke the law and stole from someone and now I need to make sure I understand the wrongfulness of my actions and how respecting others will allow me to also respect myself*
Paying restitution	*While I need this money that I must take from my paycheck each month, I acknowledge that my criminal actions resulted in damage to someone else and I must take the responsibility to pay them back so that I can look myself in the mirror and not be ashamed*
Doing community service	*Having to do 100 hours of community service seems unfair but when I think about it I am actually serving my community, the community that I harmed, by committing a crime against one of its members; I will make sure that my community service is meaningful to me and to the people that I am helping and giving back to*
Going on a prison tour	*I hated having to do this but after going I realize how important it was to see the result of the path in which I was heading if I continued in my criminal behavior*
Completing treatment	*This seemed like such a waste of time and they kept insisting on getting an assessment and a treatment plan; even though I hated doing it I appreciate their persistence because my addiction was actually a big part of my life that was holding me back from getting on the right track*

In the End: Why Are We Here?

The informal structure of the reparative board process allows board members to challenge offenders to think beyond the immediate consequences of their criminal offending in order to recognize the various impacts that their offense has not only on their victim but also the victim's family as well as their own family and the community surrounding them.[24] This also allows for flexibility in the interaction between board members and offenders and creates the ability to devise strategies that are tailored to the particular needs and circumstances of offenders.

In this context, board members encourage, challenge, reprimand, and provide assistance to offenders while holding them accountable throughout their period of supervision. Their immediate goal is to help the offender understand and learn about the impact of crime on victims and the community. By gaining a clear understanding and an empathetic view of the dynamics of offending and victimization, the offender will be in a better position to genuinely experience remorse and willingly take measures to restore and make whole the victim of the crime as well as make amends to the community.[25] Moreover, the reparative board process is also set up to help offenders learn ways to avoid reoffending in the future. The open dialog that occurs between board members and offenders allows for the development of a relationship of trust and respect, which opens the door for the learning process to emerge and flourish. While the offender is continuously reminded that they are under formal supervision and that their behavior has formal consequences which can have a long-term impact on their future in terms of being formally labeled as a criminal offender, they are also reminded that this program is built on the role of volunteers from the community who genuinely care about them and have a vested interest in their success. This indeed is the ultimate goal of the reparative board process and is highlighted in Box 8.2.

Box 8.2: Restorative Justice in Action—

Reflections from Restorative Justice Board Members

The following excerpt is taken from the journal of a criminal justice student doing an independent study on restorative justice reparative boards:

My knowledge and understanding of the restorative justice process has been profoundly influenced by my research into the volunteer role of citizen reparative boards in the process of supervising participating offenders. As I continue with my research, my work is significantly enriched by the opportunity to gain a better overview of the reparative board process through a qualitative dialog between myself and several board members. Through this dialog, I have come to the following shared meaning of the act of reparation and restoration that can take place during board meetings:

- Restorative justice board members are volunteer citizens who truly care about the welfare of the clients that come before them. This is the motivation for their continued participation every month and for taking the time to experience this process in action and see the benefits of its outcome

- There is a genuine concern to see that this type of program continues within the community as a chance for first-time offenders to gain forgiveness and avoid a felony label and its potential for social obstacles

- Board members see their participation as integral to helping probationers get the support they need to navigate their period of supervision and see them succeed by not only meeting their court-ordered obligations but by also transforming into law-abiding citizens that feel remorse, and truly appreciate this opportunity for repairing their lives

- One aspect of participation that board members mention as fulfilling is their supportive role in complementing formal probation supervision by acting as an additional collateral contact and source of accountability to offenders

- The reparative board process allows criminal justice intervention to take on a human approach, where offenders are seen as human beings, bridging the divide between community and law enforcement and avoiding the pitfalls of labeling, stereotyping, and making assumptions about people

- The restorative part of this process is epitomized by the emotional aspect of the client-board member continuum of interaction and dialog; the exchanges that occur bring to the table a plethora of feelings that would otherwise be suppressed or completely absent from formal criminal justice interventions where there is no room for sadness, frustration, anger, resentment, pride, sympathy, and compassion

Source: Hass, Natalie. (2017). Interview with Greene County Restorative Justice Board Members. Reflection journal prepared for independent study research paper, Department of Criminology and Criminal Justice, Missouri State University.

Evaluating Reparative Boards

When considering the successful implementation of the reparative board model, programmatic evaluation in the research literature has been quite scant. Nevertheless, we can rely on the degree to which the structure and design of reparative boards align with the core principles of good restorative justice practice. There are three core principles of restorative justice practice that are very often used as benchmarks for measuring success in program design and implementation.[26] These core principles can be divided into three key dimensions: repairing harm, encouraging dialog between stakeholders, and transforming the role of community and government.

Repairing the Harm

In a very direct and precise way, this core value of good restorative justice practice forms the basis of the reparative board process. The role of community members in the various encounters that take place between them and the offenders that appear on their board is to instill a strong sense of accountability whereby the offender is compelled to make amends for the harm done to the victim and the community. This is seen as a critical step for the offender to accept responsibility for their actions, stop making excuses, and begin taking steps that will change their way of thinking and acting. Repairing harm takes on a new meaning in the context of the restorative justice reparative board setting. The one-on-one meeting that takes place between an offender and a formal supervision officer is enhanced by the collective accountability that is produced when an offender comes before an entire group of individuals who share in a common sentiment and expectation and will not entertain making excuses and the lack of progress.

By holding offenders accountable for their actions, board members focus on making sure that the offender completes their obligation to pay back any financial loss to the victim. Moreover, they emphasize to the offender that their actions also impacted the community in which they live and that they are obligated to restore the loss experienced by that community through their community service hours. This in turn transforms community service from being a mere punishment to one of repairing harm that was done, whereby the offender can see their service to the community as a way of using their time and energy as well as their talents to restore the loss that was caused by their criminal behavior.[27] Community service hours are tracked and verified for accuracy each month, and board members will hold offenders accountable for their goals in completing community service.

Moreover, board members monitor and verify restitution payments as set by the court at each board meeting. Offenders are continuously reminded of their need for compliance and board members ensure that any lack of compliance is accompanied by a warning for some type of sanction but also by an effort to teach and remind offenders the importance of accepting responsibility for their actions and the need for them to repair the harm and damage done to the victim by their crime and their obligation to correct the loss.

Encouraging Dialog between Stakeholders

The reparative board program is designed and implemented with community stakeholders in mind. The use of a community reparative board as an integral part of the offender's supervision epitomizes the development of encounters that allow offenders to come face to face with volunteer members of the community in order to develop a shared understanding of the impact of crime. In doing this, ordinary citizens participating in the reparative board process are provided with the unique opportunity to have a direct impact on the offender by instilling within them a sense of disapproval and shaming that is derived from their authoritative capacity while at the same time showing them the care and acceptance that is derived from mutual respect and responsibility.

The reparative board program therefore provides members of the community with education and training in the restorative justice process and thereby equips them to play a significant role in monitoring the supervision of an offender and their progress in meeting certain established goals.[28] The structure of the meetings convened encourages dialog between offenders, board members, as well as the probation officer who oversees the program, in order to address the needs of offenders, identify any deficits they might be experiencing, encourage compliance, and provide positive feedback when tasks are completed in a timely manner.

Transforming the Role of Community and Government

Very often within the context of restorative justice, we use the word transformation, implying a complete change and conversion of roles that challenge traditional mechanisms of justice, law, and order. We use this word because the essential elements of restorative practices rely on the support and cooperation of officials and leaders within the justice system to ensure the proper implementation of programs and practices. The participation of community members on reparative boards as key decision-makers in the restorative justice process reflects this ideology of transformation. A major emphasis in the reparative board process is to place responsibility on board members in making judgments and decisions in holding offenders accountable for their actions.

Within this process, offenders are often required to engage in writing assignments where they are to reflect on such concepts as remorse and respect. These writing assignments or reflection journals are submitted to board members for discussion and approval. While they are requirements for successful completion of the program, they are not mere requirements but are in fact learning exercises that create opportunities for dialog and discussion whereby the formal role of board members transcends enforcement and becomes one of educator, counselor, and concerned citizen.[29] Within this context, offenders are more likely to fully understand the wrongfulness of their behavior and not just put up a front to complete the program and avoid further penalties.

In a very direct and impactful way, we have seen throughout this chapter that restorative justice reparative boards are designed to give offenders the opportunity to fully understand the consequences of making criminal choices as well as ponder the potential impact of going down a path defined by a career in crime. Board members convey to offenders a sense of urgency. By communicating to offenders that this is their last chance at having their records wiped clean and being restored to the full privileges and advantages of citizenship and acceptance, the reparative board process represents the core value of restorative justice theory and practice. As a close to this chapter, we leave you with the reflections of researchers on the design and implementation of the Greene County, MO, Restorative Justice Program reparative board process (see Box 8.3).

Box 8.3: Research in Restorative Justice —
Forgiveness, Repair, and Healing in Greene County, MO

An examination of the program design and implementation of the Greene County Restorative Justice Program reveals that there is a clear linkage between restorative justice principles as set forth by Bazemore and Schiff's core principles of good restorative justice practice. At the heart of Missouri's Restorative Justice Program in Greene County is a collaborative approach that emphasizes the strengthening of informal networks of social control. The core principles of repairing harm, involving stakeholders, and transforming the role of community and government are put into practice by enhancing the availability of community resources to offenders in repairing the harm caused by their crime and accepting responsibility for their actions. A major component of this program emphasizes the need for a genuine transformation in attitude and value system of offenders as a necessary step in the direction of law-abiding behavior and community reintegration.

An ideological component of restorative justice focuses on granting offenders the opportunity for mercy in exchange for their acceptance of responsibility and their willingness to participate in rehabilitation and restitution programs. Thus, the mercy granted is conditional upon the fulfillment of those contractual obligations set forth in the restorative justice agreement. Offenders who are referred to Greene County Restorative Justice are provided with various opportunities to participate in programs and services that are designed to divert them away from traditional juvenile and criminal justice systems. The goal of is not to police the behavior of offenders, but rather to hold them accountable, encourage compliance with supervision and treatment requirements, and empower them in their ability to achieve successful reintegration.

The concept of **conditional mercy** is communicated to offenders by board members at every opportunity, especially when signs of setback, failure, and non-compliance begin to emerge. Offenders are continuously reminded of the ominous outcome of their failure to take advantage of the opportunity to participate in the restorative justice process and avoid formal prosecution. The goal is not to threaten offenders with imminent punishment, but rather to show them the ability of the board to impose sanctions and recommend their termination from the program, and the choice to exercise leniency, based on their attitude and behavior.

The design and operation of the restorative justice program in Greene County is therefore consistent with the theoretical claim that formal intervention of the criminal justice system stigmatizes individuals by imposing upon them a permanent deviant label, criminal, further separating them from society and hindering their steps towards positive reintegration. Efforts are therefore geared towards this goal, with various opportunities for offenders to comply with the program requirements of restorative justice, receive treatment services that are needed, participate in conflict resolution, attend resume building/job placement fairs, enhance their money management skills, and develop a better understanding of the interactive role between the offender, victim, and community in achieving restorative justice.

Source: Hass, A. Y., & Saxon, C. E. (2012). From the inside/out: Greene county jail inmates on restorative reentry. *International Journal of Offender Therapy and Comparative Criminology*, 56(7), 1037–1062.

Chapter Summary

Where did the concept of reparative boards originate?

Community reparative boards were first implemented in the state of Vermont in 1995. They emerged mainly in response to rapidly rising rates of incarceration throughout the state. The goal and design of the Vermont model of restorative justice developed around a need to address crime victims and the harm they experienced while at the same time encouraging offenders to take responsibility in repairing this harm and involving communities in this process of restoration.

What are the basic elements of this restorative justice component?

Restorative justice reparative boards are built on the concept of citizen engagement and therefore involving members of the community in the administration of justice is the key component of their operation. Typically, a community justice reparative board is comprised of a small group of citizen volunteers that are recruited from a variety of avenues within the community. Board meetings are usually held once a month and consist of face-to-face meetings that vary in length with offenders who have been referred to participate in a restorative justice program. The meetings are designed to discuss with offenders the conditions and obligations of their sentencing agreement as well as review their monthly progress and compliance. A caseload supervisor is also present at the meetings, engages in the dialog when necessary, and coordinates the various components of the offender's supervision plan and restorative justice agreement.

How do reparative boards work?

Reparative board meetings are fairly informal and are usually held in a conference room where everyone sits in a circle around the table or some other set up which allows individuals to be facing one another in order to create dialog and build a relationship of mutual respect and trust. Offenders that are newly assigned to the board and are meeting board members for the first time begin with introductions and a brief description of the circumstances of their case. Board members also introduce themselves and begin to discuss with the offender the events that led up to their current involvement in this program as well as what they hope to get out of the experience. The voluntary role of board members is reiterated, and offenders are told that they are there to help them through the program and make sure that they stay on track and become successful. This dynamic helps to maintain the balance between gaining compliance and ensuring that offenders are held accountable, putting community reintegration at the heart of this program.

Is this restorative justice practice an effective approach?

An evaluation of the design and implementation of the reparative board process indicates that it aligns well with key dimensions of successful restorative justice programming. The various encounters that emerge between offenders and members of the reparative board encourage a strong sense of accountability whereby the offender takes on the responsibility of repairing the harm done to the victim and the community. Moreover, this type of program provides ordinary citizens with the unique opportunity to have a direct impact on offenders by imparting a sense of disapproval and shaming while at the same time showing care and acceptance. Moreover, by placing responsibility on board members to make judgments and decisions and holding offenders accountable for their actions, the restorative justice reparative board process reflects an ideology of transformation.

Key Terms

Standard Probation
Risk Management Probation
Reparative Probation
Community Justice
Conditional Mercy

Critical Thinking Questions

1. What aspects of the reparative board process do you find most intriguing? How do these aspects contribute to the successful implementation of this type of program within restorative justice?

2. How do you feel about becoming a citizen volunteer on a reparative board in your community? Would you be able to balance your role as an authority figure and also as a support mechanism for the offenders that appear before you? Why or why not?

3. Compare this type of restorative justice intervention with others that we have discussed. Do you find that there are strengths to this approach over others? Are there weaknesses?

References

1. Center for Justice and Reconciliation. Retrieved from http://restorativejustice.org/.

2. Restorative justice. Vermont Department of Corrections. Retrieved from http://doc.vermont.gov/justice/restorative-justice.

3. Humphrey, J. A., Burford, G., & Huey, M. P. *Reparative versus standard probation: Community justice outcomes*. Retrieved from http://www.doc.state.vt.us/about/reports/reparative-v-probation/view?searchterm=PROBATION.

4. Ibid.

5. Szabo, A. (2016, June). Bringing justice back into the community: The case of Vermont, US. Presentation at the 9th international conference of the European Forum for Restorative Justice, Realising restorative justice: Human rights and personal realities. Leiden, Netherlands, 24th June 2016; *Community justice*. (n.d.). Vermont Department of Corrections. Retrieved from http://doc.vermont.gov/justice.

6. *Restorative justice panels*. (n.d.). Burlington Community Justice Center, City of Burlington, Vermont. Retrieved from https://www.burlingtonvt.gov/CJC/Restorative-Justice-Panels/.

7. *Community Restorative Boards*. National Institute of Justice. Office of Justice programs. Retrieved from https://www.nij.gov/topics/courts/restorative-justice/promising-practices/pages/community-restorative-boards.aspx.

8. *Promising Practices in Restorative Justice*. National Institute of Justice. Office of Justice programs. Retrieved from https://www.nij.gov/topics/courts/restorative-justice/promising-practices/pages/community-restorative-boards.aspx.

9. Evans, C. B., Smokowski, P. R., Barbee, J., Bower, M., & Barefoot, S. (2016). Restorative justice programming in teen court: A path to improved interpersonal relationships and psychological functioning for high-risk rural youth. *Journal of Rural Mental Health*, 40(1), 15.

10. Kohm, L. M., & Haefner, A. R. (2016). Empowering love and respect for child offenders through therapeutic jurisprudence: The teen courts example. *Sociology and Anthropology*, 4(4): 212–221.

11. Rossner, M., & Bruce, J. (2016). Community participation in restorative justice: Rituals, reintegration, and quasi-professionalization. *Victims & Offenders*, 11(1), 107–125.

12. Crocker, D. (2016). Balancing justice goals: Restorative justice practitioners' views. *Contemporary Justice Review*, 19(4), 462–478.

13. Hoyle, C., & Rosenblatt, F. F. (2016). Looking back to the future: Threats to the success of restorative justice in the United Kingdom. *Victims & Offenders*, 11(1), 30–49.

14. Knox, C., & Quirk, P. (2016). Community restorative justice. In *Public policy, philanthropy and peacebuilding in Northern Ireland* (pp. 151–181). Palgrave Macmillan UK.

15. Szabo, A. (2016, June). Bringing justice back into the community: The case of Vermont, US. Presentation at the 9th international conference of the European Forum for Restorative Justice, Realising restorative justice: Human rights and personal realities. Leiden, Netherlands, 24th June 2016.

16. Clear, T. R., & Karp, D. R. (1998.) The community justice movement. In D. R. Karp (Ed.), Community justice: An emerging field (pp. 3–30). Lanham, MD: Rowman and Littlefield Press.

17. Harbin, A., & Llewellyn, J. (2016). Restorative justice in transitions: The problem of "the community" and collective responsibility. In K. Clamp (Ed.), *Restorative justice in transitional settings* (pp. 133–151). Routledge.

18. This dialogue was transcribed from a restorative justice board meeting in Greene County, Missouri.

19. Hipple, N. K., Duwe, G., & Northcutt Bohmert, M. (2016). Evaluating restorative justice circles of support and accountability (COSA): Can social support overcome structural barriers? *International Journal of Offender Therapy and Comparative Criminology*, 62(3), 739–758.

20. Maruna, S., & LeBel, T. P. (2015). 5 Strengths-based restorative approaches to reentry. *Positive Criminology*, 23, 65.

21. Hannem, S. (2013). Experiences in reconciling risk management and restorative justice: How circles of support and accountability work restoratively in the risk society. *International Journal of*

Offender Therapy and Comparative Criminology, 57(3), 269–288.

22. Ward, T., Fox, K. J., & Garber, M. (2014). Restorative justice, offender rehabilitation and desistance. *Restorative Justice, 2*(1), 24–42.

23. Kaufman, A. (2016). Restorative justice: New ways to look at old ideas. *Can. L. Libr. Rev., 41,* 12.

24. Bazemore, G., & Schiff, M. (2015). *Restorative community justice: Repairing harm and transforming communities.* Routledge.

25. Hass, A. Y., & Lucas, S. (2013). The impact of the Greene County Juvenile Justice VIP (Victim Impact Panel) on offender development of remorse and empathy. *Psychology Research, 3*(9), 529.

26. Bazemore, G., & Schiff, M. (2003). *Juvenile justice reform and restorative justice: Building theory and policy from practice.* Portland, OR: Willan Publishing.

27. Wood, W. R. (2015). Soliciting community involvement and support for restorative justice through community service. *Criminal Justice Policy Review, 26*(2), 131–155.

28. Johnstone, G. (2013). *Restorative justice: Ideas, values, debates.* Routledge.

29. Hass, A. Y., & Saxon, C. E. (2012). From the inside/out: Greene County jail inmates on restorative reentry. *International Journal of Offender Therapy and Comparative Criminology, 56*(7), 1037–1062.

Section Three

Restorative Justice in Various Contexts

In the previous section, we examined the five core models most frequently associated with restorative practice: victim-offender dialogs or mediations, family group conferences, victim impact panels, peacemaking circles, and reparative boards. As we move into our next section, we will be exploring ways in which restorative justice and restorative practices are implemented within specific systems, agencies, organizations, and movements.

Our coverage of the implementation of restorative practices will include all levels of the juvenile and criminal justice systems, including policing, courts, probation, prison, and prisoner reentry. After examining common ways of implementing a restorative approach to juvenile and criminal justice, we will also examine the possibilities of using restorative practices in cases involving special victims, such as sexual crimes, bias crimes, and abuse.

We will also step outside the bounds of juvenile and criminal justice by exploring the ways in which restorative practices are used in schools to address conflict, prevent crime, and address various problems. Lastly, we will examine the utilization of restorative principles and practices in transitional justice movements to address mass violence and community rebuilding.

Chapter 9

Restorative Justice in Policing and the Courts

In this chapter, we will explore the following questions ...

• *What is the difference between the juvenile and criminal justice systems, and how does restorative justice connect to them?*

• *In what ways can restorative justice function within a policing or law enforcement agency?*

• *In what ways can restorative justice function within a juvenile, criminal, or tribal court?*

Restorative Justice, Juvenile Justice, and Criminal Justice

Now that we have examined what restorative justice is, as well as the processes by which it is most commonly implemented, it is time for us to begin taking a closer look at the ways in which restorative justice is applied in specific contexts such as policing, the courts, criminal justice agencies, and even prisons. As we learned in Chapters 4–8, there are essentially five core processes that we associate with restorative justice: victim-offender mediations and dialogs, family group conferences, victim impact panels, peacemaking circles, and reparative boards. As we have seen, each of these five models can be easily adapted when communities create a restorative justice program or process that works with their particular needs and available resources. In this light, it is clear that restorative justice is not necessarily defined by these five models but is instead the application of restorative values and principles to a community's shared response to crime or conflict. Due to the fact that restorative justice is most aptly described as an approach to justice rather than a specific program, model, or system, we continue to see it applied in new and different ways within, alongside, and outside of the juvenile and criminal justice systems.

As illustrated by Figures 9.1 and 9.2, though they share many of the same elements and processes, the juvenile justice system and the criminal justice system are not the same thing. Since 1899, when the first juvenile court was established in Illinois, it has been common practice in the U.S. to separate juvenile offenders and adult offenders.[1] In light of this, not only is the juvenile justice system operated separately from the adult criminal justice system, but we tend to refer to criminal acts committed by juveniles as acts of delinquency rather than crimes, and instead of holding a juvenile in jail or prison we refer to juvenile correctional institutions by a variety of terms such as juvenile detention centers, residential placements, and residential treatment centers.[2]

Though these two systems are distinct from one another, restorative processes relate to each one in similar ways. In fact, when we study the ways in which individual restorative processes connect to formal systems of justice we see that they are often implemented in one of three ways: they function to divert cases away from these systems (diversion), they are incorporated into the systems themselves (incorporation), or they operate parallel to the systems (parallelism). Let's explore each of these in more detail.

Diversion

In the context of juvenile and criminal justice, **diversion** is a term used to describe an effort to place low-risk offenders in community-based programs that can address their needs outside of the formal justice system and its agencies.[3] In other words, a diversion program can move an offender outside the scope of juvenile and criminal justice, which not only allows them to avoid labels such as "delinquent," "criminal," or "felon," but may also provide them with access to community-based resources that could better address issues related to their offense or problematic behavior (such as drug treatment or cognitive behavioral therapy).

Diversion can occur before adjudication, which means that the offender's case is never formally processed by the court; however, it can also occur after adjudication in order to keep an offender out of prison or shorten their time on probation. When an offender is diverted into a restorative justice program and participates in a process such as a victim-offender mediation or family group conference, this typically means that the offender and victim are in full control over the restorative process and reparation/action plan (if applicable). In other words, a juvenile or criminal justice agency is not necessarily supervising their involvement in the program or influencing potential outcomes. That being said, diversion programs are often set up to allow the juvenile or criminal justice system to pursue the offender's case should they fail to successfully complete the diversion program.

Incorporation

Instead of diverting an offender away from the juvenile or criminal justice system, restorative justice can also be directly incorporated into justice agencies or institutions (such as courts, probation, and prisons). **Incorporation** simply means that the juvenile or criminal justice system utilizes a restorative process such as a sentencing circle, reparative board, or victim impact panel as part of their formal response to the offense.

When a restorative process is used in this way the victim's involvement (if applicable) still remains voluntary; however, an offender may be ordered, or feel pressured, to participate. The juvenile or criminal justice system will also oversee the restorative process to some degree, meaning the process could be facilitated by someone working in the system, the system may impose guidelines concerning the reparation/action plan (if applicable), and the system will likely supervise the completion of the plan (possibly imposing sanctions if the offender fails to comply with it). Restorative processes that are incorporated in this way bring up important questions about whether or not restorative justice can be effective if offenders feel coerced to participate from fear of sanctions or other punitive alternatives. If a restorative process is facilitated by someone working within the system (such as a police officer or probation officer) it can also bring up questions about whether or not the community is sufficiently included in the process which, as we know from Chapter 1, is an important aspect of restorative justice.

Parallelism

Sometimes restorative justice works alongside the juvenile or criminal justice system without diverting an offender out of the system or becoming part of the system itself. We refer to this as **parallelism**, meaning the restorative process occurs while an offender is involved in the juvenile or criminal justice system, but it is facilitated by a person or organization outside of that system and is completely voluntary. An example might be a victim impact panel that occurs within a prison but is organized by a community-based organization. While inmates could be invited to participate in this restorative program, their participation or lack of participation would in no way impact their court-imposed sentence. A community-based organization could also offer to organize family group conferences for juveniles on probation while ensuring that the conferences are simply an available resource and not something a juvenile or family is required to engage in.

Restorative Justice and Justice Systems

In the chapters ahead, we will be taking a closer look at how restorative justice works in relation to juvenile and criminal justice systems, including a fuller exploration of restorative justice within policing, the courts, probation, and correctional institutions. While we don't believe you need to be an expert on these systems in order to explore the ways in which restorative justice works within (or alongside) them, we do believe you should have at least a fundamental understanding of how these systems work. To help ensure that, we have created a basic flow chart for both the juvenile justice system and the criminal justice system within the United States, showing not only how offenders typically move through these systems but the points at which restorative justice is most commonly introduced (see Figures 9.1 and 9.2).

As seen in Figures 9.1 and 9.2, an offender can be referred to a restorative justice process at almost any point during, or in place of, their formal involvement with the justice system, making restorative processes and programs highly adaptable and easy to implement on a case-by-case basis throughout a community's various organizations

Figure 9.1: Restorative Justice and the Juvenile Justice System

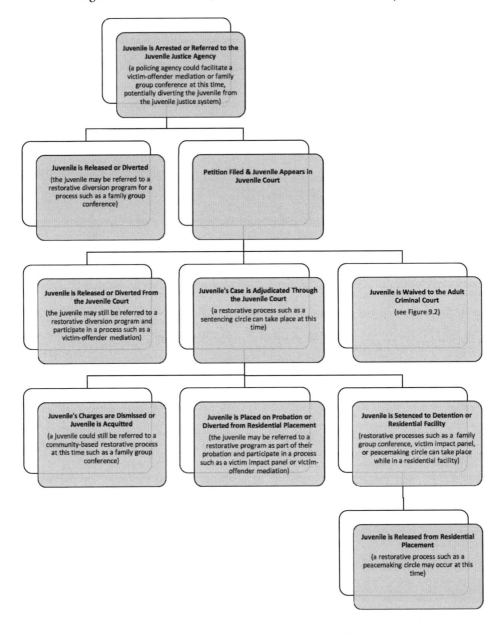

and agencies. One could argue, however, that this kind of intermittent implementation of restorative justice does little to transform the systems themselves. In other words, despite their occasional inclusion of restorative processes and programs, most juvenile and criminal justice systems remain rooted in retributive and rehabilitative values, which inevitably begs the question of whether or not a system or agency could be built upon restorative values and goals instead (see Box 9.1).

Figure 9.2: Restorative Justice and the Criminal Justice System

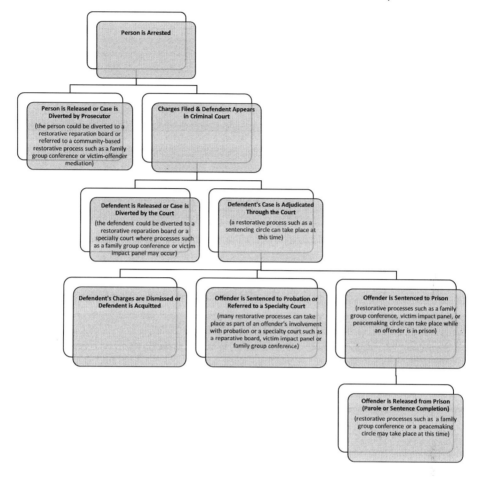

Box 9.1: Restorative Justice in Action—
Balanced and Restorative Justice Model

One example of implementing restorative justice systematically is the Balanced and Restorative Justice Project (BARJ). This project is a model for the implementation of restorative justice in local juvenile justice systems, but it was also formed to provide local agencies with the technical support and training needed to make them more restorative.

The BARJ Project was initiated in 1992 when the Office of Juvenile Justice and Delinquency Prevention contracted with Florida Atlantic University to help them expand their existing technical assistance program. As a result of this collaboration, the BARJ Project was created.

The BARJ model consists of three performance objectives or goals: competency development, community protection, and offender accountability. Each of these three goals are presented as equally important within the context of juvenile justice, making balanced attention to these three objectives essential to the model's efficacy and implementation.

- **Competency development** is rooted in the assertion that juvenile offenders should leave the juvenile justice system more capable of being responsible and productive members of society than when they entered the system.

- **Community protection** refers to the community's right to individual and collective safety from the threat of crime, delinquency, and violence.

- **Offender accountability** affirms that when a crime occurs, an offender becomes obligated to their victim, and so justice should include an effort to restore what victims have lost and make space for the direct involvement and input of victims in the justice process.

An essential part of the BARJ model is the equal investment in each of the core performance objectives listed above, giving juvenile justice systems and agencies a practical framework from which to begin a systemic shift towards restorative justice.

Source: Office of Juvenile Justice and Delinquency Prevention. (1995). Balanced and restorative justice: Program summary. Retrieved from https://www.ncjrs.gov/pdffiles/bal.pdf.

Restorative Systems, Institutions, and Agencies

As we begin to take a closer look at institutions and agencies related to juvenile and criminal justice, we will see that while restorative processes frequently work within these organizations and systems it is also possible for a system, institution, or agency to not only partner with restorative justice but become restorative itself. In other words, while restorative justice is rarely adopted systemically, it is certainly possible for an institution (such as a prison or school) or an agency (such as policing or probation) to construct its organizational culture upon restorative principles and processes in an effort to make restorative justice the guiding force behind its goals, policies, and practices. While experiments with this kind of restorative transformation are rare, there exists a growing body of literature devoted to describing both real-world attempts at this kind of systemic implementation, as well as the theoretical rationale behind how and why restorative justice could be implemented in this way.

Models for Restorative Systems

One such theorist is Daniel Van Ness, who has proposed four different models for a restorative system of justice, which he refers to as the "unified model," the "dual track model," the "safety net model," and the "hybrid model" (see Figure 9.3).[4] Ac-

Figure 9.3: Restorative Systems: The Four Models

Unified Model	Dual Track Model	Safety Net Model	Hybrid Model
Fully Restorative	Separate & Cooperative	Mostly Restorative	Integrated & Collaborative

Source: Adapted from Van Ness, D. W. (2002). The shape of things to come: A framework for thinking about a restorative justice system. In E. G. M. Weitekamp & H. Kerner (Eds.), *Restorative justice: Theoretical foundations* (pp. 1–20). Devon, UK: Willan Publishing.

cording to Van Ness, the "**unified model**" represents a system that is entirely restorative in its values, policies, and operations.[5] In other words, existing systems rooted in retribution and punishment would be completely replaced by a system guided by restorative principles and practices.

The "**dual track model**" supports two separate systems of justice that can work alongside one another and cooperate whenever possible.[6] This type of model recognizes that restorative justice may not be appropriate for all situations, victims, or offenders, and so two distinct pathways toward justice would exist and could overlap if needed.

As Van Ness describes it, the "**safety net model**" borrows from the first two models.[7] In other words, the system would be predominantly restorative in nature; however, alternatives would remain accessible if restorative justice failed to meet the needs or circumstances of a particular case or offender. In this kind of model, restorative justice is seen as the ideal track towards justice, but other options remain in place to act as a *safety net* or alternative if needed.

Lastly, the "**hybrid model**" refers to the integration of restorative justice within the conventional justice system. Unlike the "dual track model," restorative justice does not operate separately in the "hybrid model." In this model, restorative justice is fully incorporated within the conventional justice system, enhancing and expanding it but not existing as an alternative to it.[8]

Implementing a Restorative System

Regardless of what model a community or agency chooses, the literature is clear that implementing restorative justice systemically is much different than implementing a single restorative program or process. As Umbreit and Carey put it, "Each agency has different resources, assets, deficits, priorities, motivations, and system environments that require varying approaches to planning changes."[9] According to Mark Carey, when we attempt to reorganize a system or agency around restorative values and processes, the system or agency must mature through three distinct developmental

Figure 9.4: The Developmental Stages of Organizational Change

Infancy
- Training
- Staff Input & Feedback
- Action Planning
- Media/Marketing

Adolescence
- Changes to Staff Recruitment
- Changes to Evaluation Strategies
- Altering Mission Statement

Adulthood
- Adoption of New Routines & Practices
- Renew Excitement/Maintain Motivation

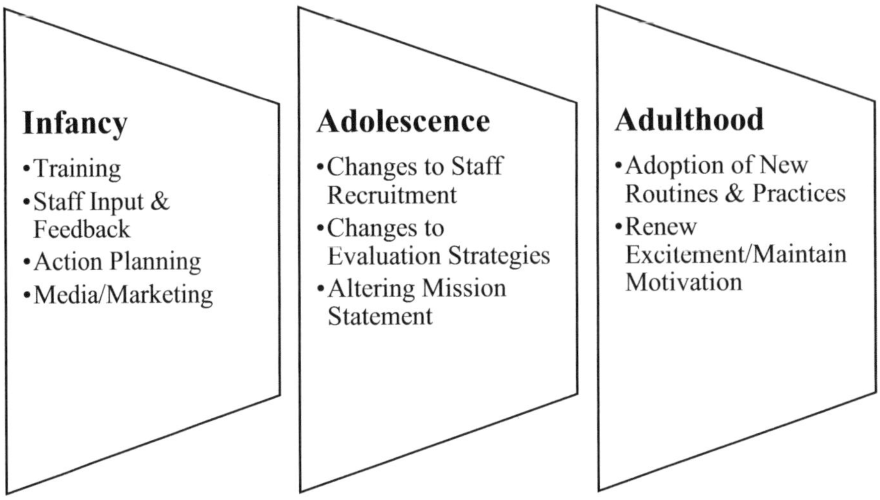

Source: Adapted from Carey, M. (2001). Infancy, adolescence, and restorative justice: Strategies for promoting organizational reform. In G. Bazemore & M. Schiff (Eds.), *Restorative community justice: Repairing harm and transforming communities* (pp. 151–169). Cincinnati, OH: Anderson Publishing.

stages that mirror human growth and development: infancy, adolescence, and adulthood (see Figure 9.4).[10]

In the "infancy" stage, energies are most focused on collecting input from personnel and generating excitement about organizational change within the system and the community.[11] In this stage, time and resources are typically devoted to training people in restorative justice and embedding their input and ideas into the reorganization process.[12]

After the initial implementation of restorative values, policies, and practices, it is common for a system or agency to experience some internal pushback or conflict regarding tensions between the old and new ways of doing things.[13] Problems might surface, fatigue might set in, and sometimes it is difficult to keep the momentum going towards restorative transformation. Carey refers to this as the "adolescence" stage.[14] Implementation can often fail in this stage; however, success is reflected in actions like the adoption of a new mission statement and changes in the recruitment and hiring processes.[15]

While it is rare for a system or agency to reach the "adulthood" stage, Carey asserts that this is the point at which the reorganization becomes more routinized.[16] Cultural and procedural changes become normal and restorative values and processes become more fully adopted within the system. At this stage, it is recommended that an agency focus time and resources on maintaining the professional staff's individual and collective motivation to remain a restorative organization while preventing problems such as complacency and stagnancy.[17]

Now that we have examined the ways in which restorative justice can connect to, interact with, and even transform the juvenile and criminal justice systems, we will focus the remainder of this chapter on two common entry points into a justice system: policing (also referred to as law enforcement) and the courts.

Restorative Justice and Policing

As shown in Figures 9.1 and 9.2, a person's entrance into either the juvenile or criminal justice system typically begins with some kind of interaction with law enforcement. In fact, police officers are often referred to as the "gatekeepers" of the criminal justice system, which essentially means that they are a person's first point of contact with the system and frequently decide who will enter it and who will not. While we typically associate restorative justice with processes that an offender (someone who has pled guilty to or been convicted of a criminal or delinquent offense) might participate in, the application of restorative justice to the realm of law enforcement is yet another way that restorative values and practices have influenced communities and systems of justice throughout the world.

As we examine the ways in which restorative justice connects to law enforcement we see that this occurs in essentially three ways: restorative processes can be embedded into traditional police work, a policing agency can be reorganized around restorative values and practices, and restorative processes can be used to address conflicts between a community and its law enforcement agency or officers. As we move forward, we will explore each of these in more detail while also identifying specific concerns and challenges that inevitably arise when we consider the concept of restorative policing.

Restorative Policing

According to Restorative Justice International (RJI), **restorative policing** is "a relational paradigm of policing that focuses on creating safer, more connected communities through restorative justice practices underpinned by restorative principles of safety, accountability, sustainability, relationship building and constructive engagement."[18] As you can see from this definition, policing from a restorative perspective is focused, in large part, on the building and maintaining of collective efficacy (see Chapter 7) and community engagement. Another thing we can take from this definition is that restorative policing is defined by the values that guide it and not necessarily by any one practice or implementation process. In this sense, much like restorative justice, restorative policing is best defined as an approach to policing rather than a prescriptive set of actions or strategies.

In the field of law enforcement different approaches to policing are often categorized as either proactive or reactive. In other words, should officers work to prevent crimes (proactive) or should they only act to address crimes that have already occurred (reactive)? As policing continues to evolve, we have seen a movement towards more proactive approaches to policing. While no one would argue against the notion that police officers need to respond to specific crimes when they occur, there is a growing sense that policing agencies should also devote time and resources to preventing crime and addressing problems through non-reactive community engagement. Perhaps the best-known example of this is **community-oriented policing**, which is an approach to law enforcement that seeks to unite police officers with the communities they serve in order to identify and address broader problems related to community safety and wellbeing (in addition to responding directly to specific acts of crime, harm, and conflict).[19] According to RJI, restorative policing can be both proactive and reactive.[20] In other words, a restorative policing agency could not only use restorative practices to actively promote and build collective efficacy within a community, but restorative practices could also be utilized when responding directly to incidents of harm or wrongdoing.[21]

The formal concept of restorative policing can be traced back to the early 1990s when the Wagga Wagga Police Department in southern Australia began facilitating family group conferences in order to address some forms of juvenile delinquency.[22] This particular process is now referred to as the **Wagga Wagga Model**, which essentially refers to the use of police-facilitated, restorative conferences to divert youthful offenders away from the formal court process. Since its initial use in Wagga Wagga, this model has been used and adapted in countries such as Canada and the U.S. to implement restorative justice within communities through local policing agencies.[23]

Embedding Restorative Processes in Police Work

As we see with the Wagga Wagga Model, one way that law enforcement agencies have of practicing restorative policing is by simply implementing a restorative approach in a very minimal and controlled way. For instance, while an agency practices a more traditional policing model, it could also begin addressing specific incidents with a restorative approach such as those involving juveniles or some instances of domestic violence (see Box 9.2 for an example). This kind of embedded approach to the implementation of restorative policing is where many agencies begin the process of exploring their own application of restorative justice.

Though no longer an active program, one example of this in the U.S. was the Woodbury Police Department in Minnesota.[24] In 1995, the Woodbury community launched the Restorative Community Conferencing Program, which sought to divert some juvenile offenders away from the juvenile court and address their cases through restorative processes such as family group conferences and victim-offender mediations.[25] Police officers were also trained to utilize the conference model while out in the field in what was called "**street diversion**."[26] In other words, rather than refer people to the restorative program in which a conference would be organized for a later date, officers were encouraged to facilitate on-the-spot conferences during a call for service if the situation seemed both amenable to the conferencing process and minor enough not to pursue through a formal conference or the court.[27]

Similar to the Woodbury conferencing process, we see the application of police-led restorative conferencing and "street diversion" in the concept of restorative cautioning, which is a term much more common in the United Kingdom than it is in the United States. **Cautioning** is a process used by policing agencies in countries such as England and Australia to divert some offenders away from the formal court process.[28] Though cautioning is not something we employ in the U.S., it is an example of a diversion process which, as we explored earlier, is a common strategy used in the U.S. and other countries to move offenders out of formal systems of justice and often spare them from socially disabling consequences such as conviction, labeling, and even imprisonment.

Though the term cautioning may cause many of us in the U.S. to think of a police warning (essentially, letting someone off the hook), cautioning, in this context, is a bit more serious than that. While police cautioning does keep a case from moving into the juvenile or criminal justice system, it can also require that the offender in the case complete certain conditions such as restitution or a letter of apology to the victim(s). Much like traditional cautioning, **restorative cautioning** also functions to divert the offender from the juvenile or criminal justice system but utilizes restorative processes such as a victim-offender mediation or family group conference to address the offense and arrive at the conditions of the caution. Unlike a traditional cautioning process, officers that facilitate a restorative caution must try to include those impacted by the offense into the process, making the inclusion of victims one of the main distinguishing factors between traditional cautioning and restorative cautioning.[29]

Box 9.2: Research in Restorative Justice—
The Bethlehem, PA, Restorative Policing Experiment

In an effort to determine the impact of restorative policing in the U.S. an experiment was conducted in Bethlehem, Pennsylvania, which is a relatively small city in the eastern part of the state. At the time of the experiment, Bethlehem's police department employed 140 officers and was already integrating community-oriented policing practices within the agency.

A diversion program was designed that targeted first-time juvenile offenders guilty of minor infractions such as misdemeanor theft, property damage, and simple assaults. The program was set up to allow juvenile offenders who qualified for the program to avoid formal adjudication through the court and instead have their case resolved through a police-led family group conference that included the offender, the victim, and other relevant family and community members.

In order to better measure the impact of the program, cases that qualified for diversion were randomly placed into one of two groups: the treatment group or the control group. Cases in the treatment group were processed through the police-led restorative justice program; however, cases in the control group were adjudicated through the court.

Over the course of the experiment, which lasted about a year and a half, researchers generated data in three ways: they observed most of the family group conferences, they surveyed police officers before and after the experiment, and they surveyed the victims, offenders, and the offenders' parents for all of the cases (those in the treatment group and the control group).

The results of the experiment showed that restorative policing did have a positive impact in Bethlehem. The officers who facilitated the family group conferences left the experiment feeling more inclined towards problem-solving and community-oriented policing practices and less inclined towards use of force. Victims who participated in the restorative justice program felt a higher rate of satisfaction than victims in the control group, and offenders in the diversion program were more motivated to complete reparative conditions/agreements such as community service and restitution.

While any program can be evaluated, experiments like the one conducted in Bethlehem allow us to directly compare outcomes within a program and outside of a program within a single setting or population. While we cannot necessarily assume that the results from this experiment would occur in any community in which we implemented restorative policing, the Bethlehem experiment gives us a glimpse into how restorative policing could be used to transform a policing agency and positively impact a community.

Source: McCold, P. (2003). An experiment in police-based restorative justice: The Bethlehem (PA) project. *Police Practice and Research*, 4(4), 379–390.

Restorative Policing Agencies

As we discussed earlier, just because a restorative process is incorporated within a justice system does not mean that the system itself becomes restorative. Similarly, just because a law enforcement agency adopts a restorative diversion program does not mean that the entire agency is restorative. The systemic transformation of a law enforcement agency that seeks to fully implement restorative policing is a process that requires time, extensive training, and a deep commitment on behalf of the agency and the community it serves.

According to Colleen McLeod, a restorative policing agency not only roots its mission, policies, and practices in restorative values, but it is characterized by elements such as high levels of community involvement, transparency, and open communication.[30] Unlike traditional policing agencies, which are typically structured around a rigid hierarchy of command, a restorative policing agency follows a flatter organizational model, resulting in fewer levels of management and a less centralized process of decision making.[31]

Figure 9.5: The Four Tracks of Implementing Restorative Policing and Agency Reform

Legislation/ Policy
guide implementation through clear legislation and/or policy

Organization/Agency
attend to the agency's structural and cultural transformation

Individual Officers
give officers direct experiences with restorative processes

Community
involve the community in restorative processes

Source: Adapted from Bazemore, G., & Griffiths, C. (2003). Police reform, restorative justice and restorative policing. *Police Practice and Research*, 4(4), 335–346.

Even if a policing agency and its officers are receptive to the concept of restorative policing, a lot can go wrong when trying to implement sustainable organizational reform. In response to common implementation issues which they identified through case studies, research literature, and their personal observations, Gordon Bazemore and Curt Griffiths recommend that an agency focus on four distinct areas when moving towards a restorative policing model.[32] These include legislation/policy, the organization/agency, the individual officers, and the community.[33]

As illustrated in Figure 9.5, Bazemore and Griffiths observed that when agencies succeed in implementing restorative policing they are typically supported by clear policy and/or legislation.[34] Not only does funding for training and implementation often accompany legislation, but a policy or legislative change can also give the agency's officers and the community a greater sense of the implementation's legitimacy and permanency.

As we often see in the realm of criminal justice, however, policy and practice don't always align. In other words, just because a community or agency mandates a shift to restorative policing does not mean the transition will succeed; the implementation will likely fail unless attention is paid to changing the agency's culture and structure. When implementing restorative policing throughout a law enforcement agency, Bazemore and Griffiths assert that not only do structural elements (such as job descriptions and roles) need to adapt to restorative values, but the agency's culture and practices need to consistently emphasize restorative principles (such as inclusion, community engagement, and participatory decision making).[35]

The final two areas to focus on when implementing restorative policing and agency reform tie into the idea that restorative policing will inevitably fail if it is not fully understood and embraced by the people most impacted by it. According to Bazemore and Griffiths, police officers who have worked within a more traditional policing model need to experience a personal conversion towards the process and goals of restorative policing, and this is best facilitated by giving them direct, personal experiences with restorative justice.[36] Research shows that officers' attitudes and practices are more likely to move towards the values and principles of restorative policing if they directly engage in a restorative process by facilitating a family group conference or victim-offender mediation.[37] This affirms that personal experiences with restorative processes are often needed to solidify training and convince individual officers that restorative policing can have successful outcomes while also maintaining officer and community safety.

Similarly, Bazemore and Griffiths state that the community must also be given the chance to directly participate in restorative processes and observe restorative policing in action.[38] As much as possible this participation needs to include community involvement in the organization and facilitation of restorative processes (such as peacemaking circles or family group conferences), and not be limited strictly to the roles of victim or offender.[39] In other words, in order for the broader community to embrace restorative policing, members need the chance to be directly involved in restorative processes and programs even if they are not personally involved in an offense.

Addressing Citizens' Complaints Restoratively

Another way in which we see restorative principles and values being applied within the realm of law enforcement is through the use of mediation to address citizen complaints against police officers and policing agencies. Trust between a community and its police force is vitally important. Not only is it important that community members feel safe with law enforcement officers, but a police force can do very little in a community if the citizens don't support the agency by reporting crimes, providing officers with critical information, and giving witness testimony in court. While law enforcement professionals do a lot to make a community safer, it is the cooperative bond between an agency and the community that leads to effective law enforcement.

Typically when a member of the community files a complaint against a police officer the issue is investigated either internally through an agency's department of internal affairs or externally by a citizen review board.[40] These options, however, can often leave both citizens and officers dissatisfied by both the process and its outcomes.[41] While citizens can often be concerned that an internal investigation will favor the officer, officers sometimes worry that external investigators will give undue weight to trivial complaints or fail to understand the situation from their perspective.[42]

The use of mediation to address citizen complaints against police officers and agencies has shown that, in some cases, a more restorative approach to these issues can increase participants' satisfaction with the process.[43] Moreover, there is also evidence to suggest that participants' satisfaction with these kinds of mediations can increase even more when the citizen complainant is Hispanic or African American.[44]

Though citizen-police mediations are typically facilitated by a professional mediator in a neutral setting,[45] it is important to note that a mediation in this context is quite different than a victim-offender mediation (see Chapter 4). As the name would suggest, a victim-offender mediation requires that there be a clear victim and a clear offender. In mediations used to address citizen complaints against the police, however, these roles are not as clearly defined.[46] The outcomes can also differ. While a victim-offender mediation will typically conclude with the offender agreeing to perform specific tasks in order to repair the harm they have done to the victim(s) and the community, the main goal of citizen-police mediations is to discuss the incident and increase understanding among all of the parties. This is one reason why citizen-police mediation programs typically focus on complaints concerning nonviolent police conduct and not necessarily on questions of severe misconduct or violent use of force.[47]

Critiques and Concerns

The use of citizen-police mediations and police-based restorative diversion programs does come with a certain amount of controversy. While diversion is frequently seen as a valuable way to unclog juvenile and criminal courts while also keeping some offenders from being unnecessarily detained or supervised, it also leads to questions and concerns regarding net-widening. **Net-widening** refers to the theory that when we implement a new process or practice in the field of criminal justice it can sometimes result in more people coming into contact with the justice system than before the new practice was implemented.[48] For example, if a police officer has the option of referring an offender to a restorative diversion program for a police-led family group conference, the officer might begin moving cases to that program that she would otherwise not pursue. Therefore, there is some concern that while police-based diversion programs can transfer some cases out of the justice system, they can also bring some people into the program that police officers would otherwise leave with a simple warning and perhaps a list of community-based resources.

Another concern regarding police-based diversion programs is that they inevitably give more power and discretion to the police with very little supervision and oversight.[49] Some argue that law enforcement should stay within the bounds of simply enforcing the law and allow the courts to do their job of determining culpability and sentencing. One fear is that some offenders may agree to a process like restorative cautioning or a family group conference out of deference to police authority or fear of harsher sanctions from the court. As is always the case when we discuss discretion in criminal justice, there is also the fear that increased police discretion could lead to more severe disparities concerning factors such as race and gender identity in the juvenile and criminal justice systems. In other words, who gets to decide who does a family group conference and who goes to court? Some contend that putting this decision into the hands of law enforcement could further degrade a community's sense that the criminal justice system is fair.

In regard to using mediation to address citizen complaints against the police, there is some concern that processes like mediation can serve to minimize what should be serious matters. Despite empirical evidence that it often results in higher rates of participant satisfaction,[50] some argue that mediation could be used to silence and disenfranchise citizens and should therefore only be used in conjunction with an investigatory process led by an individual or entity empowered to make decisions and impose formal consequences.

Taking into account all of the concerns about restorative policing, communities and agencies continue to seek new ways of defining police work, building trust and cooperation between citizens and officers, and creating strategies to increase collective efficacy and strengthen community bonds. While restorative policing practices are far from perfect, and often fail to be implemented in a sustainable way, efforts to make policing more inclusive, transparent, and collaborative are an important way that restorative justice is continuing to expand its reach throughout the world.

Restorative Justice and the Courts

While different countries structure their courts in different ways, the U.S. employs a **dual court system** that grants jurisdiction to either state or federal courts based on what type of case needs to be heard and, in regard to the criminal justice system, what law has been breached.[51] Juvenile and family courts are situated within the state court system, in addition to various types of civil courts. Certain Native American reservations and tribal communities also operate **tribal courts** which can, to a varying degree, claim jurisdiction over certain crimes if they are committed on tribal land and involve a member of the tribe.[52]

When we examine the ways in which restorative justice functions within the courts, three distinct patterns emerge from the literature. The first is peacemaking courts (or peacemaking ceremonies) used within Native American tribal courts. The second is the use of peacemaking circles, specifically sentencing circles, within juvenile and criminal courts. And the third is the use of restorative processes, such as family group conferences or victim impact panels, in specialty courts (often referred to as problem-solving courts or treatment courts). Let's explore each of these in more detail.

Peacemaking Courts

While the process itself can vary, peacemaking ceremonies are common within aboriginal groups and Native American tribes to address issues such as conflict, crime, and violence.[53] Though the term *peacemaking court* is not necessarily applied to every aboriginal peacemaking ceremony, it can be used to describe the use of such a process within the context of a tribal court.[54]

One such process is the **Navajo Nation Peacemaking Court** (also referred to as the Navajo Nation Peacemaking Program), which is heavily rooted in the tribe's culture, spirituality, and values. As seen in Figure 9.6, there are four different types of participants in the Navajo peacemaking process: the peacemaker, the decision-makers,

Figure 9.6: Navajo Peacemaking Participants

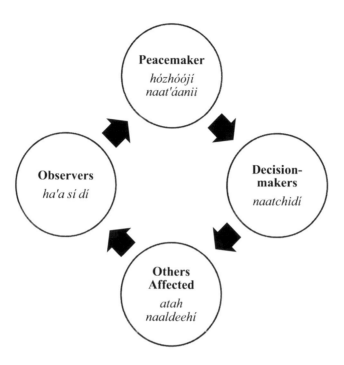

Source: Adapted from The Peacemaking Program of the Judicial Branch of the Navajo Nation. (2013). *Plan of operations.* Retrieved from http://www.navajocourts.org/Peacemaking/Plan/PPPO2013-2-25. pdf.

others impacted by the conflict or harm, and community observers.[55] The peacemaker, or *hózhóójí naat'áanii*, is typically a tribal elder whose job is to move the participants toward harmony and reconciliation.[56] Their role is one of healer, tasked with purifying the participants, affirming their connection to the community and their deities, and eliminating the evil forces at the root of the conflict or harm.[57]

The decision-makers, or *naatchidí*, are the community members who are most directly impacted by the conflict and who will have the task of deciding what will be done in order to repair the harm and restore harmony.[58] Other people, referred to as *atah naaldeehí*, are those who are personally connected to the *naatchidí* and have been directly impacted by the conflict.[59] During the peacemaking ceremony, they are invited to contribute their knowledge and experiences regarding the conflict; however, they are not involved in the final decision-making process.[60] Lastly, there are observers, known as *ha'a sí dí*, who are invited to attend the peacemaking process but do not actively participate in the ceremony.[61]

The Navajo peacemaking ceremony can take approximately 4–6 hours to complete and can be divided into three stages.[62] The first is the opening prayer in which the peacemaker calls upon supernatural forces to help the group reach harmony and reconciliation.[63] Next the peacemaker moves into the diagnosis stage in which they identify the conflict and offer a relevant teaching in Navajo values.[64] Next, the plan is discussed, and participants determine how harmony can be restored while creating a consensual plan for reconciliation.[65] To conclude the process the peacemaker offers a closing prayer, signifying the end of the process and once again reinforcing the sacredness of the ceremony and the group.[66]

While U.S. courts are typically set up in an adversarial way, meaning parties are encouraged to argue in court and try to persuade judges and juries to declare their side the winner, the Navajo peacemaking court is designed to facilitate reconciliation, consensual decision making, and the direct participation of a community (including its norms, values, and spiritual traditions). Aboriginal approaches to justice and peacemaking can't help but encourage us to take a closer look at the role of religion and spirituality in restorative and community justice. In Box 9.3 we'll take a closer look at this question and ask ourselves if restorative processes are rooted in aboriginal peacemaking ceremonies (which they certainly are), are a community's spiritual traditions and teachings an important element in restorative justice?

Box 9.3: Restorative Justice: Let's Take a Closer Look ...
Does Spirituality Have a Place in Criminal Justice?

In an effort to distinguish restorative justice from the many ways in which it can be falsely categorized and misunderstood, Michael L. Hadley (2001) once wrote:

> Restorative Justice, with its principles of repentance, forgiveness, and reconciliation, is instead a deeply spiritual process. It is never the easy way out; neither for the offender, the victim, nor the community. It requires all of us to come to grips with who we are, what we have done, and what we can become in the fullness of our humanity (p. 9).

It is perhaps unsettling and strange for those of us living in the U.S. to consider justice as a "spiritual process." Even though justice is a common theme in all of the world's major religions and spiritual traditions, the value we place on both the freedom of religion and the separation of church and state have secularized our legal system to the point of presenting law as a violation of the state versus harm and wrongdoing towards a person or local community (Hadley, 2001). While there is certainly a place for restorative justice within a secular criminal justice system, Hadley (2001) and others would question the efficacy of a restorative process within a system that prizes punishment over reconciliation and representation over direct participation and inclusion.

As our glimpse into the Navajo peacemaking process illustrates, aboriginal approaches to justice do not seek to divorce justice from the spiritual traditions, rituals, and roles of a community. Quite the opposite. These things are fully embedded into the process and used to remind participants of what they have in common, as well as the ways in which they are connected.

So, what do you think? Is there a place for religious or spiritual practices within criminal justice? In other words, if we are convening a family group conference with a Muslim or Christian family, is it appropriate to allow them to open and close their conference with prayer? While we are rightfully suspicious of the idea of forcing participants to engage in a spiritual or religious process, what if the inclusion of religious or spiritual practices in the restorative justice process is important to the family or group involved? Do we allow it, and, as the Navajos would do, make it a central part of the process, or do we insist that it remain separate or excluded from the process altogether?

Sources: Hadley, M. L. (2001). Introduction: Multifaith reflection on criminal justice. In M. L. Hadley (Ed.), *The spiritual roots of restorative justice*. Albany, NY: State University of New York Press.

Peacemaking (Sentencing) Circles

As we discussed in Chapter 7, peacemaking circles are a group process that communities can easily adapt to their specific needs and cultural norms. Peacemaking circles can take many forms; however, the type of circle process that we typically find utilized within the courts is a sentencing circle. In a **sentencing circle**, the people impacted by an offense (including the offender, the victim, family, friends, community members, and criminal justice professionals) come together to discuss what happened and create a sentencing plan.[67] Sentencing circles can only take place if the offender has admitted their responsibility for the offense, and are a way for courts to proactively attempt to address the problems motivating an offense rather than simply impose punishment.[68] Sentencing circles are an excellent example of what happens when the tribal court peacemaking process is adapted into a U.S. court.[69] While the process naturally becomes more secularized, elements of aboriginal peacemaking such as inclusion, group problem solving, and consensus decision making are, inarguably, critical parts of the sentencing circle process.

Specialty Courts

One way in which we have seen U.S. courts move toward a problem-solving approach versus a retributive one is through the use of specialty courts. **Specialty courts** (also referred to as problem-solving courts or treatment courts) are court programs that typically target one type of offender or offense, such as drug treatment courts which focus solely on cases involving drug use and addiction. These court programs typically include community-based supervision (or probation) and mandate that of-fenders engage in therapeutic services in an effort to treat the underlying causes of crime while attempting to prevent and address chronic criminal offending.[70] They come in many varieties such as mental health courts, veterans' courts, homeless courts, and domestic violence courts.

The use of specialty courts is one of nine models that Susan Daicoff associates with the "**comprehensive law movement.**"[71] According to Daicoff, this movement seeks to advance a humanistic, therapeutic, and holistic approach to the law and is exemplified in concepts and practices such as specialty courts, therapeutic jurispru-dence (see Chapter 1), and restorative justice.[72] There is some debate as to whether specialty courts are an example of restorative justice or simply a framework in which it can be practiced and applied. While some would say that treatment courts are restorative,[73] others suggest that this isn't necessarily the case.[74] As is the case with any practice or process, the degree to which it exemplifies restorative justice rests with the values and principles from which the process is designed and administered. Restorative justice, therefore, is best described as a tool which can function well within the framework of a specialty court; however, a specialty court is not necessarily always restorative. That being said, specialty courts are another way that restorative justice can be implemented within the court system. By including restorative processes such as family group conferences and peacemaking circles into a treatment court pro-gram or designing a treatment court around restorative values such as inclusion and consensus decision making, we can clearly see the increasing influence of restorative justice within our judicial system.

Now that we have explored some of the ways in which restorative justice can func-tion within law enforcement and the courts, we will move our attention to the field of corrections by examining the use of restorative justice in probation, parole, and prisons.

Chapter Summary

What is the difference between the juvenile and criminal justice systems, and how does restorative justice connect to them?

Since the inception of the United States' first juvenile court in 1899, juvenile delin-quency and adult criminal violations have been addressed separately in the U.S. justice system. Restorative justice processes typically work within or alongside the juvenile and criminal justice systems in one of three ways: they divert cases away from the system (diversion), they are incorporated into the systems themselves (incorporation), or they operate alongside the systems (parallelism). In addition to the implementation of individual restorative justice programs and processes, we also discussed the making of fully restorative systems, institutions, and agencies, examining different models and strategies for the systemic implementation of restorative justice.

In what ways can restorative justice function within a policing or law enforcement agency?

In regard to restorative policing, we examined the three ways in which restorative values and processes are known to function within law enforcement agencies. Police departments sometimes operate restorative diversion programs for specific kinds of cases such as juvenile offenses and domestic violence. In addition, some agencies have attempted a more systemic reorientation to a restorative policing model by not only embedding restorative diversion practices into their law enforcement work, but by transforming their own internal policies, roles, and recruitment practices to better align with restorative values and principles. Lastly, some agencies utilize a mediation process to address citizen complaints concerning police officers and their agencies. While restorative policing practices are not always embraced or implemented in a sustainable way, the existence of these practices illustrates a modern movement towards more proactive, community-oriented policing models.

In what ways can restorative justice function within a juvenile, criminal, or tribal court?

We examined three ways in which restorative justice functions within U.S. juvenile, criminal, and tribal courts. Aboriginal peacemaking ceremonies can be used in tribal courts to address crimes and conflict within an aboriginal community or tribe. The Navajo peacemaking court is an example of this, which is a peacemaking ceremony heavily rooted in Navajo culture and spirituality. As we discussed in Chapter 7, sentencing circles can also be utilized in U.S. juvenile and criminal courts to promote a problem-solving, inclusive approach to addressing the needs of victims and offenders while trying to prevent future and chronic offending. Lastly, we explored the rise of specialty courts (also called problem-solving courts or treatment courts) as part of the comprehensive law movement, which can incorporate restorative processes such as family group conferences and peacemaking circles into an offender's court-mandated, therapeutic programing.

Key Terms

Diversion
Incorporation
Parallelism
Unified Model
Dual Track Model
Safety Net Model
Hybrid Model
Restorative Policing
Community-Oriented Policing

Wagga Wagga Model
Street Diversion
Cautioning
Restorative Cautioning
Net-Widening
Dual Court System
Tribal Court
Peacemaking Court
Navajo Nation Peacemaking Court
Sentencing Circle
Specialty Courts
Comprehensive Law Movement

Critical Thinking Questions

1. When you consider Van Ness's four models for restorative systems, which one would you most like to see implemented in your own community? The unified model, the dual track model, the safety net model, or the hybrid model? Be sure to explain your answer.

2. If you ran a local policing agency and wanted to implement restorative policing, what concerns do you think your community and officers might have about the change? How would you address those concerns?

3. What concerns, if any, do you have about using mediation to address conflicts between the community and police officers? In what ways might a restorative approach to addressing these conflicts lead to positive outcomes for the agency and the community?

4. Identify three different types of specialty courts (such as veterans' courts and drug treatment courts). Try to imagine how you could use a specific restorative process (such as a peacemaking circle or family group conference) in each of the court programs you have identified.

References

1. Stohr, M. K., & Walsh, A. (2016). *Corrections: The essentials* (2nd ed.). Thousand Oaks, CA: Sage.

2. Ibid.

3. Development Services Group. (2017). *Diversion from formal juvenile court processing.* Retrieved from https://www.ojjdp.gov/mpg/litreviews/Diversion_Programs.pdf.

4. Van Ness, D. W. (2002). The shape of things to come: A framework for thinking about a restorative justice system. In E. G. M. Weitekamp & H. Kerner (Eds.), *Restorative justice: Theoretical foundations* (pp. 1–20). Devon, UK: Willan Publishing.

5. Ibid.

6. Ibid., see 4.

7. Ibid., see 4.

8. Ibid., see 4.

9. Umbreit, M. S., & Carey, M. (1995). Restorative justice: Implications for organizational change. *Federal Probation, 59*(1), para 9.

10. Carey, M. (2001). Infancy, adolescence, and restorative justice: Strategies for promoting organizational reform. In G. Bazemore & M. Schiff (Eds.), *Restorative community justice: Repairing harm and transforming communities* (pp. 151–169), Cincinnati, OH: Anderson Publishing.

11. Ibid.

12. Ibid., see 10.

13. Ibid., see 10.

14. Ibid., see 10.

15. Ibid., see 10.

16. Ibid., see 10.

17. Ibid., see 10.

18. Restorative Justice International (RJI). (2016). White paper on restorative policing, page 1. Retrieved from http://www.restorativejusticeinternational.com/assets/RJI-White-Paper-on-Restorative-Policing-01-JUL-16pdf.pdf.

19. Mays, G. L., & Ruddell, R. (2008). *Making sense of criminal justice: Policies and practices.* New York, NY: Oxford University Press.

20. Restorative Justice International (RJI). (2016). White paper on restorative policing. Retrieved from http://www.restorativejusticeinternational.com/assets/RJI-White-Paper-on-Restorative-Policing-01-JUL-16pdf.pdf.

21. Ibid.

22. Bazemore, G., & Umbreit, M. (2001, February). A comparison of four restorative conferencing models. *Juvenile Justice Bulletin.* Retrieved from https://www.ncjrs.gov/pdffiles1/ojjdp/184738.pdf.

23. Ibid.

24. Hines, D., & Bazemore, G. (2003). Restorative policing, conferencing and community. *Police Practice and Research, 4*(4), 411–427.

25. Ibid.

26. Ibid., see 24, page 416.

27. Ibid., see 24.

28. Young, R., & Hoyle, C. (2003). New, improved police-led restorative justice? Action-research and the Thames Valley police initiative. In A. von Hirsch, J. Roberts, A. E. Bottoms, K. Roach, & M. Schiff (Eds.), *Restorative justice & criminal justice: Competing or reconcilable paradigms?* (pp. 273–291). Portland, OR: Hart Publishing.

29. Ibid.

30. McLeod, C. (2003). Toward a restorative organization: Transforming police bureaucracies. *Police Practice and Research, 4*(4), 361–377.

31. Ibid.

32. Bazemore, G., & Griffiths, C. (2003). Police reform, restorative justice and restorative policing. *Police Practice and Research, 4*(4), 335–346.

33. Ibid.

34. Ibid., see 32.

35. Ibid., see 32.

36. Ibid., see 32.

37. McCold, P. (2003). An experiment in police-based restorative justice: The Bethlehem (PA) project. *Police Practice and Research*, *4*(4), 379–390.

38. Bazemore, G., & Griffiths, C. (2003). Police reform, restorative justice and restorative policing. *Police Practice and Research*, *4*(4), 335–346.

39. Ibid.

40. Walker, S., & Archbold, C. (2000). Mediating citizen complaints against the police: An exploratory study. *Journal of Dispute Resolution*, 2000(2).

41. Bartels, E. C., & Silverman, E. B. (2005). An exploratory study of the New York City civilian complaint review board mediation program. *Policing: An International Journal of Police Strategies & Management*, *28*(4), 619–630.

42. Schaible, L. M., De Angelis, J., Wolf, B., & Rosenthal, R. (2012). Denver's citizen/police complaint mediation program: Officer and complainant satisfaction. *Criminal Justice Policy Review*, *24*(5), 626–650.

43. Ibid.

44. Ibid., see 42.

45. Ibid., see 42.

46. McLaughlin, E., & Johansen, A. (2002). A force for change? The prospects for applying restorative justice to citizen complaints against the police in England and Wales. *The British Journal of Criminology*, *42*, 635–653.

47. Walker, S., Archbold, C., & Herbst, L. (2002). Mediating citizen complaints against police officers: A guide for police and community leaders. U.S. Department of Justice. Retrieved from http:// www.au.af.mil/au/awc/awcgate/doj/mediate_citiz_police.pdf.

48. Prichard, J. (2010). Net-widening and the diversion of young people from court: A longitudinal analysis with implications for restorative justice. *The Australian and New Zealand Journal of Criminology*, *43*(1), 112–129.

49. Braithwaite, J. (2002). *Restorative justice and responsive regulation*. New York, NY: Oxford University Press.

50. Schaible, L. M., De Angelis, J., Wolf, B., & Rosenthal, R. (2012). Denver's citizen/police complaint mediation program: Officer and complainant satisfaction. *Criminal Justice Policy Review*, *24*(5), 626–650.

51. Rennison, C. M., & Dodge, M. (2018). *Introduction to criminal justice: Systems, diversity, and change* (2nd ed.). Thousand Oaks, CA: SAGE.

52. Adams, D., Minton, T., Motivans, M., Perry, S. W., & Strong, S. (2017). *Tribal crime data collection activities, 2017*. Bureau of Justice Statistics, Department of Justice. Retrieved from https:// www.bjs.gov/content/pub/pdf/tcdca17.pdf.

53. Winfree, L. T. (2002). Peacemaking and community harmony: Lessons (and admonitions) from the Navajo peacemaking courts. In E. G. M. Weitekamp & H. Kerner (Eds.), *Restorative justice: Theoretical foundations* (pp. 1–20). Devon, UK: Willan Publishing.

54. Ibid.

55. The Peacemaking Program of the Judicial Branch of the Navajo Nation. (2013). *Plan of operations*. Retrieved from http://www.navajocourts.org/Peacemaking/Plan/PPPO2013-2-25.pdf.

56. Winfree, L. T. (2002). Peacemaking and community harmony: Lessons (and admonitions) from the Navajo peacemaking courts. In E. G. M. Weitekamp & H. Kerner (Eds.), *Restorative justice: Theoretical foundations* (pp. 1–20). Devon, UK: Willan Publishing.

57. Ibid.

58. The Peacemaking Program of the Judicial Branch of the Navajo Nation. (2013). *Plan of operations*. Retrieved from http://www.navajocourts.org/Peacemaking/Plan/PPPO2013-2-25.pdf.

59. Ibid.

60. Ibid., see 58.

61. Ibid., see 58.

62. Winfree, L. T. (2002). Peacemaking and community harmony: Lessons (and admonitions) from the Navajo peacemaking courts. In E. G. M. Weitekamp & H. Kerner (Eds.), *Restorative justice: Theoretical foundations* (pp. 1–20). Devon, UK: Willan Publishing.

63. Ibid.

64. Ibid., see 62.

65. Ibid., see 62.

66. Ibid., see 62.

67. Pranis, K. (2005). *The little book of circle processes: A new/old approach to peacemaking.* Intercourse, PA: Good Books.

68. Dickson-Gilmore, J., & La Prairie, C. (2005). *Will the circle be unbroken? Aboriginal communities, restorative justice, and the challenges of conflict and change.* Toronto, Canada: University of Toronto Press.

69. Butterwick, S. J., Connors, T. P., & Howard, K. M. (2015, June). Tribal court peacemaking: A model for the Michigan state court system? *Michigan Bar Journal: Alternative Dispute Resolution,* p. 34–38.

70. National Institute of Justice (1999, July). *Therapeutic jurisprudence and the emergence of problem-solving courts.* Retrieved from http://ndcrc.org/sites/default/files/therapeutic_jurisprudence_and_the_emergence_of_problem-solving_courts.pdf.

71. Daicoff, S. (2005). Law as a healing profession: The "comprehensive law movement." *Pepperdine Dispute Resolution Law Journal, 6*(1), 1–62.

72. Ibid.

73. Fulkerson, A. (2009). The drug treatment court as a form of restorative justice. *Contemporary Justice Review, 12*(3), 253–267.

74. Baldwin, J. M., & Rukus, J. (2015). Healing the wounds: An examination of veterans' treatment courts in the context of restorative justice. *Criminal Justice Policy Review, 26*(2), 183–207.

Chapter 10

Restorative Justice, Corrections, and Prisoner Reentry

In this chapter, we will explore the following questions ...

- *What is the difference between community-based and institutional corrections, as well as recidivism and criminal desistance?*

- *In what ways is restorative justice being implemented by juvenile and adult probation agencies?*

- *In what ways is restorative justice being implemented within jails and prisons?*

- *In what ways can restorative justice support the reentry and social reintegration process after incarceration?*

Corrections, Recidivism, and Criminal Desistance

The field of corrections in both the juvenile and criminal justice systems encompasses a wide range of offenders, offenses, and sentencing options. Everything from an informal juvenile probation program to death row in a state prison falls under the umbrella of corrections. Our understanding of corrections can be broken down into community-based corrections and institutional corrections. As the names of these categories might suggest, **community-based corrections** refers to court-ordered offender supervision that occurs within the community, such as probation and parole. **Institutional corrections**, on the other hand, refers to the detention, incarceration, or institutionalization of either a suspected or convicted offender in a facility such as a jail, prison, or juvenile detention center.

While the main function of corrections is to supervise offenders during the completion of their court-imposed sentence, the term *corrections* also implies that during that sentence an offender is somehow being reformed, taught a lesson, or otherwise dissuaded from committing the offense again. In this light, when we examine and evaluate correctional strategies we often do that by investigating offender recidivism and criminal desistance. **Recidivism** is defined as the measurement of criminal relapse or re-offense. In other words, when a convicted offender completes their sentence and then commits a new crime, we refer to the offender as a recidivist. On the contrary, when an offender succeeds in moving away from criminal behavior, we refer to this as **criminal desistance**.

In this chapter, we will examine the relationship between restorative justice and corrections by exploring ways in which restorative practices are implemented in juvenile and adult probation, jails, and prisons, and also the process of prisoner reentry and reintegration. Beginning with Box 10.1, we will also explore whether or not empirical data supports the use of restorative justice in community-based and institutional corrections by examining how restorative programs and practices impact offender recidivism and desistance, as well as other outcomes that are important to communities, families, and victims.

Box 10.1: Research in Restorative Justice—
   Analyzing Restorative Justice Programs in
   Juvenile Justice and Corrections

In partnership with the U.S. Department of Justice, David B. Wilson, Ajima Olaghere, and Catherine S. Kimbrell of George Mason University conducted a wide-scale meta-analysis in which they examined outcomes from eighty-four evaluations of restorative justice in juvenile correctional programs. Using ninety-nine published studies as their data source, the researchers were able to assess outcomes such as offender recidivism, program completion, and participant satisfaction.

The studies under review evaluated a wide range of restorative programs and processes, including sentencing circles, victim-offender mediations, family group conferences, restorative cautioning, teen courts, victim impact panels, and reparative boards. While the analysis indicated that dialog processes such as victim-offender mediations and family group conferences may reduce juvenile recidivism, this outcome was less clear in regard to victim impact panels, teen courts, and reparative boards. Apart from recidivism, the studies did show positive perceptual outcomes. Not only did juveniles in restorative programs feel a greater sense of fairness and satisfaction with the correctional process, but victims did as well.

The analysis also examined the research methodologies utilized in the studies, finding that weak sampling strategies often led to inconclusive or unreliable research results. The meta-analysis only utilized quantitative research findings, which also limited the researchers' ability to give deeper meaning and context to their conclusions. Overall, the meta-analysis not only supports the continued examination and evaluation of restorative juvenile justice programs, but highlights the need for more qualitative data, longitudinal data, and randomized samples. The analysis also emphasizes the need for more process evaluations of restorative justice programs. Unlike impact evaluations that explore the effects and outcomes of something, process evaluations examine the way a program works, as well as its adherence to its intended design. The meta-analysis found that programs including a preparatory process (such as a pre-mediation meeting) lowered recidivism more effectively than programs without a preparatory process, indicating that variables related to process and implementation may impact outcomes connected to restorative justice and are therefore in need of more direct, probative study.

Source: Wilson, D. B., Olaghere, A., & Kimbrell, C. S. (2017). *Effectiveness of restorative justice principles in juvenile justice: A meta-analysis.* Retrieved from https://www.ncjrs.gov/pdffiles1/ojjdp/grants/250872.pdf.

Restorative Justice in Juvenile and Adult Probation

As we learned in Chapter 9, not only do the juvenile and adult criminal justice systems operate separately in the United States, but the dual court system also means that state and federal courts address different law violations, dispense their own sentences, and therefore require distinct systems of corrections. Due to this, probation agencies in the U.S. provide supervision for one of three offender populations: juveniles, adults sentenced in state courts, or adults sentenced in federal courts.

The most recent available data from the Bureau of Justice Statistics tells us that in 2015 there were approximately 3,789,800 adults on probation in the U.S.[1] Though the U.S. incarcerates its citizens at a higher known rate than any other country in the world, probation remains its most frequently imposed sanction when addressing criminal and delinquent behavior in both juveniles[2] and adults.[3] Unlike incarceration, probation allows offenders to remain in their community while completing their court-imposed sentence. This often includes restrictions such as not handling a firearm, not traveling outside of the county, and not consuming alcohol; however, it can also include active requirements such as paying restitution, maintaining employment, attending substance abuse treatment, or engaging in community service. Probation's goals of maintaining an offender's positive social ties with family members or employers while also requiring the offender to give back to their victim(s) and community through mandates such as restitution and community service make it highly conducive to the implementation of restorative justice processes and programs that aim to address crime through inclusive, collaborative, and reparative practices. It is therefore no surprise that restorative justice has a long history of working within juvenile and adult probation to provide offenders with opportunities to develop empathy, repair the harm they have caused to their victims, and to integrate positively into their local communities.

John Augustus and the Origins of Modern Probation

Though probation was not formalized at the federal level in the United States until 1925 with the passing of the National Probation Act, the concept began in Massachusetts as early as 1841 when a cobbler named John Augustus offered to take over the supervision of a man on the verge of being sentenced to prison. Despite having no previous ties to him, Augustus rose in court to post his bail and petition the judge to release the offender into his custody, promising to keep him sober and help him secure both housing and employment. The judge decided to give Augustus three weeks, and after those three weeks the judge declared the offender reformed and imposed only a fine upon him.[4] And thus began the practice of probation, of diverting offenders away from prison, giving them a precise timeframe in which to meet certain requirements and goals, and providing them with community-based supervision and support. Before he died in 1859, with the help of community donors and volunteers within his city of Boston, Augustus helped between 1,800–2,000 children and adults stay out of jail, remain sober, and find employment.[5]

While Augustus was the inspiration for the subsequent formalization of probation in his home state of Massachusetts, as well as the implementation of community-based corrections throughout the United States, it is important to note that Augustus and early probation officers were community volunteers, not state employees or officers of the court. While the eventual professionalization of probation officers was, arguably, a positive evolution for many reasons, the origin of probation is a story of community involvement and direct participation in the criminal justice system. It is also a story of mercy; a story of community members seeking justice in personal transformation and repair instead of punishment; a story of keeping families and communities intact while addressing crime, substance abuse, and poverty. It is, in other words, a story of both restorative and community justice, one of recognizing both the potential for offender accountability and reparation, but also the value of a community's direct participation in addressing crime and preventing future harm.

Implementing Restorative Justice in Probation

While probation remains a practice rooted in the community, as well as committed to giving certain offenders an opportunity to avoid prison, it has also become heavily associated with the juvenile and criminal justice systems, as well as judicial punishment. Restorative programs and processes can therefore be implemented alongside or within probation as a way of restoring the community's direct role in community-based corrections and criminal justice, as well as providing opportunities for offenders to take accountability and demonstrate a desire to restore themselves, their victim(s), and their communities.

As we discussed in Chapter 9, while restorative programming can be used to divert offenders away from formal systems of justice or certain sentences (such as incarceration), it can also be incorporated within those systems, or it can be implemented alongside (or parallel to) those systems. In community-based corrections we see restorative justice being utilized in all three of these ways. Let's inspect some examples.

Diversion

While probation itself can be seen as a sentencing option that diverts offenders away from imprisonment, probation agencies typically oversee some diversion programs that move offenders even further away from the traditional justice system. For example, while standard probation still results in an adult offender establishing a formal criminal record, options such as pretrial diversion and deferred adjudication can provide a way for some offenders to avoid establishing a record or even making a formal guilty plea. **Pretrial diversion**, sometimes also referred to as deferred prosecution, moves an offender into a probation-based program without requiring them to enter a formal plea in court. If the offender successfully completes the requirements of a pretrial diversion program then the charges against them are dropped; however, if they fail to complete the diversion program the prosecutor can propel their case into court and adjudicate it normally. **Deferred adjudication** is quite similar in that it also provides the offender with an opportunity to avoid a formal criminal record; however, unlike deferred prosecution, deferred adjudication does require that an offender enter a guilty plea in court. The court, however, suspends their entry of that plea while the offender is given time to complete the diversion program. If the offender successfully completes the diversion requirements, the charges against them are dismissed and a formal record of their guilty plea is not established. However, if they fail to complete the diversion requirements, the court can impose sentencing on them in response to their original guilty plea.

Community-based restorative justice programs work very well in diversion cases such as pretrial diversion and deferred adjudication. Since probation agencies are typically overwhelmed by already high caseloads, community-based organizations (with the help of local volunteers) can handle the facilitation of processes such as victim-offender mediations, family group conferences, or victim impact panels that might be appropriate elements for these kinds of diversion programs.

Reparative boards can also function well in diversion cases. Though a reparative board is typically facilitated by a probation officer, it can utilize community-based volunteers to help shoulder the labor involved in running the program and expose offenders to local community members and resources.

Incorporation

Even if an offender is placed on traditional probation as a result of their conviction, restorative justice can still be a part of their probation requirements. For example, if the victim of a juvenile offender is willing to participate in a victim-offender mediation then that process may be used to collaboratively determine requirements for the offender that a probation officer will then supervise, such as the amount of restitution or community service. In some cases, these processes might even be facilitated by juvenile or criminal justice professionals such as police or probation officers rather than community-based volunteers, counselors, or social workers. Regardless of the facilitation model, when restorative justice is incorporated into probation it means that participation in the restorative process is part of the offender's sentence.

Victim impact panels are a popular way of incorporating a restorative process into probation. Unlike mediation and conferences, which require some degree of voluntary consent on the part of both the victim and offender, offenders on probation who participate in victim impact panels are frequently compelled to do so. While this does appear to betray a core value of restorative justice and, as we discussed in Chapter 1, result in some victim impact panels falling on the lower end of the restorative justice spectrum, it is an example of how restorative justice can be institutionalized and incorporated into the formal justice system while still providing opportunities for offenders to develop empathy and reflect on the impact of their actions.

Parallelism

The use of entirely voluntary, community-based restorative processes that are not incorporated into an offender's prosecution or probation are rare, but they do exist. One of the major functions of both juvenile and adult probation are to connect people in need to supportive, community-based resources such as mental health counseling, support groups, and educational assistance. Local organizations that facilitate restorative justice processes can therefore offer their services to juveniles and adults even if that service is not technically part of the offender's probation or diversion program. For example, a local organization may offer to facilitate family group conferences for juvenile or adult offenders who think the process might be beneficial for themselves or their family. Though the conference might include some discussion of the offense that initiated the conference, in these cases the conference is not necessarily linked to the juvenile and criminal courts or agencies such as probation and parole. Though action plans or mediated agreements can still emerge from these kinds of restorative processes, they are not supervised by a juvenile or criminal justice agency in the way they would be if they were incorporated within probation or part of a diversion program.

Peacemaking circles can also be implemented as a parallel restorative justice process. For example, if a juvenile offender has impacted students and staff in their school, a circle process could be used, apart from juvenile probation, to reintegrate the offending student back into school and provide everyone with an opportunity to discuss the impact of the offending student's behavior (see Chapter 12). Mediations and conferences could also be used in this way if fewer stakeholders are involved and the offense impacted a smaller group of people.

Community-Agency Collaborations

Whether a restorative justice process is part of a diversion program, folded into probation, or implemented apart from the juvenile or criminal justice systems, it typically involves some kind of collaboration between a community-based organization and a juvenile or criminal justice agency. A major gap in the literature on restorative justice concerns how these collaborations work, what can derail them, and what can make them successful.

As we've presented throughout this book, restorative justice is rooted in different values than traditional approaches to justice. It does not recognize punishment, which is the cornerstone of retributive systems of justice, and it pursues goals beyond public safety. While these differences do not necessarily make restorative justice incompatible with juvenile and criminal justice systems in the U.S., they can lead to tensions when organizations committed to restorative values try to work with juvenile and criminal justice agencies and professionals that may have different perspectives, principles, and goals.

One example of this kind of collaborative tension can be seen in restorative action plans and mediated agreements.[6] When a process like a family group conference or victim-offender mediation results in commitments made by the offender (such as restitution payments or community service), probation agencies are often the entity that supervises the offender's completion of those commitments even if a community organization facilitated the process. However, the nature of these agreements can sometimes highlight divergent goals between a restorative community organization and a court or probation agency. While restorative justice seeks to empower individuals to determine how the harm caused by crime can be repaired, traditional systems of justice purport to value principles such as consistency and proportionality. While the juvenile and criminal justice systems in the U.S. are rampant with examples of disproportionate and inconsistent sentencing, they may have some legitimate concerns about restorative agreements containing a diverse range of commitments for similar offenses. For instance, if two offenders both commit a similar act of property damage, but one offender agrees to 25 hours of community service through a victim-offender mediation process while another agrees to 100 hours, the probation agency overseeing the two cases may be concerned about fairness.

Though we still have much to learn concerning how to most effectively implement community-agency collaborations between local organizations, courts, and probation agencies, efforts to address tensions between restorative values or goals and those of traditional justice systems add much to our collective dialog about justice, what it means, and the extent to which offenders, victims, and community members should be directly involved in discerning it. In this light, the implementation of restorative justice can be seen as a means of strengthening a community and braiding local resources and community members into a society's systems of justice. As we discussed earlier, this extension of justice away from formal practices and systems and into the hands of the community is the birthplace of community-based corrections and probation. Though probation has become a highly institutionalized and professionalized practice, it can be argued that restorative justice is picking up where John Augustus left off by challenging the status quo and asking all of us to explore questions about what justice means and the role a community should have in facilitating it.

Restorative Justice in Jails and Prisons

While most offenders in the U.S. are sentenced to community-based corrections, over 2.2 million people are detained or incarcerated in U.S. jails and prisons,[7] and approximately 48,000 juveniles are held in detention and residential placement facilities.[8] Though we might be tempted to assume that people sentenced to time in prison are all violent, this is not the case. Only 53% of state inmates and 7–8% of federal inmates are serving sentences for violent crimes, meaning that drug, property, and public order crimes account for a large amount of U.S. prison sentences.[9]

Unlike a prison, which only houses offenders convicted of a felony, approximately 63% of the people detained in U.S. jails are defendants who have not yet been convicted of a crime.[10] In other words, it is important to note the difference between a jail and a prison. While **jails** typically detain individuals charged, but not yet convicted of a crime, **prisons** are institutions where offenders are sent to serve a court-imposed sentence of incarceration. Jails and prisons can therefore be significantly different institutions with different populations, regulations, challenges, and goals.

While restorative justice is more commonly associated with community-based corrections, restorative processes and programs can be implemented within jails and prisons, and the institutions themselves can even be structured around restorative values, practices, and principles. There are five ways in which restorative justice can operate within a correctional institution:

- Restorative Programming
- Restorative Living
- Restorative Discipline
- Restorative Units and Dorms
- Restorative Prisons

Let's examine each of these in greater detail.

Restorative Programming

The most prominent way in which restorative justice is implemented within juvenile and adult correctional institutions is through programming. Programming is important in institutional life. Not only does it give inmates positive ways to occupy their time, but it can also help meet a range of religious, educational, vocational, and therapeutic needs. Restorative processes such as victim impact panels, family group conferences, and victim-offender dialogs work well within prisons because the goals of these models do not necessarily conflict with a court-imposed sentence. In other words, an offender can be sentenced to a term of incarceration by the court and still find value in exploring the impact of their offense through deep listening and facilitated dialog.

Victim Impact Panels and Programs

Victim impact panels can be organized and brought into a correctional institution as a way of developing empathy and providing inmates with an opportunity to understand the impact of their own crimes. As we explored in Chapter 6, victim impact panels are unique in that offenders hear from victims other than their own. Not every case, offender, or victim is appropriate for a victim-offender dialog, and so impact panels can often be the next best option when trying to provide victims with a chance to tell their story and offenders with a chance to learn more about the impact of crime.

In a prison setting, victim impact panels can be organized by community members who want to bring restorative programming into the institution. Victim impact panels are most effective when the victim narratives mirror the crimes committed by the participating offenders;[11] however, some would question whether one panel experience is enough to facilitate offender transformation. In response to this concern, victim impact panels are sometimes embedded within broader victim impact trainings or awareness programs that center on victim narratives but include multiple classes and activities that afford the participants a better opportunity to reflect on their own crimes and apply new learning and insights.

One example of this is the Prison Fellowship International's Sycamore Tree Program, which is a six-session victim impact awareness program utilized in various correctional facilities around the world.[12] During the program, surrogate victims come into the prison environment to meet with small groups of offenders and share their stories of crime while a facilitator helps the inmates explore topics such as accountability and making amends in relation to their own criminal acts.[13]

Prison Fellowship International is the organization responsible for the creation of the Sycamore Tree curriculum, as well as the training of community volunteers who operate the program as both victims and facilitators.[14] The program has been shown to have a positive effect on both victims and offenders, resulting in an increased understanding and empathy on the part of offenders and a change in offenders' attitudes regarding crime and offending.[15] While more research is needed to explore how these outcomes may affect institutional conduct violations, recidivism rates, and successful prisoner reentry, the Sycamore Tree Program is proving to be very successful in regards to short-term empathy development and attitudinal change.

Victim-Offender Dialogs and Conferences

While victim-offender mediations are often used in relatively minor crimes in order to allow the victim and offender to collaboratively form an agreement as to how the offender can repair the harm they have done, some crimes are too serious to be handled in this way. In cases that involve crimes such as sexual assault and homicide, it is important that the government intervene swiftly to ensure the safety of not only the surviving victims, but the wider community and also the offender. That being said, the traditional justice system often leaves needs unmet in the victim, the offender, and the community. For instance, after violent crime, victims often need answers to their questions as well as an opportunity to feel empowered after a crime, and potentially a court process, have left them feeling powerless.[16] Offenders might need opportunities to not only learn about the impact of their crime, but express remorse to the people most deserving of it.[17]

Community-based organizations can work in collaboration with state and federal prisons to bring the victims of violent crime together with their offenders even after that offender has been sentenced and incarcerated (see Box 10.2). While all victim-offender mediations, conferences, and dialogs should include a healthy amount of preparation work with all of the potential participants, this is especially important in cases of violent crime. Facilitators of these dialogs often spend months preparing both the victim and the offender for their encounter with one another, while also discerning whether it is appropriate for a future dialog to take place.[18] Due to the fact that these dialogs are not tied to the criminal justice system, they can occur years, or even decades, after the crime at a time when the participants feel ready to meet one another. While not every victim or offender of violent crime may feel the need to participate in a dialog process like this, those that do are frequently satisfied with the experience and grateful that the opportunity was available.[19]

Box 10.2: Restorative Justice: Let's Take a Closer Look ...
  Can Victim-Offender Dialogs Work in
  Cases of Violent Crime?

While it is relatively easy for people to support the use of victim-offender mediations in minor cases that involve juvenile, first-time offenders, the use of victim-offender dialogs in cases of homicide or sexual assault is often met with resistance, skepticism, and doubt. Perhaps violent offenders are seen as unchangeable and beyond help, or perhaps our instinct is to protect the victims of violent crime from ever having to see or think about their offender again (even if they tell us they want or need to). Whatever the case may be, it is not uncommon for people and communities to draw a line at violent crimes and begin to withdraw their support for victim-offender dialogs and restorative justice.

In her book, *After the Crime: The Power of Restorative Justice Dialogues between Victims and Violent Offenders*, Susan L. Miller provides us with a glimpse into the motivations and experiences of victims and offenders who choose to participate in victim-offender dialogs after violent crimes. Miller's book is a unique presentation of case studies that emerged from a qualitative research study that utilized intensive interviews to evaluate the Victims' Voices Heard program that facilitates restorative dialogs between the victims of crime and their incarcerated offenders.

The cases presented in Miller's study range from rape and sexual molestation to murder, and involve crimes between strangers, friends, and family members. Not only are the case studies presented in her book powerful and compelling, but her data analysis gives us reason to reconsider our doubts about the utility of restorative dialogs after violent crime, showing that perhaps restorative encounters can provide even these victims and offenders with needed opportunities to express emotion and remorse while also moving towards acceptance, healing, clarity, and, for some, forgiveness.

What do you think?

- What do you think might motivate a victim of violent crime to meet with their offender? What needs might they have that only a restorative encounter could help them meet?

- What might motivate an offender to participate in a restorative dialog with their victim?

- What kind of emotional, mental, or spiritual preparation would a victim and offender need in order to meet with one another after a violent crime?

Source: Miller, S. L. (2011). *After the crime: The power of restorative justice dialogues between victims and violent offenders.* New York, NY: New York University Press.

Restorative Living

Another avenue by which restorative justice can find its way into correctional institutions is through the concept of restorative living. Unlike a program or process such as a victim impact panel, victim-offender dialog, or family group conference, **restorative living** refers to the personal application of restorative values such as respect, care, inclusion, and accountability to one's day-to-day life, relationships, and interactions.[20] Restorative living is something inmates can make a personal commitment to doing as a way of transforming themselves, their relationships, and the prison community. Inmates committed to restorative living can even form bonds with one another, give one another support, and mentor one another.[21] While malignant subcultures, such as gangs, can often increase violence and exploitation in prisons, restorative living can provide the basis for positive, pro-social inmate relationships devoted to personal improvement and rehabilitation.

Restorative Discipline

Restorative discipline is a concept we will explore in greater detail in Chapter 12; however, it bears mentioning here as another potential way in which restorative justice can be implemented within prisons and other correctional facilities. In a nutshell, **restorative discipline** is a way of approaching problematic behavior by focusing less on how the behavior violates rules and more on how it affects other people and relationships.[22] In other words, like restorative justice, it is about using conflict and rule violations as opportunities to explore impact, develop empathy, and strengthen social bonds.

Any situation in which human beings live or work together will result in rules being broken and conflicts erupting. Prison is, of course, no exception. Therefore every correctional institution has its own set of policies and procedures concerning inmate and staff discipline. In regard to inmate discipline, institutional procedures that address conduct violations and inmate grievances are often viewed by the inmate population as illegitimate and unfair,[23] and punishments emerging from these procedures often involve furthering an inmate's experience of isolation and deprivation by withdrawing privileges, suspending them from programs, and moving them into segregation or solitary confinement. Based on research evaluating the effects of restorative discipline on college campuses, we know that restorative approaches to conduct violations often result in an increased perception of procedural fairness and participant satisfaction.[24] It stands to reason, therefore, that adopting a restorative approach to discipline in correctional institutions might yield better outcomes than current processes and procedures.

Some examples of ways in which restorative discipline could be implemented within jails, prisons, and youth detention facilities include reparative boards, peacemaking circles, and mediations. By including inmates in the disciplinary process as members of the institutional community, training them in restorative principles and values, and giving them input in regard to disciplinary outcomes, it is possible that a restorative approach to inmate conflicts and conduct could result in improved behavioral records and an increased sense of fairness in regard to institutional policy.[25]

Restorative Units and Dorms

One way of implementing restorative living and restorative discipline within a correctional facility without reorganizing the entire institution is to limit the implementation to a single housing unit or dorm. Though we will explore the concept of a restorative prison a little later in this chapter, the small-scale implementation of a restorative dorm allows an institution to not only experiment with restorative justice but reserve it for inmates who freely choose to live out restorative principles and values. Let's look at some real-world examples.

Grand Cache Restorative Justice Living Unit

The Grand Cache Restorative Justice Living Unit (RJU) is a unit housed within the Grand Cache Institution in Canada that integrates restorative principles and practices into its strategies and operations.[26] In order to be a part of this unit, offenders must complete an application and are only accepted into the unit if they are assessed to be doing so voluntarily and with a sincere motivation to commit to the principles of the unit.[27] In the unit, inmates are given opportunities for autonomy and responsibility, and also participate in weekly meetings in which they are encouraged to share openly about themes such as the impact of crime, anger, forgiveness, faith, and identity.[28]

W.C. Holman Honor Dorm

The W.C. Holman Honor Dorm is a faith-based housing unit within the W.C. Holman Correctional Facility in Atmore, Alabama, that utilizes restorative values and principles in its management and structure.[29] The honor dorm began in 1999 to allow a space for inmates wanting to focus on change and rehabilitation from criminal deviance.[30] The dorm itself operates with its own administrative structure, connected to that of the prison, but also inclusive of community representatives and reliant upon the inmates themselves assisting with supervision and administrative tasks.[31]

The inmates housed in the honor dorm engage in a structured way of life rooted in restorative values such as respect and integrity and supported by restorative processes such as peacemaking circles and a cultural emphasis on conflict resolution and relationships.[32]

RSVP: Resolve to Stop the Violence Project

The Resolve to Stop the Violence Project (RSVP) is a dorm in a San Francisco jail that utilizes restorative justice principles and programming to provide inmates with the skills and treatment they need to develop greater empathy and desist from criminal behavior upon release.[33] Some of the programming offered at the RSVP dorm includes education, group sharing, counseling, role-playing, theatre, and victim awareness dialogs.[34] The structure of RSVP was originally designed by a coalition comprised of ex-offenders, activists, victims, social workers, law enforcement officers, and probation officers, and is operated in partnership by the local sheriff's department and a community-based, non-profit organization.[35]

The victim impact process is a vital component of the RSVP dorm. Much like the victim impact panels we explored earlier, victims of crime are brought into the dorm to speak with the inmates about how crime has affected their lives, and the inmates are then encouraged to dialog with them and explore the impact of their own actions.[36] Drawing on the concept of restorative discipline, internal conflicts in the dorm are also managed in a restorative way.[37] When disputes arise, peer support is utilized to help diffuse and address the conflict, and mediation is used to resolve the dispute.[38]

While a restorative approach to institutional management may not work for every inmate, voluntary restorative housing units have shown to result in positive changes in offender attitudes and behavior,[39] as well as a reduction in inmate violence and correctional costs.[40]

Figure 10.1: Edgar and Newell's Six Elements of Organizational Culture in Correctional Institutions

Adapted from Edgar, K., & Newell, T. (2006). *Restorative justice in prisons: A guide to making it happen.* Winchester, UK: Waterside Press.

Restorative Prisons

Considering the success of restorative housing units within jails and prisons, the inevitable question emerges concerning whether or not an entire correctional institution could be rooted in restorative principles and values. In their book, *Restorative Justice in Prisons: A Guide to Making It Happen*, Kimmett Edgar and Tim Newell suggest that our current understanding of prisons and prison management is fundamentally incompatible with restorative justice.[41] Foundational principles such as coercion, punishment, control, and separation which define prison culture are inarguably at odds with restorative principles such as inclusion, accountability, voluntary consent, and collaboration. It is therefore important that any movement towards the implementation of a restorative prison include a complete transformation of institutional culture.

According to Edgar and Newell, there are six elements to the organizational culture of correctional institutions (see Figure 10.1).

1. *Power Structures*: refers to how people within the institution are classified and how power is distributed

2. *Organizational Structures*: refers to how the organization is structured, as well as how decisions are made, communicated, and implemented

3. *Control Systems*: includes strategies that maintain order and communicate the power distribution, such as pay structures and disciplinary systems

4. *Routines and Rituals*: refers to individual and group actions that reinforce cultural norms and the power distribution

5. *Myths and Stories*: refers to narratives that communicate and reinforce cultural values and norms

6. *Symbols*: includes signs and emblems that support order and cultural identity, such as logos, uniforms, and job titles[42]

According to Edgar and Newell, in order to effectively transition a penal culture from a punitive model to a restorative one, each dimension of the correctional culture needs to be influenced by restorative principles and values.[43] Edgar and Newell also suggest that routines, stories, and symbols are commonly the most resistant elements to cultural change and may require the most time and energy to transform; however, these elements are also most successfully changed as a result of positive outcomes, the creation of new stories, and the validation of new routines and symbols.[44] In other words, just as we examined in Chapter 9 with restorative policing, the most effective way to transform the attitudes of the people who work within a changing agency or institution is by giving them not only training, but personal experiences with restorative models, processes, and encounters.

While the movement towards a restorative institution must, of course, include the people who live and work within it, the transformation of a prison must also include the wider community. Not only is it important that a community understand and support the purpose and goals of its justice system and its institutions, but a restorative prison will also inevitably include greater interaction with the community than a traditional prison. For example, a restorative prison would facilitate the voluntary inclusion of direct and surrogate victims in institutional programming in order to provide inmates with opportunities to explore the impact of crime, and it would also provide inmates with meaningful ways to give back to the community and its members through service and work projects.[45] Inevitably, a restorative prison would also focus a great deal on the eventual social reintegration of its inmates by investing in inmate visitation during incarceration and also reentry planning.[46]

Through the restorative prison reform efforts of countries like Belgium,[47] we see that the concept of a restorative prison is not necessarily pure fantasy; however, the implementation of this kind of large-scale reform is not to be underestimated in that it requires not only systemic and institutional change, but the transformation of a society's collective understanding of the meaning and purpose of correctional intervention.

The Promise and Potential Pitfalls of Restorative Justice in Prisons

Research illustrating the outcomes of restorative programs in prisons does indicate the ability of processes like victim awareness programs and victim-offender dialogs to result in positive changes regarding offender attitudes and short-term behavioral change.[48] It is also believed that the utilization of restorative justice in prisons can lead to positive changes regarding staff and inmate relations in the correctional setting, as well as a stronger relationship between communities and prisons.[49] While the hope exists for positive outcomes when implementing restorative justice in prisons, potential pitfalls also exist when considering such a drastic shift in correctional culture and policy. One possible pitfall we've explored already is the difficulty involved in organizational and cultural change. Many theorists question our ability to reconcile the apparent philosophical disparities between incarceration and restorative justice, and so a legitimate question emerges as to whether or not the institutionalization of restorative justice might lead to the erosion of restorative values and principles kept philosophically pure, if you will, by the placement of restorative justice outside of the criminal justice system. In light of this concern, it is wise to look at the examples available, such as Belgium, that have utilized restorative justice consultants to help organize transitions to restorative corrections and thereby maintain its integrity and values in the face of inevitable challenges and pressures to compromise in regard to the meaning and goals of restorative justice.[50]

Another potential concern is increased strain and stress on the part of correctional personnel during a cultural transition to restorative policies and practices within a prison environment. In their research on stress and correctional officers, Dowden and Tellier[51] found conflicting professional goals to be a source of workplace stress within the correctional setting. In the United States they found that often correctional officers will feel a tension between punitive and rehabilitative goals within the penal system, and this tension can result in unnecessary strain on correctional personnel.[52] Considering the inevitable tension involved in transitioning a correctional institution from a punitive culture to a restorative one, it is reasonable to assume that this kind of workplace stress would be a foreseeable challenge within prisons and would likely lead to some staff confusion, turnover, and strain.

As we can see, there are a variety of ways in which restorative values and practices can be implemented within jails and prisons. The spectrum includes everything from a single victim impact panel all the way to a fully restorative correctional institution. Though we are more prone to see restorative justice at work in community-based corrections, it is clear that these processes and principles do have a place in correctional institutions. However, what about the process of releasing someone from institutional supervision? Next, we will explore the use of restorative justice when an offender reenters society after a period of detention, institutionalization, or imprisonment.

Restorative Justice, Prisoner Reentry, and Social Reintegration

For the majority of offenders in U.S. prisons, their experience with the criminal justice system does not end after incarceration. Most adult inmates leave prison under some kind of community-based supervision such as parole or federal pre-release, and those leaving jail are often placed on probation. In the juvenile justice system, youth in residential placement often have access to aftercare services. Despite these practices, the transition from institutional corrections typically does not lead to criminal desistance, with approximately 77% of adult inmates finding themselves rearrested within five years after their release from prison.[53] Due to the high rate of recidivism amongst former prisoners, it is clear that incarceration in the U.S. is failing to effectively transform criminal offenders and their communities, and is therefore failing to effect sustainable public safety within and outside of the prison environment. As we explored above, some proponents of restorative justice feel that restorative processes and principles have the power to transform institutional corrections so that they can produce better outcomes in regards to criminal desistance; however, others question whether restorative justice is conducive to institutional policy, expressing concern that the correctional environment is more apt to negatively influence restorative justice than restorative justice is to influence or change the correctional environment. Regardless of whether or not restorative justice has the ability to transform institutional corrections, it certainly has much to offer victims, communities, and former offenders once a period of incarceration is over and the social processes of reentry, reintegration, and (sometimes) reconciliation begin.

Former prisoners face many barriers upon their release from prison. These obstacles can include social stigma, unemployment, and the lack of necessities such as housing and transportation.[54] Shackled with significant gaps in work history and by the pervasive distrust society has of people convicted of crime, former offenders are significantly less likely to find a job than someone without a criminal conviction once they are released from prison, a fate even worse for young Black men.[55] Social reentry after prison is often made even more difficult for certain felons such as drug and sex offenders, who often face legislative barriers in the form of state and federal laws intent on denying these felons access to educational assistance and various types of social welfare designed to help people in poverty maintain housing and feed their families.[56] The vast majority of felons in the U.S. also face the temporary loss of their voting rights, and in some states this can even become permanent after an offender has completed their court-imposed sentence.[57]

While prisoner **reentry** typically includes a former offender's process of leaving prison and securing basic needs such as employment and housing, the process of social reintegration is one that not only involves the offender, but their family, neighborhood, wider community, and, in some cases, their victim(s). As we examine all of the ways in which barriers to successful and sustainable reentry are socially constructed and enforced, it is clear that social reintegration after prison is a process that extends beyond the needs of the former offender and requires a certain amount of focus on that offender's relationships. In other words, **social reintegration** is an interpersonal process that requires something more than merely the former offender's intention to desist from crime and behave as a law-abiding citizen; it requires the acknowledgement of harm, the building of trust, and a society's willingness to restore the former offender's place within the community. In this light, it can be argued that a restorative approach to reentry and reintegration may be ideally equipped to accommodate the various needs and relationships at the heart of prisoner reentry and reintegration. Let's examine what we know about reintegration and desistance from crime before exploring the ways in which restorative justice can, and is, being used to support the people and communities impacted by crime and incarceration.

Criminal Desistance and Restorative Reentry

When we examine the theoretical and empirical literature on criminal desistance, we see that the pathways out of crime can be as varied as the roads into it. That being said, the role of identity is significant in determining which offenders successfully move away from crime and which ones reenter the criminal justice system. As Shadd Maruna contends, criminal desistance refers to sustained change rather than a single transformative moment.[58] Much like abstinence from drugs or alcohol, abstinence from crime is a maintenance process that involves a renegotiation of how former offenders see themselves and how they are seen by others.[59] While theories related to criminal desistance have emphasized various factors (such as maturation, informal social control, and self-control), it is widely believed that desistance from crime requires an integrated approach that addresses both the individual and social elements of prisoner reentry and reintegration.[60]

While rehabilitative approaches to corrections and prisoner reentry tend to concentrate on the offender and, in some cases, their family, the focus on community, inclusion, and direct participation that we find in restorative justice can be an important component of an integrated approach to a former offender's desistance from crime.[61] As we discussed in Chapter 1, a restorative approach to justice does not view crime solely as a violation of law, but instead sees crime in terms of the harm it has caused, the people and relationships it has impacted, and the obligations it has created on the part of the offender. In that light, a restorative approach to prisoner reentry can support social reintegration because it better acknowledges and accommodates the social networks in which crime occurs. By focusing on relationships, reparation, and dialog, restorative processes like peacemaking circles and family group conferences can provide offenders, victims, families, and communities with opportunities to address the impact of crime, as well as the impact of incarceration and reentry.[62] Let's explore some examples.

Restorative Reentry Programs and Practices

The restorative reentry process is best supported by dialog-centered practices such as circles and conferences that can provide participants with an opportunity to discuss needs related to the offender's crime, incarceration, and reentry. As we discussed in Chapter 7, **reintegration circles** can be convened during an offender's incarceration or after their release from prison in order to provide participants with an opportunity to identify their needs and create a shared action plan related to the offender's release from prison and desistance from crime.[63] These processes typically borrow from the peacemaking circle and family group conferencing models we explored in Chapters 5 and 7 to create a restorative process uniquely focused on the needs and concerns related to an offender's transition out of the juvenile or criminal justice system (see Box 10.3).

Box 10.3: Restorative Justice in Action— Huikahi Restorative Circles

Though the term "reentry" might imply that an inmate has already been released from prison, the reentry and reintegration process should begin while an offender is still incarcerated. Not only do the processes of criminal desistance and successful reentry take time and planning but focusing on one's release and transformation can also be a good way for an inmate to cope with imprisonment and prison life.

In Hawai'i, the Huikahi Restorative Circle program helps both male and female inmates create a comprehensive, integrated reentry plan while they are still in prison. Ideally, the circle process utilized in this program functions a lot like the family group conferences we explored in Chapter 5. Family members, supportive friends, and at least one prison staff-person are convened by a facilitator to gather with the inmate and discuss the impact of their crime and everyone's needs concerning the reentry process. The group then works together to create a reentry plan that will not only address the offender's practical needs such as housing, education, and employment, but also ways in which the offender can restore the people and relationships they have harmed.

The Huikahi Restorative Circle program was first implemented in a minimum-security male prison in 2005; however, the following year it was expanded to a women's prison that houses medium- and maximum-security level inmates. The reentry plans generated through the program can include both short- and long-term goals and ideally address not only the immediate needs of reentry, but also the necessary maintenance of desistance, and the rebuilding of trust and relationships harmed by the offender's crime, and incapacitation.

Much like a family group conference, Huikahi Restorative Circles are as inclusive as possible, inviting even children into the dialog process to give voice to their own needs and concerns. Follow-up circles are also held to continue modifying the plan and preparing the participants for the inmate's release.

As is the case with any restorative dialog process, sometimes important stakeholders are either unable or unwilling to participate. In these cases, a modified process is made available to inmates eager to be involved in the program. In the modified program, inmates gather with one another to craft individual reentry plans and support one another's efforts and goals.

> While the Huikahi Restorative Circle model requires further evaluation and wider implementation, evaluative research results show the model to be a promising way of using one's time in prison as a way of preparing for one's release.
>
> Source: Walker, L. (2010). Huikahi restorative circles: Group process for self-directed reentry planning and family healing. *European Journal of Probation*, 2(2), 76–95.

Approaches to restorative reentry can also be geared towards offenders at high risk for re-offense and social stigma. As we explored in Box 7.2 (see Chapter 7), **Circles of Support and Accountability** (COSA) pair high-risk sex offenders up with a group of community volunteers willing to support and assist the offender during their reentry process.[64] Similar to the reparative board model we explored in Chapter 8, Circles of Support and Accountability convene a group of community members with a single offender in order to help them set, meet, and maintain goals related to their reentry, reintegration, and desistance.[65] Keeping in line with the reciprocal nature of social reintegration, the COSA model also helps address and alleviate community fears associated with releasing high-risk felons, such as sex offenders, from prison.

Like an offender, a victim can also experience social isolation as a result of crime, as well as practical, social, and psychological needs related their offender's incarceration and release from prison. While practices like victim-offender mediations and dialogs can help victims during the reentry process, not all victims are able or willing to meet with their offender. In these cases, support circles, like those we explored in Chapter 7, can be a way to focus attention on the needs of a victim without including the offender in the process. **Support circles** are a specific type of peacemaking circle in which individuals gather with someone, such as a crime victim, in order to support that person through a particular experience or event.[66] Support circles can convene multiple times and, though this isn't a requirement, they can include the drafting of plans of support in which members of the circle make commitments concerning specific ways in which they can help meet the needs of the primary member.

While it is exciting to see all of the ways that restorative justice can plug into community-based corrections, institutional corrections, and prisoner reentry, there are some crimes that often make people begin to doubt the efficacy and purpose of restorative processes. Cases involving intimate partner violence, sexual assault, and hate crimes strike many of us as beyond the reach of restorative values and practices. In Chapter 11, we will explore these types of cases in greater detail and ask ourselves whether or not restorative justice has anything to offer the victims and offenders of crimes rooted in power, control, and prejudice.

Chapter Summary

What is the difference between community-based and institutional corrections, as well as recidivism and criminal desistance?

After an offender has been sentenced by the court, they move into the correctional arm of the juvenile and criminal justice systems. Corrections in the U.S. include both community-based and institutional corrections. While community-based corrections refers to practices such as probation and parole, we associate institutional corrections with an offender's detention in jail, prison, or juvenile residential placement.

While community-based corrections keeps an offender in their community, and institutional corrections removes them from their community, both correctional strategies seek to prevent future crime, limit recidivism (or re-offense), and promote criminal desistance (an offender's movement away from deviant and criminal behavior).

In what ways is restorative justice being implemented by juvenile and adult probation agencies?

While the U.S. incarcerates its citizens at a higher known rate than any other country in the world, an even greater number of offenders find themselves on probation or parole. After exploring the origins of modern probation, we examined ways in which restorative justice is implemented within community-based corrections through diversion programs, the incorporation of restorative programs within probation, and the provision of restorative processes to offenders apart from their correctional requirements. We also examined the role of community-agency collaborations in bringing restorative justice to community-based corrections, citing gaps in our understanding of these collaborations, and the tensions that can arise between restorative and correctional goals.

In what ways is restorative justice being implemented within jails and prisons?

We identified five ways in which restorative justice can be implemented within institutional corrections: restorative programming, restorative living, restorative discipline, restorative units and dorms, and restorative prisons. In regard to restorative programming, we examined the use of victim impact panels and training programs, such as the Sycamore Tree Program, that seek to develop an inmate's empathy and give victims the chance to share their experiences. We also explored the use of victim-offender dialogs with incarcerated offenders in cases of violent crime.

We were introduced to the concept of restorative living, which refers to an inmate's personal decision to live out restorative values such as respect, accountability, and inclusion, and explored the way this can affect prison life and serve as the basis for positive, pro-social inmate relationships. In regard to inmate conduct, we also explored restorative discipline and the ways in which a restorative approach to conflict and rule violations can be implemented within a jail or prison.

Lastly, we examined the implementation of restorative housing units and prisons, and considered the elements involved in transitioning punitive institutions into restorative ones. We reviewed specific examples of these kinds of restorative implementations such as the Grand Cache Restorative Justice Living Unit in Canada and the Resolve to Stop the Violence Project in California.

In what ways can restorative justice support the reentry and social reintegration process after incarceration?

After detailing some of the barriers former inmates face after their release from prison, we discussed the difference between prisoner reentry and social reintegration. While reentry refers to a former offender's need to secure basic needs such as employment and housing, social reintegration is a reciprocal process that includes the rebuilding of trust between a former offender and their community. We explored the ways in which restorative justice can help support offenders, their families, their communities, and their victims with the process of reentry through such practices as reintegration circles, victim-offender dialogs, and circles of accountability and support.

Key Terms

Community-Based Corrections
Institutional Corrections
Recidivism
Criminal Desistance
Pretrial Diversion
Deferred Adjudication
Jail
Prison
Restorative Living
Restorative Discipline
Reentry
Social Reintegration
Reintegration Circles
Circles of Support and Accountability
Support Circles

Critical Thinking Questions

1. When a restorative process, such as a victim-offender mediation, is incorporated into an offender's diversion program or probation, the mediation is facilitated by either a trained community volunteer or a juvenile/criminal justice professional (such as a police or probation officer). What do you see as the potential risks and benefits of using criminal justice professionals to facilitate restorative processes? What about the potential risks and benefits of a community volunteer facilitator?

2. What are your thoughts about restorative prisons? Can you imagine a fully restorative prison being implemented within the U.S.? Why or why not?

3. Make a list of needs you think might be associated with prisoner reentry and reintegration on the part of the offender, their family, and their victim. How do you think restorative processes could be used to help address these needs?

References

1. Kaeble, D., & Bonczar, T. P. (2016). *Probation and parole in the United States, 2015.* Bureau of Justice Statistics, Department of Justice. Retrieved from https://www.bjs.gov/content/pub/pdf/ppus 15.pdf.

2. Hockenberry, S., & Puzzanchera, C. (2017, April). *Juvenile court statistics, 2014.* Office of Juvenile Justice and Delinquency Prevention, Department of Justice. Retrieved from https://www.ojjdp.gov/ojstatbb/njcda/pdf/jcs2014.pdf.

3. Kaeble, D., & Bonczar, T. P. (2016). *Probation and parole in the United States, 2015.* Bureau of Justice Statistics, Department of Justice. Retrieved from https://www.bjs.gov/content/pub/pdf/ppus 15.pdf.

4. Rennison, C. M., & Dodge, M. (2018). *Introduction to criminal justice: Systems, diversity, and change* (2nd ed.). Thousand Oaks, CA: SAGE.

5. Ibid.

6. Saxon, C. (2013, July). *Consistency and proportionality in victim-offender mediation agreements.* Retrieved from http://www.mediate.com/articles/SaxonC1.cfm.

7. Carson, E. A., & Anderson, E. (2016). *Prisoners in 2015.* Bureau of Justice Statistics, Department of Justice. Retrieved from https://www.bjs.gov/content/pub/pdf/p15.pdf.

8. Office of Juvenile Justice and Delinquency Prevention. (2015). *Juveniles in corrections.* Department of Justice. Retrieved from https://www.ojjdp.gov/ojstatbb/corrections/qa08201.asp?qaDate=2015.

9. Carson, E. A., & Anderson, E. (2016). *Prisoners in 2015.* Bureau of Justice Statistics, Department of Justice. Retrieved from https://www.bjs.gov/content/pub/pdf/p15.pdf.

10. Minton, T. D., & Zeng, Z. (2016). *Jail inmates in 2015.* Bureau of Justice Statistics, Department of Justice. Retrieved from https://www.bjs.gov/content/pub/pdf/ji15.pdf.

11. Fors, S. W., & Rojek, D. G. (1999). The effect of victim impact panels on DUI/DWI rearrest rates: A twelve-month follow-up. *Journal of Studies on Alcohol*, 514–520.

12. Feasey, S., & Williams, P. (2009). An evaluation of the Sycamore Tree Programme: Based on an analysis of crime pics II data. Prison Fellowship International. Retrieved from http://www.pfi.org/media-and-news/news/an-evaluation-of-the-sycamore-tree-programme.

13. Ibid.

14. Ibid., see 12.

15. Ibid., see 12.

16. Miller, S. L. (2011). After the crime: The power of restorative justice dialogues between victims and violent offenders. New York, NY: New York University Press.

17. Ibid.

18. Ibid., see 16.

19. Ibid., see 16.

20. Toews, B. (2006). The little book of restorative justice for people in prison: Rebuilding the web of relationships. Intercourse, PA: Good Books.

21. Ibid.

22. Amstutz, L. S., & Mullet, J. H. (2005). The little book of restorative discipline for schools: Teaching responsibility; creating caring climates. Intercourse, PA: Good Books.

23. Butler, M., & Maruna, S. (2016). Rethinking prison disciplinary processes: A potential future for restorative justice. *Victims & Offenders, 11*, 126–148.

24. Karp, D. R., & Sacks, C. (2014). Student conduct, restorative justice, and student development: Findings from the STARR project: A student accountability and restorative research project. *Contemporary Justice Review, 17*(2), 154–172.

25. Butler, M., & Maruna, S. (2016). Rethinking prison disciplinary processes: A potential future for restorative justice. *Victims & Offenders, 11*, 126–148.

26. Petrellis, T. R. (2007). *The restorative justice living unit at Grande Cache institution: Exploring the application of restorative justice in a correctional environment.* Correctional Service Canada. Retrieved from http://www.csc-scc.gc.ca/text/rsrch/reports/r189/r189-eng.shtml.

27. Ibid.

28. Ibid., see 26.

29. Swanson, C. (2009). *Restorative justice in a prison community: Or everything I didn't learn in kindergarten I learned in prison.* Plymouth, UK: Lexington Books.

30. Ibid.

31. Ibid., see 29.

32. Ibid., see 29.

33. Schwartz, S. (2009). *Dreams from the monster factory: A tale of prison, redemption and one woman's fight to restore justice to all.* New York, NY: Scribner.

34. Mirsky, L. (2010). Dreams from the monster factory: A restorative prison program for violent offenders. Retrieved from http://www.realjustice.org/uploads/article_pdfs/54371_dreams.pdf.

35. Ibid.

36. Schwartz, S. (2009). *Dreams from the monster factory: A tale of prison, redemption and one woman's fight to restore justice to all.* New York, NY: Scribner.

37. Mirsky, L. (2010). Dreams from the monster factory: A restorative prison program for violent offenders. Retrieved from http://www.realjustice.org/uploads/article_pdfs/54371_dreams.pdf.

38. Ibid.

39. Petrellis, T. R. (2007). *The restorative justice living unit at Grande Cache institution: Exploring the application of restorative justice in a correctional environment.* Correctional Service Canada. Retrieved from http://www.csc-scc.gc.ca/text/rsrch/reports/r189/r189-eng.shtml.

40. Mirsky, L. (2010). Dreams from the monster factory: A restorative prison program for violent offenders. Retrieved from http://www.realjustice.org/uploads/article_pdfs/54371_dreams.pdf.

41. Edgar, K., & Newell, T. (2006). *Restorative justice in prisons: A guide to making it happen.* Winchester, UK: Waterside Press.

42. Ibid.

43. Ibid., see 41.

44. Ibid., see 41.

45. Goulding, D., Hall, G., & Steels, B. (2008). Restorative prisons: Towards radical prison reform. *Current Issues in Criminal Justice, 20*(2), 231–242.

46. Ibid.

47. Stamatakis, N., & Vandeviver, C. (2013). Restorative justice in Belgian prisons: The results of an empirical research. *Crime, Law, and Social Change, 59*(1), 79–111.

48. Feasey, S., & Williams, P. (2009). An evaluation of the Sycamore Tree Programme: Based on an analysis of crime pics II data. Retrieved from http://www.pfi.org/media-and-news/news/an-evaluation-of-the-sycamore-tree-programme.

49. Dhami, M. K., Mantle, G., & Fox, D. (2009). Restorative justice in prisons. *Contemporary Justice Review, 12*(4), 433–448.

50. Bastiansen, R., & Vercruysse, J. (2002). Commentary on responding to the crisis. *Prison Service Journal, 140,* 18–20.

51. Dowden, C., & Tellier, C. (2009). Predicting work-related stress in correctional officers: A meta-analysis. In M. Stohr, A. Walsh, & C. Hemmens (Eds.), *Corrections: A test/reader* (pp. 202–222). Los Angeles, CA: Sage.

52. Ibid.

53. Durose, M. R., Snyder, H. N., & Cooper, A. D. (2015, September). *Multistate criminal history patterns of prisoners released in 30 states.* Bureau of Justice Statistics, Department of Justice. Retrieved from https://www.bjs.gov/content/pub/pdf/mschpprts05.pdf.

54. Hattery, A., & Smith, E. (2010). *Prisoner reentry and social capital: The long road to reintegration.* Plymouth, UK: Lexington Books.

55. Pager, D. (2007). *Marked: Race, crime, and finding work in an era of mass incarceration.* Chicago, IL: The University of Chicago Press.

56. Middlemass, K. M. (2017). *Convicted and condemned: The politics and policies of prisoner reentry.* New York, NY: New York University Press.

57. Pettus, K. I. (2013). *Felony disenfranchisement in America: Historical origins, institutional racism, and modern consequences* (2nd ed.). Albany, NY: State University of New York Press.

58. Maruna, S. (2001). *Making good: How ex-convicts reform and rebuild their lives.* Washington, DC: American Psychological Association.

59. Ibid.

60. Healy, D. (2012). The dynamics of desistance: Charting pathways through change. New York, NY: Routledge.

61. Bazemore, G., & Erbe, C. (2004). Reintegration and restorative justice: Towards a theory and practice of informal social control and support. In S. Maruna & R. Immarigeon (Eds.), *After crime and punishment: Pathways to offender reintegration* (pp. 27–56). Portland, OR: Willan Publishing.

62. Bazemore, G., & Maruna, S. (2009). Restorative justice in the reentry context: Building new theory and expanding the evidence base. *Victims and Offenders, 4,* 375–384.

63. Pranis, K. (2005). *The little book of circle processes: A new/old approach to peacemaking.* Intercourse, PA: Good Books.

64. Bates, A., Macrae, R., Williams, D., & Webb, C. (2012). Ever-increasing circles: A descriptive study of Hampshire and Thames Valley circles of support and accountability 2002–09. *Journal of Sexual Aggression, 18*(3), 355–373.

65. Hannem, S., & Petrunik, M. (2007). Circles of support and accountability: A community justice initiative for the reintegration of high risk sex offenders. *Contemporary Justice Review, 10*(2), 153–171.

66. Pranis, K. (2005). *The little book of circle processes: A new/old approach to peacemaking.* Intercourse, PA: Good Books.

Chapter 11

Restorative Justice and Special Victims

In this chapter, we will explore the following questions ...

- *What are the needs of victims after crime, and to what extent are those needs met or unmet by the conventional criminal justice system?*
- *Can restorative justice processes be safe and effective for victims of relationship abuse and violence?*
- *What can restorative justice processes offer to victims of sexual assault and violence?*
- *Are cases involving bias and hate crimes appropriate for restorative justice dialogs?*

Identifying the Needs of Victims after Crime

A common criticism of conventional criminal justice systems is that they often neglect the victim while focusing on the needs and rights of the offender and the state.[1] In fact, it could be argued that restorative justice exists, in part, to challenge this dynamic by moving victims more directly into the justice process, and bringing their needs into the center of our understanding of what justice means in our society. While we have examined many ways in which restorative justice can enhance our conceptualization and practice of justice, it is important that we also examine its potential limitations. While we will explore these limitations with greater care and intention in Chapter 14, we are sure that while reading this book you have had some of your own doubts and concerns about the limits of restorative justice. For instance, what about cases in which the offender does not admit guilt or feel remorse? What about cases motivated by hate and prejudice? And what about cases involving crimes rooted in an offender's desire to dominate and control their victim(s)? Can a restorative approach have a positive impact in cases like these? Is it emotionally and physically safe to bring these kinds of victims and offenders together? As demonstrated in Box 11.1, these important questions and concerns require special consideration as we continue to explore different applications of restorative justice in the real world. In this chapter, we will examine what the literature has to say about the efficacy of restorative justice in cases involving sexual assault, relationship abuse, and hate crimes in an effort to explore our concerns and better understand the potential boundaries of a restorative approach to justice.

Box 11.1: Restorative Justice: Let's Take a Closer Look ...
Should Restorative Justice Processes Be
Used to Address Elder Abuse?

As is the case with other forms of domestic violence and relationship abuse, incidents of elder abuse often go unreported. Senior citizens can frequently be physically and socially dependent on their caregivers, a fact that can often lead to feelings of shame and fear that prevent some victims from reporting abusive treatment. Additionally, seniors can understandably be reluctant to notify law enforcement about abuse because they do not necessarily want their caregiver (who is often a family member) to be arrested or punished.

Elder abuse can take many forms. Not only can it include verbal and physical abuse, but it can also manifest as financial abuse, the taking or selling of property, psychological manipulation, neglect, and even sexual assault.

In an effort to identify and address incidents of elder abuse, while remaining sensitive to the needs and concerns of its victims, the community of Waterloo in Ontario, Canada, created the Elder Abuse Response Team (EART). Rooted in restorative values and practices, EART works to prevent elder abuse and increase reporting through community education, while also facilitating processes to respond to incidents of elder abuse when they occur. While EART supports a variety of responses to elder abuse, the team tries to address as many cases as possible through restorative justice practices like peacemaking circles. In a peacemaking circle, participants can gather to discuss the abusive behavior, explore its impact on the victim and community, and make a plan to not only repair the harm but also prevent future abusive treatment.

Elderly victims who have taken part in peacemaking circles report satisfaction with the process. Not only do they frequently feel that the process was fair, but they express appreciation that the process focused on the needs of the abusive relative or caregiver as well as their own. It is important to note that cases referred to a peacemaking circle have to pass through a screening process, and not every case involving elder abuse is appropriate for restorative justice. This could be due to an offender who is not willing to acknowledge their harm, or a victim who is cognitively unable to fully participate or consent to participate.

What do you think?

• Based on what you learned in Chapters 4–8, what types of restorative processes do think might be effective in cases of elder abuse?

• If you were running a restorative justice program for elderly victims of abuse, what kinds of factors would you look for in your screening process in order to determine whether or not restorative justice could be a safe and effective way of addressing the case? What would your screening process be like?

Source: Groh, A., & Linden, R. (2011). Addressing elder abuse: The Waterloo restorative justice approach to elder abuse project. *Journal of Elder Abuse & Neglect, 23*, 127–146.

As we see in Box 11.1, not all crimes are alike. Some crimes take place between strangers while others occur within families, some offenders target property while others target persons, and some crimes result in trauma while others simply cause inconvenience. While not all crimes are alike, there is a significant amount of overlap in the needs of victims after crime. Regardless of victim characteristics (such as age, race, and gender identity), or even the type of criminal offense (such as theft or assault), victimization creates many of the same needs in all of us when we experience it.[2]

In the realm of criminal justice, we often measure the impact of victimization through the summation of losses caused directly by an offense. For instance, medical needs due to physical injury, mental health needs due to psychological trauma, or the need to replace or repair property after damage or theft all represent needs that emerge from losses we can directly attribute to one's victimization from crime.[3]

Other needs, however, relate less to a victim's direct experience of the crime and more to the criminal justice system and what happens after the offense. For instance, multiple surveys of crime victims have shown us that they often express needs related to advocacy, legal representation, and information.[4] Information about the investigation, the court case, sentencing, and the location of the offender can be extremely important to a crime victim, and gaps in this kind of information can cause increased anxiety, fear, and frustration.[5] For the family members of homicide victims, detailed information about the crime itself can also be tremendously important in their personal effort to understand and accept their loss.[6] Research also shows us that victims need to experience the criminal justice system as a fair and inclusive process,[7] and that they also need meaningful opportunities to have their experience and emotions affirmed by others.[8]

The Victim Experience: Impact, Adjustment, and Reorganization

According to Howard Zehr, a prominent figure in the restorative justice field, crime victims that have experienced trauma generally pass through three stages of victimization: *Impact, Adjustment,* and *Reorganization.*[9] The *Impact* stage occurs during and immediately after the crime when the victim typically feels intense confusion, helplessness, and fear.[10] This is followed by the *Adjustment* stage, during which the victim begins to cope with the experience, and frequently moves into emotions such as anger, guilt, and anxiety.[11] Coping strategies can range from helpful strategies

Figure 11.1: The Three Stages of Victimization and Adjustment

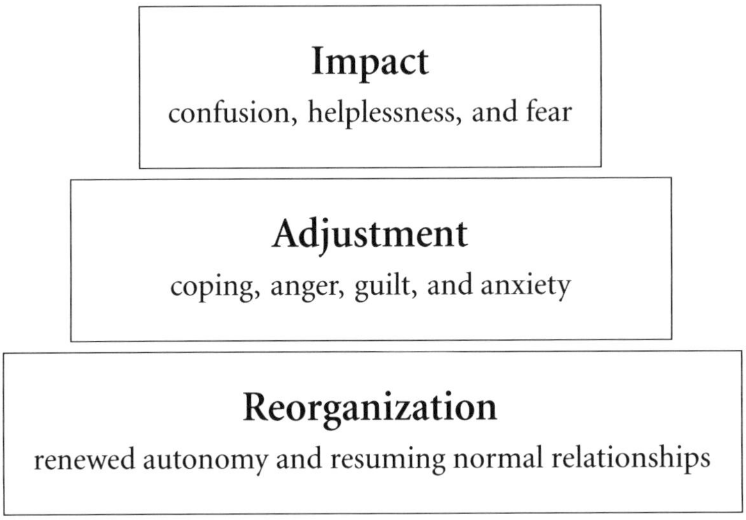

Impact
confusion, helplessness, and fear

Adjustment
coping, anger, guilt, and anxiety

Reorganization
renewed autonomy and resuming normal relationships

Adapted from: Zehr, H. (2005). *Changing lenses: A new focus for crime and justice* (3rd ed.). Scottdale, PA: Herald Press.

(such as working with a licensed counselor or participating in a support group) to potentially destructive strategies (such as compulsive behaviors like overeating and abusing drugs). With help and support, victims can then transition into the *Reorganization* stage in which they regain their sense of autonomy and resume normal relationships.[12] According to Zehr, if victims do not find helpful opportunities to heal and move into the *Adjustment* and *Reorganization* stages they become much more likely to develop long-term, chronic problems such as post-traumatic stress disorder (PTSD), clinical depression, and addiction.[13] Therefore, a victim-centered or victim-inclusive approach to justice must provide opportunities for victims to have their physical and psychological needs met so that they can move through these stages and adjust to their experience in a supportive and restorative way.

The Limitations of Conventional Criminal Justice for Crime Victims

As mentioned above, though a victim-centered approach to justice may sound ideal in many ways, conventional criminal justice systems are often designed around the needs and rights of the state and the offender, not the victim(s). Research shows that even when a community implements victim support services outside of the criminal justice system, some victims still lack the resources to meet their needs after experiencing a crime.[14] Victims are also frequently dissatisfied with the criminal justice system as a whole, citing gaps in information, a perceived leniency towards the offender, and a sense that their voices are not adequately included in the process.[15] As we explored in Chapter 10, these are typically good reasons to implement restorative justice programs alongside traditional correctional responses to traumatic and violent crimes. While violent crimes may not be appropriately addressed solely through a victim-offender dialog or family group conference, these kinds of practices can supplement the criminal justice system and provide meaningful ways to better meet the needs of victims and offenders even after an offender has been sentenced to probation or imprisonment.

As Susan Herman asserts in her book *Parallel Justice for Victims of Crime*, the criminal justice system (and, by extension, many restorative justice programs as well) fail victims by excluding unresolved cases that lack an arrest.[16] In other words, if an offender is not apprehended, many crime victims can never hope to seek compensation, restoration, or justice. While Herman is right to highlight the inability of restorative justice to address many of the needs victims have in these kinds of cases,[17] it is possible that processes rooted in restorative principles and values could be designed for victims of unsolved cases in ways that conventional, offender-focused systems of justice cannot hope to achieve.

Another important limitation of the conventional criminal justice system is its reliance on victim reporting in order to initiate investigation and prosecution. Based on victimization surveys, it is believed that a significant number of crimes go unreported by victims in the United States.[18] This can occur for a variety of reasons, including a victim's sense that the crime was minor enough not to warrant involving the police, or a victim's fear that reporting might put them in greater danger or bring harm to their offender.[19] For example, victims of domestic violence, sexual assault, and hate crimes can be reluctant to report due to a fear of retaliation, social exposure, and stigma.[20] Victims in minority communities such as immigrants and people of color can also be cautious about reporting crime due to a fear of the police and the broader criminal justice system, as well as a desire not to be seen in their community as someone who is cooperating with the police or perpetuating prejudicial stereotypes.[21] In an effort to increase reporting, not only can restorative processes be used to help develop trust between law enforcement agencies and minority communities (see Chapter 9), but, as we will explore below, some advocates of restorative justice contend that the use of restorative processes in cases of family violence could increase reporting by providing an alternative to the punitive approach of retributive justice systems and better meeting the needs of families harmed through abuse and violence.

Restorative Justice in Cases of Relationship Abuse and Violence

It likely comes as no surprise that the use of restorative processes in cases involving relationship abuse and violence (including domestic violence, family violence, dating violence, and intimate partner violence) is a highly controversial application of restorative justice. As we have explored throughout this book, restorative justice can be an enormously effective way of providing opportunities for offenders to be accountable to their victims, and for victims to share their experience and seek restitution; however, the open and inclusive nature of restorative justice can make its participants more vulnerable than they might otherwise be in a structured court process. For example, some argue that offenders lose important rights by participating in a victim-offender mediation rather than securing legal representation in a court;[22] and, especially in cases involving repeat victimization and abuse, many argue that victims require greater advocacy and protection from their offenders than a restorative process can provide.

As we explore these concerns, it is important that we acknowledge the difference between an incident of violence (even if it occurs in the home between partners or family members) and our traditional understanding of relationship abuse. Unlike most crimes, **relationship abuse** is defined as a pattern of behavior motivated by one person's desire to dominate and control another person. This dynamic of power, control, and manipulation is what leads many to not only doubt the ability of restorative justice to effectively address crimes related to abuse, but to also question whether the use of restorative justice in these cases might cause further harm or even perpetuate an offender's power and control.[23] Let's continue by examining common concerns about the use of restorative justice in cases of abuse, how those concerns can be addressed, and what the research literature can contribute to our understanding of outcomes related to the use of restorative justice to address crimes motivated by power and control.

Common Concerns about Restorative Justice in Cases Involving Abuse

We will explore general criticisms of restorative justice in Chapter 14; however, some concerns expressed in the literature tie directly to the use of restorative justice in cases involving abuse. One of the most obvious issues relates to the physical and emotional safety of participants. Not only are victims of relationship abuse at an elevated risk of physical violence and homicide when they seek help and leave the relationship or home,[24] but honest and productive discourse may be unlikely when an abusive offender has an established pattern of manipulation with a victim and the community. In other words, while participants should always be screened and prepared for restorative practices such as mediations and conferences, abusive dynamics are not always easily detected by outsiders such as program coordinators and facilitators. Therefore, in the context of a restorative process, those dynamics could be used to further harm a victim and reinforce oppressive roles.

There is also a concern that diverting abuse cases to restorative programs falsely associates these cases with minor crimes such as theft or property damage simply because less serious crimes are referred to restorative justice programs more frequently than violent felonies. The referral itself can therefore send an unintended message to the victim that their victimization is not as important to the community and therefore unworthy of a formal, punitive response. To victims disempowered by abuse, this perception can be a harmful one that could, potentially, make the restorative process even more vulnerable to offender manipulation or participant distrust.

Though some scholars and practitioners question the necessity of this belief, restorative justice is often seen as the opposite of punishment and retribution.[25] While apologies are not a requirement of restorative justice, the approach inarguably emphasizes reconciliation, harmony, and restoration above conflict, discord, and unilaterally-imposed sanctions. In abusive relationships, however, apologies can be a manipulative tactic used to solicit forgiveness, influence perceptions, and perpetuate emotional control.[26] There is a legitimate fear, therefore, that victims of abuse may enter a restorative justice process with a sense that they should forgive their abuser and move towards reconciliation, a fear that supports extreme caution when considering the application of restorative justice in cases of abuse.[27]

Another area of concern is the community. A distinguishing element of restorative justice is its inclusion of community members directly in the restorative process. Some advocates and scholars assert that communities can sometimes, directly or indirectly, participate in the oppression of abuse victims, including the minimizing of their experiences and their voices.[28] In other words, the role of community in restorative justice is to express and reinforce social norms; however, it is important to acknowledge that social norms are sometimes supportive of gender and racial oppression.[29] There is, therefore, concern that we cannot necessarily implement restorative justice while assuming that community members will support the needs and desires of abuse victims.

Addressing Concerns through Practice, Research, and Adaptation

Despite the concerns presented above, restorative justice programs have been implemented to address cases of relationship abuse and violence, and some evaluative research has been conducted to test its use in response to these types of crimes. This research, however, is not only limited, but results are often contradictory, and measurements are typically focused on participants' perceptions rather than short- and long-term behavioral outcomes.[30] As we explore in Box 11.2, it is important when evaluating restorative justice programs that we examine variables beyond offender recidivism. While conventional correctional strategies are commonly focused solely on offenders' attitudes and behavior, restorative justice programs are more inclusive and therefore need to be evaluated on how well they meet a range of victim, community, and offender needs. In this light, it is important to note that while research remains inconclusive regarding the efficacy of restorative processes in regards to offender transformation, there is empirical evidence that female abuse victims are often empowered through restorative processes.[31] While we tend to evaluate restorative justice programs based on how well they compare to their conventional criminal justice counterparts (as illustrated in Box 11.2), more research is both needed and warranted in order to ascertain the effect of restorative justice programs on victims of relationship abuse and violence.

Box 11.2: *Research in Restorative Justice — Comparing Batterer Intervention Programs with a Restorative Approach to Addressing Domestic Violence Offenders*

It is not uncommon, particularly in misdemeanor cases of domestic violence, for the court to order an offender to complete a batterer intervention program (BIP). These programs can be relatively short-term (lasting only a handful of weeks) or they can run for up to a year. Typically, these programs are designed for male offenders and focus on changing their attitudes and behavior through education and cognitive behavioral therapy techniques. Research evaluating BIPs have not shown a compelling link between program completion and behavioral change; however, the intervention continues to be a popular way of addressing these kinds of crimes.

Though the use of restorative justice in cases of domestic violence remains highly controversial, one such program was created in 2004 through a collaborative design process involving experienced restorative justice practitioners and experts in domestic violence. The Circles of Peace program was implemented in Arizona as an alternative to a local BIP, and an experiment was initiated to determine if the restorative program would have a greater positive impact on recidivism.

In Circles of Peace, offenders meet weekly with a facilitator for approximately 26 sessions. In each session others are invited into the process, such as trained community members, family members, and supportive friends. Victims are also invited into some of the sessions but are not required to participate. The goal of the Circles of Peace program is to create a plan regarding how the offender can change their behavior, maintain those changes, and restore their victim(s) and community. Unlike a traditional BIP, which tells offenders what to do and how to change, the Circle of Peace program utilizes restorative practices to include the offender in the plan for change and repair.

In an effort to compare the Circles of Peace program with the BIP model, over the course of two years domestic violence offenders in Santa Cruz County, Arizona, were randomly assigned to either a batterer intervention program or the Circles of Peace program. Recidivism rates were then assessed 6, 12, 18, and 24 months after each offender was placed in their respective program.

Though the results of the experiment were not particularly significant, they do tell us something concerning how we perceive restorative justice in cases of domestic violence, as well as how we compare restorative programs to other types of interventions. Though the experiment did suffer from a relatively small sample size and high attrition rates, findings showed that recidivism was roughly the same between the two programs. While these findings do illustrate that perhaps an unwillingness to consider restorative practices when addressing relationship abuse is unfounded, the study inspires a larger question about how we evaluate restorative interventions. Though conventional criminal justice strategies are focused on preventing future crime, restorative justice seeks a broader range of goals. Through inclusion and participatory decision making, restorative programs can, ideally, not only change offending behavior, but improve relationships, reduce conflict, improve communication skills, and empower individual participants. In other words, when evaluating these programs, it is important to explore outcomes beyond recidivism and examine changes in all of the participants, not just the offender. While this comparative study certainly provides us with reason to continuing pursuing and evaluating restorative alternatives to batterer intervention programs, it also demonstrates the need for more comprehensive evaluations that measure a range of potential outcomes.

Source: Mills, L. G., Barocas, B., & Ariel, B. (2013). The next generation of court-mandated domestic violence treatment: A comparison study of batterer intervention and restorative justice programs. *Journal of Experimental Criminology*, 9(1), 65–90.

Some concerns about the use of restorative justice in abuse cases can be resolved through the application of certain restorative processes over others, as well as procedural and practical adaptations that can minimize the risks of participants. For example, some scholars and criminal justice professionals encourage the use of restorative practices like family group conferencing and sentencing circles in these cases, while discouraging the use of direct victim-offender mediations.[32] Some of the issues we explored above, such as the potential for offender manipulation and the possibility that victims may feel pressured to forgive or reconcile, are more likely in victim-offender mediations and dialogs than other kinds of processes. In sentencing circles, for example, criminal justice professionals are active participants in the process,[33] and community-based professionals such as child welfare advocates and social workers are often involved in family group conferences.[34]

Creative process adaptations such as the Dialogue Impact Program through Domestic Violence Safe Dialogue in Portland, Oregon, also addresses many of the concerns about the safe use of dialogic practices when addressing abuse.[35] This program facilitates dialogs between victims of abuse and perpetrators; however, the participants are unrelated to one another. In other words, an abuse victim can engage in a facilitated dialog process with a surrogate offender in order to share their story and ask general questions to someone who has engaged in abusive behavior. The former abuser can listen to a victim's experience of abuse, use the information to help them better understand the impact of their own actions, and participate in a program that affords them the opportunity to lend help and support to a victim that resembles their own.

While it is unclear whether restorative justice is an appropriate way to address crimes involving relationship abuse and violence, the need for an alternative to the traditional criminal justice system and its correctional strategies is apparent. While we may have doubts and concerns about an abuse victim's safety within a restorative justice process, we know that these victims are often neglected and harmed by our courts and law enforcement agencies. Female victims from minority communities are especially distrustful of the courts and family welfare organizations, making alternatives to these formal systems appear more promising in the context of cases involving abuse.[36] When asked for their opinion concerning a specific restorative justice program for abuse cases, female victims voiced many of the same concerns we explored above: fears about safety, coercion, and the role of community.[37] However, they also voiced dissatisfaction with, and distrust in, conventional responses to relationship violence, envisioning instead a restorative, victim-centered approach to these cases that included an expansion of community-based resources, financial assistance, meaningful prevention efforts, and community education.[38] While restorative processes may not be equipped to address all of these needs, it is easy to imagine ways in which restorative justice and its advocates could have something to contribute to this kind of community-based, multi-faceted approach to addressing relationship abuse and violence within a community.

Restorative Justice in Cases of Rape and Sexual Assault

Cases involving sexual abuse and violence also lead to important questions concerning the safe and effective application of restorative justice. Unlike relationship abuse, which is typically understood as a pattern of abusive behavior, **sexual abuse** is defined as any act of sexual contact that is unwanted and nonconsensual, ranging from indecent exposure to forcible rape, and including both repeated acts of victimization and isolated incidents.[39] Much like relationship abuse, victims of sexual abuse can include both children and adults; however, unlike relationship abuse, which occurs within families and intimate partnerships, sexual violence can occur between any two people, including strangers, acquaintances, and family members.

Due to their traumatic nature, sex crimes result in a variety of emotional, social, and physical needs in victims, which are often impossible for the conventional criminal justice system to fully address. As Mary Koss presents it, victims of sex crimes have both "justice needs" (such as compensation, information, and the experience of being believed and validated), as well as "survivor needs" (such as safety, physical and mental healthcare, housing, employment, and education).[40] It is important, therefore, that the holistic response to sex crimes include procedures to address not only the needs of the offender and the community, but the full range of victims' needs as well.

Concerns regarding the use of restorative justice programs to address sexual abuse are essentially identical to concerns about its use in cases of relationship abuse. Since these crimes are similarly rooted in an offender's desire for power and control, and victims are often traumatized by the actions of their perpetrator, apprehension regarding victim coercion, the physical and emotional safety of participants, and the role of community members are common issues that arise in the literature on restorative justice and sexual abuse.

Empirical evidence concerning the use of restorative justice in these cases is sparse in large part because the implementation of restorative justice in these cases is so rare. Victims of sexual abuse are often intentionally excluded from restorative justice programs[41] most likely due to the concerns we've explored throughout this chapter, as well as the need for the specialized training of program coordinators and facilitators if sex crimes were to be referred to their programs. Though meager in quantity and scope, evaluative research examining restorative justice in cases of sexual abuse and violence has generated some positive results. While it is important to remember that these kinds of research findings are not necessarily generalizable due to the broad range of crimes that fit under the umbrella of sexual abuse, as well as the fact that restorative justice programs often differ procedurally from one another, research has found that restorative justice programs may lead to outcomes preferable to conventional criminal justice systems in areas such as offender recidivism, participant satisfaction, and the emotional safety of victims.[42]

Proponents of restorative justice in cases of sexual abuse assert a similar rationale as those who support its use in addressing relationship abuse and violence. Much like relationship abuse, sexual abuse cases are perceived to be regularly mishandled by the conventional criminal justice system, making alternatives like restorative justice more appealing.[43] Even victim advocates, while cautious about restorative justice, tend to support the ways it diverts from conventional legal practice by fully including victims, validating their experiences, and encouraging offender accountability (versus the imposition of responsibility).[44]

The use of victim-offender dialogs appears to be more prevalent in sexual abuse cases than cases involving repeated relationship abuse; however, due to the extreme trauma that many victims of sexual abuse endure, these cases can be good candidates for peacemaking circle models such as healing circles and support circles.[45] As we discussed in Chapter 7, healing circles and support circles allow for the use of restorative practices even if the participation of a victim or offender is impossible or undesirable. Both **healing circles** and **support circles** can therefore be used to gather supportive community members around a sexual abuse victim in order to provide that victim with short- or long-term support, encouragement, and comfort.[46]

Survivor impact panels have also emerged in the field of restorative justice in an effort to include cases of relationship abuse and sexual assault. **Survivor impact panels** operate in the same way as victim impact panels by giving survivors of abuse and sexual violence the opportunity to share their experience with a group of offenders who have committed similar crimes.[47] While evaluative research is needed to examine the precise procedures and effects of these restorative justice programs, survivor impact panels are another example of how existing restorative processes can be adapted to include cases involving sexual abuse.

Restorative Justice and Hate Crimes

In addition to cases involving relationship and sexual abuse, concerns over safety and efficacy also abound as we consider the use of restorative justice to address crimes motivated by bias and hate. While hate crimes can include a range of offending behaviors (including harassment, property damage, assault, and homicide), they are distinct from other crimes through the motivation and intent of the offender. A **hate crime** is defined as any crime committed in order to bring harm to a victim because of their identity, including their age, race, ethnicity, sexual orientation, gender, and religion.[48] While perpetrators of hate crimes all target their victims due to their identity and group affiliation, these offenders can be motivated by a variety of impulses, including the desire for a quick thrill, a perceived obligation to retaliate against the victim's group, or even a deep-seated mission to kill or harm as many members of the targeted group as possible.[49]

Much like terrorism, one of the consequences of hate crimes is the widespread fear it can spark in the victim and their community. In this sense, it can be argued that the net of victimization in these cases is much wider than we see in other instances of crime, which is, perhaps, one of the reasons why victims of hate crimes are often dissatisfied by conventional systems of justice.[50] This widespread victimization is also one of the reasons why proponents of restorative justice feel that, when partnered with proper screening and sufficient preparation, restorative justice can be an integral part of a community's response to incidents of bias and hate.[51]

Box 11.3: Restorative Justice in Action—
       Using Restorative Justice to Address Anti-Muslim
       Threats in Eugene, Oregon

After the September 11, 2001, terrorist attacks in the United States, which led to the deaths of approximately 3,000 people, anti-Muslim sentiments sparked widespread fear throughout the country's Muslim community. These fears were not unfounded, as many Islamic centers and mosques received threats, and there was a significant spike in assaults on Muslim and Middle Eastern citizens.

One such incident occurred in Eugene, Oregon, where, immediately after learning of the attacks, Christopher Younce, a 33-year-old resident of Eugene, placed two calls to the local Islamic Cultural Center. In the first call he spoke directly with the center's director, Tammam Adi, cursing and threatening all Muslims with death. When he called again, no one picked up the phone and so Younce left a threatening message which was later retrieved by the director's wife. Terrified by the threats, Tammam Adi enlisted the help of the Human Rights Commission, the calls were traced, and Younce was taken into police custody.

At the time of this incident, a community organization in Eugene had already established and been successfully operating the Community Accountability Board, a restorative justice program that sometimes worked in collaboration with the local district attorney's office. After examining the case, the prosecutor's office contacted the program and asked its director, Ted Lewis, if he would consider facilitating a restorative dialog between Christopher Younce and Tammam Adi.

After meeting privately with Younce, as well as Tammam Adi and his wife, Lewis brought both sides together for their first of two facilitated dialogs on October 10, 2001. The process resembled a peacemaking circle more than a traditional victim-offender mediation because not only were the direct stakeholders present with their support persons, but the dialog also included both the assigned and referring prosecutors, a police officer, twelve members of the Community Accountability Board, a probation officer, and a representative from the Human Rights Commission. After the first dialog, the participants agreed to a second session in the hopes that they could reach a better understanding of one another and a way forward from the crime.

During the second dialog, an agreement was reached between the two parties that provided Younce with meaningful ways in which he could repair the harm he had done to not only Tammam Adi and his wife, but the wider community in Eugene. In the agreement Younce committed to:

- Write a public letter of apology
- Attend two lectures about Islam
- Cooperate in news reports about the case
- Continue counseling (which Younce had begun prior to the dialog)
- Share his story with youth in the local juvenile detention center

Though it is important to remain cautious when initiating a restorative dialog after a hate crime, the case in Eugene, Oregon, shows us that when the offender is remorseful, victims are open and willing, a community is protective and supportive, and everyone is well prepared for the encounter, restorative justice can be a highly transformative way to address hate while building collective efficacy, reinforcing norms and values, and providing a way for offenders and victims to reconnect to the community after a crime rooted in ignorance, fear, and prejudice.

Source: Umbreit, M. S., Lewis, T., & Burns, H. (2003). A community response to a 9/11 hate crime: Restorative justice through dialogue. *Contemporary Justice Review*, 6(4), 383–391.

While it may be true that restorative justice dialogs can provide victimized people and communities with an opportunity to share their experiences and participate directly in the shaping of justice (see Box 11.3), the use of restorative encounters in cases involving hate and prejudice certainly has its critics. Concerns about the use of restorative justice in these cases often mirror the concerns we have already explored in regard to abuse and sexual violence, including doubts about the offender's inclination towards remorse and accountability, as well as the emotional and physical safety of the participants.

A concern unique to these crimes is the ability of victims and offenders to effectively and productively dialog despite their cultural and ideological differences, especially if supportive participants who share and reinforce those differences join the primary participants in the restorative justice process.[52] Though verified through multiple restorative justice cases involving hate crimes that these differences can not only be overcome, but that prejudices motivating the offender can actually be softened or transformed through dialog,[53] some critics believe that these cultural divides can put participants at an increased risk for emotional harm and revictimization. However, scholars and practitioners experienced in cross-cultural mediations contend that preparation, along with a willingness to engage conflict and discomfort while remaining flexible and committed to increased understanding and sustainable resolution, can lead to highly productive and transformative dialogs despite ethnic, religious, and ideological divides.[54] In fact, while hate crimes require an offender to see their victim as inferior and undeserving, storytelling through dialog is an enormously effective way of humanizing others,[55] a point that seems only to support the careful and conscientious use of restorative justice processes in cases involving crimes motivated by bias and hate.

While we tend to think of extremely violent crimes when we hear the phrase *hate crime*, it is important to note that most hate crimes are relatively minor when compared to incidents of homicide or mass killings. Behaviors like graffiti or threatening phone calls (as seen in Box 11.3) are common in offenders motivated by prejudice.[56] While these incidents can instill intense fear in the victim and wider community, these offenders are not necessarily outside the reach of attitudinal and behavioral transformation.

A cogent point introduced by Tali Gal is that we, as a society, tend to be more protective of some victims than we are of others.[57] One of the reasons why we can often begin to withdraw our support for restorative justice when faced with cases involving abuse, sexual assault, and hate is that perhaps we feel an increased responsibility to protect victims we perceive as highly vulnerable, such as child victims, victims of abuse and sexual trauma, and victims of bias and prejudice. While our intentions may be admirable, and our caution warranted, it is also important to ask ourselves if by protecting these victims of oppression, power, and control we are simply furthering that control instead of empowering them, listening to their needs, and supporting their path toward justice. Without a doubt, addressing these cases through restorative processes requires discernment, effective screening, and skilled facilitation, but, above all, it requires a willingness to reimagine what justice can mean in the lives of crime victims.

Chapter Summary

What are the needs of victims after crime, and to what extent are those needs met or unmet by the conventional criminal justice system?

While the scope and intensity of needs can differ among crime victims, these needs are typically understood to include direct losses (such as medical attention and the repair or replacement of property), as well as needs related to a victim's experience after the crime (such as the need for information, advocacy, and the validation of their feelings and experiences).

We examined Howard Zehr's three stages of victimization, which include *Impact*, *Adjustment*, and *Reorganization*. While the *Impact* stage occurs immediately after the crime, victims often need help and support in identifying beneficial coping strategies in the *Adjustment* stage and moving into the *Reorganization* stage during which victims regain their sense of autonomy and resume normal relationships.

We also explored limitations of the conventional criminal justice system in its effort to meet the needs of crime victims. While victims can often see their needs unmet by the criminal justice system, the system also fails to support victims in cases that do not result in an offender's arrest and prosecution. Additionally, crimes can frequently go unreported due to a variety of factors including a victim's distrust of law enforcement or fear that involving the police may result in further harm or retaliation.

Can restorative justice processes be safe and effective for victims of relationship abuse and violence?

We explored a variety of concerns about the use of restorative justice in cases involving relationship abuse and violence. For example, one common concern is the emotional and physical safety of participants in the restorative justice process, especially due to the established pattern of manipulation on the part of the abusive offender towards the victim and the community. Another concern is the fear that by referring abuse cases to restorative justice programs rather than seeking punishment through the conventional criminal justice system, victims already disempowered by abuse and violence will perceive the diversion of their case as an indication that the community does not affirm their victimization or take it as seriously as other cases.

Due to the fact that restorative justice is often seen as the opposite of retribution, we also confronted the possibility that a victim might feel pressured to reconcile with their abuser or accept their abuser's apology within the context of a restorative justice dialog. Since apologies are a common tactic in abusive relationships when an offender is trying to manipulate and control their victim, this possibility can be highly problematic and potentially harmful.

Lastly, we examined the role of community members in restorative justice processes. While the community is represented in restorative practices partly to express and maintain social norms, it must be noted that social norms can sometimes support racial and gender oppression within a society. It is therefore a concern that community members may serve to minimize abusive behaviors or support oppressive roles when included in restorative justice dialogs.

In an effort to address these concerns, we examined the outcomes and limitations of research related to the use of restorative justice in cases of abuse, and we also explored creative adaptations for these cases, such as the facilitation of dialogs between surrogate victims and offenders. Due to contradictory research findings, we are unable to ascertain the efficacy and safety of restorative justice processes in cases of relationship abuse; however, by exploring the perceptions and experiences of abuse victims, it is clear that alternatives to the criminal justice system are needed in order to meet the special needs of these victims.

What can restorative justice processes offer to victims of sexual assault and violence?

Many of the concerns connected to the implementation of restorative justice in cases of relationship abuse are identical to those in cases of sexual abuse and violence. Since these crimes are similarly rooted in an offender's desire for power and control, and victims are often traumatized by the actions of their perpetrator, concerns regarding victim coercion, the physical and emotional safety of participants, and the role of community members are common issues associated with the use of restorative justice in cases involving sexual abuse.

It is highly unusual for restorative justice to address these kinds of cases, which leads to the fact that we have very little empirical evidence concerning the safety and efficacy of restorative justice in this context. However, the research we have suggests that the implementation of restorative justice in sexual abuse cases may promote participant satisfaction and criminal desistance, indicating that further experimentation and evaluation of restorative justice in these cases is warranted.

Are cases involving bias and hate crimes appropriate for restorative justice dialogs?

While hate crimes can often be relatively minor offenses (such as graffiti or threatening phone calls), they cause widespread fear in the victim and the victim's community and are therefore seldom adequately addressed through conventional criminal justice processes. In addition to concerns related to participant safety and doubts about the offender's level of remorse, we also examined apprehension about the productivity of cross-cultural dialogs and the ability of restorative justice to transform deep-seated bias and hate on the part of the offender. Similar to all of the special victims cases we examined in this chapter, research indicates that while we should be cautious about the implementation of restorative justice in response to hate crimes, the use of effective screening, flexible process models, and participant preparation can result in the safe use of restorative justice even in cases rooted in oppression, power, and control.

Key Terms

Relationship Abuse
Sexual Abuse
Healing Circle
Support Circle
Survivor Impact Panel
Hate Crime

Critical Thinking Questions

1. Try to imagine a case involving relationship abuse or sexual violence that you would not recommend to a restorative justice program. What are the offender characteristics, victim characteristics, or aspects of the crime that lead you to doubt the safety and efficacy of a restorative process?

2. What are your thoughts about the Dialogue Impact Program we explored for use in cases of relationship abuse and violence in which a victim is paired with a surrogate offender in order to share their story and seek information? What do you see as the potential benefits and risks of such a program?

3. What specialized skills or training would you recommend for restorative justice facilitators before pursuing a case involving a hate crime?

References

1. Herman, S. (2010). *Parallel justice for victims of crime*. Washington, DC: The National Center for Victims of Crime.

2. Gal, T. (2011). *Child victims and restorative justice: A needs-rights model*. New York, NY: Oxford University Press.

3. Daigle, L. E., & Mufti?, L. R. (2016). *Victimology*. Thousand Oaks, CA: Sage Publications.

4. Newmark, L. C. (2004). Crime victims' needs and VOCA-funded services: Findings and recommendations from two national studies. Retrieved from https://www.ncjrs.gov/pdffiles1/nij/grants/214263.pdf.

5. Ibid.

6. Miller, S. L. (2011). After the crime: The power of restorative justice dialogues between victims and violent offenders. New York, NY: New York University Press.

7. Zehr, H. (2005). *Changing lenses: A new focus for crime and justice* (3rd ed.). Scottdale, PA: Herald Press.

8. Gal, T. (2011). *Child victims and restorative justice: A needs-rights model*. New York, NY: Oxford University Press.

9. Zehr, H. (2005). *Changing lenses: A new focus for crime and justice* (3rd ed.). Scottdale, PA: Herald Press.

10. Ibid.

11. Ibid., see 9.

12. Ibid., see 9.

13. Ibid., see 9.

14. Newmark, L. C. (2004). *Crime victims' needs and VOCA-funded services: Findings and recommendations from two national studies*. Retrieved from https://www.ncjrs.gov/pdffiles1/nij/grants/214263.pdf.

15. Ibid.

16. Herman, S. (2010). *Parallel justice for victims of crime*. Washington, DC: The National Center for Victims of Crime.

17. Ibid.

18. Ruback, R. B., & Thompson, M. P. (2001). *Social and psychological consequences of violent victimization*. Thousand Oaks, CA: Sage Publications.

19. Ibid.

20. Rennison, C. M., & Dodge, M. (2018). *Introduction to criminal justice: Systems, diversity, and change* (2nd ed.). Thousand Oaks, CA: Sage Publications.

21. Condon, M. (2010, Summer). Bruise of a different color: The possibilities of restorative justice for minority victims of domestic violence. *Georgetown Journal on Poverty Law & Policy, XVII*(3), 487–506.

22. Acorn, A. (2004). *Compulsory compassion: A critique of restorative justice*. Vancouver, BC: The University of British Columbia Press.

23. Stubbs, J. (2002). Domestic violence and women's safety: Feminist challenges to restorative justice. In H. Strang & J. Braithwaite (Eds.), *Restorative justice and family violence* (pp. 42–61). New York, NY: Cambridge University Press.

24. Ibid.

25. Daly, K. (2002). Sexual assault and restorative justice. In H. Strang & J. Braithwaite (Eds.), *Restorative justice and family violence* (pp. 62–88). New York, NY: Cambridge University Press.

26. Stubbs, J. (2007). Beyond apology? Domestic violence and critical questions for restorative justice. *Criminology & Criminal Justice, 7*(2), 169–187.

27. Stubbs, J. (2002). Domestic violence and women's safety: Feminist challenges to restorative justice. In H. Strang & J. Braithwaite (Eds.), *Restorative justice and family violence* (pp. 42–61). New York, NY: Cambridge University Press.

28. Gaarder, E., & Presser, L. (2008). A feminist vision of justice? The problems and possibilities of restorative justice for girls and women. In D. Sullivan & L. Tifft (Eds.), *Handbook of restorative justice: A global perspective* (pp. 483–494). New York, NY: Routledge International.

29. Ibid.

30. Cheon, A., & Regehr, C. (2006). Restorative justice models in cases of intimate partner violence: Reviewing the evidence. *Victims and Offenders, 1*, 369–394.

31. Pelikan, C. (2010). On the efficacy of victim-offender mediation in cases of partnership violence in Austria, or: Men don't get better, but women get stronger: Is it still true? *European Journal on Criminal Policy & Research, 16*, 49–67.

32. Presser, L., & Gaarder, E. (2000). Can restorative justice reduce battering? Some preliminary considerations. *Social Justice, 27*(1), 175–195.

33. Belknap, J., & McDonald, C. (2010, July). Judges' attitudes about and experiences with sentencing circles in intimate-partner abuse cases. *Canadian Journal of Criminology and Criminal Justice,* 369–395.

34. Morris, A. (2002). Children and family violence: Restorative messages from New Zealand. In H. Strang & J. Braithwaite (Eds.), *Restorative justice and family violence* (pp. 89–107). New York, NY: Cambridge University Press.

35. Domestic Violence Safe Dialogue. (n.d.). *Dialogue impact program.* Retrieved from https://dvsdprogram.com/dialogue-program/.

36. Hayden, A., & van Wormer, K. (2013). Restorative justice and gendered violence. In K. van Wormer & L. Walker (Eds.), *Restorative justice today: Practical applications* (pp. 121–130). Thousand Oaks, CA: Sage Publications.

37. Rubin, P. (2010). A community of one's own: When women speak to power about restorative justice. In J. Ptacek (Ed.), *Restorative justice and violence against women* (pp. 79–102). New York, NY: Oxford University Press.

38. Ibid.

39. Oudshoorn, J., Jackett, M., & Amstutz, L. S. (2015). *The little book of restorative justice for sexual abuse: Hope through trauma.* New York, NY: Good Books.

40. Koss, M. P. (2010). Restorative justice for acquaintance rape and misdemeanor sex crimes. In J. Ptacek (Ed.), *Restorative justice and violence against women* (pp. 218–238). New York, NY: Oxford University Press.

41. Ibid.

42. Oudshoorn, J., Jackett, M., & Amstutz, L. S. (2015). *The little book of restorative justice for sexual abuse: Hope through trauma.* New York, NY: Good Books.

43. Hayden, A., & van Wormer, K. (2013). Restorative justice and gendered violence. In K. van Wormer & L. Walker (Eds.), *Restorative justice today: Practical applications* (pp. 121–130). Thousand Oaks, CA: Sage Publications.

44. Curtis-Fawley, S., & Daly, K. (2005, May). Gendered violence and restorative justice: The views of victim advocates. *Violence Against Women, 11*(5), 603–638.

45. Oudshoorn, J., Jackett, M., & Amstutz, L. S. (2015). *The little book of restorative justice for sexual abuse: Hope through trauma.* New York, NY: Good Books.

46. Pranis, K. (2005). *The little book of circle processes: A new/old approach to peacemaking.* Intercourse, PA: Good Books.

47. Domestic Violence Safe Dialogue. (n.d.). *Survivor impact panel.* Retrieved from https://dvsdprogram.com/survivor-impact-panelll/.

48. Gerstenfeld, P. B. (2018). *Hate crimes: Causes, controls, and controversies* (4th ed.). Thousand Oaks, CA: Sage Publications.

49. Ibid.

50. Walters, M. A. (2014). *Hate crime and restorative justice: Exploring causes, repairing harms.* Oxford, UK: Oxford University Press.

51. Coates, R. B., Umbreit, M. S., & Vos, B. (2006, March). Responding to hate crimes through restorative justice dialogue. *Contemporary Justice Review, 9*(1), 7–21.

52. Walters, M. A. (2014). *Hate crime and restorative justice: Exploring causes, repairing harms.* Oxford, UK: Oxford University Press.

53. Gavrielides, T. (2012). Contextualizing restorative justice for hate crime. *Journal of Interpersonal Violence, 27*(18), 3624–3643.

54. LeBaron, M., & Pillay, V. (2006). *Conflict across cultures: A unique experience of bridging differences.* Boston, MA: Intercultural Press.

55. Walters, M. A. (2014). *Hate crime and restorative justice: Exploring causes, repairing harms.* Oxford, UK: Oxford University Press.

56. Ibid.

57. Gal, T. (2011). *Child victims and restorative justice: A needs-rights model.* New York, NY: Oxford University Press.

Chapter 12

Restorative Justice in Schools

In this chapter, we will explore the following questions …

- *What is the difference between restorative justice, restorative discipline, and restorative practices, and how are the three related?*
- *What is the connection between student discipline, juvenile delinquency, and crime?*
- *What are the underlying goals and principles of restorative discipline?*
- *How are restorative practices used in elementary and secondary schools?*
- *How are restorative practices used in higher education?*

Restorative Justice, Discipline, and Practices

Following the rising popularity of restorative justice in both juvenile and criminal justice systems, educators inevitably began to make connections between restorative processes (such as victim-offender mediation) and programs that had already proven effective in school settings (such as peer mediation and conflict resolution programs).[1] In the late 1990s, a movement began to emerge in countries such as Canada, the United States, and New Zealand that sought to apply restorative models and principles to student discipline, as well as prevalent problems in schools such as bullying and peer conflict.[2] In the wake of this movement two new concepts began to surface in the literature: restorative practices and restorative discipline.

As restorative processes and models began to move beyond the scope of criminal justice, there arose a need for terminology that would allow for the application of restorative justice in situations unrelated to crime. In order to address this need, the concept of restorative practices emerged. **Restorative practices** is a term we use to refer to any model, program, or process designed to implement restorative principles and values (such as inclusivity, collective efficacy, and participatory decision making) within a specific community, group, or institution. In other words, it is an umbrella term which can include restorative justice but is not limited to situations, contexts, or agencies associated with crime or delinquency.[3] For example, while a restorative practice such as a peacemaking circle can be used in the sentencing process for a criminal offender, it can also be used to address a problem or conflict within a community, school, or organization that has no connection to crime. In both contexts we are employing a restorative practice, but only one (the sentencing circle) is an example of restorative justice.

Figure 12.1: The Interconnected Nature of Restorative
Practices, Justice, and Discipline

Similarly, the term **restorative discipline** originated in order to specifically refer to the implementation of a restorative approach to student discipline and collaborative problem solving in schools.[4] While restorative discipline and restorative justice can sometimes work hand in hand, student discipline frequently addresses behavioral issues that do not rise to the level of crime or delinquency. In other words, while restorative justice and restorative discipline can certainly overlap, they remain distinctly different from one another in regard to the needs and issues that each address.

As shown in Figure 12.1, when we consider these three terms (restorative justice, restorative practices, and restorative discipline) we see that while all of these concepts are interrelated, their differences provide us with a fuller, more holistic understanding of how restorative principles and values can be applied to address a wide range of needs and broadly influence the culture of a community, organization, or institution.

This evolution of the restorative approach to community building, group decision making, and problem solving is a striking indication of the increasing influence of restorative justice in areas outside the purview of crime and juvenile delinquency. As restorative practices continue to be implemented in more and more ways, we see restorative practitioners and scholars not only envisioning the concept of a restorative system of justice (see Chapter 9), but restorative schools, restorative agencies, and even a restorative city (see Box 12.1). In this chapter, we will be looking at the ways in which restorative processes can be used in schools (including college campuses) to support the juvenile and criminal justice systems, address student discipline, solve problems, communicate behavioral norms, and transform the culture of educational communities.

Box 12.1: Restorative Justice in Action—
Hull, a Restorative City

Hull is a community in the United Kingdom with a population of approximately 250,000 people. After the collapse of the city's fishing industry, Hull entered a period of social decline and increasing poverty. In response to a city in desperate need of restoration and revitalization, the International Institute for Restorative Practices (IIRP) and the Hull Centre for Restorative Practices (HCRP) began a partnership aimed at making Hull the world's first restorative city.

With approximately 57,000 children living in Hull, efforts were initially targeted towards ensuring that agencies and professionals working with children in areas such as education, policing, and family services began taking a restorative approach to their organizational and institutional goals, services, and policies. The rationale behind this plan was to invest heavily in youth as a way of transforming the future of the city.

Since implementing restorative practices in Hull, crime has decreased well below national averages, schools have shown tremendous improvements in academic outcomes and student retention, and adults and children alike are increasing their resiliency and collective efficacy in regard to interpersonal conflict and group problem solving. Though the work of the HCRP continues to grow and expand in Hull, the community already exists as a real-world example of what can happen when restorative practices, restorative discipline, and restorative justice are all used in tandem to create a truly *restorative* city.

You can learn more about Hull by visiting HCRP's website at: http://www.hull centreforrestorativepractice.co.uk/.

Source: Mirsky, L. (2009). *Hull, UK, on track to becoming a restorative city*. International Institute for Restorative Practices. Retrieved from http://www.iirp.edu/ eforum-archive/4411-hull-uk-on-track-to-becoming-a-restorative-city.

Student Discipline, Juvenile Delinquency, and Crime

As mentioned above, there is a clear overlap between restorative justice and restorative discipline. In part, this is because crime can sometimes occur within schools; however, this is also due to the fact that research frequently shows us that there is a connection between a student's success in school and their likelihood of ending up in the criminal justice system as an adult. It is therefore important that we take some time to explore the ways in which school discipline, school safety, juvenile delinquency, and crime are connected.

As we discussed in Chapter 9, while the two systems contain many of the same elements and procedures, the juvenile justice system in the U.S. operates apart from the adult criminal justice system. We also tend to view juvenile offenders differently than we do adults, referring to their crimes as "acts of delinquency" and empowering the juvenile court to address status offenses in addition to criminal acts. **Status offenses** include behaviors such as skipping school and running away from home that are illegal for juveniles but not adults,[5] and are one of the clearest ways in which school disciplinary issues can directly connect to the juvenile justice system.

As we also see in the adult criminal justice system, the strategies we use to address and prevent juvenile crime often shift in response to public opinion about juvenile justice, as well as programming innovations in the field. While the juvenile justice system in the U.S. was originally designed to have a rehabilitative focus rather than a retributive one, that approach began to change in the mid-1980s when a perceived increase in violent juvenile crime began to have an effect on public and political opinion concerning the ways in which we respond to juvenile offenders.[6] For example, between 1987 and 1993, the U.S. saw the number of juveniles arrested for murder increase by 110 percent, an increase which led many to begin calling for an emphasis on punishment and deterrence within the juvenile justice system rather than treatment and social reintegration.[7] In the decade following 1985, juvenile detention centers in the U.S. increased their number of detained youth by 74 percent, even though many of those youth had not been arrested for a violent crime but had instead been detained due to status offenses or drug use.[8]

Following severe spikes in the mid-1990s, the number of juveniles arrested in the U.S. has been steadily declining since that time, with particularly dramatic decreases since 2010.[9] We are also seeing fewer juveniles held in detention and residential placement than was the case in the 1990s. In fact, between 1997 and 2013, 48 percent fewer juveniles were placed in residential treatment facilities in the U.S.,[10] which we can likely attribute to both a steady decrease in the number of juvenile arrests, as well as a growing emphasis in many states on alternatives to detention and community-based diversion programs.

Zero Tolerance Policies

Many attribute the swelling of juvenile justice referrals in the mid-1990s to the passing of the **Gun-Free Schools Act** of 1994 and, with it, the pervasive introduction of zero tolerance policies in schools throughout the United States. Among other things, the Gun-Free Schools Act required states receiving federal financial assistance for education to create their own laws and policies mandating the automatic expulsion of any student caught bringing a gun to school. While few of us would argue that bringing a gun to school isn't a serious offense worthy of thorough investigation and potentially significant consequences, **zero tolerance** policies in schools quickly evolved to include harsh penalties such as suspension, expulsion, and even arrest for a host of rule violations related to student misconduct, contraband, and behavior.[11]

After over two decades of observing zero tolerance policies in action, many have questioned the effects of punitive approaches to student discipline. Increased risk for arrest has even been linked directly to a juvenile's experience with school disciplinary procedures such as expulsion. For instance, in a study published in 2014 researchers found that juveniles who were suspended or expelled from school were more likely to be arrested despite controlling for factors such as past behavioral problems and delinquency within their peer groups.[12]

The increased use and reliance upon harsh disciplinary policies in schools has also been challenged in regard to its connection to the adult criminal justice system, including incarceration. While most juvenile offenders mature out of their delinquent behaviors after adolescence or early adulthood, the likelihood of this can be influenced by factors such as the age at which they began offending, race, gender identity, type of offending, and the type of programming or interventions youth encounter within the juvenile justice system.[13] Another important factor related to adult offending and incarceration is one's success while in school, including the completion of high school and one's level of involvement with punitive school disciplinary procedures.[14] While high school graduation rates in the U.S. are dependent on a variety of factors related to schools, families, and communities, the enactment of zero tolerance policies has, inarguably, led to the expulsion of many students, resulting in their transfer to alternative schools or their eventual failure to graduate.

Racial and Sexual Minority Students

A common finding in the research literature concerning school success, student discipline, and criminal justice is that racial and sexual minority students are repeatedly shown to be at greater risk for student discipline and involvement with the juvenile justice system. The **school-to-prison pipeline** is a term frequently used to articulate the way that school disciplinary practices, such as suspension and expulsion, have been linked to students' increased risk of being moved into alternative schools, failing to graduate, and ending up in prisons as adults.[15] Research examining student discipline in schools frequently shows that there exists a racial disparity in how students are impacted by disciplinary policies in the U.S.[16] This research illustrates that children of color are more likely than white students to find themselves suspended or expelled for nonviolent reasons such as truancy and disobedience.[17] Racial minority students (particularly Black and Hispanic students) may also face much harsher penalties, such as out-of-school suspension, for their first conduct violation at a significantly higher rate than white students.[18] While much of this literature is focused on the experiences of Black male students, there is also evidence to suggest that Black girls are routinely criminalized and pushed out of mainstream schools for behaviors that do not necessarily result in such extreme responses toward white students.[19]

In addition to racial minority students, research also points to the increased risk of sexual minority youth for involvement in the juvenile justice system due, in part, to their treatment in schools. While school attendance is often viewed as something that decreases a juvenile's risk for delinquency and arrest, sexual minority youth (including, but not limited to, lesbian, gay, transgender, genderqueer, and intersex children and teens) often feel less connected to their schools due to bullying and harassment, as well as unsafe and un-affirming policies and practices such as the lack of gender neutral bathrooms or private locker rooms.[20] Gender non-conforming youth can also find themselves being referred to juvenile justice agencies by their families and schools for insubordination if their gender expression does not conform to specific social norms concerning factors such as how they choose to dress or cut their hair.[21] Much like racial minority students, research indicates that LGBTQ+ youth are also more likely than other students to be separated from their schools and held in juvenile detention for status offenses (such as truancy), as well as nonviolent acts of delinquency (such as prostitution).[22]

School Safety and Student Discipline

Despite the wealth of literature challenging the imposition and application of zero tolerance policies in schools, the topic of school safety and security remains an important factor to consider regarding student discipline and how it is administered. Despite the fact that national, standardized data collection concerning violence in schools did not begin in the U.S. until 1989,[23] the data we have do indicate that victimization within schools is on the decline, and has been since 1992.[24] Victimization, however, can include both violent and property crime, and when we examine violent crime alone we see that this has actually increased in schools between 2010 and 2013.[25] Despite this increase, however, public schools in the U.S. remain relatively safe spaces when it comes to violent victimization, which begs the question of whether school safety standards can be maintained, or even improved, without the harsh approach to student discipline that we see utilized in most U.S. public schools. As we will see, some schools are using the concept of restorative justice to further limit practices such as detention, suspension, and expulsion by replacing them with restorative practices like mediation, peacemaking circles, and family group conferences.

The Goals and Principles of Restorative Discipline

A common criticism of the criminal justice system is that it focuses too much on the offender and neglects the needs and experiences of both the community and the victim(s). In other words, judicial punishment (whether it comes in retributive or rehabilitative forms) tends to be predominantly concerned with isolating, treating, and responding to the offender and often fails to focus on the true impact of the offender's behavior or the relationships that were harmed by the crime. In many ways,

Figure 12.2: Comparing Common Punishments in Schools and the Criminal Justice System

School	Criminal Justice
Detention	Jail
In-School Suspension	Probation
Out-of-School Suspension	Prison
Expulsion	Life Sentence in Prison without Parole
Expulsion and Transfer to an Alternative School	Prison and Parole

it is this very aspect of the justice system and judicial punishment that restorative justice seeks to challenge and change.

The criminal justice system, however, is not the only context in which we respond to problematic social behavior. We also do this in our homes, our schools, our workplaces, and any organization in which humans interact with one another. This means that a restorative approach can be implemented in almost any institution. This is especially true for organizations concerned with addressing social behavior and teaching social skills, such as schools. It should therefore be no surprise that when we compare the ways in which schools and the criminal justice system respond to offensive behavior we see quite a bit of overlap in the strategies that each use to teach discipline, impose punishment, and exert social control. As Figure 12.2 illustrates, we can easily see correlations between school-based disciplinary practices such as detention and suspension and criminal justice strategies such as jail and probation.

What unites these various approaches to discipline and punishment is a focus on the wrongdoer (versus the people and relationships impacted), as well as an emphasis on social isolation and removal (versus social reintegration). As Brenda Morrison writes:

> Too often our institutional designs have failed to recognise the importance of collective processes to individual lives, and when individuals don't fit into our social institutions, typically we find ways to exclude them rather than create opportunities to build mutual understanding through the enhancement of social relationships.[26]

In a nutshell, this is what restorative discipline seeks to do. **Restorative discipline** is a way of approaching problematic behavior in youth by focusing less on how the behavior violates rules and more on how it affects other people and relationships.[27] A restorative approach to education and student discipline points to an effort to inten-

Figure 12.3: The Social Discipline/Social Control Window

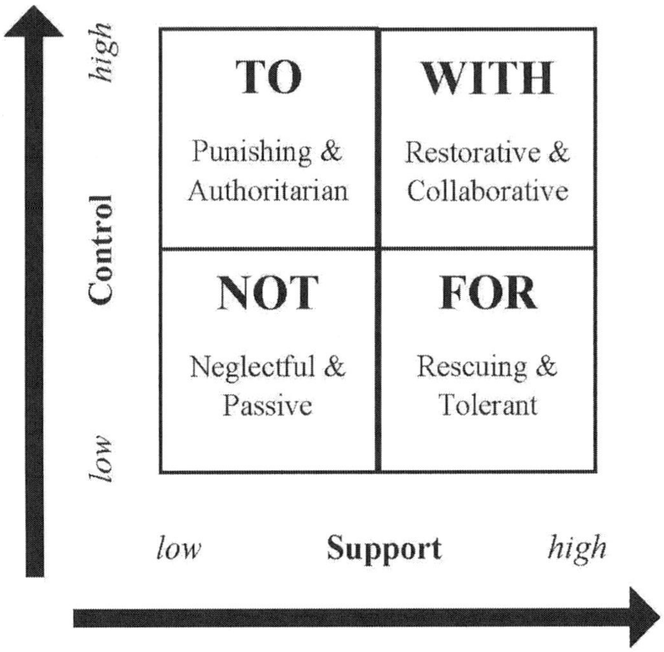

Source: Adapted from the following two sources: Hansberry, B. (2016). *A practical introduction to restorative practice in schools: Theory, skills, and guidance.* Philadelphia, PA: Jessica Kingsley Publishers Wachtel, T. (2016). *Defining restorative.* International Institute for Restorative Practices. Retrieved from http://www.iirp.edu/images/pdf/Defining-Restorative_Nov-2016.pdf.

tionally create opportunities for students to develop empathy and reflect directly on how their actions impact others, especially in the social contexts of conflict, wrongdoing, and misconduct. Evans and Vaandering refer to this as prioritizing "social engagement rather than social control."[28]

Restorative Discipline:
A Supportive Approach to Social Control

When we examine the different ways of trying to control social behavior or develop social discipline in youth, a popular way of illustrating these various approaches is seen in the "social control window" (also frequently referred to as the "social discipline window"). As presented in Figure 12.3, this illustration provides us with the means of examining how different methods of social discipline vary depending on the way each method relates to control and support. For example, an authoritarian approach to discipline is defined by its high degree of control and low degree of support; how-

Figure 12.4: The Social Scope of Restorative Discipline

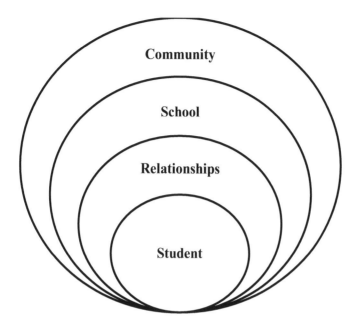

ever, a restorative approach is defined by maintaining high degrees of both support and control.

As demonstrated by the "social control window" (see Figure 12.3), when faced with problematic or harmful behavior in students, educators have the option of addressing that behavior by doing something *to* the student, *with* the student, *for* the student, or *not* doing anything at all.[29] Unlike what the other approaches might suggest, a restorative approach asserts that control and support do not need to contradict or efface one another if educators are to effectively confront and address student misconduct. Instead, restorative discipline supports collaborative practices and the direct inclusion of students in processing and addressing their behavior so that they can actively participate in their own social and moral development.

Restorative Discipline: Common Goals and Guiding Principles

While different theorists and practitioners articulate the goals of restorative discipline in slightly different ways, it is clear that the restorative approach to addressing student conduct is not simply focused on the offending student, but more broadly includes the student, their relationships, the school, and even the wider community (see Figure 12.4). Though we lack one single, standard way of articulating or implementing restorative discipline in schools, when we look at the literature on this subject common goals and guiding principles do emerge. For example:

- **Restorative discipline is inclusive.** Much like restorative justice, it attempts to bring in relevant stakeholders (such as the offending student, peers, teachers, administrators, and family members) when addressing important problems.[30]

- **Restorative discipline is collaborative.** Rather than imposing punishment or treatment plans on a student or student's family, a restorative approach tries to include the student directly in the creation of action plans intended to address their problematic behavior.[31]

- **Restorative discipline focuses on social reintegration rather than isolation.** While a restorative approach to discipline seeks to clarify and confront wrong-doing and harm, the intent is not to socially isolate the offending student, but rather to reintegrate that student in positive social environments such as peer groups, classrooms, and the school itself.[32]

- **Restorative discipline sees conflict and misconduct as potentially transformative and educative.** While restorative educators don't necessarily rejoice over student misconduct and conflict, these situations are seen as a natural, inevitable, and normal part of social life and development. As much as possible, restorative discipline seeks to use these situations to support important goals such as empathy development, healthy socialization, and even organizational transformation.[33]

- **Restorative discipline focuses on harm and is responsive to individual and group needs.** A defining characteristic of both restorative justice and restorative discipline is a focus on harm and impact versus specific rule violations. While restorative schools and classrooms still rely on specific rules and policies to set behavioral expectations, harm and impact are emphasized when responding to rule violations, and the needs of all are considered when determining how violations will be addressed.[34]

As mentioned above, restorative discipline is multi-layered in its overall scope when addressing social problems and concerns. As shown in Figure 12.4, while a traditional approach to discipline would likely focus solely on the problem student and their offending behavior, restorative discipline takes a more layered, holistic approach to investigating and addressing harm and wrongdoing. Not only do restorative educators and administrators have an interest in the individual needs and concerns of the offending student and their peers, but there is also an emphasis on the nature and health of relationships (including those between students, their families, teachers, and staff), and interest in the ways in which the school and community can contribute to the prevention of future harm and misconduct. As our exploration continues, we will examine specific ways in which restorative discipline and practices are implemented within educational institutions, including elementary schools, secondary schools, and college campuses.

Restorative Practices in Elementary and Secondary Schools

When we begin to examine the different ways in which restorative practices and restorative discipline are being used in elementary and secondary schools, we see that these practices can be classified as either informal or formal.[35] **Informal restorative practices** refer to the use of restorative practices and the application of restorative principles in day-to-day classroom and school activities.[36] Some examples of informal restorative practices might include:

- Using circles to discuss course content and facilitate collaborative learning[37]
- Using questions and guidance that help students develop their agency and self-confidence (rather than only telling them what to do)[38]
- Using circles or conferences to develop and reinforce classroom values and intentions
- Using circles to begin and end each school day[39]
- Using conferences to quickly address small-scale conflicts between students before they escalate and become serious disciplinary issues[40]

While informal practices are a way of embedding restorative principles and processes into a school's routine activities, **formal restorative practices** are used when something goes wrong and there is a need to clearly identify and address harm and severely problematic behavior.[41] Some examples of formal restorative practices might include:

- Using a peacemaking circle to address an ongoing, severe conflict within a group or classroom[42]
- Using a dialog process (such as a conference or mediation) to address harm that one person has done to another[43]
- Using a conference process to bring in a student's family if that student is struggling behaviorally, socially, or academically[44]

While restorative discipline could fall under the umbrella of both informal and formal restorative practices, it is more commonly associated with formal practices and the need to address behavior that extends beyond expected, everyday classroom conflict or disruption.

Informal restorative practices can be used to support a school's desire to implement formal restorative practices and/or a restorative approach to student discipline. Informal practices normalize restorative principles and processes and implant them firmly into a school's social and academic culture. Whether restorative or not, informal and formal practices within a school work hand in hand to communicate norms and values to students and staff. For example, just like telling a disruptive second grader to go sit in the corner prepares that student for future disciplinary practices such as detention and suspension, having an informal conference with a disruptive student can also prepare them for future disciplinary practices such as a family group conference should their behavior escalate and become more problematic. In other words, the practices a teacher uses to demonstrate social norms and processes should mirror the way a school addresses serious problems and conflict. Therefore, when a school attempts to implement a broad restorative approach to discipline, informal classroom practices should align to support and normalize that approach.

Examples of Restorative Practices in Elementary and Secondary Schools

As is the case with restorative justice, restorative practices in schools take many forms and function in many different ways; however, the restorative process models most frequently utilized in schools include peacemaking circles, reparative boards, and conferencing. Let's explore some examples.

Peacemaking Circles

Peacemaking circles are a common process used in restorative schools and classrooms. As we explored in Chapter 7, circles are not only highly adaptable to different situations and groups, but they also work well when larger groups need to discuss an issue rather than a small number of individuals. Talking circles are therefore a popular way of implementing restorative practices in schools both informally and formally. In other words, not only can talking circles be embedded into a classroom's daily routine (informal), but they can also be convened to intentionally address problematic and disruptive issues or conflicts that are affecting the class as a whole (formal).[45] As we examined in Chapter 7, a **talking circle** is a type of peacemaking circle that provides a community or group with an opportunity to discuss important issues with one another. These dialogs are typically facilitated by a circle keeper and the use of a talking piece ensures that every member of the circle has an equal chance to speak and contribute to the dialog.[46]

In addition to talking circles, another common use of peacemaking circles in schools are reintegration circles. While we explored the use of reintegration circles in Chapters 7 and 10 in the context of an offender's social reintegration after serving time in prison, these circles can also be used in a school setting when a student is returning to the school or classroom after being temporarily removed through practices such as detention or suspension.[47] A **reintegration circle** is a process in which a returning student, and possibly their parents, can convene with teachers, school administrators, and perhaps even other students to discuss the reentry and reintegration of the returning student into the academic and social life of the school.[48] Agreements can be formed through a reintegration circle that specify what the returning student will do to repair the harm they have caused to individuals or the school, and plans of support can also be created to help address the needs of the returning student, or other individuals, in regards to the reentry and reintegration process.[49]

Conferences and Mediations

While circles are effective in bringing larger groups (such as classrooms) together for intentional sharing and dialog, sometimes more intimate processes are needed in order to address an individual student's behavior. Common problems in schools such as truancy and bullying often don't need to be addressed within the larger classroom community but need specialized attention outside of the classroom setting. A **truancy conference** (also referred to as a truancy circle) brings a truant student together with their family, teachers, and school staff to discuss the problem and brainstorm solutions.[50] Rather than punishing the student, a truancy conference convenes to support the student, generate understanding about the motivations behind their behavior, and create a plan to increase school attendance.[51]

While a truancy conference in many ways mirrors a family group conference (see Chapter 5), bullying in schools can often be addressed by utilizing and adapting the model for victim-offender mediation. As we explored in Chapter 4, a victim-offender mediation brings an offender together with their victim(s) to discuss the impact of the crime and create a plan for repair and restoration. Restorative schools can use a similar process to address bullying between students.[52] A facilitated peer-to-peer mediation or conference to address instances of bullying can be used in schools when it is deemed safe to do so; however, due to the nature and impact of bullying (including the abusive power dynamics often at play) this is not always the case. In some ways, concerns about using direct mediation to address bullying in schools connect to the concerns many people have about using victim-offender mediation in cases involving intimate partner violence (see Chapter 11). Bullying, much like intimate partner violence, is an example of relationship abuse and therefore cannot always be addressed in the same way we address social conflicts. Schools can therefore adapt this model by holding private conferences with both the bullying student and the bullied student without bringing the two together.[53] While this kind of conferencing process may differ from victim-offender mediation, it can be used to pursue similar goals such as exploring impact, identifying harm, and collaboratively addressing safety, repair, and restoration.

Reparative Boards

As we discussed in Chapters 8 and 10, reparative boards are commonly implemented within probation agencies as a way to increase community participation in the juvenile and criminal justice systems. In a similar way, reparative boards can be used within schools to increase student participation in disciplinary policies and practices. One example of this is a model referred to as a fairness committee. A **fairness committee** is a reparative board that includes a mix of students, teachers, and school staff who meet to discuss specific cases of students violating school policies and make decisions concerning how those violations will be addressed.[54] These committees can adjudicate cases involving academic success (such as truancy or skipping homework), as well as cases involving problematic social behavior (such as vandalism and disrespectful speech).[55] Not only do school-based reparative boards increase the trans-

Figure 12.5: The Whole School Approach to Restorative Schools

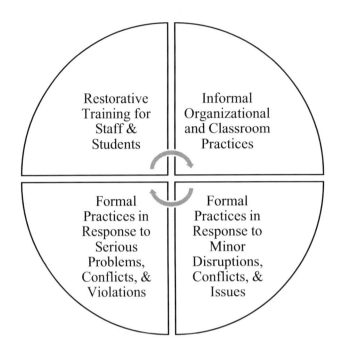

parency and inclusivity of a school's approach to student discipline, but they also facilitate direct participation and collective efficacy within a school community.

Implementing Restorative Practices in Schools

As stated earlier, restorative practices in schools can be either informal or formal, and often the informal practices are the key to successfully implementing formal, disciplinary practices. This is referred to in the literature as the **"whole school" approach.**[56] Essentially this means that a school does not just use restorative practices when addressing severely problematic behavior by students, but seeks to implement these practices in everyday organizational and classroom activities, when addressing school-wide issues and decisions, and also when addressing problems with staff.[57] In other words, as seen in Figure 12.5, with the "whole school" approach, restorative values and practices permeate every part of a school and its operations, making them the foundation of that school's academic, social, and professional culture.

In line with the "whole school" approach are the six elements of sustainable, restorative implementation outlined by Lisa Cameron and Margaret Thorsborne.[58] Within their six elements we see an emphasis on both policy and practice, informal and formal practices, and staff and student participation. Their suggested guidelines for implementation are as follows:

"Professional development in restorative justice philosophy and practices for all staff including those with a non-teaching role"[59]

According to Cameron and Thorsborne,[60] everyone who works in the school should be educated and trained in restorative values and practices, as well as those who support the school and interact with students such as parents and volunteers.

"Development and maintenance of a cohort of highly skilled conference facilitators"[61]

Not only should teachers be well trained in restorative practices, but a school should identify, train, and sustain continued training for a special group of teachers and staff who can support and facilitate formal restorative practices when needed.

"Use of restorative processes for dealing with incidents of inappropriate behavior and high-level conflict for staff"[62]

According to Cameron and Thorsborne[63] it is important that professional issues and conflicts are addressed similarly to those within the student body. In other words, if punitive responses to staff issues and conflicts remain in place, restorative values and practices will struggle to take root in a school's daily operations and culture.

"Provision of restorative justice philosophy and practice within pre-service teacher education"[64]

If a community hopes to implement a restorative approach to school management, teaching, and student discipline, then teachers should be introduced to this approach when they are receiving their own education and preparing to become teachers. Therefore, the inclusion of restorative discipline and practices in university-level teaching curriculums will naturally support the implementation of restorative schools within a community.

"State policy development"[65]

Schools are typically part of a broader school system within a district or state. While schools can find ways to implement restorative practices without the aid and support of their city or state, schools can often be accountable to external district and state policies. In light of this, according to Cameron and Thorsborne,[66] a school is more likely to succeed in implementing restorative practices if district and state policy guides or supports that implementation.

"School policy development"[67]

Lastly, Cameron and Thorsborne[68] assert that a school must develop its own policy that states how restorative practices will be implemented and evaluated. The process of developing this policy should also be as collaborative as possible by directly including stakeholders such as parents, teachers, staff, administrators, and even students.

As is the case with any implementation of restorative values and practices (whether that be restorative justice, restorative policing, restorative prisons, or restorative schools), it is vitally important that attention is paid to the cultural transformation of the institution, community, or organization in addition to the practical application of restorative models and processes. A restorative implementation cannot hope to be sustained if it is executed in an authoritarian way, or if the values of a community or organization simply don't align with restorative principles. Implementing restorative values and practices within a community or school that is comfortable with a punitive or authoritarian approach is not easy and will not happen overnight. It requires commitment, collaboration, inclusion, and a collective recognition that punishment is not the most effective way to discipline and teach students.

Adapting Restorative Practices to Accommodate Special Needs and Differences

As we've explored in previous chapters, it is important when implementing restorative practices in any context that we be prepared to adapt to the people and communities with which we are working. As we consider ways to utilize restorative practices in schools, it is inevitable that we may need to address student conduct and conflict between students of different ages, physical abilities, social development, and cognitive abilities. In a nutshell, the restorative approach to addressing social conflict and rule violations is focused on exploring how the behavior or misconduct has impacted other people, but what if one or more of the students involved are limited in their ability to understand that impact or communicate their experience?

Students with special needs encompass a range of limitations and difficulties that can require us to adapt restorative practices and processes in order to make them more accessible for people who behave, think, and/or communicate differently than the average person their age (see Box 12.2).[69] Therefore, before utilizing a restorative practice in a school setting, it is important to understand the potential limitations and special needs of the students involved in the incident or issue being addressed. Often restorative processes can be altered in the way they are structured or facilitated in order to accommodate different needs among the participants.[70] Different approaches to student preparation can also be utilized before a restorative process takes place in order to maximize the student's comfort level and involvement.[71] Students without special needs may also need to be prepared prior to the restorative process in order to better understand how or why another student may be limited in their ability to communicate, make decisions, or demonstrate empathy.

There is no denying that restorative practices do require certain abilities when it comes to social skills, communication, and cognition; however, there is also no denying that inclusion (and therefore accessibility) is a restorative value, and so adapting to the special needs of students is an essential part of implementing and modeling a restorative approach to issues, problems, and relationships within schools.

Box 12.2: Restorative Justice: Let's Take a Closer Look ...
Can Restorative Practices be Helpful for Students with
Special Needs and Low Levels of Empathy?

In 2010, Caryn Saxon designed a restorative program for a young girl in middle school named "Hannah" (not her real name) who was diagnosed with Asperger's Syndrome. Hannah's condition, which is now referred to as one variation of Autism Spectrum Disorder, meant that she struggled with social skills and also had a limited ability to feel and express empathy. After harming a neighbor and classmate, Hannah was referred to a victim-offender mediation program, but it was determined that it would not be a suitable process for Hannah because she would likely struggle to meet social expectations and fully understand the impact of her actions. Learning about Hannah's love of art, Caryn Saxon, the victim-offender mediator assigned to Hannah's case, therefore decided to design a program specifically for Hannah that might help her explore the impact of her problematic behavior toward her classmate. The *Impact Through Art* program was conceived and, after the appropriate needs assessment and preparation, Caryn and Hannah met to do art, make paper, and process Hannah's offense. What follows is an excerpt from Caryn's journal following her *Impact Through Art* session with Hannah.

> *Hannah arrived and she was really excited by the room. She immediately got herself a big sheet of paper and started collecting some markers and paints. I sat down across from Hannah and explained that we would be making paper a little later on, but that we had some other things to do first.*
>
> *I began by giving her a hunk of purple clay, keeping a brown hunk for myself. I asked her if she was familiar with the idea of a begging bowl and she said she had made one before. I told her to take the clay into her hands and begin to shape a bowl while she thought about what she wanted to get out of our session together. We worked with our clay in silence. I then gave her a thin strip of white paper and asked her to write down one thing she wanted to get out of our session, and put it in her begging bowl. We put our bowls aside.*
>
> *I gave Hannah the large sheet of paper and told her she was free to fill that space in any way she liked. She began by painting her name and then a large blue form that ended up taking the shape of a cloud. While she was working I asked her to tell me the story about breaking into her classmate's home. While she recounted the details she painted her hand purple and pressed it onto her paper, right in the middle of a large blue cloud shape. After we got through most of the details of what she had taken, I asked her to tell me who had been affected by what she had done. During this time her face was much less expressive and she appeared rather de-*

tached (more so than she had when we began our session). She first mentioned that the mom and dad of the classmate's family had been affected. I asked her to name someone else. She mentioned their daughter who had been a friend of hers that she had played with before. She began leafing through the magazine clippings and gluing selected pictures onto her paper. She next mentioned her sister. She said she had gone into the house initially on her own and then went to get her sister and bring her there, after which they both took items from the house. Lastly she mentioned her own parents. I asked her how she thought her parents felt about what had happened and she said they were mad and angry. After some silence she said they were disappointed, and then she added that they were embarrassed.

I handed Hannah another small strip of white paper and told her that I wanted her to write a message to the man and woman whose house she stole from and put it in her begging bowl.

We took a little break from discussing the offense and we both worked on some art. She continued using paints and I worked on a small collage. After we had been playing for a while, I handed Hannah another piece of white paper and asked her to write a message to her friend who lived in the house and put it in her begging bowl.

Hannah returned to her original paper and continued to add collage elements to it, and I put together a couple of cards using paper scraps. After a short while, I handed Hannah another piece of scrap paper and asked her to write a message to her sister and put it in the begging bowl. I then asked her to do the same for her mother and then her father.

It was finally time to make our paper. I explained the process to Hannah and told her we would be using one of her art pieces (if she wanted to), as well as her begging bowl messages in our paper pulp. We began to create the basics for our pulp. We tore apart some tissue paper scraps, Hannah ripped up one of her art pieces and we made our first batch of pulp. We added some cotton to our blender, and Hannah put in some tissue paper, some of her art work, and we blended it together. We continued until we had a good amount of pulp in our water basin. I showed her how to hold the dackle and make a sheet which she did really well. We drained off the water, flipped it over and Hannah, using the sponge, worked hard to get as much water out of the paper as she could. I showed her how to tell if the paper was ready to be released from the dackle and suddenly we had our first sheet done. Hannah was thrilled. She made five sheets in all. During about the third batch of pulp I asked her to get her begging bowl and add her messages to the blender. I told her that this was really meaningful and asked her if she understood why I felt that way. She said she wasn't sure, and so I told her that these messages represented something harmful she had done but that we were going to take that experience and make something better out of it. She said that was "cool."

When we were done I thanked Hannah for coming and for doing art with me. She asked me if I wanted to know what she had written for her begging bowl in terms of what she wanted to get out of the session. I said sure. She said she had written, 'that I will learn to make paper and have fun, thank you.' I said I thought we had succeeded in that and she agreed.

- What do you think? Was this process successful in giving Hannah the opportunity to explore the impact of her offense?
- Based on what you know about Hannah, what could Caryn have done differently to make her session with Hannah even more impactful and restorative?
- What about the classmate and family Hannah had harmed? What additional response to Hannah's offense might be necessary in order to restore the family, and what might Hannah be able to do on their behalf?

Source: Caryn E. Saxon, journal excerpt from *Impact Through Art* field notes.

Restorative Practices in Higher Education

While the vast majority of colleges and universities still utilize traditional, retributive approaches to student discipline, the use of restorative practices within these institutions is becoming increasingly popular.[72] Despite the fact that students attending these schools are typically adults, universities still maintain rules and policies concerning student conduct, and, therefore, must formally address rule violations, conflicts, and even crimes that occur on their campuses. Issues that might be addressed in this way can include everything from sexual assault and stalking to hosting a loud party or cheating on an exam.

Since institutions of higher education are even more decentralized than elementary and secondary schools, the supportive interplay between formal and informal practices is less likely to exist. In other words, on most college and university campuses, classroom practices are less likely to be influenced by school administrators and policies than might be the case in other types of schools. Due to this, when we examine the application of restorative practices in higher education, we find that these typically consist of formal, highly organized disciplinary practices that utilize existing restorative process models or are designed to uphold restorative principles and values while addressing specific instances of student misconduct.

Regarding the need to respond to student misconduct, institutions of higher education are commonly focused on creating processes that are fair and effective while also being educative and focused, in part, on student development and learning.[73]

As we explored earlier in this chapter, research shows that authoritarian, retributive approaches to discipline are less effective than collaborative, restorative ones (see Figure 12.3). As discussed in Box 12.3, research also indicates that retributive approaches are less educative and facilitative of student development and accountability within college campuses.[74] It is therefore no surprise that more and more universities are taking notice of restorative practices and applying them to student judicial affairs and cases of conflict and misconduct.

Box 12.3: Research in Restorative Justice — The STARR Project

In 2014, David R. Karp and Casey Sacks published findings from their STARR Project, a research study examining the impact of restorative practices when used in cases involving student misconduct on college campuses. Karp and Sacks collected evaluative survey data from 18 different college campuses, which ranged from public to private, small to large, and secular to religious. In all, they examined 659 cases involving alleged student misconduct.

The STARR Project was a comparison study that evaluated six specific outcomes using three different approaches to student misconduct hearings. The three approaches Karp and Sacks evaluated included what they termed the *Model Code Hearing*, the *Restorative-Oriented Administrative Hearing*, and *Restorative Justice Practice*.

> The *Model Code Hearings* were traditional in nature and involved either a one-on-one meeting between the student offender and a conduct officer or a meeting between the student offender and a panel of board members that included staff, faculty, and other students. The *Model Code Hearings* followed a traditional process of applying sanctions to the student offender such as restrictions, suspension, and even expulsion.
>
> The *Restorative-Oriented Administrative Hearings* followed the traditional model but implemented some restorative elements. For example, in these hearings a conduct officer would discuss the misconduct with the student offender and support them in identifying the harm they caused, as well as strategies for repairing it. Karp and Sacks refer to this approach as a hybrid model that incorporated elements of the *Model Code Hearing* and *Restorative Justice Practice*.
>
> *Restorative Justice Practice* deviated from the *Model Code Hearing* by bringing directly into the process members of the campus community who had been impacted by the student offender's misconduct. A facilitated dialog would take place between the student offender and affected community members with the goal of identifying ways in which harm could be repaired and trust restored.

Regardless of the approach taken to address the offending student's misconduct, the surveys employed by Karp and Sacks measured the perceptions and outcomes of student offenders, conduct officers, and other participants involved in the process. Through the surveys, six dependent variables were examined in order to measure the impact of each approach on factors related to student development and educative sanctioning. These variables included:

- Just Community/Self-Authorship
- Active Accountability
- Interpersonal Competence
- Social Ties to the Institution
- Procedural Fairness
- Closure

Findings from the data analysis employed by Karp and Sacks revealed that the approach to the conduct process was the most significant factor when measuring student learning after misconduct, and that *Restorative Justice Practice* was the most effective approach for all six dependent variables, including perceptions regarding fairness, social reintegration, and student offender accountability.

The STARR Project remains the largest comparative, evaluative analysis of restorative approaches to student misconduct on college campuses. While we still have a lot to learn when it comes to student discipline in college, this analysis indicates that the use of restorative discipline and practices are a promising way of addressing misconduct while promoting student development.

Source: Karp, D. R., & Sacks, C. (2014). Student conduct, restorative justice, and student development: Findings from the STARR project: A student accountability and restorative research project. *Contemporary Justice Review*, 17(2), 154–172.

Examples of Restorative Practices in Colleges and Universities

Much like elementary and secondary schools, peacemaking circles, reparative boards, and conferencing are the most prevalent restorative processes used in higher education;[75] however, impact panels and direct mediation have also found their way into restorative college practices.[76] Let's explore some examples.

Peacemaking Circles, Conferences, and Mediations

Circles, conferences, and mediations are dialog processes that can be used in a variety of ways on university campuses to address social issues, student conflicts, academic challenges, and also misconduct. As we explored in Chapter 7, circles can be a highly effective process when facilitating dialogs within large groups. In this way, colleges can use circles to support a range of needs such as discussing alcohol abuse in a residential housing unit or providing students with the chance to speak and listen to one another about sensitive campus and community issues.[77]

Conferences and mediations are typically convened when an incident includes and impacts a smaller group of people. Not only can these processes be implemented in cases involving student misconduct, but campus offices and departments can also use mediation or conferencing to address and resolve disputes between roommates, faculty members, and student groups.[78] As we explored in Chapters 4 and 5, these kinds of processes typically result in a mediated agreement or action plan in which the parties identify their individual and collective commitments to resolving the conflict, repairing harm done to one another or the community, and preventing future harm and wrongdoing.[79]

Reparative Boards

Boards are a common way in which college campuses address student judicial affairs and misconduct. A typical judicial board usually consists of faculty, staff, and students who convene to adjudicate incidents of student misconduct by hearing from the offending student and applying appropriate sanctions to their case (such as community or university service, academic probation or suspension, or letters of apology).[80] A restorative adaptation of this model is referred to as an integrity board. An **integrity board** also consists of faculty, staff, and students; however, members are trained in restorative values and practices and focus less on the application of prescribed sanctions and more on working with the offending student to identify and explore how the misconduct has impacted others and what can be done to reestablish trust between the student and their campus community.[81] In other words, not only are punitive sanctions replaced with plans for repair and restoration, but there is also an emphasis on the social and academic reintegration of the offending student.[82]

Impact Panels

As we explored in Chapter 6, impact panels are a restorative way of addressing serious issues such as drunk driving or sexual assault without bringing victims into direct contact with their own offenders. Similarly, this process can be used on college campuses to help students develop empathy and explore the impact of their actions without necessitating the involvement of people they have directly harmed. For example, members of a fraternity could be asked to attend an impact panel on initiation rituals and hazing practices. Similarly, students guilty of violating campus drug or alcohol policies could attend a panel on substance abuse, and students guilty of violating sexual conduct policies could be required to attend a survivor's impact panel on sexual assault (see Chapter 11).

As we've explored throughout this chapter, though the two can sometimes be conflated, discipline is distinctly different from retributive punishment. Discipline is not necessarily defined by its intent to restore balance or impose pain; it is intended to teach, to shape behavior, and to reinforce norms and expectations. It is intended to correct someone who has deviated. As we have seen, the evidence indicates that perhaps a restorative approach to discipline is more effective at achieving these ends than retributive punishments that isolate people and impose pain and disconnection. As we see the widening implementation of restorative practices and principles in our schools and other organizations, it will be interesting to see if communities that adopt this approach may one day see a reduction in overall crime, violence, and harm.

As our exploration of restorative practices in schools has shown us, the concept of restorative justice can be applied to issues, problems, and institutions unrelated to crime. Gerry Johnstone refers to this as the "downward expansion" of restorative justice, the stretching of restorative values and practices to address routine problems in families, communities, and organizations.[83] Johnstone also asserts that there is an "upwards expansion" as well, a movement to explore what a restorative approach can do to address problems with even greater social significance than crime, such as war, human rights violations, and systemic social injustice.[84] As we move forward into Chapter 13, we will examine these issues in greater detail while exploring the ways in which restorative justice and practices are being used to address them.

Chapter Summary

What is the difference between restorative justice, restorative discipline, and restorative practices, and how are the three related?

While restorative justice refers to the application of restorative values, principles, and processes to incidents of crime and juvenile delinquency, restorative discipline is the application of this same restorative approach to student discipline in schools. Restorative practices, on the other hand, refer to any model, program, or process that is designed in order to implement restorative principles and values within an organization, agency, institution, or community. While restorative practices, restorative discipline, and restorative justice can all overlap with one another, and all are rooted in the same values and principles (such as inclusivity, accountability, and collaboration), they are also distinctly different from one another in regard to the contexts in which they are used.

What is the connection between student discipline, juvenile delinquency, and crime?

Not only do common approaches to student discipline (such as detention and suspension) frequently mirror traditional responses to crime and juvenile delinquency (such as probation and incarceration), but research also shows that a student's involvement with school-based disciplinary procedures, as well as their failure to complete high school, can put them at greater risk for later involvement with the juvenile and criminal justice systems. The connection between student discipline, juvenile delinquency, and crime can also be seen in the implementation and effect of policies such as the Gun-Free Schools Act of 1994 and the zero tolerance policies that flooded local schools after it became law. While these policies were intended to keep schools safe, history has shown that they also resulted in more students failing to complete school, moving into alternative schools, and becoming involved in the juvenile justice system.

What are the underlying goals and principles of restorative discipline?

Restorative discipline is a way of approaching problematic behavior in youth by focusing less on how the behavior violates rules and more on how it affects other people and relationships. Common goals and guiding principles of restorative discipline include:

- Inclusivity
- Collaboration
- Focus on social reintegration
- Conflict as potentially transformative and educative
- Focus on harm
- Responsive to individual and group needs

Unlike traditional, retributive approaches to student discipline that typically focus solely on the offending student, restorative discipline takes a more layered, holistic approach to investigating and addressing harm and wrongdoing by focusing on relationships and the wider environment.

How are restorative practices used in elementary and secondary schools?

In elementary and secondary schools, restorative practices can be categorized as either informal or formal. Informal restorative practices refer to the application of restorative principles in routine classroom and school-wide activities. Formal restorative practices are used to address issues or problems that exist outside the scope of normal activities and expectations.

Some common examples of restorative practices in schools include peacemaking circles, reparative boards, and conferencing. When implementing restorative practices and student discipline in elementary and secondary schools, it is important to consider the ways in which informal practices can support the formal implementation of restorative discipline. This is referred to as the "whole school" approach, which means that a school does not just use restorative practices when addressing severely problematic behavior by students but seeks to implement these practices in everyday organizational and classroom activities, when addressing school-wide issues and decisions, and also when addressing problems with staff.

How are restorative practices used in higher education?

While the vast majority of colleges and universities still utilize traditional, retributive approaches to student discipline, the use of restorative practices within these institutions is becoming increasingly popular. One explanation for this is that institutions of higher learning share an expressed desire to utilize processes when addressing student misconduct that are fair and effective while also resulting in student development and learning. Research studies, such as the STARR Project, indicate that restorative practices are better at facilitating student development, social reintegration, and perceptions of fairness than traditional, retributive approaches to student discipline in colleges and universities.

Examples of restorative practices in higher education include the use of circles, conferences, and mediations to address conflict and harm involving both small and large groups, as well as integrity boards and impact panels.

Key Terms

Restorative Practices
Restorative Discipline
Status Offenses
Gun-Free Schools Act
Zero Tolerance
School-To-Prison Pipeline
Informal Restorative Practices
Formal Restorative Practices
Talking Circle
Reintegration Circles
Truancy Conference
Fairness Committee
"Whole School" Approach
Integrity Board

Critical Thinking Questions

1. After reading Box 12.1 on the concept of a "restorative city," why do you think it might be important for a community to commit fully to restorative values and processes instead of only implementing them in isolated ways? Do you think this city-wide approach to restorative justice and practices is critical to the effective implementation of restorative justice? Why or why not?

2. In what ways, if any, do you think traditional, retributive student discipline in elementary and secondary schools reflects retributive punishment in the criminal justice system? What connections can you identify between student discipline and offender punishment?

3. Imagine that you are a middle school teacher and one of your students was just caught cheating on a test in class. Using the "Social Discipline Window" in Figure 12.3, try to articulate how you might address your student's behavior using each quadrant in the window. In other words, what would an authoritarian response be, a restorative response, a neglectful response, and a rescuing response? After generating your four options, which response do you think would be most effective and why?

4. Without using an example from this chapter, try to come up with an idea for an informal restorative practice and a formal restorative practice that could be utilized in a high school.

5. Imagine that you are in charge of addressing frequent noise violations by a specific group of students in a college campus dorm. How might you utilize a restorative practice or process to address the problem?

References

1. Evans, K., & Vaandering, D. (2016). The little book of restorative justice in education: Fostering responsibility, healing, and hope in schools. New York, NY: Good Books.

2. Ibid.

3. Wachtel, T. (2016). *Defining restorative*. International Institute for Restorative Practices. Retrieved from http://www.iirp.edu/images/pdf/Defining-Restorative_Nov-2016.pdf.

4. Amstutz, L. S., & Mullet, J. H. (2005). The little book of restorative discipline for schools: Teaching responsibility; creating caring climates. Intercourse, PA: Good Books.

5. Stohr, M. K., & Walsh, A. (2016). *Corrections: The essentials* (2nd ed.). Thousand Oaks, CA: Sage.

6. Bayens, G., & Smykla, J. O. (2013). *Probation, parole, & community-based corrections: Supervision, treatment, & evidence-based practices*. New York, NY: McGraw-Hill.

7. Ibid.

8. Ibid., see 6.

9. Office of Juvenile Justice and Delinquency Prevention. (n.d.). *Law enforcement and juvenile crime*. Retrieved from https://www.ojjdp.gov/ojstatbb/crime/JAR.asp.

10. Hockenberry, S. (2016, May). *Juveniles in residential placement, 2013*. Retrieved from http://www.ncjj.org/pdf/Juvenile%20Arrests%20Bulletins/249507.pdf.

11. Aull, E. H. (2012). Zero tolerance, frivolous juvenile court referrals, and the school-to-prison pipeline: Using arbitration as a screening-out method to help plug the pipeline. *Ohio State Journal on Dispute Resolution*, *27*(1), 179–206.

12. Monahan, K. C., VanDerhei, S., Bechtold, J., & Cauffman, E. (2014). From the school yard to the squad car: School discipline, truancy, and arrest. *Journal of Youth and Adolescence*, *43*(7), 1110–1122.

13. Loeber, R., Farrington, D. P., & Petechuk, D. (2013). Bulletin 1: From juvenile delinquency to young adult offending. Retrieved from https://www.ncjrs.gov/pdffiles1/nij/grants/242931.pdf

14. Weissman, M. (2015). *Prelude to prison: Student perspectives on school suspension*. Syracuse, NY: Syracuse University Press.

15. Ibid.

16. Simson, D. (2014). Exclusion, punishment, racism and our schools: A critical race theory perspective on school discipline. *UCLA Law Review*, 506–523.

17. Simmons, L. (2017). The prison school: Educational inequality and school discipline in the age of mass incarceration. Oakland, CA: University of California Press.

18. Fabelo, T., Thompson, M. D., Plotkin, M., Carmichael, D., Marchbanks III, M. P., & Booth, E. A. (2011). Breaking schools' rules: A statewide study of how school discipline relates to students' success and juvenile justice involvement. Retrieved from https://csgjusticecenter.org/wp-content/uploads/2012/08/Breaking_Schools_Rules_Report_Final.pdf.

19. Morris, M. W. (2016). *Pushout: The criminalization of black girls in schools*. New York, NY: The New Press.

20. Conover-Williams, M. (2014). The queer delinquent: Impacts of risk and protective factors on sexual minority juvenile offending in the U.S. In D. Peterson & V. Panfil (Eds.), *Handbook of LGBT communities, crime, and justice* (pp. 449–472). New York, NY: Springer.

21. Ware, W. (2015). Rounding up the homosexuals: The impact of juvenile court on queer and trans/gender-non-conforming youth. In E. A. Stanley & N. Smith (Eds.), *Captive genders: Trans embodiment and the prison industrial complex* (2nd ed., pp. 97–104). Oakland, CA: AK Press.

22. Wilber, S. (2015). Lesbian, gay, bisexual and transgender youth in the juvenile justice system: A guide to juvenile detention reform. Retrieved from http://www.aecf.org/m/resourcedoc/AECF-lesbiangaybisexualandtransgenderyouthinjj-2015.pdf.

23. Carlton, M. P. (2017, July). *Summary of school safety statistics*. Retrieved from https://www.ncjrs.gov/pdffiles1/nij/250610.pdf.

24. Zhang, A., Musu-Gillette, L., & Oudekerk, B. A. (2016, May). *Indicators of school crime and safety: 2015*. Bureau of Justice Statistics, Department of Justice. Retrieved from https://www.bjs.gov/content/pub/pdf/iscs15.pdf.

25. Carlton, M. P. (2017, July). *Summary of school safety statistics*. Retrieved from https://www.ncjrs.gov/pdffiles1/nij/250610.pdf.

26. Morrison, B. (2001). The school system: Developing its capacity in the regulation of a civil society. In H. Strang & J. Braithwaite (Eds.), *Restorative justice and civil society* (pp. 195–210). Cambridge, UK: Cambridge University Press, p. 202.

27. Amstutz, L. S., & Mullet, J. H. (2005). The little book of restorative discipline for schools: Teaching responsibility; creating caring climates. Intercourse, PA: Good Books.

28. Evans, K., & Vaandering, D. (2016). The little book of restorative justice in education: Fostering responsibility, healing, and hope in schools. New York, NY: Good Books, p. 12.

29. Hansberry, B. (2016). A practical introduction to restorative practice in schools: Theory, skills, and guidance. Philadelphia, PA: Jessica Kingsley Publishers.

30. Smith, D., Fisher, D., & Frey, N. (2015). Better than carrots or sticks: Restorative practices for positive classroom management. Alexandria, VA: ASCD.

31. Thorsborne, M., & Blood, P. (2013). Implementing restorative practices in schools: A practical guide to transforming school communities. London, UK: Jessica Kingsley Publishers.

32. Amstutz, L. S., & Mullet, J. H. (2005). The little book of restorative discipline for schools: Teaching responsibility; creating caring climates. Intercourse, PA: Good Books.

33. Evans, K., & Vaandering, D. (2016). The little book of restorative justice in education: Fostering responsibility, healing, and hope in schools. New York, NY: Good Books.

34. Amstutz, L. S., & Mullet, J. H. (2005). *The little book of restorative discipline for schools: Teaching responsibility; creating caring climates*. Intercourse, PA: Good Books.

35. Smith, D., Fisher, D., & Frey, N. (2015). Better than carrots or sticks: Restorative practices for positive classroom management. Alexandria, VA: ASCD.

36. Ibid.

37. Ibid., see 35.

38. Ibid., see 35.

39. Amstutz, L. S., & Mullet, J. H. (2005). *The little book of restorative discipline for schools: Teaching responsibility; creating caring climates*. Intercourse, PA: Good Books.

40. Smith, D., Fisher, D., & Frey, N. (2015*). Better than carrots or sticks: Restorative practices for positive classroom management*. Alexandria, VA: ASCD.

41. Ibid.

42. Ibid., see 40.

43. Ibid., see 40.

44. Ibid., see 40.

45. Evans, K., & Vaandering, D. (2016). *The little book of restorative justice in education: Fostering responsibility, healing, and hope in schools*. New York, NY: Good Books.

46. Pranis, K. (2005). *The little book of circle processes: A new/old approach to peacemaking*. Intercourse, PA: Good Books.

47. Amstutz, L. S., & Mullet, J. H. (2005). *The little book of restorative discipline for schools: Teaching responsibility; creating caring climates*. Intercourse, PA: Good Books.

48. Riestenberg, N. (2012). Circle in the square: Building community and repairing harm in school. St. Paul, MN: Living Justice Press.

49. Ibid.

50. Ibid., see 48.

51. Ibid., see 48.

52. Amstutz, L. S., & Mullet, J. H. (2005). *The little book of restorative discipline for schools: Teaching responsibility; creating caring climates*. Intercourse, PA: Good Books.

53. Ibid.

54. Hantzopoulos, M. (2013). The fairness committee: Restorative justice in a small urban public high school. *The Prevention Researcher*, *20*(1), 7–10.

55. Ibid.

56. Hopkins, B. (2004). *Just schools: A whole school approach to restorative justice*. Philadelphia, PA: Jessica Kingsley Publishers.

57. Thorsborne, M., & Blood, P. (2013). Implementing restorative practices in schools: A practical guide to transforming school communities. London, UK: Jessica Kingsley Publishers.

58. Cameron, L., & Thorsborne, M. (2001). Restorative justice and school discipline: Mutually exclusive? In H. Strang & J. Braithwaite (Eds.), *Restorative justice and civil society* (pp. 180–194). Cambridge, UK: Cambridge University Press.

59. Ibid., page 189.

60. Ibid., see 58.

61. Ibid., see 58, page 190.

62. Ibid., see 58, page 191.

63. Ibid., see 58.

64. Ibid., see 58, page 192.

65. Ibid., see 58, page 192.

66. Ibid., see 58.

67. Ibid., see 58, page 193.

68. Ibid., see 58.

69. Burnett, N., & Thorsborne, M. (2015). Restorative practice and special needs: A practical guide to working restoratively with young people. Philadelphia, PA: Jessica Kingsley Publishers.

70. Ibid.

71. Ibid., see 69.

72. Darling, J. (2011). *Restorative justice in higher education: A compilation of formats and best practices.* Retrieved from https://www.skidmore.edu/campusrj/documents/Darling-2011-campus-programs.pdf.

73. Lowery, J. W., & Dannells, M. (2004). Contemporary practice in student judicial affairs: Strengths and weaknesses. In D. R. Karp & T. Allena (Eds.), *Restorative justice on the college campus: Promoting student growth and responsibility, and reawakening the spirit of campus community* (pp. 16–26). Springfield, IL: Charles C. Thomas, Publisher, LTD.

74. Karp, D. R., & Sacks, C. (2014). Student conduct, restorative justice, and student development: Findings from the STARR project: A student accountability and restorative research project. *Contemporary Justice Review, 17*(2), 154–172.

75. Karp, D. R. (2013). The little book of restorative justice for colleges and universities: Repairing harm and rebuilding trust in response to student misconduct. Intercourse, PA: Good Books.

76. Darling, J. (2011). *Restorative justice in higher education: A compilation of formats and best practices.* Retrieved from https://www.skidmore.edu/campusrj/documents/Darling-2011-campus-programs.pdf.

77. Goldblum, A. (2009). Restorative justice from theory to practice. In J. Meyer Schrage & N. Geist Giacomini (Eds.), *Reframing campus conflict: Student conduct practice through a social justice lens* (pp. 140–154). Sterling, VA: Stylus Publishing.

78. Warters, W. C. (2000). Mediation in the campus community: Designing and managing effective programs. San Francisco, CA: Jossey-Bass.

79. Warters, W. C. (2004). Applications of mediation in the campus community. In D. R. Karp & T. Allena (Eds.), Restorative justice on the college campus: Promoting student growth and responsibility, and reawakening the spirit of campus community (pp. 77–91), Springfield, IL: Charles C. Thomas, Publisher, LTD.

80. Karp, D. R. (2004). Integrity boards. In D. R. Karp & T. Allena (Eds.), Restorative justice on the college campus: Promoting student growth and responsibility, and reawakening the spirit of campus community (pp. 29–41). Springfield, IL: Charles C. Thomas, Publisher, LTD.

81. Ibid.

82. Ibid., see 80.

83. Johnstone, G. (2011). *Restorative justice: Ideas, values, debates* (2nd ed.). New York, NY: Routledge, page 144.

84. Ibid.

Chapter 13

The Role of Restorative Justice in Transitional Justice Contexts

In this chapter, we will explore the following questions …

- *In what ways is transitional justice distinct from restorative justice, and in what ways do the two overlap?*

- *What are the needs of victims and communities after mass violence, and how can restorative practices help address those needs?*

- *In what ways is our understanding and practice of restorative justice evolving in relation to transitional justice?*

Expanding the Scope of Restorative Justice

As we stated in the conclusion to Chapter 12, not only can the principles and processes of restorative justice be applied to behavior and conflict unrelated to crime (like we see with restorative discipline in schools), but it can also be used to address problems and events on a greater scale than crime (such as genocide, human rights violations, and systemic injustice). Gerry Johnstone refers to this as the upwards and downwards expansion of restorative justice.[1] In other words, while restorative justice can be applied in a downward direction to address conflicts and issues in families, organizations, schools, and communities, it can also expand upwards to address mass violence and systemic oppression.

While Chapter 12 focused on the downward expansion of restorative justice, in this chapter, we will examine the ways in which restorative principles and processes are applied to transitional and social justice movements throughout the world in an effort to address systemic injustice, rebuild war-torn communities, and help people heal after traumatic experiences of mass violence and structural oppression.

Understanding Transitional and Restorative Justice

When we consider common applications of restorative justice what typically comes to mind are juvenile or criminal justice cases involving relatively minor offenses and first- or second-time offenders. In light of this, it might be difficult to imagine the placement of restorative practices in contexts so large-scale and horrific that even conventional criminal justice systems cannot handle the severity and scope of the legal and civil violations involved. When a state, country, or region is involved in human rights abuses such as mass violence, mass rape, and genocide, there is a need to not only stop the abuses and account for the harm, but a need to restructure and rebuild the government and its institutions in order to prevent future oppression and atrocities. Since the late 1980s, these processes in places such as Latin America, South Africa, and Rwanda have been referred to as transitional justice. **Transitional justice** is a coordinated set of interventions implemented after periods of political oppression, mass violence, or state-sponsored human rights violations that seeks to acknowledge what happened, identify offenders, restore victims, and transform the systems and conditions that helped facilitate injustice and abuse. While transitional justice and restorative justice are distinct concepts, some of their values, intentions, and practices do overlap, making restorative justice a frequent partner in transitional justice contexts.

Similarities between Transitional Justice and Restorative Justice

As we can see in its definition, transitional justice does share some common traits with restorative justice. For example, both surface from individual and collective needs following crime and conflict, both emphasize acknowledgement and truth-telling, and both seek to repair harm and prevent it from recurring.

In part, both concepts also exist due to the inherent limits of criminal justice and traditional judicial process. While restorative justice has taken root as an alternative to traditional juvenile and criminal justice strategies because of the failure of these systems to fully include and satisfy relevant stakeholders, transitional justice often operates outside of the traditional criminal justice system for a few reasons. For instance, one of the clear aims of transitional justice is to transform oppressive or violent systems in communities divided by war and conflict. In other words, these processes are often taking place in settings where there is very little trust in existing government institutions;[2] and, therefore, too much association with those institutions (such as a criminal justice system) can corrupt or taint the perceived legitimacy of transitional justice. Additionally, in contexts that necessitate transitional justice, there are often innumerable cases of atrocities and crimes such as rape, assault, and murder. An attempt to process each incident through traditional means would therefore overload the judicial system and immobilize progress.[3]

Criminal justice systems also operate within a restricted set of parameters. In order to initiate criminal justice proceedings there must be evidence to prove an incident of direct victimization as defined through law. However, societies impacted by mass violence cannot necessarily define harm in this limited way. Harm caused by witnessing violence or living under the threat of genocide or rape may not be acknowledged by a criminal justice system, but a transitional justice process must include these victims and account for their experiences.[4] Furthermore, transitional justice is not only concerned with responding to incidents of violence, but also rebuilding and transforming a nation or society. In other words, the scope of transitional justice clearly expands beyond the reach of criminal justice and conventional judicial process.

Both transitional justice and restorative justice also value procedural principles such as inclusion and practices such as narrative storytelling. As we've noted throughout this book, a defining aspect of restorative justice is inclusion, an unwavering belief that victims, offenders, and community members all need a place at the table as we discern how to address a criminal offense. Similarly, transitional justice programs are designed to include as many community members as possible when determining the scope and impact of violent abuses, as well as a region's path toward a more democratic and open government. In fact, as we examine in Box 13.1, there is often a great effort made towards including even children in transitional justice programs, especially if their experiences help a community understand the effects of mass violence and oppression, or child victims are in need of support and reparations.[5]

Box 13.1: Restorative Justice: Let's Take a Closer Look ... Should Children Be Included in Transitional Justice Outreach Programs?

As we've explored in Chapter 13, the term *transitional justice* refers to a variety of strategies that communities can use to address incidents of internal conflict, violence, and oppression that are typically so great in their scale that conventional criminal justice systems cannot adequately intervene. In the context of transitional justice, processes like truth and reconciliation commissions that allow community members to gather information, share their experiences, and publically dialog about these incidents are frequently called outreach programs. While outreach programs tend to be highly inclusive of community members affected by the violence and conflict, there does remain some debate as to whether or not children should be included or shielded from transitional justice processes.

According to the International Center for Transitional Justice (www.ictj.org), there is no doubt that children are greatly affected by the conflict and violence addressed through transitional justice processes. Not only do they often directly experience violence and loss, but they also depend on adults who have suffered through trauma, terror, and brutality. In other words, it is impossible to deny that children in post-conflict communities hold knowledge about these incidents and are therefore a key part in understanding their consequences and impact, as well as potentially deserving of justice and reparations. While transitional justice processes should always be planned and implemented with the participants' emotional and physical safety in mind, this can be especially important as we consider the inclusion of children in transitional justice outreach programs.

According to Clara Ramírez-Barat of the International Center for Transitional Justice, when including children in the transitional justice process, it is wise to identify at least one official staff member who can focus on attending to the needs of children included in outreach programs. Programs involving children should also be facilitated or supervised by adults with whom they are familiar, and guardian consent for their participation should be sought. The potential need for aftercare services or monitoring should also be considered, especially if, during the program, children share difficult experiences or memories that may trigger symptoms of traumatic stress.

While creative outreach programs can be helpful for participants of any age, embedding creativity and art into youth-centered programs can be a great way to help children express their emotions and memories while also remaining responsive to their developmental and cognitive abilities. For example, asking children to share their experiences through painting or crafts might be an effective way to include children in a process like a truth and reconciliation commission without requiring them to participate in the formality of a transitional justice program designed for adults.

What do you think?

What are the risks and benefits of including children in a process of transitional justice? What are the risks and benefits of not including children?

Consider and identify three needs that children in a post-conflict community might have. What is one way we could include children in the transitional justice process in order to meet those needs?

Source: Ramírez-Barat, C. (2012, November). *Engaging children and youth in transitional justice processes: Guidance for outreach programs.* Retrieved from https://www.ictj.org/sites/default/files/ICTJ-Report-Children-Youth-Outreach-2012.pdf.

As we explore the overlap between transitional and restorative justice, we see that both approaches also emphasize the importance of storytelling. Unlike a conventional criminal justice process, which is most concerned with the analysis of evidence that can prove or disprove the violation of law, transitional and restorative justice do not necessarily question the violation of law or human rights but instead seek to understand the impact of these transgressions. Practices associated with restorative justice (such as victim-offender dialogs) and transitional justice (such as truth and reconciliation commissions) are typically designed to facilitate the open sharing of experiences.[6] In this way, many restorative practices can become highly effective strategies within a transitional justice framework.

Differences between Transitional Justice and Restorative Justice

While restorative and transitional justice share some common values and goals, they also differ in some fundamental ways. The clearest distinction lies in their scope. Restorative justice addresses crime by prioritizing relationships. Not only is it interested in examining how harm occurs, but it also attempts to include all relevant stakeholders in the process, and empowers those stakeholders to determine the nature and severity of the harm caused by crime. Ultimately, its goal is to repair the harm and restore relationships between victims, offenders, and the community. While transitional justice often shares these goals, it does so on a massive scale, and stretches beyond the restoration of relationships into the construction of stable and participatory government. In other words, while transitional justice programs can be focused on individuals and neighborhoods, the true scope is much broader, and there is an expressed interest in preventing future oppression and harm through peacebuilding and profound systemic change.

Transitional justice also strays from restorative justice concerning voluntary participation. While participation in specific programs (such as truth and reconciliation commissions) might be voluntary, transitional justice initiatives are typically imposed within a region after civil conflict and mass violence.[7] While traditional judicial process operating within a stable government can easily sweep in and adjudicate any cases that a restorative justice program is unable to successfully address, transitional justice does not share this luxury. After incidents of genocide or mass violence, there is not necessarily a system in place that can address the vast needs within the affected region, nor one that can simultaneously facilitate the rebuilding of a country's political infrastructure. In light of these conditions, transitional justice as a whole is not a voluntary endeavor.

Transitional and restorative justice also deviate in regards to their relationship with the state, including the government, its agencies, and its systems. As we explored in Chapters 9 and 10, restorative justice programs typically relate to a state's justice system in one of three ways: diversion, incorporation, or parallelism. In cases of transitional justice, however, the state is often a direct stakeholder in the conflict and violence.[8] In other words, it has most likely participated in the violence or otherwise sanctioned it through inaction, funding, or other forms of support. While restorative justice programs relate to the state and its systems through partnership and collaboration, transitional justice relates to the state as an offending party and seeks to expose its harm and transform its foundation.

Lastly, while some common transitional justice programs (such as truth and reconciliation commissions, which we will explore more below) align ideologically with restorative justice concerning the pursuit of reconciliation over retribution, transitional justice is not inherently opposed to punishment. Under the umbrella of transitional justice, we can find punitive processes such as special courts and tribunals that seek accountability through punishment operating right alongside restorative, dialog-based programs that facilitate peace and reconciliation.

While restorative and transitional justice have their similarities, it is clear that they are not direct mirrors of one another. Instead, restorative practices can inform pragmatic strategies regarding some of the goals associated with transitional justice. In other words, restorative practices can support transitional justice, especially concerning the design and implementation of dialog-based processes that can help people share their experiences of victimization and seek reparation, collective safety, and shared stability.

Meeting the Needs of Victims and Communities after Mass Violence

As we learned in Chapter 11, violent crime creates many needs in the lives of victims, including the need for safety and compensation, the need to express and share their experiences, and the need to understand the motive and details of the crime.[9] In light of this, one of the most important challenges faced by transitional justice lies in the design and implementation of processes and programs equipped to meet these needs on a massive scale when victims can include the populations of entire communities, regions, and ethnic groups. In fact, in transitional justice settings, it is difficult to identify anyone not affected by trauma and victimization.

Trauma exposure can come in direct and indirect forms. We can exhibit symptoms of traumatic stress after personally experiencing a traumatic event, such as witnessing the murder of a loved one. However, we can also experience traumatic stress from simply hearing about such events, a phenomenon known as **traumatic countertransference**.[10] In whatever form it takes, trauma exposure can affect us in a multitude of ways. Increased anxiety, depression, a dampening of creative thought, feelings of helplessness, fatigue, and emotional numbing are just some of the detrimental effects of trauma exposure.[11] While these consequences of violence and victimization are daunting enough when we consider crime victims in stable regions such as the United States, imagine entire communities where trauma has spread like a virus and the needs of victims outweigh the availability of the conventional resources used to address them. This is referred to as **collective trauma**, meaning traumatic experiences that are shared by large groups of people after which common repercussions such as feelings of anger, helplessness, and terror spread throughout the group and can even affect future generations.[12]

Restorative Practices in Transitional Justice Contexts

As we noted earlier, transitional justice not only aims to rebuild broken and oppressive systems of governance, but to provide victims and community members with opportunities to share their experiences and seek reparation. These latter goals are the point at which restorative justice and transitional justice most commonly intersect. As detailed in Box 13.2, established restorative models such as peacemaking circles and victim-offender dialogs can be supportive and effective strategies when addressing needs in small, community-based settings.[13] Whether reintegrating former child soldiers into a village, or reconciling neighborhoods divided by civil war and genocide, restorative practices designed to facilitate safe and productive dialogs can be a helpful part of a larger transitional justice movement.

Box 13.2: Research in Restorative Justice—

> *Assessing the Use of Restorative Peacemaking Circles to*
> *Reintegrate Former Child Soldiers in the*
> *Democratic Republic of Congo*

While it is important to examine the needs of victims and communities after collective trauma and mass violence, the principles of restorative justice also suggest that we should give equal attention to the needs of perpetrators. The use of child soldiers by armed militias in the Democratic Republic of Congo is a practice that dates back to 1996 and the ousting of President Mobutu Sese Seko. When child soldiers either escape or are expelled from these armed groups, the process of resettlement and reintegration can be a difficult one. Not only do communities need justice and accountability, but resettlement can also be further strained by shame, confusion, distrust, abuse, and poverty.

In an effort to better understand the challenges of former child soldier resettlement and reintegration, Jean Chrysostome K. Kiyala spent seven months in North Kivu Province in the Democratic Republic of Congo conducting a longitudinal, exploratory study aimed at measuring the importance of justice and accountability in communities harmed by child soldiers, as well as perceptions regarding the use of a restorative peacemaking circle process to facilitate community building and the reintegration of children transitioning out of the armed forces.

Through a series of interviews, focus groups, and questionnaires, Kiyala's study included two phases of data collection that generated both quantitative and qualitative data. The second phase of data collection evaluated an interactive workshop that trained former child soldiers, victims, and community members in restorative justice and peacemaking circles. Role plays were used in the training to give participants a chance to experience the peacemaking circle process before evaluating its use in aiding the resettlement process for former child soldiers.

While the majority of people in the study's sample expressed support for holding child soldiers accountable for their crimes, 68.5% of the sample agreed that restorative justice is an effective way to seek and facilitate justice. Only 16.8% of the sample disagreed with this idea. In regard to the ability of restorative justice to impact the reconciliation process between former child soldiers and war victims, 83.4% of the sample agreed that it would. The majority of the sample also agreed that restorative justice processes could prevent children from joining armed groups.

While Kiyala's study included a fairly large sample for a regional, largely qualitative study, we cannot necessarily generalize the findings to other communities directly impacted by war and child soldiers. However, the study does present us with another example of how restorative justice can be applied to processes of transitional justice, community peacebuilding, and offender reintegration while supporting the restorative assertion that inclusive dialog is essential to personal and collective healing after crime and violence.

Source: Kiyala, J. C. K. (2015). Challenges of reintegrating self-demobilised child soldiers in north Kivu province: Prospects for accountability and reconciliation via restorative justice peacemaking circles. *Human Rights Review, 16,* 99–122.

In order to address these same needs on a larger scale, truth and reconciliation commissions (TRCs) have emerged as a model associated with both transitional and restorative justice. Though TRCs often differ from one another in both scope and process, a **truth and reconciliation commission** is generally defined as a temporary committee, which is granted authority by the state, and tasked with investigating and reporting on the impacts of mass violence and oppression within a specific society or region.[14] The first known TRC originated in Argentina in 1983 in order to investigate state-sponsored human rights abuses from the previous decade. Named *The National Commission on the Disappearance of Persons*, this body established the investigative model that would later be adapted by countries such as Chile, El Salvador, and South Africa; and would come to be known as a truth and reconciliation commission.[15]

A defining feature of TRCs is that they require the active participation of community members directly affected by the abuses under investigation.[16] Among other things, a TRC is a process grounded in truth-telling that provides space for oppressors to acknowledge their abuses and victims to give voice to their suffering and loss. They are rooted in the hope that by providing an official space to account for atrocities such as mass violence and genocide, a country can achieve a clearer sense of what occurred, victims can find some peace and reparation, and a future path towards reconciliation can begin.[17] This emphasis on storytelling and accountability is what connects truth and reconciliation commissions to restorative justice, and leads many to refer to TRCs as examples of restorative justice in action.

TRCs, however, are not without their critics. Much like restorative justice, truth and reconciliation commissions inspire critical dialogs concerning the validity of justice when divided from retribution and punishment. TRCs are not judicial authorities; they do not prosecute, formally determine guilt, or render punishment. Instead, their focus is on establishing the truth, providing platforms for victims, and, if so empowered, distributing reparative compensation to survivors.[18] While the existence of a TRC does not necessarily erase the possibility of retributive justice, some TRCs, such as that in South Africa, have provided prosecutorial amnesty to perpetrators willing to come forward and participate truthfully in the TRC.[19] This practice has been criticized as a form of injustice; however, supporters of amnesty point to its ability to facilitate truth-telling and future reconciliation, which, as advocates of restorative justice would also assert, may better meet the needs of victims than conventional penalties such as imprisonment.[20]

Broadening Our Understanding of Restorative Justice

While truth and reconciliation commissions are often presented in the literature as a restorative practice for societies pursuing transitional justice, it is important to remind ourselves that transitional justice and restorative justice differ in more ways than they connect. However, the evolving partnership between restorative and transitional justice movements has led to a continued expansion in our understanding of the boundaries within which restorative justice can effectively function. As we stated earlier in this chapter, while restorative justice can certainly stretch down into the realm of everyday conflicts, perhaps it can also stretch up into the realm of social justice, systemic oppression, and structural violence.

One of the main critiques of transitional justice is that, in practice, it does not focus enough on social inequalities and cultural attitudes that breed atrocities like mass violence, civil war, and genocide.[21] Indeed, many contend that despite its intentions, transitional justice either overlooks social justice issues like poverty and racism that highlight the distribution of wealth and privilege within a society, or fails to actively address them.[22] For example, while a process like a TRC might report on the need to address economic inequality or prejudicial attitudes within a society, those recommendations may never materialize in the implementation of actual programming or policy.[23]

In response to these concerns, the concept of **transformative justice** has emerged to emphasize the importance of not only politically transitioning societies broken and divided by violent conflict, but also transforming the systems, policies, and social attitudes that led to that division. While transitional justice is a relatively short-term process that can perhaps initiate this goal, proponents of transformative justice argue that more time, as well as a clearer focus on socioeconomic and cultural conditions, is needed in order to more effectively move a society towards sustainable reconciliation and equality.[24]

The question, therefore, emerges as to whether or not restorative practices can help facilitate social justice, structural change, and cultural transformation in addition to supporting the short-term goals of transitional justice. As we see in Box 13.3, there exists some precedent for adapting the truth and reconciliation commission model to address not only a single event, but also a relevant social justice issue like racism.[25] It therefore stands to reason that other restorative practices such as peacemaking circles, victim-offender dialogs, and community reparative boards could also be utilized or adapted to address social justice concerns outside of transitional settings in stable countries such as the United States. While we still have much to explore concerning the role of restorative justice in these kinds of movements, it is clear that if restorative justice truly is a pathway towards peacebuilding and reconciliation, then its practices and principles have much to offer us beyond cases of delinquency, crime, and criminal justice.

Now that we have explored the potential of restorative justice, it is important that we take some time to examine its limitations. In our next chapter, we will take a look at common doubts and criticisms concerning restorative justice, including its limitations and shortcomings.

Box 13.3: Restorative Justice in Action— Greensboro Truth and Reconciliation Commission: Using the TRC Model to Address Inequality and Racism in the U.S.

Though it is common to associate truth and reconciliation commissions (TRCs) with transitional justice and changes in a region's political structure, the model can also be applied outside of a political transition in order to address incidents of public violence and collective trauma. One example occurred in the year 2000 when a group of citizens and private funders initiated the Greensboro Truth and Reconciliation Commission (GTRC) in Greensboro, North Carolina. The Greensboro TRC was organized in order to explore the causes and consequences of events on November 3, 1979, that led to the murder of five people and the wounding of ten others at the hands of local members of the Ku Klux Klan. Despite efforts on the part of law enforcement and local government in Greensboro to thwart their work, the GTRC convened and issued a report of its findings and recommendations in 2006, inspiring questions about whether or not the TRC model can be effective in contexts outside of transitional justice and without local political support.

On November 3, 1979, a group of approximately fifty activists gathered to protest against racism and unfair labor practices in Greensboro. During their rally, a counter group of Ku Klux Klan members drove through their gathering while shouting racial slurs and threats. The activists shouted back, and fighting began to erupt between some of the protestors and some of the Klan members. Armed Klan members began firing their weapons and within moments five of the protestors had been killed, and ten others had been shot and wounded. The murdered victims included César Cause, Mike Nathan, Bill Sampson, Sandy Smith, and Jim Waller. Despite the fact that the murders had been filmed by local television crews, the arrested Klan members were acquitted, and no one was held criminally responsible for the injuries and deaths in Greensboro.

The murders and acquittals had a terrorizing and destructive effect on many people in Greensboro. It widened racial divisions in the community and increased distrust in local law enforcement. From the events, there arose a need to acknowledge the truth of what happened in 1979, and examine ways to prevent it from happening again. Despite these needs, however, the GTRC experienced a tremendous amount of resistance from the local city council and law enforcement agency, including refusals to cooperate and efforts to intimidate and dissuade community members and organizations from participating.

In many ways, the GTRC was a grassroots investigation intent on building an accurate historical narrative concerning the events on November 3, 1979, and the years that followed. Based on their findings, the commission process also empowered its members to create, document, and share their recommendations for institutional, governmental, and community-based reforms in the hopes that their work might help pave the way for individual and collective transformation.

Source: Inwood, J. (2012). Righting unrightable wrongs: Legacies of racial violence and the Greensboro truth and reconciliation commission. *Annals of the Association of American Geographers, 102*(6), 1450–1467.

Chapter Summary

In what ways is transitional justice distinct from restorative justice, and in what ways do the two overlap?

While restorative and transitional justice share some common traits such as an emphasis on inclusion and a desire to prevent future harm, the two are also distinctly different from one another. Transitional justice is a coordinated set of interventions implemented after periods of political oppression, mass violence, or state-sponsored human rights violations that seeks to acknowledge what happened, identify offenders, restore victims, and transform existing systems and conditions that led to the injustice and abuse. Though they differ dramatically in scope, both restorative and transitional justice value the role of storytelling in the process of healing and reconciliation, and both operate, in part, due to the limits of conventional judicial process.

Differences between transitional and restorative justice include their scope, their relationship to the state, their focus on voluntary participation, and their connection to punishment. While transitional and restorative justice do share some common objectives, the ultimate goal of transitional justice is to move a society into a new system of governance. While restorative practices can help support this goal, the aims of transitional justice go far beyond those of restorative justice.

Additionally, while restorative justice typically collaborates with the state and its systems, these bodies are often treated as oppressors and perpetrators in transitional justice contexts. Lastly, while an important tenet of restorative justice is voluntary participation, this is not necessarily the case in transitional justice, and while restorative justice does not acknowledge punishment as an effective means towards repairing harm and meeting needs, some transitional justice programs do emphasize punishment as an important part of justice and accountability.

What are the needs of victims and communities after mass violence, and how can restorative practices help address those needs?

In many ways, the needs of victims after mass violence overlap with the needs of other violent crime victims. Among other things, survivors of these acts typically need answers to their questions, physical safety, and compensation for their losses. Communities riddled by prolonged periods of extreme violence and fear can also suffer from collective trauma, the sharing of traumatic experiences by large groups of people which can result in widespread feelings of anger, helplessness, and terror that can even spread to future generations.

A variety of established restorative practices such as victim-offender dialogs and peacemaking circles can prove helpful within the framework of transitional justice; however, we explored the truth and reconciliation commission (TRC) as a common example of restorative practice within a transitional justice setting. With its origins in Argentina's 1983 *National Commission on the Disappearance of Persons*, a truth and reconciliation commission is a temporary committee, granted authority by the state, and tasked with investigating and reporting on the impacts of mass violence and oppression within a specific society or region. While each truth and reconciliation commission can vary in both its goals and procedures, the model is fundamentally grounded in truth-telling and inclusion. Each TRC is rooted the hope that by providing an official space in which it can account for atrocities such as mass violence and genocide, a country can achieve a clearer sense of what occurred, victims can find some peace and reparation, and a future path towards reconciliation can begin.

In what ways is our understanding and practice of restorative justice evolving in relation to transitional justice?

Some critics of transitional justice contend that, due to its short-term nature, it does not go far enough in transforming the social and cultural factors that can lead to violence and oppression. In response to these concerns, the concept of transformative justice has emerged to focus on changing the systems, policies, and social attitudes that lead to division, domination, and discord within a society. An emerging question concerning restorative justice lies in whether or not its practices and principles can be applied to social justice movements aimed at addressing inequalities in the distribution of wealth and privilege within and among communities and nation groups.

Key Terms

Transitional Justice
Traumatic Countertransference
Collective Trauma
Truth and Reconciliation Commission (TRC)
The National Commission on the Disappearance of Persons
Transformative Justice

Critical Thinking Questions

1. What are the main similarities and differences between restorative justice and transitional justice?

2. Go online and investigate a real-world example of transitional justice that utilized a truth and reconciliation commission (TRC). What was the nature of the conflict in the region, what kinds of abuses and violence occurred, and what were the main outcomes of the TRC? After researching a specific example of a TRC, would you identify it as a restorative process? Why or why not?

3. Come up with at least three concrete ways in which restorative practices could be implemented in order to address a social justice issue in the United States (such as racism, transphobia, or economic inequality). Do you think your ideas would lead to substantive changes in society? Why or why not?

References

1. Johnstone, G. (2011). *Restorative justice: Ideas, values, debates* (2nd ed.). New York, NY: Routledge.

2. Cunneen, C. (2001). Reparations and restorative justice: Responding to the gross violation of human rights. In H. Strang & J. Braithwaite (Eds.), *Restorative justice and civil society* (pp. 83–98). Cambridge, UK: Cambridge University Press.

3. Johnstone, G. (2011). *Restorative justice: Ideas, values, debates* (2nd ed.). New York, NY: Routledge.

4. Llewellyn, J. L., & Philpott, D. (2014). Restorative justice and reconciliation: Twin frameworks for peacebuilding. In J. L. Llewellyn & D. Philpott (Eds.), *Restorative justice, reconciliation, and peacebuilding* (pp. 14–36). New York, NY: Oxford University Press.

5. Ramírez-Barat, C. (2012, November). *Engaging children and youth in transitional justice processes: Guidance for outreach programs.* Retrieved from https://www.ictj.org/sites/default/files/ICTJ-Report-Children-Youth-Outreach-2012.pdf.

6. Porter, E. (2016). Gendered narratives: Stories and silences in transitional justice. *Human Rights Review, 17*(1), 35–50.

7. Rohne, H., Arsovska, J., & Aertsen, I. (2008). Challenging restorative justice: State-based conflict, mass victimisation and the changing nature of warfare. In I. Aertsen, J. Arsovska, H. Rohne, M. Valiñas, & K. Vanspauwen (Eds.), *Restoring justice after large-scale violent conflicts: Kosovo, DR Congo, and the Israeli-Palestinian case* (pp. 3–45). New York, NY: Routledge.

8. Clamp, K., & Doak, J. (2012). More than words: Restorative justice concepts in transitional justice settings. *International Criminal Law Review, 12*, 339–360.

9. Gal, T. (2011). *Child victims and restorative justice: A needs-rights model.* New York, NY: Oxford University Press.

10. Herman, J. (1997). Trauma and recovery: The aftermath of violence—from domestic abuse to political terror. New York, NY: Basic Books.

11. Lipsky, L. (2009). Trauma stewardship: An everyday guide to caring for self while caring for others. Oakland, CA: Berrett-Koehler Publishers.

12. Yoder, C. (2005). *The little book of trauma healing: When violence strikes and community security is threatened.* Intercourse, PA: Good Books.

13. Kiyala, J. C. K. (2015). Challenges of reintegrating self-demobilised child soldiers in north Kivu province: Prospects for accountability and reconciliation via restorative justice peacemaking circles. *Human Rights Review, 16*, 99–122.

14. Hayner, P. B. (2001). Unspeakable truths: Transitional justice and the challenge of truth commissions (2nd ed.). New York, NY: Routledge.

15. Ibid.

16. Ibid., see 14.

17. Rotberg, R. I. (2000). Truth commissions and the provision of truth, justice, and reconciliation. In R. Rotberg & D. Thompson (Eds.), *Truth v. justice: The morality of truth commissions* (pp. 3–21). Princeton, NJ: Princeton University Press.

18. Crocker, D. A. (2000). Truth commissions, transitional justice, and civil society. In R. Rotberg & D. Thompson (Eds.), *Truth v. justice: The morality of truth commissions* (pp. 99–121). Princeton, NJ: Princeton University Press.

19. Kiss, E. (2000). Moral ambition within and beyond political constraints: Reflections on restorative justice. In R. Rotberg & D. Thompson (Eds.), *Truth v. justice: The morality of truth commissions* (pp. 68–98). Princeton, NJ: Princeton University Press.

20. Ibid.

21. Mullen, M. (2015). Reassessing the focus of transitional justice: The need to move structural and cultural violence to the centre. *Cambridge Review of International Affairs, 28*(3), 462–479.

22. Evans, M. (2016). Structural violence, socioeconomic rights, and transformative justice. *Journal of Human Rights, 15*, 1–20.

23. Ibid.

24. Daly, R. (2002). Transformative justice: Charting a path to reconciliation. *International Legal Perspectives, 12,* 73–183.

25. Inwood, J. (2012). Righting unrightable wrongs: Legacies of racial violence and the Greensboro truth and reconciliation commission. *Annals of the Association of American Geographers, 102*(6), 1450–1467.

Section Four

The Future of Restorative Justice

To fully understand something, it is important to explore, not only our own doubts and concerns, but the critiques of others. As we conclude our journey into the history, intentions, and current applications of restorative justice, we will identify and examine specific limitations, pitfalls, and critiques of the restorative approach to crime, such as net-widening and the ability of restorative justice to integrate further into the juvenile and criminal justice systems.

We will also focus on the future of restorative justice, including the need to explore gaps in empirical approaches to measuring the efficacy of restorative policies and practices, as well as the need for advocates of the restorative approach to address common concerns and criticisms in order to further the spread of restorative justice in formal and informal processes used to address conflict and crime within local communities, systems, and agencies.

Chapter 14

A Critical Look at Restorative Justice

In this chapter, we will explore the following questions ...
* *What are some of the pitfalls of implementing restorative justice programming?*
* *Are there limitations to the use of peacemaking alternatives?*
* *How do we answer the skeptic's questions about this approach?*

Restorative Justice: Pitfalls to a Positive Approach

Throughout this textbook, we have presented restorative justice as a constructive alternative to the traditional model of justice, one which aims to reestablish the broken connection between the victim, the offender, and the community as a whole. It is a compassionate approach to justice which acknowledges that crime is a symptom of human suffering and therefore recognizes the need for reparation and healing. In doing this, we are in a sense challenging social norms and values associated with the concepts of punishment and retribution by promoting the ideals of forgiveness and reparation. With this challenge, however, it is necessary to address some of the pitfalls that can hinder the progress of implementing restorative justice ideals and integrating policies and practices that complement traditional forms of justice.

The Pitfall of Widening the Net

The concept of **net-widening** is used to describe the process whereby there is an increase in the formal or informal contact with the criminal justice system.[1] While the aim of diversion type programs such as restorative justice might be to avoid mechanisms of social control that might increase the criminogenic effects of formal contact with the criminal justice system, some critics of such programming suggest that an opposite effect might occur. Since restorative justice is often implemented in settings where formal criminal justice interventions may not have been initiated, the argument is made that this places individuals who might not have otherwise been legally sanctioned under the net of social control, which often disproportionately puts a certain category of individuals under scrutiny and places conditions and demands that can be lengthy and intrusive.[2] Moreover, program administrators seeking high rates of success for their initiatives, will often "seek out" certain cases that are not necessarily in need of formal proceedings but could benefit from restorative justice programming. These cases will most likely yield a success but do not necessarily reflect the more difficult cases in need of management and intervention.

While these dynamics merit attention, it may not always be a bad thing to widen the net of social control for the benefit of providing reparation to crime victims and their communities. Studies show that interventions targeting individuals before they become a part of formal criminal justice proceedings will in the long run produce more desirable outcomes by increasing compliance, reducing recidivism, and enhancing victim satisfaction with the results.[3] This is coupled with the fact that restorative justice intervention, although sometimes "catching" more individuals in its symbolic net, is by far a less costly alternative to formal sanctioning within a traditional criminal justice setting.[4] Thus, when addressing this potential pitfall, it is important to recognize the need to cast the net of restorative justice uniformly by ensuring that programs are structured in a manner that addresses client needs and targets communities for intervention in a wide variety of settings.

The Pitfall of Avoiding Justice

Some skeptics of restorative justice policy and practice have noted that one of the most difficult aspects of digressing from traditional forms of criminal justice intervention is that there is no clear way of defining justice.[5] Within a courtroom trial, the outcome is equated with a judicious balance that is embedded in laws and statutes that have been developed by experts and agreed upon through lengthy proceedings with significant oversight. With this observation, we must recognize the difference in *setting a goal* of justice and *achieving an outcome* of true justice. As we aspire to defend the innocent and ensure that the guilty are punished, we ultimately rely on justice being served by enacting the law based on fact finding, testimonials, the presentation of evidence, and the opinion of various experts, advocates, scholars, and observers.[6] While this process may be based on a textbook definition of justice, it neglects the human side of interaction that is based on ideals set upon a higher standard of fairness, balance, and equity.

Perhaps if we agree on process and hope for outcome, then we see that the restorative justice approach to reconciliation, repair, and healing, while idealistic, ensures that the mechanisms implemented towards achieving those goals are based on notions of justice that treat those individuals who are directly involved in the conflict as active participants in its resolution and not mere bystanders with no role or voice. Perhaps this is the ultimate and ideal form of justice, and while far from perfect, narrowing the gap between the ideal and the actual may be the ultimate goal we strive for when seeking fairness and defining justice for victims of crime.[7] With that goal as a standard, restorative justice must continue to thrive and seek its rightful place as an embedded feature within established criminal justice processes.

The Pitfall of a Blurred Vision of Reconciliation

A final pitfall we want to explore is that associated with the concept of reconciliation and what it actually means and implies. While we may not always be concerned
with mending a broken relationship between a victim and an offender that is caused
by criminal offending, reconciliation can expand into areas of repair that are necessary for victim healing, as well as offender reintegration into the community.
Skeptics of restorative justice have argued that a major shortcoming of its application
in a wide variety of settings is its failure to integrate the fact-finding phase of the
criminal justice process and focus exclusively on outcome and penalty.[8] This focus
on dispute resolution in favor of attempts to gather information and present evidence
may compromise the reconciliation process whereby offenders might feel that the
outcome is forced or absent of all the facts. Whether creating dialog, mediating
restitution, engaging in a peacemaking circle, or participating in a victim panel
presentation, the orientation of outcome is premised on the admission of guilt to
the offense.

We see here that in order to ensure active reconciliation that has a long-term impact
on creating a judicial balance as well as mend the broken relationship between victim,
offender, and community, we must therefore ensure appropriate case selection where
restorative justice compliments and does not replace official fact-finding proceedings
that might be integral to proper restorative outcomes. So, while we acknowledge that
the premise and practice of restorative justice focuses on resolution and not why or
how a crime occurred, or if the offender indeed is guilty of that crime, its focus on
reconciliation acknowledges that limitation and sets a higher standard of ideals when
it comes to bringing together victims, offenders, and communities in a forum for
repair that may disable the adversarial nature of justice but enables an effective,
creative process of dialog and understanding that has withstood the test of scientific
scrutiny over time.[9]

Limitations to the Use of
Peacemaking Alternatives

While we have clearly established the value of restorative justice alternatives as a
method and approach to dispute resolution within various contexts, we must acknowledge and address the criticism of restorative justice that is not applicable in
certain circles of justice. While this might be the case, we must not view it as a limitation, but rather as a cautious approach to implementation that is guided by an
understanding of when and how to apply restorative justice methodologies.[10] With
that idea in mind, let's turn to a closer examination of those circumstances in which
restorative justice might be limited in its application, bearing in mind that we are
not merely talking about case types but rather circumstances surrounding cases.

When Restorative Justice Is Not Right for Victims

While it may seem unthinkable to suggest that the ideals of restorative justice would not resonate well with victims of any crime, we must remember that the practical application of restorative justice principles rests upon the premise of voluntary victim participation.[11] Throughout this text, we have seen the value of victim participation in restorative justice processes in terms of achieving healing from the loss and devastation of crime, feeling a sense of fairness and equity, repairing a broken relationship and holding offenders accountable for their actions. Why then would some victims be reluctant to participate in these processes?

The Hurt Is Too Deep

One factor that has been associated with victim non-participation in restorative justice processes is the nature of their relationship to the offender, which can often result in a type of hurt that is too deep for the encounters that are offered through forums such as mediation, circles, or victim impact panels.[12] In such cases, the victim may not want to continue to engage in a relationship with the offender where separation or the severing of ties may be a better or more productive alternative to their welfare in the long run. Reconciliation is based on the assumption that the victim and the offender are amenable to continuing a relationship, whether superficial or intimate ... however, the established condition is that the maintenance of the relationship is beneficial to the healing of the victim. In cases where the hurt is too deep due to its integral connection between the criminal behavior and the emotional health of the victim, alternatives such as therapy, counseling, and behavioral interventions might be a better choice.[13]

There Is Too Much Anger

Sometimes hurt and anger can collide; however, for the purpose of clarification and informed discussion, we present them here separately because while anger can be diffused in a restorative justice encounter, that anger must be such that it does not overwhelm and sabotage those processes.[14] Because restorative justice intervention is often an immediate intervention that takes place after the commission of a crime, the anger, frustration, and rage associated with the offense may need some time to subside. Regarding intangible destruction and hurt, the anger may be more intensified, and a victim might choose or desire to hold on to that anger and refuse to encounter the offender for the goal of reparation or reconciliation. Certainly, restorative justice programming is contingent upon volunteerism, and in cases where anger might interfere with the ability to effectively participate, its refusal would be appropriate in such circumstances.

There Is Not Enough Commitment

Another consideration for circumstances where participation in restorative justice dialog and encounter may not be productive are cases where the victim is not able to show commitment due to time restrictions or the perception that these processes will interfere too much with their daily lives and routines. Some victims perceive the suffering and inconvenience that the crime has caused to be sufficient disruption to their daily lives and wish to put it behind them and not become further involved in any other program or obligation related to that event.[15] Under these circumstances, the sense of commitment to the values, ideals, and practices of restorative justice become diluted and their positive impact will dissipate as they become viewed as an unnecessary burden in addition to the original victimization.

There Is a Fear of Retaliation

One dynamic of victim-offender interaction that is counterproductive under any circumstance is the fear of retaliation.[16] In many cases, merely being in the presence of the offender can retraumatize the victim. Holding the offender accountable in such cases through formal criminal justice mechanisms will deflect the victim's feeling of personal responsibility for bringing them to justice and the outcome of their punishment. With restorative justice interventions, that accountability is in effect transferred onto the victim, and this may evoke feelings of further hostility on the part of the offender in certain types of cases such as sexual assault, for example.[17]

When Restorative Justice Is Not Right for Offenders

Restorative justice has offered us a powerful approach that relies on creative and innovative methods of intervention focusing on dialog, repair, and reintegration. It is difficult to conceive of these processes as falling short of an umbrella method of intervention that should apply to all cases at all times. We have seen, however, that there are instances where this model of justice may not be one size fits all, and while its customization may offer hope and solutions to bring conflict resolution to groundbreaking levels, it is not always the best choice for victims. Likewise, there are certain cases where restorative justice may not be right for offenders. We turn now to a brief look at when and why restorative justice alternatives may not be an appropriate approach in responding to criminal offending.[18]

When Offenders Are Reluctant

We cannot emphasize enough the role of volunteerism and the acceptance of responsibility as key components the absence of which would compromise the integrity and efficiency of restorative justice process.[19] While accepting responsibility for harm done can be translated into mere words in a courtroom setting to alleviate the outcome of sentencing and the penalty phase of a trial, restorative justice processes require actions and not simply the expression of artificial or superficial statements. Thus, the participation of offenders in restorative justice programming cannot simply be the proverbial "fire escape from hell" or "get out of jail free" card without the offender being committed to the program and fully willing to participate in all aspects of program rules and requirements.[20] They cannot be hesitant or reluctant due to the often excessive obligations and time commitment, as well as the need to engage in dialog and encounters where they are held accountable for their actions.

When Repair Is Not Possible

Does the failure to repair a broken relationship indicate a breakdown in the mechanisms of restorative justice? Some critics would argue that it does.[21] However, under these circumstances, we would like to submit that there are certain conditions that make restorative forms of reconciliation unlikely to bring out reparation. The path of restorative justice can be a bumpy one and acknowledging responsibility for one's actions means an unconditional willingness to make amends and repair a harm that has been done. This willingness implies a sincere indication that the offender wants to change their ways and mend the relationships that have been broken.[22]

This process very often means that offenders take on a personal role of humility, make an emotional commitment, and deal with the shame and guilt that can be associated with restorative encounters. Moreover, it can imply that an offender see the victim as a real person, a process which is brought about through self-awareness of one's action and a heightened sense of empathy.[23] If an offender is unwilling to engage in such resolution, then restorative processes will be counterproductive, as a genuine reparation of harm cannot be achieved and the material aspect of repair will be better served as part of a binding court-ordered resolution outside of any possibility for restorative intervention.

When Remorse Is Not Genuine

Some critics of restorative justice note that there are certain cases where restorative justice can bring about more harm to the victim when offenders simply comply with program requirements to be able to cast themselves in a more favorable light and avoid further forms of punishment.[24] This can be the case, for example, where restorative justice is used with incarcerated violent offenders as part of reentry programming, or to get early release credit, as we've discussed in Chapter 10. This can also occur during the presentencing process, where offenders are offered restorative justice diversion alternatives in order to avoid formal charges.

Throughout this text, we have advocated the application of restorative justice in various contexts and settings, as a mechanism of dispute resolution that focuses on dialog, repair, and healing. As any mechanism of intervention, however, we must acknowledge its limitation in uses when participants in these processes are not genuine in their motives and intentions. Restorative justice is about process and experience. It is not about writing an apology letter to a victim, it is about experiencing the type of genuine remorse that transforms behavior and brings about reconciliation.[25] From our experience as restorative justice board members for many years, we have had the opportunity to read many letters of apology written by offenders as part of their restorative justice program requirements. These letters must reflect true remorse and show a clear acceptance of responsibility on the part of the offender. If not, the concept is explained to them in detail, and they are asked to write the letter again to reflect this sentiment. Even then, it is difficult to gauge true remorse, and we leave the evidence of long-term change, improvement, and criminal desistance as measures that provide us with a glimpse of understanding as we explore some answers to the skeptic's questions in the section to come.

A Skeptic's View of Restorative Justice and a Brief Defense

The implementation of a restorative justice paradigm requires a significant divergence in theory and practice from traditional models of justice, which focus on fact finding, the rule of law, and the exacting of punishment. Restorative justice processes require an empathetic and supportive understanding of human interactions, which aims at bringing about reconciliation to broken relationships, mending hurt caused by offending, increasing accountability, and providing support and assistance during discussions and dialog aimed at reparation.[26] With such high ideals, some critics note that there are structural barriers that can potentially weaken restorative processes. What are these barriers and how can they be overcome? Let's take a closer look.

The Problem of Definition

When we consider the vast scope of the meaning of *justice*, adding the word *restorative* brings about an even greater burden of outcome that may place the two terms at odds with one another. Skeptics of the application of restorative processes within the realm of criminal justice argue that there is confusion at best and a lack of understanding as to the meaning of the term restorative justice.[27] Some argue that restorative justice refers to a set of ideals that reflect desired outcomes of certain processes, and there is very little agreement on what those outcomes should be and how they are achieved in a practical sense. This lack of a firm identity, arguably, creates confusion and a disconnect in the theoretical application and empirical assessment of restorative justice policy and practice.

A consideration of this argument leads us to take a look back at what we have learned throughout this text. The problem of defining restorative justice does not lie in our lack of a historical and philosophical grounding of the concept, for we have seen throughout our discussions that restorative justice practices and ideals have been implemented in various contexts for decades and centuries. For critics, the problem of defining restorative justice lies in a confusion over its fundamental approach. While there can be a need for the building of concrete definitions and meanings when advocating for a specific paradigm or approach, we must see that the strength of restorative justice lies in its way of challenging established mechanisms of criminal justice by changing the way we think about crime, respond to offenders, and help victims.[28] This implies a constant change of ideals that cannot be restricted within the box of definition nor confined by strict adherence to meaning for to do this would be to limit the expansive vision of restorative justice as a mechanism of transformation.

Victim Centered or Offender Centered?

Throughout our textbook, we have presented restorative justice as a model of intervention that focuses on the reparation of harm done to victims of crime. The mechanisms for achieving this reparation involve offenders playing an active role in the process of making things right.[29] For this reason, some skeptics of restorative justice programs and practices note that victims play a secondary role as "pawns" or tools used by program administrators in the process of rehabilitating offenders, and are sometimes even coerced or coaxed into participating in processes they would rather avoid.[30] Whether participants on impact panels or active negotiators in circles, the focus of the process is to achieve an outcome that brings about change and transformation in the behavior and attitude of the offender with the goal of criminal desistance.

This criticism, while presenting us with a valid concern, can be addressed by placing the values and ideals of restorative justice at the heart of program intervention. While the foundation of restorative justice is built upon the restoration of relationships through dialog and communication, this restoration cannot rely on the participation of offenders in programming without also including victims in the process.[31] With that said, we submit that while the intention of criminal desistance is an outcome of restorative justice processes, that outcome is built upon a victim-centered approach that relies on voluntary, non-coercive methods of participation whereby victims are given a chance to be heard, healed, and restored with a variety of remedies.[32] Moreover, true restorative justice by definition is inclusive, and therefore, bringing offender, victim, and community together to repair a harm through safe and respectful dialog implies that we are removing the depersonalization of crime and actually holding offenders directly accountable for their actions by elevating the role of crime victims and community in the process of reparation.

Dealing with Penalty and Not Process

One structural obstacle that critics note about restorative justice theory and practice is the inherent disconnect between procedure and outcome.[33] When we consider the historical context of restorative justice evolution and development, as well as modern forms of application, we see that the restorative justice interventions begin after there has been an admission of guilt, with little or no regard to elements of fact finding surrounding the criminal event. Skeptics of this approach argue that the omission of procedure from the stages of conflict resolution can leave offenders and even victims with a lack of trust and confidence in the outcome of justice, making the question of what crime was committed and the circumstances surrounding that crime vague and unresolved.[34]

We wish to address this proposed criticism by arguing that what is viewed as a weakness in restorative justice theory and practice can actually be regarded as its inherent strength. The adversarial process of traditional criminal justice intervention, with its focus on procedure, evidence, and established guidelines of the law, can serve to limit the participatory and consensual aspect of restorative justice that allows for creative dialog and the expression of feelings, which can ultimately lead to conflict resolution without bypassing facts.[35] Thus, while we cannot expect restorative justice to replace the adjudication process of formal courts, we can indeed argue that in many circumstances, it can complement court proceedings through a focus on outcome that is a product of communication, mutual respect, agreement, and the active participation of both victims and offenders in the reconciliation and resolution process.

Balance for One but Not Balance for All

Restorative justice is about achieving balance as we have emphasized throughout our text. We acknowledge that this balance, sometimes quite illusive, can take time and effort to exact results that are both creative and transformative in their effect. For this reason, some critics of restorative justice processes argue that the overall balance is sometimes tipped in the favor of some but not others, resulting in an ambiguous state of intervention for some offenders.[36] The ideals of justice may overstep the boundaries of traditional court interventions, where an offender has a clear understanding of guidelines, knows what to expect, and can depend on objective criteria when completing their period of supervision. With restorative justice, the expectations are imbedded in philosophical principles that require a degree of maturity and empathy. This can make it difficult for some offenders to achieve compliance with such high standards for participation.

While we acknowledge that restorative justice processes can often place a greater burden of participation on the part of offenders, family members, victims, and even members of the community, this investment of time and effort has the potential for more profound outcomes in terms of creating permanent solutions within conflict resolution and reconciliation that go beyond the band-aid efforts of traditional interventions.[37] The specific mechanisms of restoration call upon the building of relationships, teaching people how to communicate, and reaching out to all those who are affected by an act of criminal offending in a way that might take time, but in the long run will have a more impactful effect in changing lives and repairing broken bonds between offenders, victims, and the community in which they live. We will discuss these long-term goals of restorative justice policy development and practice in our final look at the future of restorative justice research and application.

Chapter Summary

What are some of the pitfalls of implementing restorative justice programming?

At the beginning of this chapter, we identified several pitfalls that restorative justice program implementation should avoid. These included the concept of net-widening, whereby individuals who might not have otherwise been legally sanctioned under the net of social control, are under scrutiny with conditions and demands that can be lengthy and intrusive. Another pitfall noted by skeptics is the difficulty in achieving traditional forms of justice that are embedded in the formal dynamics of courtroom trial and procedures. Finally, restorative justice has been criticized for its failure to integrate the fact-finding phase of the criminal justice process into the dispute resolution process, which may compromise the reconciliation process, because offenders might feel that the outcome is forced or absent of all the facts.

Are there limitations to the use of peacemaking alternatives?

In this chapter, we examined various circumstances in which restorative justice may not be the appropriate intervention for victims and also for offenders. With regard to victims, we identified particular cases that may need alternative forms of intervention: when the hurt from the crime is too deep, when there is too much anger toward the offender, when there is not enough commitment to the process, and when the victim fears retaliation from the offender. Regarding offenders, we also noted that restorative justice mechanisms of intervention may not be suitable in cases where offenders are reluctant to participate, when full, genuine reparation cannot be achieved, and when remorse for the harm committed is not sincere.

How do we answer the skeptic's questions about this approach?

The research literature has noted several skeptical accounts as to the structural integrity of restorative justice theoretical application. These criticisms have revolved around the arguments over defining the meaning of restorative justice principles and practices, the secondary role of victims as tools used by program administrators, the inherent disconnect between procedure and outcome, and the ambiguous state of intervention and expectation that can lead to difficulty in achieving compliance for some offenders. Our understanding of the fundamental ideals of restorative justice provides us with a valid defense to these claims. We have established that the strength of restorative justice lies in its way of challenging established mechanisms of criminal justice by changing the way we think about crime, respond to offenders, and help victims, and not by building concrete definitions and meanings that confine creative thinking. Moreover, restorative justice processes are built upon a victim-centered approach that relies on voluntary, non-coercive methods of participation whereby victims are given a chance to be heard, healed, and restored with a variety of remedies. We also noted that the inherent disconnect between procedure and outcome can be viewed as a strength, as it allows for a departure from the adversarial process of traditional criminal justice intervention in favor of a participatory and consensual dialog and the expression of feelings, which can ultimately lead to conflict resolution without bypassing facts. This has the potential for more profound outcomes in terms of creating permanent solutions.

Key Terms

Net-Widening

Critical Thinking Questions

1. You are a lobbyist for an organization advocating restorative justice inside maximum-security prisons. What types of criticism are you facing? How would you defend this approach to justice?

2. What do you think of the concept of "net-widening"? Are there merits to the idea that this can lead to the unfair treatment of certain categories of individuals over others? How would you avoid this pitfall in the administration of restorative justice interventions?

3. How do you see the definition of restorative justice today? Does this definition match the historical vision of restorative justice?

4. In what ways is the application of restorative justice difficult in terms of achieving true justice? Are we more concerned with the ideal and compromising procedure? How do we reconcile the two?

References

1. Prichard, J. (2010). Net-widening and the diversion of young people from court: A longitudinal analysis with implications for restorative justice. *Australian & New Zealand Journal of Criminology*, *43*(1), 112–129.

2. Gross, J. (2010). The effects of net-widening on minority and indigent drug offenders: A critique of drug courts. *U. Md. LJ Race, Religion, Gender & Class, 10*, 161.

3. Brennan, I. R., Green, S., & Sturgeon-Adams, L. (2016). Early diversion and empowerment policing: Evaluating an adult female offender triage project. *Policing and Society*, 1–17. Huck, J. L., & Morris, C. S. (2016). Jail diversion and recidivism: A case study of a municipal court diversion program. *Criminal Justice Policy Review*. doi: 0887403415619986.

4. Sherman, L. W., Strang, H., Mayo-Wilson, E., Woods, D. J., & Ariel, B. (2015). Are restorative justice conferences effective in reducing repeat offending? Findings from a Campbell systematic review. *Journal of Quantitative Criminology, 31*(1), 1–24.

5. Skitka, L. J., Bauman, C. W., & Mullen, E. (2016). Morality and justice. In C. Sabbagh & M. Schmitt (Eds.), *Handbook of social justice theory and research* (pp. 407–423). Springer New York.

6. D'Amato, A. (2011). On the connection between law and justice. *Northwestern University School of Law Scholarly Commons*. Retrieved from http://scholarlycommons.law.northwestern.edu/cgi/viewcontent.cgi?article=1001&context=facultyworkingpapers.

7. Johnstone, G. (2013). *Restorative justice: Ideas, values, debates*. Routledge.

8. Morris, A. (2002). Critiquing the critics: A brief response to critics of restorative justice. *British Journal of Criminology, 42*(3), 596–615; Boucher, D. (2015). The limits of distributive justice: A brief exploration of restorative justice. In Routledge Studies in Social and Political Thought: Vol. 105. C. Boison & M. C. Murray (Eds.), *Distributive justice debates in political and social thought: Perspectives on finding a fair share*. Routledge.

9. Braithwaite, J. B. (2016). *Restorative justice and responsive regulation: The question of evidence*. RegNet Working Paper No. 51, School of Regulation and Global Governance.

10. Karp, D. R., & Frank, O. (2016). Anxiously awaiting the future of restorative justice in the United States. *Victims & Offenders, 11*(1), 50–70.

11. Zernova, M. (2016). *Restorative justice: Ideals and realities*. Routledge.

12. Van Camp, T., & Wemmers, J. A. (2016). Victims' reflections on the protective and proactive approaches to the offer of restorative justice: The importance of information. *Canadian Journal of Criminology and Criminal Justice, 58*(3), 415–442.

13. Van Camp, T. (2016). Understanding victim participation in restorative practices: Looking for justice for oneself as well as for others. *European Journal of Criminology*. doi: 1477370816682981.

14. Zebel, S., Schreurs, W., & Ufkes, E. G. (2017). Crime seriousness and participation in restorative justice: The role of time elapsed since the offense. *Law and Human Behavior, 41*(4), 385–397.

15. Keenan, M. (2016, October). Restorative responses to sexual violence: Challenging perceptions. In *International Association of Women Police (IAWP) Conference, 9–13 October 2016, Barcelona, Spain*.

16. Cohen, R. L. (2016). Restorative justice. In *Handbook of social justice theory and research* (pp. 257–272). Springer New York.

17. Jülich, S., & Thorburn, N. (2017). Sexual violence and substantive equality: Can restorative justice deliver? *Journal of Human Rights and Social Work*, 1–11.

18. Hoyle, C., & Willis, R. (2016). The challenge of integrating restorative justice into the "deep-end" of criminal justice. In T. G. Blomberg, J. M. Brancale, K. M. Beaver, & W. D. Bales (Eds.), *Advancing criminology and criminal justice policy*, (pp. 324–336). Routledge.

19. Bazemore, G., & Schiff, M. (2015). *Restorative community justice: Repairing harm and transforming communities*. Routledge.

20. Cohen, R. L. (2016). Restorative justice. In C. Sabbagh & M. Schmitt (Eds.), *Handbook of social justice theory and research* (pp. 257–272). Springer New York.

21. Hoyle, C., & Rosenblatt, F. F. (2016). Looking back to the future: Threats to the success of restorative justice in the United Kingdom. *Victims & Offenders, 11*(1), 30–49.

22. Harris, N. (2017). Shame in regulatory settings. In P. Drahos (Ed.), *Regulatory theory: Foundations and applications* (pp. 59–76). Acton, Australia: ANU Press.

23. Worth, P., Gavrielides, T., Smith, M., Ntziadima, A., & Gouseti, I. (2015). The psychology of restorative justice: Creating the inner and outer space for change—An observation of restorative justice meetings. In T. Gavrielides (Ed.), *The psychology of restorative justice: Managing the power within* (pp. 203–226). Routledge.

24. Robinson, J., & Hudson, J. (2015). Restorative justice: A typology and critical appraisal. *Willamette J. Int'l L. & Dis. Res., 23*, 335.

25. Halsey, M., Goldsmith, A., & Bamford, D. (2015). Achieving restorative justice: Assessing contrition and forgiveness in the adult conference process. *Australian & New Zealand Journal of Criminology, 48*(4), 483–497.

26. Zernova, M. (2016). *Restorative justice: Ideals and realities.* Routledge.

27. Daly, K. (2016). What is restorative justice? Fresh answers to a vexed question. *Victims & Offenders, 11*(1), 9–29.

28. Knox, C., & Quirk, P. (2016). Community restorative justice. In *Public Policy, Philanthropy and Peacebuilding in Northern Ireland* (pp. 151–181). Palgrave Macmillan UK.

29. Ward, T. (2017). Restorative justice and the dual role problem confronting practitioners. In E. Zinsstag & M. Keenan (Eds.), *Restorative responses to sexual violence: Legal, social and therapeutic dimensions* (pp. 92–107). Routledge.

30. Takagi, P., & Shank, G. (2004). Critique of restorative justice. *Social Justice, 31*(3), 147–163.

31. Ibid., see 7.

32. Van Camp, T., & Wemmers, J. A. (2013). Victim satisfaction with restorative justice: More than simply procedural justice. *International Review of Victimology, 19*(2), 117–143.

33. Takagi, P., & Shank, G. Critique of restorative justice. *Social Justice, 31*(3), 147–163. Retrieved from https://www.socialjusticejournal.org/pdf_free/97Takagi.pdf.

34. Mika, H., Achilles, M., Halbert, E., & Amstutz, L. S. (2004). Listening to victims: A critique of restorative justice policy and practice in the United States. *Fed. Probation, 68*, 32.

35. Van Camp, T., & Wemmers, J. A. (2013). Victim satisfaction with restorative justice: More than simply procedural justice. *International Review of Victimology, 19*(2), 117–143.

36. Acorn, A. E. (2004). *Compulsory compassion: A critique of restorative justice.* UBC Press.

37. Weitekamp, E. G. M., & Parmentier, S. (2016). Restorative justice as healing justice: Looking back to the future of the concept. *Restorative Justice: An International Journal, 4*(2), 141–147.

Chapter 15

What Lies Ahead?
The Future of Restorative Justice

In this chapter, we will explore the following questions ...
- *What are some future directions for restorative justice research and policy?*
- *Where do we see restorative justice in society?*
- *How do we conclude this journey of understanding?*

The Future of Restorative Justice Theory, Research, and Practice

We have seen throughout this text that restorative justice principles and practices have been applied in a variety of shapes and forms in different contexts around the world. Despite an increase within academia in the attention given to restorative justice theory and research, there continues to be a gap in awareness amongst practitioners, politicians, and policy makers as well as the general public in terms of its applicability and usage. Conceptual tensions regarding the definition of restorative justice coupled with a gap between theoretical principles and practical application have proved to be barriers to the adoption of restorative justice programs within the criminal justice system. The future of restorative justice therefore lies in the ability of scholars and researchers to guide the development and understanding of restorative justice theory, research, and practice to better inform its purpose, scope, and application. We turn now to a better look at this endeavor.

Micro-Level Considerations in Restorative Justice Theory, Research, and Practice

The direction of restorative justice has been embedded in a history and tradition of human interaction, dialog, and emotions. The success of interventions based on principles of restorative justice are equated with outcome and satisfaction with processes designed to build trust, alter behavior, and bring about transformation.[1] Practically speaking, we would, at the micro level, want to consider the defining of successful outcome as evidenced by the integrity of the practice itself. However, in the real world where programmatic initiatives are implemented and funded for tangible and measurable outcomes, the success of restorative justice has been traditionally considered in terms of evidence of best practice.[2] The direction of restorative justice research, theory, and practice is therefore best served, at the micro level, to focus on reducing recidivism and bringing about restoration to victims and their communities.

The Question of Recidivism

Throughout our discussions of restorative justice principles and practice as applied in various contexts, we have seen that a major draw of programmatic initiatives has been the successful reduction in offending behavior. Whether the context is within a school, workplace, police station, treatment center, courtroom, or prison, the goal of altering behavior is at the forefront, and the desistance of problematic behavior is seen as the hallmark of success.[3]

With that in mind, we must strive to establish tangible and measurable outcome measures for a reduction in behaviors that lead to conflict, hostility, and criminal offending. Restorative justice research and theoretical application must accomplish this task with a comprehensive focus on those aspects of program design and implementation aimed at reducing formal contacts with the criminal justice system, diverting offenders from formal labeling, decreasing incidents of violence and aggression, and increasing compliance with treatment.[4] Thus, while a significant amount of research on restorative justice theory and practice focuses on participant satisfaction and views of the process, there needs to be a balanced approach that encompasses offender behavior, with rigorous evaluation studies that are methodologically sound building confidence in this approach to dealing with crime and conflict in society.[5]

The Question of Restoration

Analyzing programmatic success must also entail a multidimensional understanding of the overall structure and function of the initiative which is implemented. With restorative justice practices, we cannot overlook the integral component of restoration, which includes the elements of repair, remorse, and resolution.[6] Placing value on these elements in terms of successful outcome is beneficial not only in determining funding for programs, but also reminds us of the need for progress in terms of restorative justice research to evaluate the extent to which certain practices align well with restorative justice theory and principles.

At the heart of developing restorative justice research, theory, and practice is therefore a need to continue a focused expansion of understanding in terms of process and outcome.[7] A compelling approach would provide an integrated perspective, which combines restorative justice process with restorative justice outcomes. Thus, while restorative justice programs may appear in different shapes and formats, the processes of restoration must be inherently connected to outcomes which bring about change and transformation—we cannot bypass one and focus exclusively on the other without connecting results with the process itself.[8]

Macro-Level Considerations in Restorative Justice Theory, Research, and Practice

Program implementation within the context of criminal justice management and organization has relied heavily on the ability of coordinators and researchers to present findings of successful outcome measures in support of the initiative.[9] This documentation has been the basis of budget allocations and continued funding of the program as a "best practice." In a climate where politics and public support are significantly intertwined, this documentation must also take into account the macro dynamic of obtaining public support and ensuring that media attention does not sway opinion in a distorted manner that misrepresents factual evidence. Thus, gaining public support and ensuring political commitment are important macro-level considerations in the expansion of restorative justice theory, research, and practice.

Convincing the Public

In a climate of law and order pervading the political arena today, gaining support for restorative justice must integrate a large-scale public education campaign into the research agenda of restorative justice scholars and advocates by directly engaging the public. This can be accomplished by developing an alliance of leadership in the areas of victims' rights, offender advocacy, law enforcement governance, politics, and educational institutions.[10] Within these domains, specific restorative principles and practices must be identified and embedded in a system-wide vision that will ultimately permeate the structure of interactions that take place throughout each component. This calls for bridging the gap between public perception of conflict resolution and restorative mechanisms of justice and removing structural barriers that would hinder the development of protocols which allow victims and offenders the opportunity to encounter one another and reconcile.[11]

Convincing the public of the value of restorative justice policies and practices also includes the delivery of an approach that is victim centered, one which places the value of reparation as a priority in outcomes, but also one that ensures that harms are addressed in a positive and proactive way which holds offenders accountable for their actions. This means bringing in the community whenever possible as stakeholders in the restorative justice process, teaching them the value of participation in the reintegration process of offenders as beneficial to building community.[12] This can be accomplished by the continued expansion of evaluation studies of restorative programs and interventions in order to provide a consistent vision and purpose which can persuade the public of their benefit to the community and ensure continued commitment to the implementation, expansion, and improvement of restorative justice practices. Restorative justice research should therefore establish the legitimacy of a restorative response to conflict resolution and criminal offending by monitoring, evaluating, and improving on programmatic goals and initiatives to ensure their proper alignment with guiding principles of restorative justice.[13]

The Role of Media and Politics

It is a widely recognized fact that media of all forms, whether social media, television, newspaper reports, or other forms of mass dissemination of information, plays an integral role in defining and shaping the public's view about crime, crime prevention, community safety, law enforcement, and policies affecting crime prevention and victimization.[14] In many instances, the media is seen as an obstacle to program alignment with a restorative justice vision as adverse propaganda can emerge to attack ideologies in favor of reparation, forgiveness, and reintegration. The resolution to this dilemma must therefore focus on the portrayal of restorative justice as a mechanism of crime control which is based on victim advocacy, community involvement, and the empowerment of individuals to restore damaged lives and relationships.

Restorative justice practitioners, advocates, and scholars have the task of building confidence in their programs and policies by promoting them to community leaders as best practices.[15] This can be accomplished through the systematic employment of empirical evidence of evaluation studies documenting the success of restorative justice in achieving balance, accountability, and reparation.[16] Building credibility through public awareness can bring to the surface the contextual elements of interventions which are restorative and elevate these successful practices as an outcome of a sound, well-guided, evidenced-based theoretical approach.

Restorative Justice in Society: A Look Ahead

Throughout our text, we have built a nexus between the practical application of restorative justice and outcomes which are linked to forgiveness, healing, repair, and reintegration. We must continue to strive towards achieving this ideal while recognizing that certain limitations, inconsistencies, and disagreements will continue to hinder the growth and progress of restorative justice values and ideals.[17] Looking into the future of restorative justice theory, research, and practice, we find that the direction and course it will take is inherently tied to its connection and relationship with the current criminal justice system. We turn now to a closer examination of the dynamics involved in characterizing the long-term trend in scope and nature of restorative justice application as determined by the relationship between restorative justice and criminal justice.

Restorative Justice: Part of Criminal Justice or Outside Criminal Justice?

Part of making any new programmatic initiative appealing to the public is using catch phrases like "new" or "innovative" when referring to restorative justice practices. The downside of this approach is the creation of a divide between programs and policies that are currently in place with the assumption that the new is replacing the old. While this may have been the initial impetus behind the emergence of restorative justice practices and their integration into criminal justice systems, it is now time to recognize that there is a need to mainstream this ideological approach into the criminal justice system in a way that bridges the divide.[18]

When we speak of restorative justice as diverting offenders away from traditional, formal mechanisms of criminal justice, we are elevating it as a complimentary approach to justice which rests solely outside of the adversarial, punitive process. This separation is supported by the argument that restorative programs can only work properly if used as a parallel of criminal justice. The argument is supported by the idea that integrating restorative justice into a punitive system of justice without a clear line of separation can compromise and marginalize the ideological basis of restorative programming and practices.[19] However, we submit that this argument, while valid, must be addressed at the procedural and implementation stages of program development to maintain the integrity of restorative justice processes while ensuring their proper and viable place within the formal criminal justice system. Restorative justice is a powerful approach, a philosophical movement which permeates so many different aspects of human interaction. For this reason, we cannot confine it to a few programmatic initiatives in a sparse setting that is barely traceable and can lead to misconceptions about its rightful place. Rather, it is necessary to acknowledge and advocate restorative justice as a philosophical method of advocacy which can embrace all aspects of criminal justice with its focus on offender accountability and reintegration, victim advocacy and support, and community restoration and sustainability.[20]

Restorative Justice: Process or Outcome?

When it comes to program implementation, the line of divide continues to be drawn with a clear distinction between process and outcome. With process, a strong emphasis is placed on values and ideals that shape the design and application of a specific program or initiative. For example, the restorative justice ideals of remorse and reconciliation define the various encounters that can take place between victims and offenders. On the other hand, with an adversarial criminal justice process, encounters between victims and offenders are often discouraged if not completely forbidden.[21]

This apparent paradox makes it difficult to recognize that the outcomes we sometimes desire when it comes to criminal justice intervention can both complement and overlap between the ideals of restorative justice and the goals of traditional methods of social control and accountability. It might best be thought of in a very simple way. When restorative justice first came to the forefront of criminal intervention, the process was new and innovative, and therefore, the outcomes were described as different, better, and more promising.[22] Now, as we move forward and advance our knowledge of justice, we are better served to align outcome with process, as the goals of empathy, remorse, repair, reconciliation, and reintegration are not only process based but are the ultimate outcome measures of success when it comes to interventions for conflict resolution and criminal desistance.[23]

Restorative Justice: Alternative to Punishment or Punishment Alternative?

The line of divide between punishment and corrections has traditionally centered upon **utilitarian** notions of justice, which focus on the goals of rehabilitation and deterrence, and the retributive model of justice, which focuses on the ideals of punishment as "**just deserts**" for harm that is done.[24] Where criminal behavior upsets the peaceful balance of society, the boundaries of punishment and correctional intervention should not be limited by such a narrow approach to justice but rather must embrace the standard of intervention based on the restoration of peace and balance to crime victims, communities, as well as those family members affected by the offender's harmful actions.

Thus, to establish restorative justice values and ideals as the hallmark of correctional interventions that are designed to resolve conflicts, achieve justice, and settle disputes, we must neither speak of it as punishment alternative nor alternative to punishment, but instead, the pillar of justice by which we build a foundation for processes designed to achieve these goals.[25] It is an undeniable fact that restorative justice programs and practices impose obligations upon offenders that are the functional equivalent of punishment. Sanctions such as community service, restitution, and participation in prison tours, victim impact panels, and family conferencing can be taxing and viewed as punitive. However, it is the manner in which these obligations are designed, assigned, and monitored which elevates them from the domain of punishment or alternative to punishment to one of reconciliation and restoration where coercive measures are only the outcome of an offender's non-compliant attitude and behavior. With that said, we are not advocating a system of justice that is devoid of the concept of punishment in its variable forms and definitions. Rather, we envision a constructive approach to conflict resolution and criminal offending which transcends the punishment and post-punishment phases of intervention and embraces the elements of dialog, interaction, and engagement in the process of repair, healing, and restoration.[26]

Our Final Thoughts

We began this journey towards a more comprehensive understanding of restorative justice theory and application by exploring its definition as a process represented by certain values, goals, ideals, and practices. We connected the concept of restorative justice to a theoretical paradigm and social movement which embraced dialog, accountability, healing encounters, and reparation of harm.[27] These ideals were reflected in the emerging spectrum of practices that have come to be known as victim-offender mediation, family group conferencing, victim impact panels, peacemaking circles, and reparative boards. Moving forward in our understanding, we explored the practical application of these restorative processes in various contexts and within the various components of criminal justice, noting the value of this approach to conflict resolution and in bringing about reconciliation, healing, and repair.[28] While it seems now that our journey has come to an end, there are some final thoughts that we wish to leave you with, thoughts that we hope will inspire your further exploration of this vast field of knowledge we have presented through this text.

A theoretical approach which embraces the ideals of repairing harm, restoring relationships, building communities, and increasing accountability should be an easy sell when it comes to putting theory into practice. However, the practical application of such intervention techniques can prove to be challenging in the least and at times face many obstacles in terms of implementation.[29] Yet, these obstacles can be overcome with the emphasis on restorative justice as neither theory nor practice alone, but rather a philosophical approach that embraces both. In our understanding of restorative justice, we must rise to the challenge of integrating restorative justice as an approach which normatively and practically prioritizes the resolution of conflicts within interpersonal relationships as the primary goal of addressing antisocial behavior.[30] By placing value on this as a priority, we see that the most promising avenue to such a successful outcome — the restoration of harm — can only be achieved by placing emphasis on making things right in terms of future behavior and not just reacting to a past action through retribution.[31]

A restorative approach to conflict resolution is a learning approach which teaches individuals accountability by actively involving them in the process of repair and resolution. This approach has a more beneficial long-term impact on the lives of community members, as well as victims and offenders, by creating a forum for problem solving that is engaging among all parties involved in a conflict based on a well-grounded principled approach.[32] We see this process as consistent with the development of a civilized citizenship which fosters care and integration rather than alienation and isolation. It is in this recognition of the value of restorative justice that we see its promise as a theoretical and practical approach to conflict resolution. It is in this direction that we hope this text has inspired you to take on a genuine interest in understanding, advocating, and pursuing this meaning of justice within your academic and professional goals and aspirations.

Chapter Summary

What are some future directions for restorative justice research and policy?

We have argued in this final chapter that the future of restorative justice lies in the ability of scholars and researchers to guide the development and understanding of restorative justice theory, research, and practice to better inform its purpose, scope, and application at both the micro and macro levels of application. At the micro level, the direction of restorative justice research, theory, and practice entails a focus on reducing recidivism and bringing about restoration to victims and their communities in order to establish tangible and measurable outcome measures for a reduction in behaviors that lead to conflict, hostility, and criminal offending. Likewise, we cannot overlook the integral component of restoration which includes the elements of repair, remorse, and resolution.

At a macro level of application where politics and public support are significantly intertwined, we must also take into account the need for obtaining community support and ensuring that media attention does not sway opinion in a distorted manner that misrepresents factual evidence. Thus, gaining public support and ensuring political commitment are important macro-level considerations in the expansion of restorative justice theory, research, and practice.

Where do we see restorative justice in society?

In this final chapter, we examined the future of restorative justice theory, research, and practice as inherently tied to its connection and relationship with the current criminal justice system. We described restorative justice as a powerful approach, a philosophical movement which permeates so many different aspects of human interaction. For this reason, we argue against its confinement to a few programmatic initiatives and instead, advance restorative justice as a philosophical method of advocacy which can embrace all aspects of criminal justice with its focus on offender accountability and reintegration, victim advocacy and support, and community restoration and sustainability.

Moreover, as we move forward and advance our knowledge of justice, we are better served to well align outcome and process, as the restorative goals of empathy, remorse, repair, reconciliation, and reintegration are not only process based but are the ultimate outcome measures of success when it comes to interventions for conflict resolution and criminal desistance. Thus, to establish restorative justice values and ideals as the hallmark of correctional interventions, we must neither speak of it as punishment alternative nor alternative to punishment, but instead, the pillar of justice by which we build a foundation for processes designed to achieve these goals.

How do we conclude this journey of understanding?

We concluded our journey of understanding with an emphasis on the challenge of practically applying restorative justice interventions in various settings. We noted that the most promising means of overcoming these challenges is to emphasize restorative justice as neither theory nor practice alone, but rather a philosophical approach that embraces both. In our understanding of restorative justice, we must therefore rise to the challenge of integrating restorative justice as an approach which normatively and practically prioritizes the resolution of conflicts within interpersonal relationships as the primary goal of addressing antisocial behavior.

Key Terms

Utilitarian
Just Desserts

Critical Thinking Questions

1. With regard to micro-level considerations in applying restorative justice theory and practice, do you think the goals of reducing recidivism and achieving restoration are competing values? Why or why not? How do we reconcile the two with one another?

2. What obstacles does restorative justice face when it comes to the macro-level dynamics of public support and the intervention of media and politics? How can these obstacles be overcome to advance restorative justice theory and practice?

3. Do you think that restorative justice application should be a part of the criminal justice system or separate from the criminal justice system? Are there benefits to one over the other? Explain your position.

4. Is restorative justice consistent with the concept of punishment? Should the benefits of this theoretical approach focus on process, outcome, or both?

References

1. Latimer, J., Dowden, C., & Muise, D. (2005). The effectiveness of restorative justice practices: A meta-analysis. *The Prison Journal*, *85*(2), 127–144.

2. Rodriguez, N. (2007). Restorative justice at work: Examining the impact of restorative justice resolutions on juvenile recidivism. *Crime & Delinquency*, *53*(3), 355–379; Bonta, J., Wallace-Capretta, S., Rooney, J., & Mcanoy, K. (2002). An outcome evaluation of a restorative justice alternative to incarceration. *Contemporary Justice Review*, *5*(4), 319–338.

3. Bouffard, J., Cooper, M., & Bergseth, K. (2016). The effectiveness of various restorative justice interventions on recidivism outcomes among juvenile offenders. *Youth Violence and Juvenile Justice*. doi: 1541204016647428.

4. Braithwaite, J. B. (2016). *Restorative justice and responsive regulation: The question of evidence*. RegNet Working Paper No. 51, School of Regulation and Global Governance.

5. Foley, T. (2016). *Developing restorative justice jurisprudence: Rethinking responses to criminal wrongdoing*. Routledge.

6. Walklate, S. *(2005)*. Researching restorative justice: Politics, policy and process. *Critical Criminology*, *13*, 165–179. Center for Justice and Reconciliation. Retrieved from http://restorativejustice.org/rj-library/researching-restorative-justice-politics-policy-and-process/6302/#sthash.1xhPHyal.dpbs.

7. Daly, K. (2016). What is restorative justice? Fresh answers to a vexed question. *Victims & Offenders*, *11*(1), 9–29.

8. Zernova, M. (2016). *Restorative justice: Ideals and realities*. Routledge; Crawford, A., & Newburn, T. (2013). *Youth offending and restorative justice*. Routledge.

9. Garrison, A. H. (2009). The influence of research on criminal justice policy making. Retrieved from https://kucampus.kaplan.edu/documentstore/docs09/pdf/picj/vol4/issue1/PICJ_V4N1_Garrison_9_22.pdf.

10. Building support. Center for Justice and Reconciliation. Prison Fellowship International. Retrieved from http://restorativejustice.org/restorative-justice/about-restorative-justice/tutorial-intro-to-restorative-justice/lesson-5-implementation-issues/building-support/#sthash.8BVQqUgt.dpbs.

11. Gerkin, P., Walsh, J., Kuilema, J., & Borton, I. (2017). Implementing restorative justice under the retributive paradigm: A pilot program case study. *SAGE Open*, *7*(1), doi: 2158244017691562.

12. Willis, R. (2016). Three approaches to community in restorative justice, explored through a young person's experiences of a youth offender team in England. *Restorative Justice*, *4*(2), 168–194.

13. Hoyle, C., & Rosenblatt, F. F. (2016). Looking back to the future: Threats to the success of restorative justice in the United Kingdom. *Victims & Offenders*, *11*(1), 30–49; Fronius, T., Persson, H., Guckenburg, S., Hurley, N., & Petrosino, A. (2016). *Restorative justice in US schools: A research review*. San Francisco, CA: WestEd Justice and Prevention Training Center.

14. Surette, R., & Kampe, K. (2016). The media and criminal justice policy and practices. In T. G. Blomberg, J. M. Brancale, K. M. Beaver, & W. D. Bales (Eds.), *Advancing criminology and criminal justice policy* (p. 428). Routledge.

15. Leonardi, L., Network, C., & Bliss, K. (2016). *Expanding the use of restorative justice: Exploring innovations and best practices*. Canadian Families and Connections Network.

16. Gregory, A., Clawson, K., Davis, A., & Gerewitz, J. (2016). The promise of restorative practices to transform teacher-student relationships and achieve equity in school discipline. *Journal of Educational and Psychological Consultation*, *26*(4), 325–353.

17. Wood, W. R., & Suzuki, M. (2016). Four challenges in the future of restorative justice. *Victims & Offenders*, *11*(1), 149–172.

18. von Hirsch, A., Roberts, J. V., Bottoms, A. E., Roach, K., & Schiff, M. (Eds.). (2003). *Restorative justice and criminal justice: Competing or reconcilable paradigms*. Bloomsbury Publishing.

Daly, K. (2000). Revisiting the relationship between retributive and restorative justice. In H. Strang & J. Braithwaite (Eds.), *Restorative justice: Philosophy to practice* (pp. 33–54). Aldershot: Dartmouth.

19. Hoyle, C., & Willis, R. (2016). The challenge of integrating restorative justice into the "deep-end" of criminal justice. In T. G. Blomberg, J. M. Brancale, K. M. Beaver, & W. D. Bales (Eds.), *Advancing criminology and criminal justice policy* (pp. 324–336). Routledge.

20. Blomberg, T. G., Brancale, J. M., Beaver, K. M., & Bales, W. D. (Eds.). (2016). *Advancing criminology and criminal justice policy*. Routledge.

21. King, M., Freiberg, A., Batagol, B., & Hyams, R. (2014). *Non-adversarial justice*. Federation Press.

22. Richards, K. (2014). A promise and a possibility: The limitations of the traditional criminal justice system as an explanation for the emergence of restorative justice. *Restorative Justice, 2*(2), 124– 141.

23. Jülich, S., & Landon, F. (2017). Achieving justice outcomes. In E. Zinsstag & M. Keenan (Eds.), *Restorative responses to sexual violence: Legal, social and therapeutic dimensions* (p. 192). Routledge. Koss, M. P. (2014). The RESTORE program of restorative justice for sex crimes: Vision, process, and outcomes. *Journal of Interpersonal Violence, 29*(9), 1623–1660.

24. Punishment. (2015, July 21). *Stanford encyclopedia of philosophy*. Retrieved from https://plato. stanford.edu/entries/punishment/.

25. Zernova, M. (2016). *Restorative justice: Ideals and realities*. Routledge.

26. Daly, K. (2013). The punishment debate in restorative justice. In J. Simon & R. Sparks (Eds.), *The SAGE handbook of punishment and society* (pp. 356–375).

27. Daly, K. (2016). What is restorative justice? Fresh answers to a vexed question. *Victims & Offenders, 11*(1), 9–29.

28. Wong, D. S. (2016). Restorative justice at different levels of the criminal justice system in China: Challenges and paths forward. *Restorative Justice, 4*(1), 10–26.

29. Shapland, J. (2014). Implications of growth: Challenges for restorative justice. *International Review of Victimology, 20*(1), 111–127.

30. Ward, T., Fox, K. J., & Garber, M. (2014). Restorative justice, offender rehabilitation and desistance. *Restorative Justice, 2*(1), 24–42.

31. Marsh, B., & Maruna, S. (2016). Desistance and restorative justice: Learning from success stories of Northern Ireland's Youth Justice Agency. *Restorative Justice, 4*(3), 369–387; Bouffard, J., Cooper, M., & Bergseth, K. (2016). The effectiveness of various restorative justice interventions on recidivism outcomes among juvenile offenders. *Youth Violence and Juvenile Justice*. doi: 1541204016647428.

32. Bazemore, G., & Schiff, M. (2015). *Restorative community justice: Repairing harm and transforming communities*. Routledge; Llewellyn, J., Archibald, B. P., Clairmont, D., & Crocker, D. (2014). Imagining success for a restorative approach to justice: Implications for measurement and evaluation. *Dalhousie Law Journal, 36*(2), 281–316.

Glossary

Aboriginal: A term used to describe a region's native, pre-colonial population.

Acephalous Societies: egalitarian societies, organized around tribes, with no central government or leadership.

Affective Empathy: the sharing of another's emotional state.

Behavioral Empathy: a conscious decision to alter one's response patterns as a direct result of experiencing cognitive and affective empathy, which create a responsive distress upon hearing of the suffering and hurt of another individual and the subsequent desire to relieve that stress by taking corrective action.

Cautioning: a process used by policing agencies in countries such as England and Australia to divert some offenders away from the formal court process.

Centralization: organization of a society in which a single, consolidated body of government or authority possesses the role of managing the allocation of resources, enforcing the rules, and protecting the common good of society.

Children, Young Persons and Their Families Act: a 1989 New Zealand act that revamped the juvenile justice system, creating a process that focused on repair of harm and creating dialog between victims, offenders, family, and community. It was an outcome of the New Zealand government's attempt to integrate Maori recommendations to restore the involvement of family and community to address juvenile delinquency. Family Group Conference (FGC)

Circle Keeper: the facilitator of a peacemaking circle whose role is to support the circle process and its participants.

Circle of Understanding: a type of peacemaking circle that is organized in order to discuss a specific incident in the hopes of coming to a better understanding of how and why it occurred.

Circles of Support and Accountability: A program that provides those coming out of prison (especially sex offenders) with community supervision and support as they work to reintegrate into society and desist from crime.

Cognitive Empathy: an understanding of another person's feelings.

Collective Efficacy: a community's sense of shared responsibility. In the context of crime, communities with high levels of efficacy have a desire to intervene when something goes wrong and express an interest in correcting social deviance and repairing harm.

Collective Trauma: traumatic experiences that are shared by large groups of people after which common repercussions such as feelings of anger, helplessness, and terror spread throughout the group and can even affect future generations.

Community Justice: according to Clear and Karp, this refers to "all variants of crime prevention and justice activities that explicitly include the community in their processes and set the enhancement of community quality of life as an explicit goal."

Community-Based Corrections: court-ordered offender supervision that occurs within the community, such as probation and parole.

Community-Oriented Policing: an approach to law enforcement that seeks to unite police officers with the communities they serve in order to identify and address broader problems related to community safety and wellbeing (in addition to responding directly to specific acts of crime, harm, and conflict).

Comprehensive Law Movement: according to Susan Daicoff, it is a movement that seeks to advance a humanistic, therapeutic, and holistic approach to the law and is exemplified in concepts and practices such as specialty courts, therapeutic jurisprudence and restorative justice.

Conditional Mercy: mercy based on an offender's actions.

Consensus Decision Making: a form of group decision making that takes everyone's needs and opinions into consideration and tries to arrive at a decision that reflects the group as a whole rather than one person or one part of the group.

Constructive Shaming: akin to reintegrative shaming, relies on the bonds that connect family members with one another to bring about a genuine, emotional desire to seek approval by correcting action that has brought about shame and humiliation not only to the individual actor but to their entire family.

Containment Theory: a theory proposed by Walter Reckless which argues that there are internal and external forces of restraint that keep individuals from breaking the law.

Creative Restitution: a term coined by Albert Eglash to describe restitution that repairs the direct harm to the victim and supports offender accountability.

Criminal Desistance: successful movement of an offender away from criminal behavior.

Deferred Adjudication: gives an offender an opportunity to avoid a formal criminal record but it does require that an offender enter a guilty plea in court (unlike with pre-trial diversion).

Deterrence: a goal of the law that seeks to prevent individuals from committing further acts of harm.

Deviance Amplification: a cycle where persistent involvement in criminal behavior is an outcome of isolation and the development of behavior patterns that reflect the values and beliefs of a deviant identity.

Differential Association Theory: presents crime as a learned behavior contingent upon the meanings or definitions we attach to the social conditions and cultural concerns or values that surround us.

Diversion: in the context of juvenile and criminal justice, it's a term used to describe an effort to place low-risk offenders in community-based programs that can address their needs outside of the formal justice system and its agencies.

Dual Court System: a court system that grants jurisdiction to either state or federal courts based on what type of case needs to be heard and, in regard to the criminal justice system, what law has been breached. This is the system the U.S. uses.

Dual Track Model: a system of justice, proposed by theorist Daniel Van Ness, that supports two separate systems of justice that can work alongside one another and cooperate whenever possible.

External Containment: referred to in *Containment Theory* as a type of restraint that exists outside of someone, such as effective supervision, parental disapproval, and sanctioning.

Family Group Conference (FGC): a restorative gathering of an offender, their family members, criminal justice or social services professionals, and those impacted by their offense to discuss how and why the offense occurred and create an action plan to repair the harm and prevent future offending.

Fairness Committee: a reparative board that includes a mix of students, teachers, and school staff who meet to discuss specific cases of students violating school policies and make decisions concerning how those violations will be addressed.

First Nations: the original, native peoples of present-day Canada.

Formal Restorative Practices: refers to the use of restorative practices to address serious problems and violations within schools.

Gun-Free Schools Act: passed in 1994, this act required states receiving federal financial assistance for education to create their own laws and policies mandating the automatic expulsion of any student caught bringing a gun to school.

Hate Crime: any crime committed in order to bring harm to a victim because of their identity, including their age, race, ethnicity, sexual orientation, gender identity, ability, or religion.

Healing Circle: a type of peacemaking circle organized for the purpose of providing care and support for someone who has been victimized by crime.

Howard Zehr: a pioneer in restorative justice theory and practice and a member of the Mennonite Central Committee who helped establish the process for implementing a program modeled on the Kitchener Experiment.

Hui: Maori word for a special meeting.

Hybrid Model: a system of justice, proposed by theorist Daniel Van Ness, that integrates restorative justice within the conventional justice system. Unlike in the "dual track model," restorative justice is fully incorporated within the conventional justice system, enhancing and expanding it but not existing as an alternative to it.

Incapacitation: the correctional practice of removing offenders from society, otherwise known as imprisonment or incarceration.

Incorporation: an effort by the juvenile or criminal justice system to utilize a restorative process such as a sentencing circle, reparative board, or victim impact panel as part of their formal response to the offense.

Informal Restorative Practices: the use of restorative practices and the application of restorative principles in day-to-day classroom and school activities.

Institutional Corrections: the detention, incarceration, or institutionalization of either a suspected or convicted offender in a facility such as a jail, prison, or juvenile detention center.

Integrity Board: consisting of faculty, staff, and students who are trained in restorative values and practices, this kind of board focuses less on the application of prescribed sanctions and more on working with the offending student to identify and explore how the misconduct has impacted others and what can be done to reestablish trust between the student and their campus community.

Internal Containment: referred to in Containment Theory as a type of restraint that exists inside of someone, such as moral reasoning, a sense of responsibility to others, and a personal sense of right and wrong.

Inuit: along with Métis and First Nations, they are the original peoples of North America in present-day Canada.

Jail: centers that typically detain individuals charged, but not yet convicted, of a crime.

Just Desserts: a focus of the retributive model of justice that is concerned with fitting punishment for the harm that is done.

Kitchener Experiment: name given to the test case of reconciliation using face-to-face mediation between the teen offenders in a 1974 vandalism spree in Ontario and their victims.

Korero: Maori word for a talk among a group to resolve a dispute.

Labeling Theory: suggests that one's identity, and therefore behavior, is largely shaped by the "labels" attached to an individual by his/her community.

Mana: in Maori society, the honor and prestige that is derived from birth and throughout a lifetime of good deeds and peaceful association with community members.

Maori: the indigenous Polynesian people of New Zealand.

Mediation: a process whereby two or more parties come together with a neutral facilitator to discuss, and attempt to resolve, shared issues and conflicts.

Mennonite Central Committee (MCC): a local chapter of the Mennonite and Brethren in Christ Churches. Mark Yantzi, a Mennonite Christian, partnered with the chapter to offer a mediated face-to-face encounter between the teen offenders in a 1974 vandalism spree in Ontario and their victims.

Métis: Along with First Nations and Inuit, they are the original peoples of North America in present-day Canada.

Monkalun: a figure in Ifugao society that fulfills the role of judge, prosecutor, and defense attorney.

Mothers Against Drunk Driving: (formerly Mothers Against Drunk Drivers) founded by Candace Lightner, this organization became the face and voice of victims throughout the country to unite against the senseless acts of violence that are the product of driving under the influence of alcohol and drugs.

National Campaign to Eliminate Drunk Driving: MADD campaign that promoted three important and creative steps in reducing the tragic and senseless act of drunk driving: support law enforcement; prevention of drunk driving through the use of interlock devices (in-car breathalyzers) and support of technology development that would keep a vehicle from operating if a driver is over the legal limit.

The National Commission on the Disappearance of Persons: this body established the investigative model that would later be adapted by countries such as Chile, El Salvador, and South Africa; and would come to be known as a truth and reconciliation commission.

Navajo Nation Peacemaking Court: heavily rooted in the tribe's culture, spirituality, and values, it is a process of reconciliation involving four types of participants (the peacemaker, the decision-makers, the others impacted by the conflict or harm and the community observers).

Net-Widening: related to the theory that when we implement a new process or practice in the field of criminal justice it can sometimes result in more people coming into contact with the justice system than before the new practice was implemented.

Opening and Closing Rituals: Peacemaking circle rituals that bring attention to the group's collective transition into and out of the circle process, reinforcing the idea that the act of engaging in a circle is a sacred or otherwise special practice.

Parallelism: refers to the use of restorative practices alongside the juvenile and criminal justice systems.

Peacemaking Circle: a dialog process that brings members of a community or group together to facilitate mutual understanding, discuss important issues, and/or make decisions.

Peacemaking Court: a term that can be used to describe the use of an aboriginal peacemaking ceremony within the context of a tribal court.

Plan of Support: a plan that details specific ways in which members of the support circle commit to providing aid, consolation, and/or help to the person at the heart of the circle process.

Pretrial Diversion: also referred to as deferred prosecution, this type of diversion moves an offender into a probation-based program without requiring them to enter a formal plea in court.

Primary Victim(s): a term used to describe the person or people most directly impacted by a crime.

Prison: institutions where offenders are sent to serve a court-imposed sentence of incarceration.

Prisoner and Community Together (PACT): an organization based in Michigan City, Indiana, that strongly advocated for, developed, and administered several community-based correctional programs to enhance the reentry process.

Rangatira: a Maori leader. This is a word made of two parts with its root being "tira" meaning to knit together and "ranga" meaning to uplift. Combined then a rangatira is someone who can uplift the people, while binding them together.

Recidivism: the measurement of criminal relapse or re-offense.

Reentry: a former offender's process of leaving prison and securing basic needs such as employment and housing.

Rehabilitation: refers to the transformation of an offender into a law-abiding member of society by addressing the underlying issues that motivated the offender to commit crime.

Reintegration Circle: a type of peacemaking circle used to foster reconciliation and the social reintegration of an offender after crime and/or following a period of separation due to detention or incarceration.

Reintegrative Shaming Theory: introduced in John Braithwaite's book Crime, Shame, and Reintegration, this theory suggests that offenders should be allowed to earn the right to re-enter society after expressing remorse, apologizing to their victim, and repairing the loss after crime.

Relationship Abuse: a pattern of behavior motivated by one person's desire to dominate and control another person.

Reparative Probation: category of probation within the Vermont Department of Corrections which includes offenders with minimal supervision requirements and conditions aside from a contract that is signed between them and the restorative justice board members. It is this category of probation that has given rise to the Vermont model of community justice.

Restorative Cautioning: a process used by some policing agencies outside of the U.S. that diverts some offenders from the juvenile or criminal justice system by utilizing restorative processes such as a victim-offender mediation or family group conference to address the offense and arrive at the conditions of diversion.

Restorative Discipline: a way of approaching problematic behavior by focusing less on how the behavior violates rules and more on how it affects other people and relationships.

Restorative Justice: An approach to justice that includes practices rooted in the idea that both the origins and outcomes of crime can be articulated as needs in communities, victims, and offenders.

Restorative Living: within correctional institutions, it is the personal application of restorative values such as respect, care, inclusion, and accountability to one's day-to-day life, relationships, and interactions.

Restorative Policing: per Restorative Justice International, it's "a relational paradigm of policing that focuses on creating safer, more connected communities through restorative justice practices underpinned by restorative principles of safety, accountability, sustainability, relationship building and constructive engagement."

Restorative Practices: a term used to describe any model, program, or process designed to implement restorative principles and values (such as inclusivity, collective efficacy, and participatory decision making) within a specific community, group, or institution.

Retribution: the means by which we seek to satisfy the desire for revenge upon an individual who has inflicted unfair harm upon someone else.

Retributive Justice: a philosophy of justice that focuses on reasonable and deserving compensation to victims, as well as punishment to offenders that is proportionate to their offense.

RISE (Re-integrative Shaming Experiments): Australian program for juvenile offenders that led to a positive change in the attitudes of offenders with regard to their desire to make things right with their victim as well as society and also with regard to their feelings of remorse and repentance.

Risk Management Probation: a type of caseload within the Vermont Department of Corrections which includes offenders that present multiple management issues, risk factors, or are a particular category of offenders such as sex offenders and domestic violence offenders.

Safety Net Model: a system of justice, proposed by theorist Daniel Van Ness, that borrows from the Unified and Dual Track models. It is predominantly restorative in nature; however, alternatives would remain accessible if restorative justice failed to meet the needs or circumstances of a particular case or offender.

School-To-Prison Pipeline: a term frequently used to articulate the way that school disciplinary practices, such as suspension and expulsion, have been linked to students' increased risk of being moved into alternative schools, failing to graduate, and ending up in prisons as adults.

Secondary Victim(s): a term used to describe indirect victims of crime such as the family members, coworkers, and friends of primary victims.

Sentencing Circle: circle process used in courts that bring together the people impacted by an offense (including the offender, the victim, family, friends, community members, and criminal justice professionals) to discuss what happened and create a sentencing plan.

Sentencing Plan: a written plan created during the sentencing circle process that details what an offender agrees to do in an effort to repair the harm experienced by the victim and community.

Sentencing Reform Bill: 1995 Canadian bill that focused on a more unified and equitable system of sanctioning criminal offenders.

Sexual Abuse: any act of sexual contact that is unwanted and nonconsensual, ranging from indecent exposure to forcible rape, and including both repeated acts of victimization and isolated incidents.

Shared Guidelines: refers to the creation of specific rules of conduct made by circle participants as a way of demonstrating important restorative values and principles such as equality and shared responsibility.

Social Bond Theory: created by Travis Hirschi, it is a type of social control theory involving bonds comprised of four interrelated elements: attachment, commitment, involvement, and belief.

Social Control Theory: argues that people are less likely to commit crimes when bonded to social groups such as families and peers that act as social controls to criminal delinquency.

Social Reintegration: an interpersonal process that requires something more than merely the former offender's intention to desist from crime and behave as a law-abiding citizen; it requires the acknowledgement of harm, the building of trust, and a society's willingness to restore the former offender's place within the community.

Social Strain Theory: argues that the degree of opportunity one has to meet goals shared and favored within one's community can determine one's likelihood to engage in deviant behavior.

Specialization: a way of organizing members of a social group whereby those who are most suited for a task, either by personal talent, skill, or other qualification, become responsible for that task, such as being a hunter, farmer, or artisan.

Specialty Courts: also referred to as problem-solving courts or treatment courts, these are court-based programs that serve as alternatives to incarceration by targeting one type of offender or offense (such as drug courts or mental health courts), and focusing on an offender's criminogenic needs.

Standard Probation: type of probation within the Vermont Department of Corrections where offenders are on a suspended sentence with a general or standard set of criteria for their period of supervision, by which they have to abide or their probation will be terminated.

Status Offenses: behaviors such as skipping school and running away from home that are illegal for juveniles but not adults.

Stratification: the division of people into distinct groups based on personal traits such as wealth, status, occupation, and religion.

Street Diversion: a form of diversion by police officers who facilitate on-the-spot conferences during a call for service if the situation seemed both amenable to the conferencing process and minor enough not to pursue through a formal conference or the court.

Subcultural Theory: attributes criminal delinquency to cultural norms and one's need or desire to behave in accordance with those norms.

Support Circle: a type of peacemaking circle that is organized in order to provide support to someone going through a difficult time in their life (such as healing from victimization or desisting from criminal behavior).

Surrogate Victims: individuals participating in victim impact panels who have not been directly involved with the offenders to whom they are speaking.

Survivor Impact Panel: operating in the same way as victim impact panels, these panels give survivors of abuse and sexual violence the opportunity to share their experience with a group of offenders who have committed similar crimes.

Talking Circle: a type of peacemaking circle that is organized so that members of a community or group can discuss an issue that concerns them, as well as share their experiences, thoughts, and feelings with each other.

Talking Piece: refers to an object that is passed around a peacemaking circle, allowing the participant holding it to speak without being interrupted.

Tapu: the sacred spiritual and moral code that affirmed the collective-based, family-centered culture of the Maori.

Techniques of Neutralization: ways in which individuals who commit harmful or illegal acts come to neutralize certain values in order to justify their behavior or negate their obligation to society and others.

Therapeutic Jurisprudence: an approach to the law and the legal system that emphasizes law, in part, as a therapeutic agent which should support psychological healing and wellbeing after crime.

Transformative Justice: concept of justice that emphasize the importance of not only politically transitioning societies broken and divided by violent conflict, but also transforming the systems, policies, and social attitudes that led to that division.

Transitional Justice: a coordinated set of interventions implemented after periods of political oppression, mass violence, or state-sponsored human rights violations that seeks to acknowledge what happened, identify offenders, restore victims, and transform the systems and conditions that helped facilitate injustice and abuse.

Traumatic Countertransference: the phenomenon of directly experiencing symptoms of traumatic stress after hearing about traumatic events.

Tribal Court: courts operated by certain Native American reservations and tribal communities that claim jurisdiction over certain crimes if they are committed on tribal land and involve a member of the tribe.

Truancy Conference: (also referred to as a truancy circle) brings a truant student together with their family, teachers, and school staff to discuss the problem and brainstorm solutions.

Truth and Reconciliation Commission (TRC): generally defined as a temporary committee, which is granted authority by the state, and tasked with investigating and reporting on the impacts of mass violence and oppression within a specific society or region.

Unified Model: a system of justice, proposed by theorist Daniel Van Ness, that is entirely restorative in its values, policies, and operations.

Utilitarian: a philosophic doctrine that argues what is right is what is most beneficial to the most people.

Vicarious Victimization: the experience of trauma caused by witnessing the victimization of another person.

Victim Impact Panels (VIPs): emerging in 1982 as part of the mission and goal of MADD, these panels provided a forum for victims to tell their story to a group of offenders and share the impact that the incident had on their lives and the lives of their families and friends.

Victim Impact Training (VIT): refers to a program that includes a victim impact panel in addition to other educational and reflective elements that focus on empathy building and offender transformation.

Victim Offender Reconciliation Project (VORP): inspired by the Kitchener Experiment, it is a program of mediated reconciliation implemented throughout Canada.

Victim-Offender Mediation (VOM): a process whereby victims are given the opportunity to meet with their offender to engage in a facilitated discussion, in a structured and safe environment.

Victimology: the scientific study of the physical, emotional, and social harm that victims experience from crime.

Wagga Wagga Model: named after the Wagga Wagga Police Department in southern Australia that developed the model in the early 1990s, it refers to the use of police-facilitated, restorative conferences to divert youthful offenders away from the formal court process.

"Whole School" Approach: refers to the implementation of both informal and formal restorative practices in schools.

Zero Tolerance: a punitive form of social control in school settings which emphasizes suspension from school, further isolating troubled teenagers and failing to address the underlying sources of the conflict.

Index